Practical Automation with PowerShell

EFFECTIVE SCRIPTING
FROM THE CONSOLE TO THE CLOUD

MATTHEW DOWST

MANNING

SHELTER ISLAND

For online information and ordering of this and other Manning books, please visit www.manning.com. The publisher offers discounts on this book when ordered in quantity. For more information, please contact

    Special Sales Department
    Manning Publications Co.
    20 Baldwin Road
    PO Box 761
    Shelter Island, NY 11964
    Email: orders@manning.com

Manning Publications Co.	Development editor: Connor O'Brien
20 Baldwin Road	Technical development editor: Michael Lund
PO Box 761	Review editor: Adriana Sabo
Shelter Island, NY 11964	Production editor: Andy Marinkovich
	Copy editor: Alisa Larson
	Proofreader: Melody Dolab
	Technical proofreader: Gonzalo Huerta-Canepa
	Typesetter: Dennis Dalinnik
	Cover designer: Marija Tudor

ISBN: 9781617299551
Printed and bound by CPI Group (UK) Ltd, Croydon, CR0 4YY

Get the eBook FREE!

(PDF, ePub, Kindle, and liveBook all included)

We believe that once you buy a book from us, you should be
able to read it in any format we have available. To get electronic
versions of this book at no additional cost to you, purchase and
then register this book at the Manning website.

Go to https://www.manning.com/freebook and follow the
instructions to complete your pBook registration.

That's it!
Thanks from Manning!

Practical Automation with PowerShell

This book is dedicated to my wife, Leslie,
who has supported me every step of the way—
not just during the writing process, but my entire career.

brief contents

contents

preface

While most people know PowerShell as a command-line tool, it is truly much more than that. If you look at Microsoft's description of PowerShell, it says that it is an automation and configuration tool/framework. PowerShell was written to be a plain text language that is easy to pick up and get started with but also a very powerful tool that you can use to automate an untold number of tasks in your environment and daily life.

However, I'm not here to sell you on PowerShell. The fact that you are reading this book shows you know what PowerShell is capable of. Instead, this book is designed to help you learn from my over-a-decade's worth of experiences in creating PowerShell-based automations and apply those lessons to your own automation needs.

Like many people in the information technology space, I started my career on the help desk and moved into a systems administrator role. No matter what position I was in, if there was a repetitive task I needed to do, I scripted it—first in VBS and then eventually in PowerShell. I was in a unique position because my background was in infrastructure, but I ultimately landed at a company that does custom application development. I learned many skills from those I worked with along the way who helped me build bigger and better automations.

Working as a consultant, I have repeatedly seen companies that are afraid of automation—not necessarily fear of automating yourself out of a job, but fear of becoming beholden to the automation. I can't tell you the number of times I've heard that some process cannot be changed because nobody knows how to update some esoteric automation that someone made years ago.

My goal in writing this book is to help others avoid that situation by creating robust, easy-to-maintain automations that will be supported for years to come.

acknowledgments

This book has taken up many evenings and weekends, so first and foremost, I would like to thank my family. I thank my wife Leslie, whose love of reading really inspired me to start down this path, not to mention her endless support along the way, and my two kids, Jason and Abigail, who spent many Saturdays and Sundays waiting for Dad to come out of the office and play.

I would also like to acknowledge Cameron Fuller, whose mentorship and support have been paramount in getting me where I am today, and the rest of my colleagues at Quisitive, who have inspired and supported me throughout this process. This includes, but is not limited to, Greg Tate and David Stein, who provided invaluable feedback during the MEAP process.

Also, this book would not have been possible without the help of my editors, Connor O'Brien and Michael Lund. Thank you, Connor, for working with me and teaching me the best ways to communicate my message for others to learn. I thought I knew a lot about writing before, but your patience and commitment to my vision helped me make the book even better than I ever imagined. Also, thanks to Michael for his technical feedback and guidance, which helped me tremendously throughout the writing process.

I'd also like to thank the reviewers and those who provided feedback through MEAP. Your feedback has been invaluable in helping me write this book for a wider audience. To all the reviewers—Aleksandar Nikolic, Alice Chang, Andreas Schabus, Anne Epstein, Anton Herzog, Bruno Sonnino, Charles Mike Shelton, Chuck Coon, Eric Dickey, Fredric Ragnar, Giuliano Latini, Glen Thompson, Glenn Swonk, Gonzalo

Huerta Cánepa, Håvard Wall, Jan Vinterberg, Jeremiah Griswold, Jérôme Bezet-Torres, Jiri Pik, Kent Spillner, Mike Haller, Milan Sarenac, Muralidharan T R, Mustafa Özçetin, Nik Rimington, Orlando Méndez Morales, Przemysław Chmielecki, Ranjit S. Sahai, Roman Levchenko, Sander Zegveld, Satej Kumar Sahu, Shawn Bolan, Sylvain Martel, Wayne A Boaz, Werner Nindl, and Zoheb Ainapore—your suggestions helped make this a better book.

Finally, I'd like to thank the PowerShell team at Microsoft and, especially, the wider PowerShell community. This book would not have been possible without all the work they do.

about this book

While the lessons in this book are written with PowerShell, the concepts taught can apply to any automation language or platform. This is done by taking you beyond how to do something and leaning more into the why. My goal is to help you take these concepts and apply them directly to your needs by showing you how to think through the automation and what needs to be accomplished so you can create efficient and maintainable automations that you can continue to use for years to come.

Who should read this book?

This book is for anyone familiar with PowerShell who would like to create enterprise-ready automations. While the concepts of this book apply to everyone, from beginners to experts, to get the most out of this book you should have some familiarity with PowerShell. You should know how to install modules, understand the basics of creating PowerShell script (.ps1), and know some core basics of the language, such as if/else conditional statements, splatting, and loops.

How this book is organized: A roadmap

This book consists of 14 chapters, broken down into three parts. Each part covers a core concept of the automation process.

Part 1 covers getting started with your automation journey:

- Chapter 1 discusses the best uses of PowerShell from an automation point of view and how to ensure you are using the correct tools for the job.
- Chapter 2 shows you how to organize your scripts and modules to make reusable tools.

Part 2 is the heart of the book, covering many different automation concepts:

- Chapter 3 covers scheduling automations and how to think about your code when it is going to be run on a schedule.
- Chapter 4 shows you how to handle secure data in your automations, including the use of password vaults.
- Chapter 5 demonstrates multiple ways you can use PowerShell for remote execution and how to apply these to real-world situations.
- Chapter 6 starts by showing you how to use logic in your code to make your automations adaptable. It then takes that concept a step further by showing you how to use external data to control the execution of an automation script.
- Chapter 7 goes in-depth into using PowerShell with a database backend, freeing you from the Excel and CSV files many companies use to store important data.
- Chapter 8 shows you how to use Azure to manage and execute your automations by combining many of the concepts from previous chapters into a single platform.
- Chapter 9 demonstrates how you can use PowerShell to interact with different solutions. These include generating a Word document from within PowerShell, communicating with a web API, and even invoking Python and passing data between the two scripts.
- Chapter 10 covers some best practices when it comes to writing PowerShell specifically for automation purposes.

Part 3 shows you how you can share and maintain your automation scripts:

- Chapter 11 covers how you can use SharePoint as a front-end for a PowerShell script and how to design scripts that need to run on end-user devices.
- Chapter 12 shows you how to use GitHub for source control and for sharing scripts with your colleagues.
- Chapter 13 teaches you the basics of using Pester to create unit and integration tests that will help ensure your scripts meet all the scenarios you designed them for.
- Chapter 14 demonstrates how to go back to a previous script and make changes to it. This includes what you need to consider beforehand and incorporating automated testing into your source control.

About the code

Unless otherwise stated, all code in this book is written to use PowerShell 7.2 or newer. Some sections still require Windows PowerShell 5.1, but these are clearly called out. In trying to write this book to be as conclusive as possible, I tried to keep the dependence on third-party platforms to a minimum. Any platform or external tools used in this book are either free or have a free trial long enough for you to complete the exercises. There is no dependence on things like Active Directory.

   To accommodate the spacing requirements for a printed book, splatting is used throughout this book. If you are not familiar with splatting, it is a way to pass a collection of parameters to a command using a hashtable. This allows you to break up the parameters into individual lines, making it more readable.

   To show the difference between a command and the output from the command, anytime output is shown, the code will be in a separate block immediately following the command and indented. Also, the output may be shortened to only show relevant data:

```
Code example
Output example
```

   You can get executable snippets of code from the liveBook (online) version of this book at https://livebook.manning.com/book/practical-automation-with-powershell. The complete code for the examples in the book is available for download from the Manning website at www.manning.com, and from GitHub at https://github.com/mdowst/Practical-Automation-with-PowerShell.

   Helper scripts are also provided in some chapters. These are typically used to help you set up your development environment to support the lessons in that chapter. Their use will be called out in the individual chapters.

liveBook discussion forum

Purchase of *Practical Automation with PowerShell* includes free access to liveBook, Manning's online reading platform. Using liveBook's exclusive discussion features, you can attach comments to the book globally or to specific sections or paragraphs. It's a snap to make notes for yourself, ask and answer technical questions, and receive help from the author and other users. To access the forum, go to https://livebook.manning.com/book/practical-automation-with-powershell/discussion. You can also learn more about Manning's forums and the rules of conduct at https://livebook.manning.com/discussion.

   Manning's commitment to our readers is to provide a venue where a meaningful dialogue between individual readers and between readers and the author can take place. It is not a commitment to any specific amount of participation on the part of the author, whose contribution to the forum remains voluntary (and unpaid). We suggest you try asking the author some challenging questions lest his interest stray! The forum and the archives of previous discussions will be accessible from the publisher's website as long as the book is in print.

about the author

MATTHEW DOWST is a Managing Consultant for Quisitive (formerly Catapult Systems) and the lead architect for their managed automation team. He has spent the last 10 years working extensively with PowerShell to help clients of all sizes automate their production workloads. In addition, Matthew is very involved in the PowerShell community, writing blogs, authoring modules, and participating in online forums. He is also the creator of the PowerShell Weekly newsletter, a weekly roundup of that week's PowerShell news.

about the cover illustration

The figure on the cover of *Practical Automation with PowerShell* is captioned "Habitante de Frascati," or "Resident of Frascati," taken from a collection by Jacques Grasset de Saint-Sauveur, published in 1797. Each illustration is finely drawn and colored by hand.

In those days, it was easy to identify where people lived and what their trade or station in life was just by their dress. Manning celebrates the inventiveness and initiative of the computer business with book covers based on the rich diversity of regional culture centuries ago, brought back to life by pictures from collections such as this one.

Part 1

If you go to any conference, read any trade publications, or just talk to others, you will hear that the future is in automation. However, automation is much more than just taking an existing manual process and writing some code to do it for you. To be genuinely successful in your automation endeavors, your automations must save you time and money. However, calculating that is more than just taking into consideration the time it takes you to do the task versus a machine. You also need to calculate in the time it takes to create and maintain the automation.

In this section, you will learn not only how to calculate the cost of automation but also how to minimize the cost of creation and maintenance. In addition, you will see how properly planning your projects and creating reusable code will save you time now and in the future.

PowerShell automation

Every day, across all industries, IT professionals are tasked to do more with less, and the best way to achieve that is through automation. However, many companies do not see IT automation as an asset. More often than not, automations are cobbled together by some sysadmin in their spare time. This often leads to situations where the automation becomes less efficient than doing the task manually, or even worse, it becomes a blocker for change.

I am sure at some point you have tried using one of the codeless automation platforms such as IFTTT, Flow, or Zapier, among others. If you are like me, you probably found the features a little too basic. They are great for personal one-off–type automations, but to really get what you need out of them and ensure they can support enterprise-level automations, they require customization beyond what their simple GUIs can provide.

This is where PowerShell can shine. PowerShell is a task automation framework with a simple and intuitive scripting language. PowerShell includes *command-lets* (cmdlets) that allow you to do similar tasks available in admin consoles and provides a framework in which tasks can be chained together to execute a series of logical steps. Cmdlets allow you to manage and automate the entire Microsoft ecosystem (Azure, Office 365, Microsoft Dynamics, etc.) and other platforms such as Linux and Amazon Web Services. By harnessing the potential of PowerShell and learning a few fundamental principles of automation, any IT professional can become an automation guru.

In addition to asking IT professionals to do more with less, the IT industry is moving to an infrastructure as code model. I have the unique experience of working for a company that specializes in infrastructure consulting and custom application development. This has given me the opportunity to work on automation projects within both specialties, and I have learned that anyone can become an automation guru with a bit of knowledge from each side.

If you are a systems administrator or other IT specialist, you are probably already familiar with working in command-line interfaces (CLIs), using batch/shell files, and running PowerShell scripts. Therefore, the leap to writing code specifically for automations is not that significant. However, you may not be as familiar with some of the supporting skills around issues such as source control and unit testing, and this book aims to help with that.

At the same time, someone with a strong development background may not be as familiar with all the idiosyncrasies of system administration. This is where PowerShell can shine because it does not rely on enterprise architecture. You can just as easily run a script on your local machine as you can on a server. This book demonstrates how you can leverage PowerShell in an organization of any size to create robust, maintainable, and secure automations.

1.1 What you'll learn in this book

This book does not simply show you how to write PowerShell scripts. There are already hundreds of resources out there on just writing code. Instead, the goal is to show you how you can use PowerShell as an automation tool by understanding

- How you can leverage PowerShell to automate repeatable tasks
- How to avoid common automation pitfalls with PowerShell
- How to share and maintain scripts for your team
- How to frontend your scripts for end users

We will achieve this goal by using real-world examples that IT professionals run into every day. You will work through the technical side of writing the code, the conceptual side of why the code is structured the way it is, and how you can apply that to your automation needs.

1.2   *Practical automation*

If you are reading this book, then it is probably safe to assume you have asked yourself, "What should I automate?" While the answer you most likely want to hear is "Everything!" the generic answer is "Any repetitive task that takes you less time to automate than perform." However, like many things in the IT field, the answer is not always so simple. You need to consider multiple factors to determine whether something is worth automating, and as you will see, it may not always be a straight return on time invested.

It is easy to say if it takes you less time to automate it than it takes to do it manually, then it is worth automating, but that is not the complete story. You need to take into consideration the following:

- *Time*—How long does it take to perform the task?
- *Frequency*—How often is the task performed?
- *Relevancy*—How long will the task/automation be needed?
- *Implementation*—How long will it take to automate?
- *Upkeep*—How much long-term maintenance and upkeep will it require?

The first two items, how long and how often, are usually the most straightforward numbers to figure out, along with the business side of things such as how long the task will be relevant. For example, if you automate a task that will go away after the next system upgrade, then you may not recoup your time invested.

The implementation time and upkeep costs can be a little more challenging to calculate. These are things you will begin to get a feel for the more you automate. Just remember to factor in the cost of the tools, platforms, licenses, etc. To determine upkeep costs, you need to consider technology-based maintenance tasks such as platform maintenance, API changes, and system upgrades.

Once you have answers to these questions, you can calculate the amount of time you can spend automating the task to determine whether it is worth your time. You can get the cost by multiplying the time by the frequency and the relevancy. Then, add your implementation plus the upkeep over the relevancy period. If your current cost exceeds your automation cost, then the task is worth automating.

$$\text{Time} \times \text{Frequency} \times \text{Relevancy} > \text{Implementation} + (\text{Upkeep} \times \text{Relevancy})$$

$$\text{Current cost} > \text{Automation cost}$$

At the beginning of your automation journey, estimating the implementation and upkeep costs can be challenging. However, this is something you will learn the more you do it. Until you become more comfortable with these estimates, a good rule of thumb is that if you think you can automate it in half the time saved, then you will be almost guaranteed a good return on your investment.

Besides the benefit of simplifying a repetitive task, there are other factors to consider when determining what to automate. Anything prone to a high degree of human error is a great candidate for automation. Working with a large data set and data transcription is a great example of two tasks that are ripe for automation. People make mistakes when typing. Those mistakes are amplified when they are dealing with lots of data in front of them. If you have ever created a complex Excel formula to manipulate some data, then you have already made a simple automation.

Even if the task at hand is not something you need to do repeatedly, creating a one-off automation may save you time. Plus, if you keep that automation, you can use it as a foundation if you have to perform a similar task in the future. An excellent example of this is string manipulation tasks. For example, say you have a text file with a bunch of poorly formatted text that you need to parse into columns and get into a spreadsheet. However, it is not that many rows, and you could transcribe it or copy/paste it in a few minutes. Or you can take it as an opportunity to hone your skills by using regular expressions, splits, substrings, indexes, replacements, or any other number of string manipulation methods. Learning to use these correctly will be an invaluable skill in your automation journey.

Another place you can look for things to automate is in tasks that you may not need to do often but that are complex and time-consuming. If the task is complex enough that you made a checklist, then you also made an automation project plan. Start by automating one of the steps, then another, and another, and so on until you have a fully automated process. The next time this task comes up, you can click a button instead of referring to a checklist or trying to remember each step of the process.

The best way to get started on your automation journey is to find a simple task that you repeatedly do and automate it. It doesn't have to be a big task or anything fancy. Just think about something that will save you time.

You can also use automation to help you overcome obstacles or handicaps that might prevent you from being as productive as you would like to be. For example, I will freely admit that I am not the most organized person when it comes to my inbox. I would like to be, but I cannot always keep on top of things. I don't like to use Outlook rules because I want to ensure I don't miss an alert, especially if I'm away from my desk. So, what ends up happening is that I quickly read through my emails, but I don't always file them right then. As a result, I end up with thousands of emails in my inbox over time. To combat this, I wrote a script that will file my emails for me. It moves messages to specific folders based on email addresses and keywords. Not only does this automation save me time and help me be more productive, but it also makes me happy, and at the end of the day, that's worth it to me.

One last thing to remember is that you do not need to automate an entire process end to end. You may very well calculate that the cost of automating a task would be greater than performing it manually. However, you may be able to automate certain portions of it to save time and give you a positive return on investment. A perfect example of this is barcodes. Barcodes allow cashiers and warehouse workers to quickly scan items instead of hand-entering product codes. RFID tags would be even quicker, but the cost of implementing them has, so far, been higher than the cost of scanning a barcode.

The more experience you get with automation, the better you will become at determining what is and what isn't worth automating. Also, as you will see in the next section, by using a phased approach with reusable building blocks in your automation processes, you can set yourself up for creating bigger and better automations down the line.

To help you get started, let's look at the four key factors you need to consider when designing an automation. These are the automation's

- Goal
- Triggers
- Actions
- Maintainability

The *automation goal* is what that automation needs to accomplish. The *trigger* is what initiates the automation actions. The *actions* are the steps taken during the automation. Finally, *maintainability* is what it will take to maintain this automation as a whole and as individual building blocks.

We can use a common real-world example to help illustrate each part of the anatomy of the automation. For example, imagine you have a web server that keeps going offline because the logs fill up the drives. These logs cannot be deleted because they are required for security audits. So, about once a week, you must find files over 30 days old, compress these old logs, and move them to long-term storage.

1.2.1 Automation goal

The *automation goal* is what you are trying to achieve with a specific automation. While the goal of the automation may seem easy to define, you need to be sure that you consider all aspects of the automation.

In our log file cleanup example, our obvious goal is to prevent the drives on the web server from filling up, but that just scratches the surface. If that were our only goal, we could simply delete the old logs. However, these logs are required for security audits. So, our goal is to create an automation process that will prevent the drives from filling up while ensuring no data is lost and that the data will be accessible on the rare occasions it is needed. This gives an overview of the automation and can be used to create a checklist when designing your actions.

For example, if we change our goal to include regular access to the data, it could change our actions. In this case, compressing the files and moving them to long-term storage would not be the best option. You could instead move the files to a larger storage array. This would make them easier to access while still preventing your drives from filling up. Now that you know what you want your automation to achieve, you can start planning the steps needed to get there.

1.2.2 *Triggers*

Triggers are what start your automation. Broadly speaking, there are two types of triggers, polling and event-based. Polling triggers check in with end points, and event triggers are initiated by an outside event. Understanding the difference between these two types of triggers and how they work will significantly impact your automation journey.

Polling triggers routinely check in with a system for specific conditions. Two typical implementations—and ones we will use throughout this book—are *monitors* and *schedules.*

A monitor checks in and waits for a specific condition to occur. This can be anything from watching an FTP site for file uploads to monitoring an inbox for emails or confirming a service is running, among many other tasks. Monitors can run continuously or on a recurring interval.

The choice to use a continuous or interval-based monitor will depend on the balance between automations needs and costs. For example, let's say you are monitoring a file share for a file to be written. If you know that the file only gets written once an hour, having your automation check every 60 seconds for it would be a waste of resources.

While a monitor might run on a regularly recurring schedule, a scheduled automation is different in that the trigger itself doesn't check for a condition before running subsequent steps. Instead, it will run every time it is scheduled. Common examples include cleaning files, data synchronization, and routine maintenance tasks. Like with a monitor, you need to carefully consider the needs of your automation when setting up your schedule.

An event trigger occurs when an outside event initiates the automation. For example, a common event trigger is an http request such as a webhook. Event triggers can also include calls from other automations, and most service desk tools have a workflow engine that can trigger automations when a particular request is received. These are just a few examples of automated event triggers, but any external interaction can be considered an event trigger.

A simple button or the execution of a command shell can be an event trigger. The critical thing to remember is that event triggers are initiated by any outside event, whereas polling triggers reach out to the end point.

Let's go back to the example of cleaning up the web server logs. You need to figure out what trigger would be best to use, polling or event. In this case, a polling trigger makes sense because the web server has no way to reach out. Now, you need to determine whether it should be a monitor or schedule. Usually, a monitor is used for issues that require immediate or near-future actions—for instance, a service has stopped or a network connection has dropped. Since cleaning up web server logs is a maintenance task, a schedule would make the most sense. Next, you need to determine your recurrence interval.

You already know that you have to clean up these logs at least once a week. Logically, a trigger with a recurring interval of less than one week would be best. You also know that a new log file gets created after a certain number of lines. You see there are about three or four logs generated daily. Therefore, a once-daily job would be a good option because anything less would be overkill and anything more would run the risk of the logs growing too large. Once you determine your trigger, it is time to move on to the core part of your automation, the actions.

1.2.3   Actions

Actions are what most people think of when they think of automation. The actions are the operations your automation performs to achieve the automation goal. Automations can consist of multiple different actions, sometimes referred to as *steps*. You can classify actions into three main categories: *logic, tasks,* and *logging*. Figure 1.1 shows the steps for the log cleanup automation.

Logic actions are the actions that control the flow of your automation. They include conditional constructs (your typical if/else conditions), loops, waits, error catching/handling, and handling of variables or other runtime data. Tasks are the actions performed against the end points. In other words, if it is not a logic or logging action, it's a task. The best way to think about it is that logic actions are the brain, and tasks are the hands.

Logging, as the name implies, is the recording of your actions. Your logging can consist of output from both logic and task actions. While logging actions could be considered tasks, I prefer to think of them separately because they are not directly involved in completing the automation goal. However, they will be directly involved in the creation of successful and maintainable automations.

Looking at our example of cleaning up log files, we can identify the actions we need to take and what type of actions they are:

1   Find logs over 30 days old (logic).
2   Create an archive file with timestamp name (task).
3   Add old files to the archive (task).
4   Remove the old files from the drive (task).
5   Record which files were removed and the name of the archive file (logging).
6   Copy the archive files to Azure Blob Storage for long-term storage (task).
7   Confirm that the copy was successful (logic). If not, stop the process, and send a notification.
8   Record the location of the new file (logging).
9   Remove the original archive file (task).

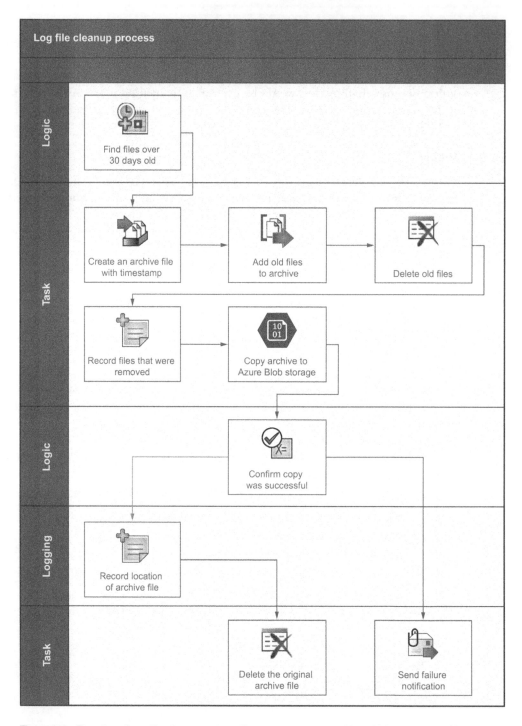

Figure 1.1   The steps for a file cleanup automation process separated by which steps are logic, tasks, and logging

1.2.4   *Maintainability*

A few years ago, I helped a customer automate their user provisioning processes. During the discovery phase, I was told users had to be created in a specific directory, left for one hour, and then moved to their proper directory. Of course, I asked why and was told it would allow the users to sync with an in-house application. It turns out the person whose job it was to add and remove users from this application decided that they would automate the process. At the time, all users existed in the same directory. So they built this automation, saving them 30 to 60 minutes of work a week. However, over time things changed.

The company had expanded and needed to provide different policies to different users, so they created different directories. They then noticed that certain users were not being created in this in-house system. By this time, the person who wrote the automation was long gone, and no one else understood how it worked. So, they would add users into the directory, wait until the hourly sync ran, and then move them to the proper directory. What had initially saved one person 60 minutes of work a week was now costing others a couple of extra minutes for each user they created, which means in the long-term, this automation was costing them more than it ever saved. This is a classic example of not planning for the future.

No one can predict the future, but you can certainly plan for it. No matter what step of the automation process you are working on, you need to ask yourself how difficult this will be to maintain. When you do this, think back on your experience and consider how the requirements might change over time.

In our log cleanup scenario, we said our first action was to find log files over 30 days old. One of the first things that should have come to mind is what happens if the drive starts filling up faster and you need to clean up logs every 14 days. How difficult would it be to make this change? If you created the number of days as a variable, it would not be difficult at all. However, if you hardcoded the number of days in your scripts, you would need to go back and make multiple changes.

Another scenario that might not be as straightforward is if a second log folder is deemed necessary. To begin, you need to ask, "How likely is this scenario?" If it is likely, you should consider whether it is worth writing the automation to handle multiple folder paths, or whether you could do something as simple as running it twice, once for each path.

Another aspect to consider is if you have to change log cleanup from daily to hourly. Again, ask yourself if this is a likely scenario. If it is, determine what it would take to change the automation to hourly. It might seem like a simple answer, say, to change the filter from days to hours, but you also need to look at how this could affect other actions. For instance, when creating the archive file, are you adding a timestamp to the name? If so, does it include hours? If it doesn't, you may create a situation in which you accidentally overwrite data.

The answers to any of these questions will depend on your unique requirements. Of course, you will not be able to predict every possible situation, but if you keep these questions in mind and know how to address them using PowerShell, you will be more prepared when changes become necessary.

You also need to be aware of getting caught in the weeds. If you noticed, my first response to any question is "How likely is this scenario?" You can get so bogged down in accounting for different scenarios that you'll never accomplish anything, or you'll make your logic so complex that no one else will understand it. It is a delicate balancing act that we will continually touch on throughout this book.

1.3   The automation process

When looking at an automation project, it is easy to get overwhelmed. People will tell you to use things like the KISS principle (keep it short and simple). While that is easy to say, it is not always easy to do in practice. It may seem nearly impossible when you have multiple systems talking to each other, complex logic, and ever-changing requirements. This is where the concepts of *building blocks* and *phases* come in. By using building blocks and phases, you can break down your complex tasks into small, simple steps.

1.3.1   Building blocks

No matter how complex the automation is, it can always be broken down into smaller, more simplified steps or building blocks. By breaking tasks down into smaller blocks, you can prevent yourself from becoming overwhelmed and provide clear goals that you can meet regularly. In addition, this concept will allow you to use portions of the automation as soon as day one and provide you with a framework to expand on your earlier work. The majority of this book will cover helping you create these different building blocks that you can use across your automations.

Building blocks also allow you to build your skills over time. As you automate more and more, your skills will continue to grow. You will learn new techniques, not just in your coding but in the overall process. You may find a better way to perform a task using PowerShell. If you used building blocks, you can go back and update all your previous automations quickly and easily.

1.3.2   Phases

The adage "You have to be able to walk before you can run" applies perfectly to the world of automation. Your first few automations you make will likely not be pretty—just like the first picture you ever drew or the first paper you wrote in school. It takes time and experience to build your skills. But that doesn't mean you cannot start reaping the benefits of automation immediately.

By breaking your automations into phases, you can create incremental benefits. Imagine you need to get from point A to point B. Sure, a car may be the fastest way to get there, but you have no idea how to build a car, let alone have the resources. So, start small and work your way up. Begin by building a skateboard. Then upgrade to a scooter, a bike, and a motorcycle and, finally, build that car. Figure 1.2 illustrates the

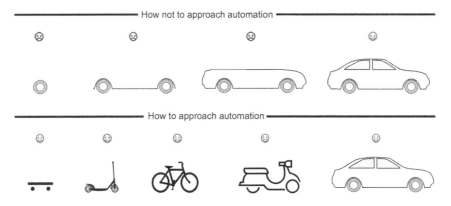

Figure 1.2   How a phased approach can allow you to start receiving benefits sooner

benefits of a phased approach to automation. Each step of the way, you will make improvements and continue to improve your process. Plus, you will see benefits from the very start, unlike if you set out to build a car from the get-go. In that situation, you would be walking the entire time until you finally built the car.

During each phase, you will most likely be creating several building blocks. Furthermore, these building blocks that you create will often be used across the different phases and improved upon from one phase to the next. For example, in figure 1.2, you learned to make a wheel in phase 1. Then, in phase 2, you improved upon that knowledge and made an even better wheel.

Phases also allow you to adapt and adjust the automation along the way. You can get feedback after each phase from the people using it. You may discover there are things you did not consider. In the scenario in figure 1.2, after you created the skateboard, people told you it was great for part of the trip but not for the really muddy parts. You can take this feedback and adjust phase 2 to include larger wheels. Contrast this with the nonphased approach of jumping right in and building the car and then finding out it gets stuck in the mud. If you didn't build the suspension and wheel wells to fit bigger wheels, you would have a ton of rework to do.

1.3.3   Combining building blocks and phases

To demonstrate the concept of building blocks and phases in a more IT-centric way, you can look at the common automation scenario of provisioning a virtual machine. While there can be a lot to this process, you can break it down into a few phases:

1 Create a virtual machine.
2 Install the operating system.
3 Configure the operating system.

While it would be great to tackle all of this at once, it would be a massive undertaking, and you would not see any benefits until the very end. Instead, you can tackle one phase at a time, providing yourself with added benefits along the way. Start with phase 1, creating a virtual machine. The building blocks for this could consist of

1 Selecting a host machine
2 Creating a blank virtual machine
3 Allocating CPU and memory
4 Attaching a network interface card to the appropriate subnet
5 Creating and attaching virtual hard disks

Once you've finished phase 1 (creating a virtual machine, shown in figure 1.3), you can move on to phase 2 while already reaping the benefits of phase 1.

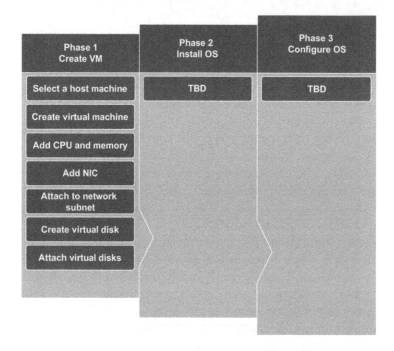

Figure 1.3   A virtual provisioning phased approach (phase 1)

In phase 2, you are going to install the operating system. Here you have a couple of options. You can create a template virtual hard disk with the operating system already installed. However, this would mean you must maintain the template, including applying patches. Also, if you have multiple hosts in different regions, it could be a pain to make sure they all stay in sync. Instead, you decided to use your configuration management tools to install the operating system. This way, your image is consistent throughout your environment and always up to date.

As you start building this part of the automation, you realize that your virtual machine needs to be on a specific subnet to receive the image. Your building blocks may be similar to this:

1 Attach to operating system deployment subnet.
2 Turn on the virtual machine.
3 Wait for the operating system to install.
4 Attach to production subnet.

Since you created a block to assign the virtual machine to a subnet in phase 1, you can reuse that code for blocks 1 and 4 in this phase. Notice that I made attaching to a subnet a separate block. This is because I've automated this exact scenario before and have run into the situation multiple times. If you combine all the resources into one block—that is, you assign CPU and memory, attach the network, and allocate the virtual hard disk—you cannot reuse it. If you want to connect to a different network, you can reassign the CPU and memory, but allocating another virtual hard disk could cause significant issues. If you do something like this, don't worry about it. Think of it as a learning experience. I still do it all the time myself. Plus, since you will have to create the building block to assign the subnet for this phase, there is no reason why you can't go back and update blocks in the previous phase. Figure 1.4 shows these developments in phase 2.

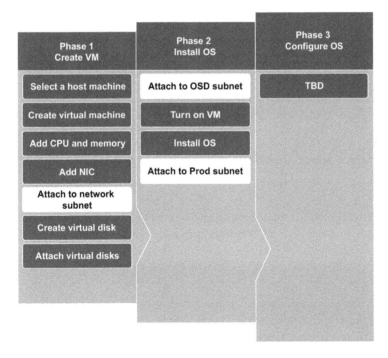

Figure 1.4   A virtual provisioning phased approach (phase 2) with shared components

Now you have two phases in production, and users are starting to see real benefits. In addition, you are learning what would benefit them in the next phase, shown in figure 1.5. You can talk to the people using the automation and discover what they would like to see in phase 3. It could be assigning a static IP address, creating secondary data drives, or any other number of things you may not have considered. Also, you don't have to stop after phase 3. You can add a phase 4 to install applications automatically.

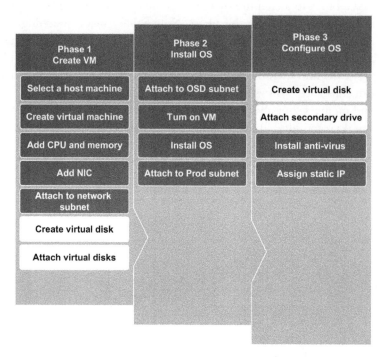

Figure 1.5   A virtual provisioning phased approach (phase 3) with shared components

The most significant benefit of combining the concept of building blocks and phases is flexibility—not just during the creation process but also down the road. If your requirements or resources change, you only need to swap out the building blocks specific to that change. The process itself and the other building blocks will remain unchanged.

Imagine if your company decided to switch to a new hypervisor or move to the cloud. In these cases, you would need to redo phase 1. In phase 2, you simply need to swap the network assignment blocks with the new ones you built. The rest of phase 2 stays the same. Alternatively, say your company decided to switch to a different operating system. There would be few to no changes in phase 1 and maybe some minor changes in phase 2. All the changes would focus on phase 3. If you've used a phased approach, no matter what gets thrown at you, you'll be able to adjust rapidly.

1.4   Choosing the right tool for the job

One of the biggest mistakes you can make when trying to automate a task is trying to make a tool do something it is not designed to do. Therefore, before you begin any PowerShell automation project, you need to determine whether it is the best tool for the job.

For example, I would not recommend using Python if you are setting up resources in Azure, not because Python is a bad tool (far from it), but because Python does not have the same native support for Azure resources. You can do it by invoking the Azure CLI through Python, but this can lead to another set of issues. Now your Python script is dependent on having the Azure CLI installed. Since the Azure CLI is a stand-alone application and not a package for Python, you will need to build specific checks into your script to ensure that the files you need are available. Also, your script is now dependent on a platform that supports both Python and the Azure CLI. This dramatically increases the complexity of your automation and makes it much less portable.

Now, if you choose PowerShell for this task, you can use the Azure PowerShell modules created and maintained by Microsoft to perform your tasks. All the functionality to check for and resolve dependency issues are built into PowerShell. With two or three lines of code, you can make your script completely portable to any other system running PowerShell.

I am not saying PowerShell is the end-all, be-all, but for certain workloads, it just makes sense. Now, with PowerShell Core, the number of tasks you can automate with PowerShell is growing larger and larger, although it still does not cover everything. If you need to do technical analysis as part of your automation, such as calculating and plotting statistical charts, I would not recommend PowerShell. In this case, the panadas library in Python is leaps and bounds above anything available in PowerShell.

1.4.1   Automation decision tree

How do you determine whether PowerShell is the right tool for the job? One way is by using the decision tree in figure 1.6.

When using a decision tree, you need to look at all aspects of the automation process you are creating. For example, let's return to our previous example of archiving old log files and add in the requirement to upload them to Azure Blob Storage. The first action was to find files over 30 days old. Running that through a decision tree would look something like this:

- Does this tool have native support for all the tasks I need to accomplish? *Yes, PowerShell has built-in functionality to work with file systems.*

There is no need to continue with the other questions because the first one is a definitive *yes*. The next few actions in the process will be similar. For instance, when creating the archive file, ask

- Does this tool have native support for all the tasks I need to accomplish? *Yes, the* `Compress-Archive` *cmdlet is native to PowerShell.*

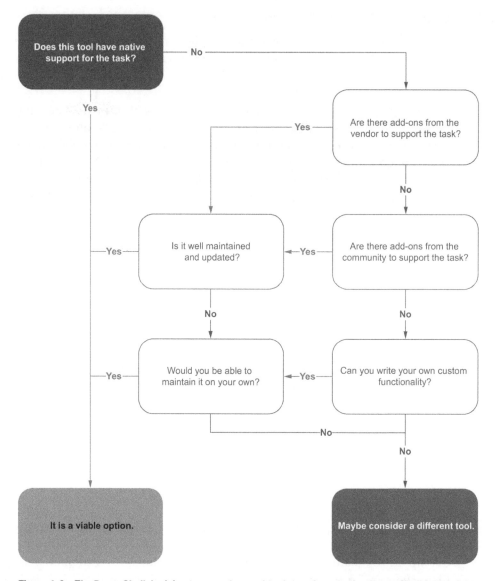

Figure 1.6   The PowerShell decision tree can be used to determine whether PowerShell is the right tool for the job.

However, not all actions will be so straightforward. Take, for example, the action to copy the files to Azure Blob Storage:

- Does this tool have native support for all the tasks I need to accomplish? *No.*
- Are there modules/add-ons from the company that can accomplish the tasks? *Yes, Microsoft has an official Azure Blob Storage module.*

Again, this is pretty cut and dried because we know Microsoft creates official Power-Shell modules to support all Azure functionality. But there will be instances, even within the Microsoft ecosystem, when the answer might not be so clear. For example, let's say that for the action to log which files are removed, you need to write these files to a SQL table:

1 Does this tool have native support for all the tasks I need to accomplish? *No.*
2 Are there modules/add-ons from the company that can accomplish these tasks? *There is a SqlServer module from Microsoft, but it does not support all the tasks I want to automate.*
3 If not, are there modules/add-ons from the community that can accomplish the tasks? *Yes. The module dbatools is available in the PowerShell Gallery.*
  a Is it maintained and updated? *The GitHub repo has over 15,000 commits and 200 contributors and is updated regularly.*
4 How difficult would it be to write custom functionality? *It is possible to query SQL directly from PowerShell using the System.Data.SqlClient class that is native in .NET.*
  a Will it be difficult to maintain? *There may be differences between .NET and .NET Core for the SqlClient class.*

As you can see, there is a multitude of ways that you can accomplish the task. It will be your job to make an informed decision on which tool or tools are best suited for the task at hand. Of course, you may find that no single tool can meet all your needs, and that is fine, too. When using PowerShell, you can easily switch between different solutions to accomplish your goals. After reading this book, you'll be able to identify tasks for which you can utilize PowerShell.

1.4.2 *No need to reinvent the wheel*

One of the great things about PowerShell is the large community that loves to share its knowledge. At the time of this writing, over 6,400 different PowerShell modules are available in the official PowerShell Gallery. There are also numerous websites, forums, and blogs dedicated to PowerShell. So, chances are, if there is something you are trying to do with PowerShell, someone has already done it or something similar.

There is no need to write every single line of code in your scripts from scratch. I encourage you to go explore what other people have done. Learn from their mistakes and experiences. I cannot tell you how many times I've seen a block of code to do XYZ, and I think to myself, "Why did they do it that way?" Then I write it another way, run into a problem, and then realize, oh, that's why the other script did that.

At the same time, do not just copy and paste code from GitHub or StackOverflow into your script and expect everything to work. Instead, look at the code. Figure out what exactly it does and how it accomplishes its task. You can then implement it into your script with the confidence that it will work and, most important, that you will be able to maintain it.

1.4.3   *Supplemental tools*

While PowerShell is capable of many things, there are a few things it cannot do. For example, it does not have a frontend that can provide forms that users can fill in. It is also not a job scheduler and does not have built-in triggers like webhooks. Although achieving some of this functionality through PowerShell is not technically impossible, it may not be practical. There are other tools out there that are built specifically for these tasks, and many of them support PowerShell.

However, as you will see throughout this book, there is no reason why you cannot combine multiple tools. For instance, in chapter 3, you will learn how to use multiple tools to schedule jobs to run, and in chapter 11, you will see how to use tools like SharePoint to create frontend forms for your automations.

JOB SCHEDULER

PowerShell does not have a built-in job scheduler. You may be aware of the `Register-ScheduledJob` cmdlet, but that only created PowerShell jobs in the Windows Task Scheduler. To achieve true cross-platform support with PowerShell Core, this functionality was removed from version 6.0 and up. Of course, you can still use Task Scheduler to schedule and run your PowerShell scripts in Windows, just like you can use Cron in Linux, but there are other tools out there that are purpose-built to handle things like automation jobs.

If you are already using tools such as Jenkins, Ansible, or Control-M, you can use PowerShell inside of these platforms to fulfill your automation requirements. The best part is that your automations will then be platform agnostic. For example, if you invested your efforts in a solution like IFTTT or System Center Orchestrator, you are now locked into those platforms. If that software is deprecated, changes its licensing, or takes away functionality, your only course of action is to recreate your entire automation. However, if you build your automations with PowerShell in Jenkins and your company decides to move to Ansible, you can easily transfer your automation scripts from one platform to another with minimal effort.

FRONTEND

The same can be said for things like frontend forms. A frontend is just a way to gather information for your automation. You can technically build forms in PowerShell, and there are instances where it makes sense to do so, but there are a lot of caveats to it. Like with job schedulers, there are numerous tools available that make creating and presenting forms simple and easy.

You can build all the actions for your automations in PowerShell and then frontend it through any means you like. For instance, you can make a SharePoint list to collect the necessary information for your automation in a few minutes. Then, all you need to do is build a simple trigger that passes the required information to your automation. If you want to move to ServiceNow, no problem. You simply remap your trigger from SharePoint to ServiceNow, and your automation will continue to function as before.

1.5 *What you need to get started today*

While PowerShell Core is a cross-platform tool, most examples in this book will be running in a Windows environment. I recommend using Windows 11 or Windows Server 2022, but you should be able to follow along using any version of Windows that supports Windows PowerShell 5.1 and PowerShell 7. Unless otherwise specified, you can assume that everything in this book is written for PowerShell 7.

You will also need an integrated development environment to write your code. Although the built-in PowerShell ISE has been the go-to for many years, it does not support PowerShell 7. If you have not already done so, I highly recommend that you switch to Visual Studio Code (VS Code). Unlike the traditional Visual Studio, VS Code is a free, lightweight code editor that is open-sourced, cross-platform, and very community-driven. In addition, it supports most common programming and scripting languages, including Windows PowerShell and PowerShell, allowing you to work with both side by side.

One thing that makes PowerShell so versatile is that it can be used across a multitude of platforms, including Windows, Linux, macOS, servers, containers, third-party platforms, and many cloud platforms. Not only can it be run on those platforms, but it can also be used to automate their management. At the time of writing, the big thing in the industry is containers. By next month or next year, who knows what it will be. This is why most of the examples in this book are designed to use your local resources.

Because most cloud-native or PaaS services have different authentication protocols or minor differences in how they handle scripts, it would be impossible to write for every potential service. Instead, this book will teach you the fundamentals that will remain the same regardless of which platform you use or manage. It will teach you how to think about, identify, and work with your chosen platform.

While some examples in this book utilize third-party platforms or cloud solutions, all platforms are either free or have a free trial you can use. These include Jenkins, Azure, SharePoint, and GitHub. You can refer to the appendix for complete details on the environments and tools used.

Summary

- PowerShell is a powerful high-level language designed with IT automation in mind that is easy to pick up and start using.
- You can use PowerShell to create reusable building blocks that can be shared between automations and among your team members.
- To create successful automations, you need to be able to conceptualize the process and plan for the future.
- PowerShell is an extensible and portable tool that makes it a perfect fit for most automation needs.
- PowerShell can work hand in hand with other tools and platforms to meet most needs you have quickly and easily.
- PowerShell has a large community and is backed by one of the largest tech companies in the world.

Get started automating 2

This chapter covers

- Applying the concept of phased automations
- Examples of how to create reusable functions
- How to store your functions in a module

In the last chapter, you read about how to make your automation project a success by using the concepts of phases and building blocks and how those apply to Power-Shell. In this chapter, you will see how to take a simple script and turn it into a reusable building block you can use anywhere. You will do this by creating a script to clean up old log files and turn it into a building block by thinking like an automator.

You will also learn how to store these building blocks for use across multiple automations. Whether you are writing a simple script to automate a repetitive task or working with a much more extensive script, knowing how to use a phased approach to your automation can save you a lot of time, money, and stress.

2.1 Cleaning up old files (your first building blocks)

In this section, you are going to write a simple script (automation) to clean up old log files. In doing so, you will apply the concept of building blocks to your script creation.

22

As always, you start with your requirements gathering. You know that you need to remove old logs to keep the drive from filling up. You also understand that the logs must be retained for at least seven years, but after 30 days, they can go into cold storage.

With that information, you can start designing phase 1. In this phase, shown in figure 2.1, you will find the files to archive, add the old files to an archive file, and then remove the old files. Now that you have your basic design, you need to start thinking like an automator.

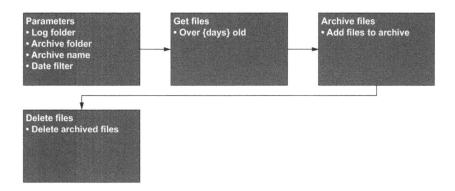

Figure 2.1   Design the first phase of the file cleanup automation by defining the required parameters and the steps to perform, such as getting the files to archive, performing the archive, and then cleaning up the archived files.

First, you need to consider what variables your automation will need. This will help you determine the parameters for your script. In this case, you are going to need to know

- The folder containing the log file
- Where to save the archive file
- What to name the archive file
- How old a file should be before being archived

The first two tasks, getting the log folder and knowing where to save the archive, are reasonably straightforward. In both cases, the input will be a folder path. However, the next two tasks require some additional considerations.

You know you need to filter the logs by date, so you only archive the files you want. Since you want to archive files over 30 days old, you can simply subtract 30 days from the current time. You can achieve this in PowerShell by using the `AddDays` method on a `DateTime` object and putting in a negative number. Since you want to make this reusable for other automations, you can make the date filter parameter a number value provided to the script. However, there are other things you will want to consider.

Because the value of the date filter needs to be a negative number, you can either expect someone using this automation to know that and enter a negative value, or you can have the script automatically flip a positive number to a negative one. However, in either case, you may potentially end up setting the date to 30 days in the future, causing your script to archive files way too soon.

Luckily, with PowerShell, there are several ways to handle this. For example, you can add logic to check whether the value is positive and have your script automatically convert it to a negative number. Alternatively, you can calculate the date using the AddDays method and confirm that the value returned is in the past. If it is not, you can throw an error message and exit the function or attempt to fix it by reversing the sign of the parameter. Both of these options can be reusable functions, but in this case, they might be overkill. Instead, a more straightforward approach is to use the parameter validation functionality, which is native in PowerShell, to ensure the value passed is within the range you want. Because positive numbers are easier for people to think about and enter, your script can require a positive number and then automatically flip it to a negative one.

While any of the approaches mentioned would be valid, we used the simplest and, therefore, less error-prone process, following the KISS principle (keep it short and simple). If, down the line, you discover that even with the validation, people keep trying to send negative values, you can adjust your script to use one of the more complex solutions. The key here is the phased approach. You have the ability to continue to evolve your script as time goes on. While this problem is easily solved using parameter validation, the next one, setting the name of the archive file, is not so straightforward.

When your automation runs, you will most likely want to create a new archive file instead of adding to an existing one. Adding to an existing archive file can be dangerous because if something goes wrong, it can affect multiple files going back days or even weeks. Also, a possible phase 2 could be to copy this archive to a cloud-based store. In this case, you would not want to recopy the same file repeatedly as it continues to grow larger. Instead, the safest bet is to create a new archive file every time the automation runs.

Because the file name needs to be unique for every execution, it makes sense to add a timestamp to the file name. This means you need to consider how often the automation will run. If it runs once a day, make the timestamp for the day, month, and year. However, if it will run multiple times a day, you may need to add the hour, minutes, and seconds, or even milliseconds, to the name. Next, you need to consider what timestamp to use. You can use the current time, but that may make it difficult to find past logs without looking inside every archive. You can use the date of your filter, but this could get confusing if you ever change the number of days in the filter. Instead, the best option is to use the timestamp from the newest file you are archiving. Now, if you need to search the archives, you can quickly determine which files would be in which archive simply by the name.

Given these needs, the archive filename cannot be a simple parameter. Instead, make a parameter for the archive filename prefix and create a building block (aka a PowerShell function) to append the timestamp value to it. The additional steps are shown in figure 2.2.

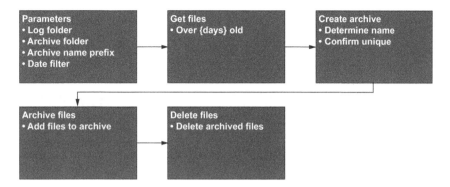

Figure 2.2 **Expand on the initial file cleanup design to include more details around the creation of the archive file.**

As this example shows, something as simple as what to name your file can have more variables than you may have initially considered. However, this serves as an excellent example of the mindset you need when creating your automations. You will see throughout this exercise examples of how to think like an automator.

2.1.1 Your first function

The code to create the timestamp, append it to the filename and folder, and confirm it is a unique file is a perfect example of when to create a function. Not only will making it a function allow you to maintain and test just that portion of the script, but its functionality can also be useful in other automations.

Just as with the larger overall automation, you start by determining your parameters. In this case, you need the archive path, the file prefix, and the date value to create the timestamp. Then you need to think about the tasks to perform.

When you think in terms of automation, you should be asking yourself questions such as what should happen if the folder in the ZipPath variable does not exist or if a file with the same name is already in the folder. To address these concerns, use some `if` conditions along with the `Test-Path` cmdlet to test the path and the file. The logic behind these decisions is shown in figure 2.3.

Now that you have the logic, you can move on to creating the function. However, before diving right in, let's cover a few best practices when creating a function.

You should always include the `[CmdletBinding()]` attribute at the beginning of any function. It provides your function with support for the default parameters to manage things such as verbose output and error handling. After the `[CmdletBinding()]` line, you should always include `[OutputType()]`. It tells PowerShell what type of value the function will return. In this case, your function will return a string value for the archive file. So you'll set the value to `[OutputType([string])]`.

Although neither the `CmdletBinding` nor the `OutputType` cmdlet is required to create a function, it is good practice to include them. As you get into more advanced functions, these will come into use, so it is good to start using them from the beginning.

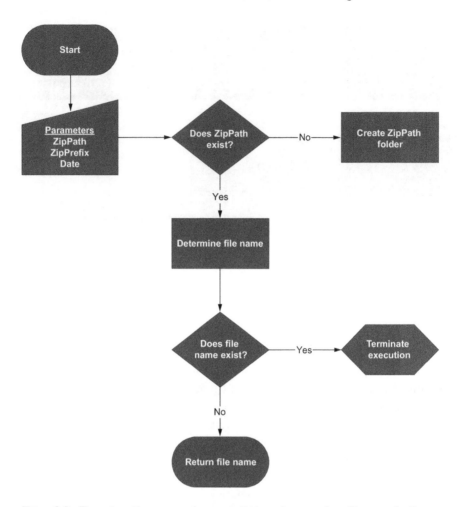

Figure 2.3   The automation process to ensure that you have a unique file name for the archive file each time the file cleanup automation runs

Next, you will define your parameters in a `params` block. For each parameter, you set whether it is mandatory and the type of value. Again, neither of these is required when writing PowerShell functions. However, when you are writing functions that will be used in automations or shared with others, it is good to include them so that people can quickly identify what values are required and what data type they should provide. Also, it helps to ensure that the proper values are passed, and if not, PowerShell's built-in error handling will help prevent unforeseen consequences if the wrong value is sent.

You should also always include the comment-based Help section. Although I leave this out in many of the examples in the book for brevity, I highly recommend you add it to all scripts and functions you create. Plus, if you are using Visual Studio Code (VS

Code), there is no excuse not to add it because VS Code can autogenerate it. Just type ## on the first line inside your function, and VS Code will outline the Help section for you. Then, you simply fill in the details.

Now let's get into the actual execution of the function, which is shown in the following listing. The first thing you want to do is check whether the folder passed in exists. Use the Test-Path cmdlet inside an if condition to do this.

Listing 2.1 Set-ArchiveFilePath function

```
Function Set-ArchiveFilePath{                          Declare the function
    [CmdletBinding()]                                  and set the required
    [OutputType([string])]                             parameters.
    param(
    [Parameter(Mandatory = $true)]            Declare
    [string]$ZipPath,                         CmdletBinding and
                                              OutputType.
    [Parameter(Mandatory = $true)]
    [string]$ZipPrefix,

    [Parameter(Mandatory = $true)]
    [datetime]$Date                      Check whether the
    )                                    folder path exists, and
                                         create it if it doesn't.
    if(-not (Test-Path -Path $ZipPath)){
        New-Item -Path $ZipPath -ItemType Directory | Out-Null
        Write-Verbose "Created folder '$ZipPath'"         Include verbose
    }                                                     output for testing
                                                          and troubleshooting.
    $timeString = $Date.ToString('yyyyMMdd')
    $ZipName = "$($ZipPrefix)$($timeString).zip"
    $ZipFile = Join-Path $ZipPath $ZipName         Set the full path of
                                                   the zip file.
    if(Test-Path -Path $ZipFile){
        throw "The file '$ZipFile' already exists"    Confirm the file
    }                                                 doesn't already exist.
                                                      Throw a terminating
    $ZipFile          Return the file                 error if it does.
}                     path to the script.
```

Labels on the left:
Define the parameters.
Create the timestamp based on the date.
Create the file name.

The Test-Path cmdlet returns True if the folder exists and False if it doesn't. In this case of the archive folder, you want to know that it does not exist. Therefore, you need to reverse the logic by adding the -not keyword to the if statement, which causes the command inside the if block to execute when it returns False. However, instead of having your automation stop if the folder does not exist, you can create it using the New-Item cmdlet.

The next part of the script will be some simple string concatenations to create the file name and set the path. When dealing with paths in any automation, it is always best to use the Join-Path cmdlet as it will automatically account for the slashes. This way, you do not have to worry whether the value passed for the folder parameter contains a slash at the end or not.

> ### Controlling function output
>
> If the `New-Item` cmdlet is not set to write to a variable, PowerShell will write it to the output stream. Anything written to the output stream of your script will be returned from your function. In this case, the function would return the output from this command and the zip file path at the end, causing all sorts of unknown issues later in the script.
>
> To prevent this from happening, add `| Out-Null` to the end of any PowerShell command to stop it from writing to the output stream. `Out-Null` does not block the error or verbose streams, so you can still use those with the command.
>
> If you added the `[CmdletBinding()]` to the beginning of the function, you can use the `-Verbose` switch when calling the function. Verbose output is not written to the output stream. Therefore, it is not returned to the script or any variables. However, when you include the `-Verbose` switch, the verbose stream will be written to the screen. This allows you to confirm that the `if` condition is working even though you need to block the output from any command.

Next, use `Test-Path` again to confirm a file with the same name doesn't already exist, except this time, you want to take action if it does, so do not include `-Not` to reverse the logic. If a file with the same name already exists, you can use the `throw` command to send a terminating error to the script, causing the entire process to halt. When designing anything for automations, you must be mindful of when you want your automation to stop if a particular condition is not satisfied. Like in the situation where a file with the same already exists, you want to terminate to prevent accidentally overwriting data. Finally, the function ends by returning the value of the archive file path by outputting the variable to the script.

2.1.2   *Returning data from functions*

When returning data from a function, it is best to save it to a variable in the function and have just that variable on the last line of the function. You may see that others use `return` or `Write-Output` in these cases. While these methods are valid ways to return values from a function to a script, they have drawbacks.

The `return` command in PowerShell is different from the `return` command you will see in other languages. Just because you use the `return` command, it does not mean that is the only value the function will return.

Remember that a function will return everything written to the output stream. Therefore, the name `return` can be misleading, especially for people used to languages like C# and Java. Also, in some situations, you will want to return multiple streams from a function. If you are in the habit of adding `return` to every function, this will cause issues.

The `return` command does have its uses since it will stop the processing of a function. You can use it to stop a function from executing under certain conditions and return the value at that time. There are multiple other ways to handle this, but if `return` works well in your situation, go ahead and use it. I would also recommend adding some comments above that line to explain your choice.

Some people prefer to use the `Write-Output` cmdlet for clarity, as it expresses what is being written to the output stream. However, others feel that, just as with the `return` command, it sets a false expectation that this will be the only value returned. Also, using the `Write-Output` cmdlet can affect the performance of your functions and has been known to cause issues with different data types.

For these reasons, it is best to use a single line with a clearly named variable to output the results to the output stream on the very last line of the function. Returning values inside `if/else` statements or having `Write-Output` cmdlets mixed in with other commands can make it very difficult to read and understand where the output is coming from. Remember, with automations, you are almost guaranteed that you will need to revisit your script or function in the future. Why not make it easier for yourself or the next person who reads the script?

2.1.3   Testing your functions

As mentioned previously, one of the best reasons to make functions is to allow for easy testing. Testing is made even easier by the fact that PowerShell saves functions to memory. This enables you to run multiple tests without worrying about dependencies or issues with other parts of your script.

To test the function you just created, we will use VS Code. If you have not already done so, open a new file in VS Code and enter the function from listing 2.1.

Press F5 to execute the code. Since the file only contains this one function, PowerShell does not execute the code; the function is simply loaded into memory. Then you can execute the function in the terminal pane for your testing. In later chapters, we will cover things like mock testing, but for now, the commands you run will perform the actions they are designed to do.

> **Helper scripts**
>
> I have included several scripts throughout this book that you can use to help with testing. These scripts are in the Help Scripts folder for each chapter or on the GitHub repository for this book. For this section, I have included the script file New-TestLog-Files.ps1. You can use this script to create a directory of dummy log files with different created and modified dates. This will allow you to test the functions and scripts in this section.

To start, you need to determine the parameters to pass for testing. In this case, you need `ZipPath` and `ZipPrefix`, which are both strings. Those can be easily passed as part of the command line. The final parameter, `Date`, requires a `DateTime` object. Here is where PowerShell's ease of use can really come in handy. Because you defined the parameter as a `DateTime` object, PowerShell is smart enough to know how to parse a properly formatted string value into a DateTime object for you. This gives you the option to either create the DateTime object before calling the function as the script will do or send a properly formatted string, which it will convert for you. Keep in mind that it must be a properly formatted string.

> **NOTE** You can get a list of string format examples by running the command (Get-Date).GetDateTimeFormats().

Once you have the values for your parameters, you are ready to begin testing. For the first test, set the ZipPath parameter to a folder you know does not exist. This allows you to test the folder creation statement in the function:

```
Set-ArchiveFilePath -ZipPath "L:\Archives\" -ZipPrefix "LogArchive-" -Date
    "2021-02-24" -Verbose
VERBOSE: Created folder 'L:\Archives\'
L:\Archives\LogArchive-20210124.zip
```

Note the -Verbose at the end of the command line. This tells the function to output any Write-Verbose statements that it executes. In this case, we received confirmation that the condition to check that the folder does not exist is true, and the folder is created. If you rerun the same command, you should see the same file name, but this time, there should not be any verbose output. This tells you that the script correctly detects that the folder exists, so it does not try to recreate it. It also shows you that the New-Item command successfully created the folder the first time you ran the function:

```
Set-ArchiveFilePath -ZipPath "L:\Archives\" -ZipPrefix "LogArchive-" -Date
    "2021-02-24" -Verbose
L:\Archives\LogArchive-20210124.zip
```

For the next test, create a zip file in the directory using the name that the previous steps returned, and then run the command once more:

```
Set-ArchiveFilePath -ZipPath "L:\Archives\" -ZipPrefix "LogArchive-" -Date
    "2021-02-24" -Verbose
Exception:
Line |
  24 |             throw "The file '$ZipFile' already exists"
     |             ~~~~~~~~~~~~~~~~~~~~~~~~~~~~~~~~~~~~~~~~~~~~
     | The file 'L:\Archives\LogArchive-20210224.zip' already exists
```

This time you will see that the function threw an exception, letting you know that the file already exists. Once your function is tested, it is ready to be added to your script. A bonus of testing is that you can create some perfect examples to include in your comment-based help.

2.1.4   Problems to avoid when adding functions to scripts

When you add a function into a script, it must go before any lines that call it because PowerShell scripts execute in sequence. Therefore, you must always have the statement declaring the function before calling it. Also, be very careful with functions stored in memory. If you run one script that loads a function into memory and then run another script in the same PowerShell session, the second script can use functions that only exist in the first script. However, if you create a new PowerShell session and then run the second script first, it will error out because it does not contain the function. It worked the first time because the first script had already loaded the function into memory. For this reason, you should always create new PowerShell sessions between tests. This prevents you from getting false positives in cases where items may be stored in memory.

Thankfully, VS Code provides a very easy way for you to do this. Simply click the little trash can icon in the terminal. This will kill the session and ask if you want to start a new one. Click Yes, and it will load a new, clean session.

2.1.5   Brevity versus efficiency

One trap that people often fall into with PowerShell is the insistence on making scripts as few lines as possible. Unfortunately, this leads to scripts with unwieldy, long commands that are impossible to read and test. As a result, they can often be less efficient than if they are broken up into multiple lines.

For example, you need to get the files to archive in the automation you are creating. This is done using the `Get-ChildItem` cmdlet which returns the files inside the specified folder. They can then be added to an archive using the `Compress-Archive` cmdlet. This task can be accomplished in a single line by piping the results of the `Get-ChildItem` cmdlet to the `Compress-Archive` cmdlet:

```
Get-ChildItem -Path $LogPath -File | Where-Object{ $_.LastWriteTime -lt $Date}
    | Compress-Archive -DestinationPath $ZipFile
```

If you combine these commands into one line, the output will be from the last command, `Compress-Archive`. Therefore, when you try to delete the files, your script will not know which files were added to the archive. You would then need to rerun the `Get-ChildItem` cmdlet to get the files to delete. Not only is this very inefficient, as you are querying the machine for the files again, but it can also lead to unintended consequences. For example, if a file has been added between the two times the `Get-ChildItem` cmdlet runs, you could end up deleting a file that wasn't archived.

That is not saying that combining commands or using multiple pipelines is a bad thing. It really just depends on the context. A good rule to remember is to only query once. If you have a command collecting data and multiple steps use that data, that command should not be repeated. Instead, the results should be saved in a variable and passed to the other commands that need it.

Besides efficiency, another good reason to break things up is for readability. For example, you can set the path, name, and timestamp in a single command, but it becomes a mess to read:

```
$ZipFile = Join-Path $ZipPath "$($ZipPrefix)$($Date.ToString('yyyyMMdd')).zip"
```

Breaking it up into a couple of lines makes it much more readable:

```
$timeString = $Date.ToString('yyyyMMdd')
$ZipName = "$($ZipPrefix)$($timeString).zip"
$ZipFile = Join-Path $ZipPath $ZipName
```

At the same time, breaking code up into too many lines can sometimes lead to large chunks that are not as clear:

```
$ZipFilePattern = '{0}_{1}.{2}'
$ZipFileDate = $($Date.ToString('yyyyMMdd'))
$ZipExtension = "zip"
$ZipFileName = $ZipFilePattern -f $ZipPrefix, $ZipFileDate, $ZipExtension
$ZipFile = Join-Path -Path $ZipPath -ChildPath $ZipFileName
```

There may be a perfectly good reason to do it this way. If you want the script to increment the file name instead of failing on a duplicate entry, it might make sense to break it down to separate variables on separate lines. Neither way is inherently right or wrong. It all depends on your context and needs.

Remember, brevity and efficiency do not go hand in hand. Just because you can achieve something with a single command doesn't always mean it is a good idea. Readability and clarity should take precedence over both.

2.1.6 *Careful what you automate*

The last step in the automation, deleting the old log files, might seem pretty straightforward. However, if the thought of deleting files via an automated script does not give you pause, then perhaps you've never heard the saying, "To err is human. To totally mess something up takes a computer." This rings especially true with automations. However, if you build them well, you can sleep soundly at night, knowing your automations will not be running wild throughout your environment.

With the cleanup of the log files, you can quickly delete all the files found by the Get-ChildItem command using the Remove-Item cmdlet. You can assume all the files were added to the archive because the Compress-Archive cmdlet did not return any errors, but we all know what assuming leads to. So, how can we ensure that each file was archived and is safe to delete? By creating a function that will do just that.

Like with everything in PowerShell and automations, there are multiple ways to achieve this. For example, the Expand-Archive cmdlet can extract the archive to another folder and check that each file matches. However, this would be very inefficient and prone to issues such as not having enough disk space to extract the files, and it will leave you with two sets of files to delete. Unfortunately, PowerShell does not have a cmdlet to look inside a zip file without extracting it. Fortunately, you are not restricted to only using PowerShell cmdlets. You can also call .NET objects directly in PowerShell. For example, you can create a function that uses the `System.IO.Compression` .NET namespace to look inside a zip file, thus allowing you to confirm each file's name and uncompressed size without needing to extract it.

How did I know to use the System.IO.Compression namespace?

After searching for ways to look inside an archive file in PowerShell and coming up empty, I performed the same search, but instead of PowerShell, I used C#. This brought me to a forum post on how to do just that. Knowing that I could dot source, I was able to re-create the C# code using PowerShell.

Like the last function, you will start this one, shown in the next listing, with the `CmdletBinding` and `OutputType` attributes. However, because you are performing a delete with no output, the `OutputType` attribute can be left blank.

Listing 2.2   Deleting archived files

```
Function Remove-ArchivedFiles {
    [CmdletBinding()]
    [OutputType()]
    param(
    [Parameter(Mandatory = $true)]
    [string]$ZipFile,

    [Parameter(Mandatory = $true)]
    [object]$FilesToDelete,

    [Parameter(Mandatory = $false)]
    [switch]$WhatIf = $false
    )
    $AssemblyName = 'System.IO.Compression.FileSystem'
    Add-Type -AssemblyName $AssemblyName | Out-Null

    $OpenZip = [System.IO.Compression.ZipFile]::OpenRead($ZipFile)
    $ZipFileEntries = $OpenZip.Entries

    foreach($file in $FilesToDelete){
        $check = $ZipFileEntries | Where-Object{ $_.Name -eq $file.Name -and
            $_.Length -eq $file.Length }
        if($null -ne $check){
            $file | Remove-Item -Force -WhatIf:$WhatIf
        }
        else {
            Write-Error "'$($file.Name)' was not find in '$($ZipFile)'"
        }
    }
}
```

Load the **System.IO.Compression.FileSystem** assembly so you can use dot sourcing later.

Get the information on the files inside the zip.

Confirm each file to delete has a match in the zip file.

If $check does not equal null, you know the file was found and can be deleted.

Add WhatIf to allow for testing without actually deleting the files.

For the parameters, you need to know the path of the zip file and the files that should be inside of it. The zip file path is a simple string, but the files to delete need multiple values. Because PowerShell is an object-oriented language and the output from the Get-ChildItem cmdlet is saved in a variable, you can pass the object as a parameter as is. This allows you to avoid the need to convert it to a string array or something similar.

Because this function performs an irreversible action, you will also want to include a WhatIf switch to help with testing. Switches work much like a Boolean value, except you don't have to include True or False after it. Just listing the parameter in your command sets it to True. WhatIf is a popular parameter included in many PowerShell cmdlets. It allows you to see what the cmdlet would do without actually performing the action. Including it in your function allows you to test the deletion process without actually removing anything.

Since you will be using a .NET class in your function, begin by adding the Add-Type cmdlet with the full name of the .NET class. This cmdlet will load a .NET namespace into your PowerShell session. This ensures that you will be able to use the dot sourcing in the other command. In this case, it is the namespace System.IO .Compression.FileSystem.

The classes in that namespace can be called directly in PowerShell by writing the class name between square brackets. You can call the methods and constructors by adding two colons. For example, to get the files inside an archive, use the OpenRead method in the System.IO.Compression.ZipFile class and save it to a PowerShell variable:

```
$OpenZip = [IO.Compression.ZipFile]::OpenRead($ZipFile)
```

Next, you need to compare the files in the archive to the files that should be in it. Using foreach allows you to go through every file, one at a time, to confirm each one is in the archive file by matching the name and file size. If found, they can be deleted. If they are not found, an error message is sent to PowerShell. However, unlike the previous function, there is no need to stop processing if a couple of files are missing. In this case, use the Write-Error cmdlet instead of the throw command. The Write-Error cmdlet sends the error back to PowerShell, but it is not a terminating error like the throw command. Instead, this error is just recorded so it can be addressed later. Because there is no output from this function, there is no need to add a variable result to the end.

2.1.7 *Putting it all together*

Now that you have created your new function (aka building block), it is time to put everything together into a single script, as shown in listing 2.3. Like with a function, your scripts should always start with comment-based help, the CmdletBinding and OutputType attributes, and a parameter block. If you need it to import any modules, place them directly after the parameters.

Listing 2.3   Putting it all together

```
[CmdletBinding()]
[OutputType()]
param(
    [Parameter(Mandatory = $true)]
    [string]$LogPath,

    [Parameter(Mandatory = $true)]
    [string]$ZipPath,

    [Parameter(Mandatory = $true)]
    [string]$ZipPrefix,

    [Parameter(Mandatory = $false)]
    [double]$NumberOfDays = 30
)

Function Set-ArchiveFilePath{          ◁── Declare your
    [CmdletBinding()]                      functions before
    [OutputType([string])]                 the script code.
    param(
    [Parameter(Mandatory = $true)]
    [string]$ZipPath,

    [Parameter(Mandatory = $true)]
    [string]$ZipPrefix,

    [Parameter(Mandatory = $false)]
    [datetime]$Date = (Get-Date)
    )

    if(-not (Test-Path -Path $ZipPath)){
        New-Item -Path $ZipPath -ItemType Directory | Out-Null
        Write-Verbose "Created folder '$ZipPath'"
    }

    $ZipName = "$($ZipPrefix)$($Date.ToString('yyyyMMdd')).zip"
    $ZipFile = Join-Path $ZipPath $ZipName

    if(Test-Path -Path $ZipFile){
        throw "The file '$ZipFile' already exists"
    }

    $ZipFile
}

Function Remove-ArchivedFiles {
    [CmdletBinding()]
    [OutputType()]
    param(
    [Parameter(Mandatory = $true)]
    [string]$ZipFile,
```

```
    [Parameter(Mandatory = $true)]
    [object]$FilesToDelete,

    [Parameter(Mandatory = $false)]
    [switch]$WhatIf = $false
    )

    $AssemblyName = 'System.IO.Compression.FileSystem'
    Add-Type -AssemblyName $AssemblyName | Out-Null

    $OpenZip = [System.IO.Compression.ZipFile]::OpenRead($ZipFile)
    $ZipFileEntries = $OpenZip.Entries

    foreach($file in $FilesToDelete){
        $check = $ZipFileEntries | Where-Object{ $_.Name -eq $file.Name -and
            $_.Length -eq $file.Length }
        if($null -ne $check){
            $file | Remove-Item -Force -WhatIf:$WhatIf
        }
        else {
            Write-Error "'$($file.Name)' was not find in '$($ZipFile)'"
        }
    }
}
```

```
$Date = (Get-Date).AddDays(-$NumberOfDays)
$files = Get-ChildItem -Path $LogPath -File |
    Where-Object{ $_.LastWriteTime -lt $Date}

$ZipParameters = @{
    ZipPath = $ZipPath
    ZipPrefix = $ZipPrefix
    Date = $Date
}
$ZipFile = Set-ArchiveFilePath @ZipParameters

$files | Compress-Archive -DestinationPath $ZipFile

$RemoveFiles = @{
    ZipFile = $ZipFile
    FilesToDelete = $files
}
Remove-ArchivedFiles @RemoveFiles
```

Set the date filter based on the number of days in the past.

Get the files to archive based on the date filter.

Get the archive file path.

Add the files to the archive file.

Confirm files are in the archive and delete.

Before you enter any of the script code and logic, enter the script functions. Although, technically, functions can go anywhere as long as they are before any commands that call them, it will make your script much easier to read and maintain if all functions are declared at the beginning. This will also make it easier to add or replace building blocks in a later phase.

For instance, in phase 2, you want to upload the archive to a cloud storage provider. You can build that function outside of this script. When you are ready to add it, you simply copy and paste it in and add a line to call it. Then, say, down the line, you change cloud providers; you can simply swap out that function with one that uploads to the other cloud, and you don't have to change anything else in your script.

Once you add the functions, you can start adding code for the script. Here, that will be setting the date filter, getting the files to archive, getting the archive file path, archiving the files, and finally deleting them.

To test this script, you need log files to clean up. If you have not already done so, run the New-TestLogFiles.ps1 included in this chapter's Helper Scripts to create the dummy log files for you to test. Next, set the values to use for your testing in the terminal:

```
$LogPath = "L:\Logs\"
$ZipPath = "L:\Archives\"
$ZipPrefix = "LogArchive-"
$NumberOfDays = 30
```

In VS Code, you can run a single line or section of your code at a time by highlighting it and pressing F8. Unlike F5, which runs the entire script, F8 only runs the section of code that is highlighted. Start testing by highlighting the functions and pressing F8. This will load the functions into memory. Next, run the lines to set the date and collect the files to archive:

```
$Date = (Get-Date).AddDays(-$NumberOfDays)
$files = Get-ChildItem -Path $LogPath -File |
    Where-Object{ $_.LastWriteTime -lt $Date}
```

You will notice there is no output. That is because the output is saved in the $files variable at this point in the script. You can check the values of each variable by entering them in the terminal window. You can also use this to confirm that your date filter is working and that only the files you want to archive are included:

```
$Date
Sunday, January 10, 2021 7:59:29 AM
$files
    Directory: L:\Logs

Mode                 LastWriteTime         Length Name
----                 -------------         ------ ----
-a---          11/12/2020   7:59 AM      32505856 u_ex20201112.log
-a---          11/13/2020   7:59 AM      10485760 u_ex20201113.log
-a---          11/14/2020   7:59 AM       4194304 u_ex20201114.log
-a---          11/15/2020   7:59 AM      40894464 u_ex20201115.log
-a---          11/16/2020   7:59 AM      32505856 u_ex20201116.log
```

Next, run the lines to set the archive path and file name and confirm that it is set as expected:

```
$ZipParameters = @{
    ZipPath = $ZipPath
    ZipPrefix = $ZipPrefix
    Date = $Date
}
```

```
$ZipFile = Set-ArchiveFilePath @ZipParameters
$ZipFile
L:\Archives\LogArchive-20210110.zip
```

Then run the line to add the log files to the archive file:

```
$files | Compress-Archive -DestinationPath $ZipFile
```

Now you are ready to test the delete function. For your first test, add the `-WhatIf` switch to the end of the command:

```
Remove-ArchivedFiles -ZipFile $ZipFile -FilesToDelete $files -WhatIf
What if: Performing the operation "Remove File" on target
    "L:\Logs\u_ex20201112.log".
What if: Performing the operation "Remove File" on target
    "L:\Logs\u_ex20201113.log".
What if: Performing the operation "Remove File" on target
    "L:\Logs\u_ex20201114.log".
What if: Performing the operation "Remove File" on target
    "L:\Logs\u_ex20201115.log".
```

You should see `What if` written to the terminal window for each file it would delete. If you check in file explorer, you should see that the files are still there. Now rerun the command without the `-WhatIf` switch:

```
Remove-ArchivedFiles -ZipFile $ZipFile -FilesToDelete $files
```

This time there should be no output. You can check File Explorer, and the files will be gone.

After running through this test, you will want to test the entire script. When performing the final test, I recommend opening a new PowerShell window and calling the script directly. This way, you can ensure there are not values or functions in memory affecting the script. To do this, run New-TestLogFiles.ps1 again to create new log files. Then open a new PowerShell terminal and run your script. If it works, you are done.

2.2   *The anatomy of PowerShell automation*

In the previous section, you created your first building block (aka function). Now we will look at how to utilize PowerShell to make that building block reusable.

Throughout this book, we will define an automation as a single script. A script, in this instance, is a single PowerShell script (ps1) file that, when executed from start to finish, will perform all the required tasks of your automation. Now you can write a PowerShell script one line after another to perform each task you need. However, doing this leaves you with a tangled mess of code that is difficult to read, make changes to, and test. Instead, use functions to break up your code into small, easily testable, and manageable pieces of code. These functions are your building blocks.

However, functions declared inside a script are only available to that script. At that point, they become specialty-use tools and not really building blocks. Of course, sometimes you need a specialty tool, and you can build those as needed, but you do not want to have to re-create general-purpose tools for every script you create.

While storing your functions in a script file is fine for very specific tasks, it limits your ability to share or reuse them outside of that individual script. The other option you have is to store functions in a script module.

A script module is a collection of functions, classes, and variables, all written in PowerShell. Script modules are great for collaborating with a team because each member can add their own functions to it. In addition, it allows you to reuse the same function in multiple different automations. As you will see later in this book, modules also lend themselves very nicely to version control and unit testing.

A script module can also be used to extend the functionality of a base or gallery module. These modules contain compiled cmdlets that you cannot change. They can also contain functions that you can change, but doing so would cause untold issues when it comes to upgrades and maintaining the code. Instead, you will see in this chapter how your custom script modules can be used to supplement the other modules. Figure 2.4 shows a diagram of a script and its modules.

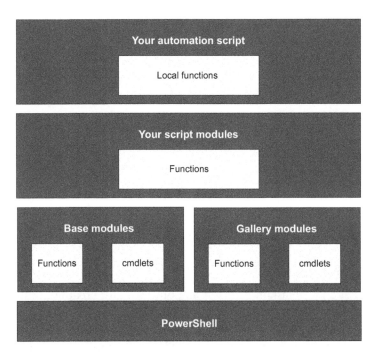

Figure 2.4   Your PowerShell script will inherit all of the script modules, base modules, and gallery modules loaded into it. It can also contain its own specialized functions if needed.

A function in PowerShell is a collection of statements that are defined in a single command. For instance, if you want to get a list of the top 10 processes using the most CPU on your computer, you can use the Get-Process cmdlet. However, running this cmdlet will return every running process in alphabetical order, but you want to sort it by top CPU utilization and limit the number of items returned. You also want to format the output to show the process ID, name, and CPU utilization with thousand separators. Now your command is starting to get pretty long and more complex.

This also may be something you want to run often. Instead of needing to remember and retype this entire command line, you can turn it into a function, as shown in the next listing, which can then be called with a single short command. You can also make your functions dynamic by defining parameters. For example, you can create a parameter to specify the number of items to return instead of hardcoding it to 10.

Listing 2.4   Get top *N* processes

```
Function Get-TopProcess{          ←───┤ Declare your
    param(                                function.
        [Parameter(Mandatory = $true)]
        [int]$TopN
    )
    Get-Process | Sort-Object CPU -Descending |     ←───┤ Run the
        Select-Object -First $TopN -Property ID,          command.
        ProcessName, @{l='CPU';e={'{0:N}' -f $_.CPU}}
}
```

Define the parameters. (annotation pointing to `param(`)

Functions can contain calls to other functions and cmdlets. You can store your functions inside your script or in a module. Once you have your function defined, you can call it like any other command in PowerShell:

```
Get-TopProcess -TopN 5
   Id ProcessName   CPU
   -- -----------   ---
 1168 dwm           39,633.27
 9152 mstsc         33,772.52
 9112 Code          16,023.08
 1216 svchost       13,093.50
 2664 HealthService 10,345.77
```

2.2.1   When to add functions to a module

The question you should be asking yourself any time you are creating a function in PowerShell is "Would this be useful in another script?" If the answer to that question is yes or maybe, it is worth considering putting it into a module. As a good rule of thumb, to ensure that your functions are reusable across multiple automations, it should perform one task that can be restarted if something goes wrong.

Take the example of an automation for archiving old logs. You want to find the old files, add them to an archive, and then delete them from the folder. You can write a single function to do that, but what happens if something goes wrong halfway through the removal process? If you restart the function, you could lose data when you re-created the archive file, and half the files are already deleted.

It is also good practice to write a function any time you find yourself writing the same lines of code again and again. This way, if you need to make a change to your code, there is only one place to update it instead of having to track down every single line you wrote it on.

However, there is also no need to go overboard with functions. If what you need to do can be done with a single command or just a couple of lines of code, wrapping it in a function could be more trouble than it is worth. It is also best not to include control logic inside of your functions. If you need your automation to take specific actions based on certain results, it is best to define that in the script.

Most modules you come across in PowerShell are system-based (for example, the Active Directory module or the Azure modules). They are all built with a specific tool in mind because they are usually created by the company or provider of that system. You can certainly stick to this pattern. It is really up to you. Nothing is stopping you from creating a module to house a bunch of different useful yet unrelated functions.

For instance, you can create a single module used for managing user accounts. This module might have functions that reach out to Active Directory, Office 365, SAP, etc. While these are all separate systems, your module can act as a bridge between them, making your user management tasks much more manageable.

Again, it depends on your needs. Plus, once you see how easy it is to create and maintain a module, there should be no hesitation in considering it.

2.2.2 Creating a script module

Creating a module in PowerShell can sometimes be as easy as renaming a file from a ps1 to a psm1, and it can be as complicated as writing cmdlets in C# that need to be compiled to a DLL. A module that does not contain a compiled code is a script module. A script module provides a perfect place to store and share a collection of related functions. We will not go in-depth into module creation, as there can be a lot to it, and there are plenty of other books and resources that cover this topic. However, I would like to cover a few essential tips and tricks that you can use to get started creating script modules today.

At its most basic, a module can be a single PowerShell script file saved as a psm1. You can paste all the functions you want into a psm1 file, save it, load it into Power-Shell, and be on your way. But this does not lend itself well to versioning or testing. So, at a minimum, you should also include a module manifest (psd1) file. The module manifest can provide details about the module, such as which functions or variables to make public. But, most important, it contains the module's version number, helping to ensure you always have the latest and greatest version.

Along with the psm1 and psd1 files, you can include additional script files (ps1) with your functions to load with the module. Instead of creating one massive psm1 file with every function, you can create a separate script (ps1) file for each function and have them loaded by the psm1.

To show you how simple this process can be, we can take our log file cleanup script from the last section and move the functions from inside the script into a module. As with anything, the first place to start is with the name. In this case, we can name the module FileCleanupTools. Then, you simply create the folder structure, psd1, and psm1 files. The top-level folder, the psd1, and the psm1 should all have the same name. If they do not have the same name, PowerShell will not be able to load them using the standard `Import-Module <ModuleName>` command. Next, under the top-level folder, you should create a folder that matches the version number.

PowerShell allows you to have multiple versions of the same module installed at the same time. This is great for testing and upgrading proposes. As long as you nest your module files in a folder with the version number, you can pick and choose which ones you want to load.

> **NOTE**   By default, PowerShell loads the highest version, so you need to include `-MaximumVersion` and `-MinimumVersion` in the `Import-Module` command if you want to load a specific version.

The psd1 and psm1 go inside the version folder. From here forward, the file and folder structure is up to you. However, the standard practice, and one that I recommend, is to create a folder named Public. The Public folder will contain the ps1 files that will house the functions. As a result, your typical module will start to look something like what you see in figure 2.5.

While this may sound like a lot to remember, you can use PowerShell to streamline your module creation process. As you just saw in the log file cleanup, PowerShell can create folders for you. PowerShell also includes the cmdlet `New-ModuleManifest` that you can use to create the psd1 file for you.

When you use the `New-ModuleManifest` cmdlet, you need to specify the module name, the path to the psd1 and psm1 files, and the module version number. You will also want to provide the author's name and the minimum PowerShell version the module can use. You can do that all at once with the script in the following listing.

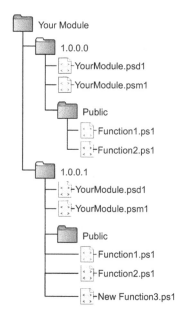

Figure 2.5   A PowerShell module folder structure with version folders

---

Listing 2.5   `New-ModuleTemplate`

```
Function New-ModuleTemplate {
    [CmdletBinding()]
    [OutputType()]
```

Create a
folder with
the same
name as the
module.

Create
a blank
psml file.

```
param(
    [Parameter(Mandatory = $true)]
    [string]$ModuleName,
    [Parameter(Mandatory = $true)]
    [string]$ModuleVersion,
    [Parameter(Mandatory = $true)]
    [string]$Author,
    [Parameter(Mandatory = $true)]
    [string]$PSVersion,
    [Parameter(Mandatory = $false)]
    [string[]]$Functions
)
$ModulePath = Join-Path .\ "$($ModuleName)\$($ModuleVersion)"
New-Item -Path $ModulePath -ItemType Directory
Set-Location $ModulePath
New-Item -Path .\Public -ItemType Directory

$ManifestParameters = @{
    ModuleVersion     = $ModuleVersion
    Author            = $Author
    Path              = ".\$($ModuleName).psd1"
    RootModule        = ".\$($ModuleName).psm1"
    PowerShellVersion = $PSVersion
}
New-ModuleManifest @ManifestParameters

$File = @{
    Path     = ".\$($ModuleName).psm1"
    Encoding = 'utf8'
}
Out-File @File

$Functions | ForEach-Object {
    Out-File -Path ".\Public\$($_).ps1" -Encoding utf8
}
}

$module = @{
    ModuleName    = 'FileCleanupTools'
    ModuleVersion = "1.0.0.0"
    Author        = "YourNameHere"
    PSVersion     = '7.0'
    Functions     = 'Remove-ArchivedFiles',
                    'Set-ArchiveFilePath'
}
New-ModuleTemplate @module
```

Create the Public
folder to store
your psl scripts.

Set the path to
the psdl file.

Set the path to
the psml file.

Create the module
manifest psdl file with
the settings supplied
in the parameters.

Create a blank psl
for each function.

Set the parameters to
pass to the function.

The name
of your
module

Your
name

The version of
your module

The minimum
PowerShell version
this module supports

Execute the function to
create the new module.

The functions to
create blank files for
in the Public folder

Now that you have your basic structure, you can add your functions to the Public
folder. To do this, create a new PowerShell script file in the folder and give it the same
name as the function. Starting with the Set-ArchiveFilePath function, create the file

Set-ArchiveFilePath.ps1. Then do the same for the `Remove-ArchivedFiles` function. Figure 2.6 shows this file structure.

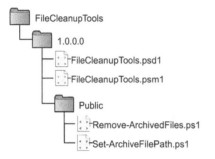

Figure 2.6   The file structure for the FileCleanupTools module

From here, you can simply copy and paste the code for each function into its respective file. Be sure that you are only bringing in the function and no other parts of the script when you copy and paste. The file should start with the `Function` keyword declaring the function, and the last line should be the curly bracket ending the function. The next listing shows what the Set-ArchiveFilePath.ps1 file should contain.

Listing 2.6   Set-ArchiveFilePath.ps1

```
Function Set-ArchiveFilePath{
    [CmdletBinding()]
    [OutputType([string])]
    param(
    [Parameter(Mandatory = $true)]
    [string]$ZipPath,

    [Parameter(Mandatory = $true)]
    [string]$ZipPrefix,

    [Parameter(Mandatory = $false)]
    [datetime]$Date = (Get-Date)
    )

    if(-not (Test-Path -Path $ZipPath)){
        New-Item -Path $ZipPath -ItemType Directory | Out-Null
        Write-Verbose "Created folder '$ZipPath'"
    }

    $ZipName = "$($ZipPrefix)$($Date.ToString('yyyyMMdd')).zip"
    $ZipFile = Join-Path $ZipPath $ZipName

    if(Test-Path -Path $ZipFile){
        throw "The file '$ZipFile' already exists"
    }

    $ZipFile
}
```

Repeat this process for any other functions you want to add to the module. One thing to note is that the script files will not automatically be loaded when you import the module. By default, PowerShell will run the psm1 file on import because it is listed as the `RootModule` in the psd1 manifest. Therefore, you need to let the module know which files it needs to run to import your functions. The easiest way to do this is by having the psm1 file search the Public folder for each ps1 file and then execute each one to load the function into your current PowerShell session.

The best part about loading the functions this way is that there is nothing you need to update or change when adding a new function. Simply add the ps1 for it to the Public folder, and it will be loaded the next time you import the module. As long as your functions are in the Public folder, you can do this by adding the code in the following listing to your psm1 file.

Listing 2.7 Loading module functions

```
$Path = Join-Path $PSScriptRoot 'Public'
$Functions = Get-ChildItem -Path $Path -Filter '*.ps1'
```
Get all the ps1 files in the Public folder.

```
Foreach ($import in $Functions) {
    Try {
        Write-Verbose "dot-sourcing file '$($import.fullname)'"
        . $import.fullname
    }
    Catch {
        Write-Error -Message "Failed to import function $($import.name)"
    }
}
```
Loop through each ps1 file.

Execute each ps1 file to load the function into memory.

If you use a different folder structure or multiple folders, you will need to update the first couple of lines so PowerShell knows which folders to look in. For example, if you add a Private folder for private functions, you can pass both folders to the `Get-ChildItem` cmdlet to return all the ps1s between them:

```
$Public = Join-Path $PSScriptRoot 'Public'
$Private = Join-Path $PSScriptRoot 'Private'
$Functions = Get-ChildItem -Path $Public,$Private -Filter '*.ps1'
```

Once you have your module file created, run the `Import-Module` command and point it to the path of your module manifest (psd1) file to import the functions into your current PowerShell session. You will need to use the full path unless the module folder is inside a folder included in the `$env:PSModulePath` environment variable. Even if it is, it is good to use the full path for testing to ensure you are loading the correct version.

Also, when you are testing a module, include the `-Force` switch at the end to force the module to reload and pick up any changes you have made. You can also provide the `-PassThru` switch to ensure that your functions are loaded:

```
Import-Module .\FileCleanupTools.psd1 -Force -PassThru
ModuleType Version  Name              ExportedCommands
---------- -------  ----              ----------------
Script     1.0.0.0  FileCleanupTools {Remove-ArchivedFiles,
                                      Set-ArchiveFilePath}
```

Once your module is ready, remove the functions from the original script and add one line of code to import the module, as shown in the following listing.

Listing 2.8   Moving functions to module

```
param(
    [Parameter(Mandatory = $true)]
    [string]$LogPath,

    [Parameter(Mandatory = $true)]
    [string]$ZipPath,

    [Parameter(Mandatory = $true)]
    [string]$ZipPrefix,

    [Parameter(Mandatory = $false)]
    [double]$NumberOfDays = 30
)

Import-Module FileCleanupTools     �⟵  Replaced functions with
                                          the command to load the
                                          FileCleanupTools module

$Date = (Get-Date).AddDays(-$NumberOfDays)
$files = Get-ChildItem -Path $LogPath -File |
    Where-Object{ $_.LastWriteTime -lt $Date}

$ZipParameters = @{
    ZipPath = $ZipPath
    ZipPrefix = $ZipPrefix
    Date = $Date
}
$ZipFile = Set-ArchiveFilePath @ZipParameters

$files | Compress-Archive -DestinationPath $ZipFile

Remove-ArchivedFiles -ZipFile $ZipFile -FilesToDelete $files
```

2.2.3 Module creation tips

There are a few things you can do to help yourself and others when you are creating a module. These include using common naming and styling, separating public and private functions, installing custom modules in PSModulePath, and listing dependencies in the manifest.

USE COMMON NAMING AND STYLING

You may have noticed by now that the majority of PowerShell commands follow the same naming conventions and style. This includes using the Verb-Noun naming pattern for cmdlets and functions (`Get-Module`, `Import-Module`, etc.). When deciding what verb to use, it is best to stick with the list of approved verbs. You can find the list of approved verbs by running the command `Get-Verb`. Also, the noun should be singular (for example, `Get-Command`, not `Get-Commands`).

Module names, parameter names, and variables use Pascal casing. With Pascal casing, each proper word in the name starts with an uppercase letter. For example, the module we just created is named FileCleanupTools. Some people will use Camel casing for local variables and Pascal for global variables, but this is not universal. Camel casing is like Pascal casing except the first word is lowercase (for example, fileCleanupTools).

Do not be afraid of long variable and parameter names. It is much better to be descriptive than short and vague. For example, a parameter named `$NumberOfDays` is much clearer than one named `$Days`.

None of these styles are required. You could create a function named `archive-File-Deleting`, and it would work fine. Of course, you would receive a warning when you import the module, but that's it. However, others who are used to the standard PowerShell naming conventions may find it challenging to find and use your functions.

SEPARATE PRIVATE AND PUBLIC FUNCTIONS

In our example, we created a folder named Public and put our functions ps1 files in it. We did this to let others know that these are functions that they can use in their scripts. There may be times when you write what are referred to as *helper functions*. These are functions that other functions in the module can call, but the users should not need to call directly. You can have helper functions for a whole host of reasons. For example, you may have a function that parses some data and is used by several functions in your module, but there would be no reason for the end user to need it. In this case, it is best to make it a private function. To do this, create a second folder in your module named Private to hold these files. Then, update the import in your psm1 to also import the Private folder.

Keep in mind that just because the files are in the Private folder doesn't mean they will be hidden. The Public and Private folder names are just suggestions. You could name them anything. However, others writing PowerShell modules commonly use these names to help keep things organized. You can put them all together in one folder, multiple subfolders, or any way you like, as long as the psm1 file can find them. To make them private, you have to delist them from the manifest (psd1) file. If you look inside the FileCleanupTools.psd1 you created earlier, you will see the line `FunctionsToExport = '*'`. This line tells the module to export all functions that match this pattern. Because the pattern is a single wildcard, everything will match. As there is no exclude line, the only way to exclude something is by not listing it. This is where the Public and Private folders come in handy. You can simply update the manifest to only include the functions from the Public folder. So it would look like this for the FileCleanupTools.psd1:

```
FunctionsToExport = 'Remove-ArchivedFiles', 'Set-ArchiveFilePath'
```

When you do this, remember to update the manifest any time you want to add a new public function.

INSTALL CUSTOM MODULES IN PSMODULEPATH

Have you ever wondered how PowerShell knows where the files are when you type `Import-Module` and just give a module name and not a path as we did in the previous example? It will do this for any module installed in a folder listed in the `$env:PSModule-Path` environmental variable. Therefore, it is best to always install your modules to a path listed there. However, be careful, as there are system (AllUsers) and user (Current-User) scopes. If you are creating an automation that will run under the system account, use the AllUsers scope. The default on Windows is `$env:ProgramFiles\PowerShell\Modules`. You can confirm what folders are included by checking the `$env:PSModulePath` variable in your PowerShell console.

LISTING DEPENDENCIES IN THE MANIFEST

There is a parameter in the manifest file named `RequiredModules`. This parameter allows you to list modules that are required for this module. For example, if you wrote a module to work with Active Directory users, you need to be sure that the Active Directory module is loaded along with your module. The problem you may run into with the `RequiredModules` parameter is that it does not import the module if it has not already been imported, and it does not check versions. Therefore, I often find myself handling module dependencies directly in the psm1 file, as in the following listing.

Listing 2.9   Importing required modules

```
[System.Collections.Generic.List[PSObject]]$RequiredModules = @()
$RequiredModules.Add([pscustomobject]@{          ⏴──┐ Create an object for
    Name = 'Pester'                                    │ each module to check.
    Version = '4.1.2'
})

                                                     Loop through each
                                                     module to check.
foreach($module in $RequiredModules){          ⏴──┘
    $Check = Get-Module $module.Name -ListAvailable      ⏴──┐ Check whether the
                                                               │ module is installed
    if(-not $check){          ⏴──────────────────────────┐   │ on the local machine.
        throw "Module $($module.Name) not found"
    }                                                   If not found, throw a
                                                        terminating error to
    $VersionCheck = $Check |                            stop this module
        Where-Object{ $_.Version -ge $module.Version }  from loading.

    if(-not $VersionCheck){
        Write-Error "Module $($module.Name) running older version"
    }

    Import-Module -Name $module.Name          ⏴──┐ Import the module into
}                                                    │ the current session.
```

If it is found, check the version.

If an older version is found, write an error, but do not stop.

While these tips are all optional, following them can help you and others down the road when you need to make changes or updates to your modules.

Summary

- Building blocks can be translated to PowerShell functions.
- Functions should only perform one action that can be restarted if something goes wrong.
- Functions should be stored in PowerShell modules to allow other automations and people to use them.

Part 2

When it comes to creating successful automations, knowing how to write a script is only part of the equation. You also need to know what to consider when you have a script that will run unattended. This includes accounting for scheduling the script, providing the appropriate permissions/credentials, storing external data, and interacting with external sources.

For instance, scheduling a script to run can seem simple, but have you considered what would happen if a part of the automation failed? Or what would happen if the script was still running when the next occurrence kicks off? Or how to handle a situation where a script is required to authenticate? Or what would happen if two instances of a script tried to write data simultaneously?

This section will answer these questions and more. It will teach you how to think like an automation expert, plan for those unexpected situations, and create the most robust automations possible.

Scheduling
automation scripts

This chapter covers

- How to schedule scripts
- Considerations for scheduled scripts
- Creating continuously running scripts

When starting their PowerShell automation journey, one of the first things everyone wants to learn about is scheduling scripts to run unattended. In this chapter, you will learn more than just how to schedule a script. You will also learn some best practices, using common real-world scenarios that will help to ensure your scheduled scripts run smoothly. The concepts and practices used in these examples can be applied to any script you need to schedule.

It is tempting to say that you can take any existing PowerShell script and schedule it with a job scheduler, but that is only part of the solution. Before jumping straight into scheduling a PowerShell script, you must ensure that your script is adequately written to handle being run unattended. This includes many of the previously covered concepts, like ensuring dependencies are met and there are no user prompts.

There are several different types of scripts you will want to run on a scheduled basis. Two of the most common are *scheduled scripts* and *watcher scripts*. A scheduled script is any script that runs on a regular basis but not so often that it is continuously running. A watcher script runs either continuously or at least every few minutes. This chapter will cover both types, including the factors to consider when coding them and the considerations to make when scheduling them.

3.1   Scheduled scripts

A scheduled script is run on a fairly regular basis but does not need to be real-time. Some good examples of these are scripts to collect inventory, check on user accounts, check system resources, run data backups, etc. No matter what your script does, you need to take care before setting it to run on a schedule.

3.1.1   Know your dependencies and address them beforehand

If your script is dependent on any modules, be sure that these are installed on the system running the script before scheduling it. You also need to be aware of how these dependencies may affect other scheduled scripts. For example, if you have two scripts that require different versions of the same module, you need to ensure that both versions are installed instead of just the highest version.

Do not try to have your scheduled script install modules because this can lead to all sorts of unintended consequences. For example, it could fail to properly install the module, causing the scheduled script to never execute successfully. Or you could create a situation where two scripts continually override each other, taking up valuable system resources and causing failures between each other.

3.1.2   Know where your script needs to execute

Knowing where your script needs to execute sounds simple, but there are situations where a script executing in the wrong environment or on the wrong server can cause problems. A typical example is ensuring that the script has network access to the required systems. For instance, if you need to connect to Amazon Web Services or Azure from an on-premises script, you need to make sure no proxies or firewalls are blocking it.

There are also situations that may not seem as obvious. For instance, if you want to force the Azure AD Connector to sync using PowerShell, that script must run on the server with the connector installed. Another issue I've run into multiple times is dealing with Active Directory replication. If you have a script that creates an Active Directory user and then connects to Exchange, you can run into problems due to replication. For example, if you create the account on a domain controller in a different site than the Exchange server, it may not see the account when your script tries to create the mailbox, causing your script to fail.

3.1.3 *Know what context the script needs to execute under*

In conjunction with knowing your dependencies and where your script needs to execute is knowing what context it needs to run under. Most job schedulers can run scripts as a particular user or as the system. If you need to authenticate with Active Directory, SQL, or a network share, chances are you will need to run under a user context. If you are collecting data about the local machine, it can run under the system account.

Knowing the context will also help in setting your dependencies. PowerShell modules can be installed at the user level or the system level. You may test your script under your account, but it fails to load the modules when run through the job scheduler. This can be because the modules are installed under your account only. Therefore, I suggest you install modules to the system level to avoid these types of problems.

3.2 *Scheduling your scripts*

As with most things in PowerShell, there are several ways you can schedule scripts to run regularly. You can use anything from the built-in Windows Task Scheduler to enterprise-level job schedulers like Control-M or JAMS. Also, many other automation platforms have built-in schedulers such as System Center Orchestrator/Service Management Automation (SMA), Ansible, ActiveBatch, and PowerShell Universal. There are also several cloud-based solutions that can run PowerShell scripts both in the cloud and in your on-premises environment. You will find these covered in chapter 8. It will be up to you to choose the tool that best fits your environment. Whichever tool you choose, the process remains the same:

1 Create your script.
2 Copy it where the scheduler can access it.
3 Ensure dependencies are met.
4 Set required permissions.
5 Schedule it.

The log file cleanup script from chapter 2 is a perfect example of a script you would want to schedule to run. You can use it to practice creating a scheduled job using the Windows Task Scheduler, Cron, and Jenkins.

> **NOTE** A copy of the script Invoke-LogFileCleanup.ps1 and the module folder FileCleanupTools are available in the Helper Script folder for this chapter.

3.2.1 *Task Scheduler*

Task Scheduler is by far the most popular tool for scheduling scripts in a Windows environment. It does have one major drawback in that there is no central console for it, but it is easy to use and has been built into the Windows operating system since Windows NT 4.0.

When setting up any job to run through Task Scheduler, you need to consider permissions to access the script file and permissions to access the required resources. For this exercise, you can assume the logs are on the local machine, so you can run it under the system account.

However, you could, for example, place the script file on a network share. Having the script in a network share is a great way to help maintain a single script file and not have individual copies on every server. The downside is that you need to ensure that Task Scheduler can access it. The best way to do this is with a service account. You never want to use your personal account for a scheduled task. Besides the obvious security risk, it's also a great way to get locked out of your account the next time you change your password. Your other options include creating a completely unrestricted share or giving each computer that runs the script explicit access to the share—each of which is a huge security risk and can make maintaining a nightmare.

If you are reading this book, you are more than likely very familiar with the Windows Task Scheduler. However, I would like to cover a few things you should consider when creating scheduled tasks for PowerShell scripts.

INSTALLING YOUR CUSTOM MODULE OPTIONS

Since this script uses functions in a custom module, you must copy the module folder somewhere the script can access it. The default paths for the PowerShell modules, which will be automatically loaded at run time, are

- *PowerShell v5.1*—C:\Program Files\WindowsPowerShell\Modules
- *PowerShell v7.0*—C:\Program Files\PowerShell\7\Modules

To install the module for Task Scheduler to use, copy the folder FileCleanupTools from chapter 2 to one of these two folders.

SECURITY OPTIONS

Typically, you want your automations to run unattended. Therefore, you want to select Run Whether User Is Logged On or Not. From there, you have two options. First, you can select Do Not Store Password to have the task run under the system context. This is fine as long as everything the script interacts with is on the local machine.

Second, if you need to interact with other systems, network shares, or anything that requires user authentication, leave Do Not Store Password unselected. Then click Change User or Group to select the service account. You will receive a prompt to provide the password when you save the task.

CREATING POWERSHELL ACTIONS

When you create an action to execute a PowerShell script, you cannot simply set the Program/Script box to the PowerShell script file (ps1). Instead, you need to set the Program/Script box to the PowerShell executable. Then your script will go in the Add Arguments box. The default paths for the PowerShell executables that will go in the Program/Script box are

- *PowerShell v5.1*—C:\Windows\System32\WindowsPowerShell\v1.0\powershell.exe
- *PowerShell v7.0*—C:\Program Files\PowerShell\7\pwsh.exe

Then, in the Add Arguments box, you provide the -File argument with the path to your script and the values to pass for any parameters:

```
-File "C:\Scripts\Invoke-LogFileCleanup.ps1" -LogPath "L:\Logs\" -ZipPath "L:
➥\Archives\" -ZipPrefix "LogArchive-" -NumberOfDays 30
```

Also, if you are using PowerShell v5.1 or below, you will most likely also want to include the -WindowStyle argument and have it set to Hidden so your script will run silently.

SCHEDULING THE TASK

Once you have created the action, you need to schedule it. Task Scheduler in Windows has multiple options for running tasks once or repeatedly. Click the Triggers tab, and click New to create a new trigger. Select Daily with a start time of 8 a.m. in the settings, and then click OK to add it to your task.

JOB LOGS

You can review the results of all past executions and see any errors in the History tab for each job. All job logs are written to the Event Viewer log Microsoft-Windows-TaskScheduler/Operational. Although there is no central console to manage jobs, you can use event forwarding to collect all the job logs into one central location.

3.2.2 *Create scheduled tasks via PowerShell*

Since Task Scheduler does not have a central console for you to see and schedule across multiple computers at once, the next best thing is to create your scheduled tasks via a PowerShell script. This will help to ensure that all computers end up with the same configuration.

When creating a scheduled task through PowerShell, you have two main options. One is to create a script that explicitly defines the required parameters, and the other is to export an existing scheduled task. Whichever way you choose, you will use the Register-ScheduledTask cmdlet that is part of the Scheduled-Tasks module. This module is included in Windows, so there is nothing special you need to install.

CREATE A NEW SCHEDULED TASK

Creating a scheduled task via PowerShell is very similar to the process of creating it in the Task Scheduler console. You set the time interval for the trigger, define the actions, assign permissions, and create the task. Using the previous example of setting the Invoke-LogFileCleanup.ps1 script to run once a day at 8 a.m., let's look at how you can create this task.

First, you need to define your trigger. This can be done using the `New-Scheduled-TaskTrigger` cmdlet. You can set triggers to run once, daily, weekly, or at logon. In this case, you will use the `-Daily` switch and set the `-At` parameter to 8 a.m.

Next, you need to define your action. This is done using the `New-ScheduledTask-Action` cmdlet. Here you need to supply the path to the executable and the arguments. Remember, the executable is the path to the PowerShell executable and not the ps1 file. Then, in the arguments, you supply the `-File` parameter, the path to the ps1, and any parameters for that ps1.

When you enter the argument, it needs to be a single string, so watch out for things like escaping quotes and spaces. It is safest to create it with single quotes on the outside and double quotes on the inside. When you create a string with single quotes in PowerShell, it takes the text between them as literal characters and does not interpret anything. You can see that in the following snippet, where the final string contains all the double quotes:

```
$Argument = '-File ' +
    '"C:\Scripts\Invoke-LogFileCleanup.ps1"' +
    ' -LogPath "L:\Logs\" -ZipPath "L:\Archives\"' +
    ' -ZipPrefix "LogArchive-" -NumberOfDays 30'
$Argument
-File "C:\Scripts\Invoke-LogFileCleanup.ps1" -LogPath "L:\Logs\" -ZipPath "L:
\Archives\" -ZipPrefix "LogArchive-" -NumberOfDays 30
```

Once you have your action and trigger defined, you can create the scheduled task using the `Register-ScheduledTask` cmdlet. These steps are shown in figure 3.1.

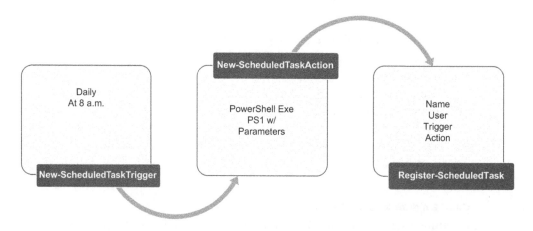

Figure 3.1   Creating a scheduled task via PowerShell by defining the trigger and action and registering it

When creating the scheduled task, you have several options to choose from when setting the permissions. By default, the schedule is set to *Run only when user is logged on*. However, since you will want it to run unattended, you will need to use the -User argument to set it to *Run whether user is logged on or not*.

When creating it through the console, you can choose to have it run as the system account or use a service account. To use the system account, set the value for the -User argument to NT AUTHORITY\SYSTEM. If you decide to use a service account, you will also need to supply the password using the -Password argument.

> **WARNING** The password argument is a plain text string, so be sure not to save it in any scripts.

One more thing to consider before creating your task is the name. I strongly recommend that you create a subfolder in the Task Scheduler Library to group similar automations. You can do this by adding the folder name followed by a backslash (\) before the task's name in the -TaskName argument.

Finally, you supply the -Trigger and -Action parameters with the trigger and action you created. You can see the code for this scheduled task in the following listing.

Listing 3.1 Creating a scheduled task

Create a Scheduled
Task trigger.

```
$Trigger = New-ScheduledTaskTrigger -Daily -At 8am          Set the Action
                                                            execution path.
$Execute = "C:\Program Files\PowerShell\7\pwsh.exe"   ←
$Argument = '-File ' +                              ←   Set the Action
    '"C:\Scripts\Invoke-LogFileCleanup.ps1"' +           arguments.
    ' -LogPath "L:\Logs" -ZipPath "L:\Archives"' +
    ' -ZipPrefix "LogArchive-" -NumberOfDays 30'

$ScheduledTaskAction = @{        ←    Create the Scheduled
    Execute  = $Execute               Task Action.
    Argument = $Argument
}
$Action = New-ScheduledTaskAction @ScheduledTaskAction

$ScheduledTask = @{                          ←    Combine the trigger
    TaskName = "PoSHAutomation\LogFileCleanup"        and action to create
    Trigger  = $Trigger                              the Scheduled Task.
    Action   = $Action
    User     = 'NT AUTHORITY\SYSTEM'
}
Register-ScheduledTask @ScheduledTask
```

> **NOTE** You may receive an access denied message when running the Register-ScheduledTask cmdlet. To avoid this, you can run the command from an elevated PowerShell session.

After you run this, you should see your scheduled task under the folder PoSHAutomation, as shown in figure 3.2.

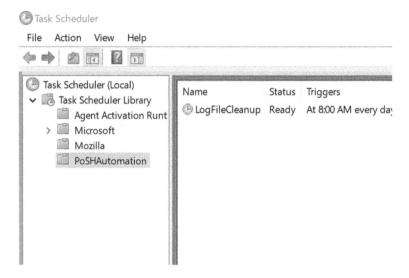

Figure 3.2   Task Scheduler with a custom folder to keep your automations separate from the rest of the scheduled tasks

EXPORTING AND IMPORTING SCHEDULED TASKS

The best way to ensure that your jobs remain consistent across multiple computers is by using the import and export functionality available with Task Scheduler. You can use the `Export-ScheduledTask` cmdlet to export any task to XML. You can then use this XML with the `Register-ScheduledTask` cmdlet to re-create the task on any other Windows computer.

You start by exporting the task and saving the XML output to a file. It is a good idea to save these to a file share so that you can easily import them to any other machine on your network. The `Export-ScheduledTask` cmdlet outputs a string with the XML data, so you can save it by piping the output to a file using the `Out-File` cmdlet:

```
$ScheduledTask = @{
    TaskName = "LogFileCleanup"
    TaskPath = "\PoSHAutomation\"
}
$export = Export-ScheduledTask @ScheduledTask
$export | Out-File "\\srv01\PoSHAutomation\LogFileCleanup.xml"
```

From there, you can recreate the task on any other computer by importing the contents of the XML file, running the `Register-ScheduledTask`, and passing in the XML string to the `-Xml` argument. However, note that even though the XML file contains the task's name, you still have to supply the -TaskName parameter. Well, luckily, you can convert XML directly to a PowerShell object. So, with a couple of extra lines of code, shown in the following listing, you can extract the name of the job from the XML to automatically populate the -TaskName parameter for you.

Listing 3.2   Importing a scheduled task

Convert the XML string to an XML object.

Import the contents of the XML file to a string.

Set the task name based on the value in the XML.

```
$FilePath = ".\CH03\Monitor\Export\LogFileCleanup.xml"
$xml = Get-Content $FilePath -Raw
[xml]$xmlObject = $xml
$TaskName = $xmlObject.Task.RegistrationInfo.URI
Register-ScheduledTask -Xml $xml -TaskName $TaskName
```

Import the scheduled task.

You can even take it one step further and import all the XML files from a single directory to create multiple jobs at once, as in the following listing. You can use the Get-ChildItem cmdlet to get all the XML files in a folder and then use a foreach to import each one of them.

Listing 3.3   Importing multiple scheduled tasks

Get all the XML files in the folder path.

```
$Share = "\\srv01\PoSHAutomation\"
$TaskFiles = Get-ChildItem -Path $Share -Filter "*.xml"

foreach ($FilePath in $TaskFiles) {
    $xml = Get-Content $FilePath -Raw
    [xml]$xmlObject = $xml
    $TaskName = $xmlObject.Task.RegistrationInfo.URI
    Register-ScheduledTask -Xml $xml -TaskName $TaskName
}
```

Parse through each file and import the job.

REGISTER-SCHEDULEDJOB

If you've been using PowerShell for a while, you may be aware of the cmdlet Register-ScheduledJob. This cmdlet is very similar to the Register-ScheduledTask cmdlet, with one major caveat. The Register-ScheduledJob cmdlet is not in PowerShell Core. The way it works is entirely incompatible with .NET Core, and starting in PowerShell 7 has been blocked from even being imported using the PowerShell compatibility transport. Therefore, I highly recommend you switch any existing scripts from Register-ScheduledJob to Register-ScheduledTask.

3.2.3   *Cron scheduler*

If you are new to Linux or just not familiar with Cron, it is the Linux equivalent of Task Scheduler—or, really, the other way around since Cron was originally built by Bell Labs in 1975. Either way, it is an excellent tool for scheduling recurring tasks on a

Linux computer and is installed by default on pretty much every major distro. It is a very robust platform with many options, but we are going to focus on how you can use it to run PowerShell scripts.

Unlike Task Scheduler, Cron does not have a GUI. Instead, you control everything through command lines and a Cron Table file, known as Crontab, containing all the jobs for that particular user on that computer. Like Task Scheduler, in Cron, you simply set the schedule, set permissions, and set the action to call your script.

The script part is easy. It is essentially the same command you used for Task Scheduler, just with paths written for Linux. For example, your command to call the Invoke-LogFileCleanup.ps1 script would look something like this:

```
/snap/powershell/160/opt/powershell/pwsh -File "/home/posh/Invoke-
LogFileCleanup.ps1" -LogPath "/etc/poshtest/Logs" -ZipPath
"/etc/poshtest/Logs/Archives" -ZipPrefix "LogArchive-" -NumberOfDays 30
```

Prior to creating your Cron job, you can test the execution using Terminal. If your command runs successfully through Terminal, you know it will run through Cron.

To create your Cron job, open Terminal and enter the command as follows:

```
crontab -e
```

This will open the Crontab file for the current user. If you want the job to run as a different user, enter the command with the -u argument followed by the account's username:

```
crontab -u username -e
```

If this is your first time opening Crontab, you may see a prompt to select an editor. Select your preferred one and continue.

Now it is time to create your job. The syntax to create the job is the Cron syntax for the schedule followed by the command. Again, we won't go into too much detail on Cron syntax as there are plenty of resources on it. Just know that it consists of five columns that represent minute, hour, day of the month, month, and day of the week, as shown in figure 3.3.

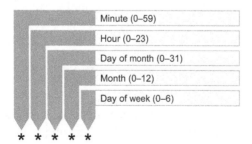

* * * * *

Figure 3.3   Cron schedule parts

To run the script at 8 a.m., just like on the Windows computer, your syntax will be
* 8 * * *. Next, enter the syntax for the time interval followed by the command to execute, similar to the following:

```
* 8 * * * /snap/powershell/160/opt/powershell/pwsh -File "/home/posh/Invoke-
LogFileCleanup.ps1" -LogPath "/etc/poshtest/Logs" -ZipPath
"/etc/poshtest/Logs/Archives" -ZipPrefix "LogArchive-" -NumberOfDays 30
```

Then save your changes and close the Crontab file. As long as the Cron service is running on your computer, this job will execute at 8 a.m. every day.

3.2.4   Jenkins scheduler

As mentioned earlier, there are numerous tools out there that can support executing
PowerShell. Jenkins is an open source automation server that, while originally built as
a continuous integration tool, has grown much larger. As with any tool, it has its pluses
and minuses. A big plus is that it has a web UI that you can use to manage all of your
jobs in one place. It also has the ability to use role-based access and store credentials.
This will allow you to give others access to execute scripts on systems or environments
without providing them with explicit permissions to that system. If you have not
already done so, take a look at the instructions in the appendix for setting up a development Jenkins server for performing these actions.

   One downside to Jenkins is that executing PowerShell on remote servers can be
tricky. Jenkins will execute the PowerShell script on the Jenkins server. But if you need it
to run the script on a different server, you will need to use PowerShell remoting or set
up each server as a Jenkins node. We will cover PowerShell remoting in depth in chapter 5, so for this example, we are fine with the script running on the Jenkins server.

   If you followed the environment setup guide in the appendix, you should be all set
to perform this exercise. We will once again schedule your disk space usage script to
run on a schedule, this time using Jenkins.

   Before you copy your script to Jenkins, there is one thing you need to change.
Jenkins does not have the ability to pass parameters to a script the same way you can
from the command line. Instead, it uses environment variables. The easiest way to
account for this is by replacing your parameter block and defining the parameters
as values. Then, set a value for each variable to an environmental variable with the
same name. This will prevent you from having to rewrite every instance where the
parameter is used inside the script. The parameters in the log file cleanup should
look like this:

```
$LogPath = $env:logpath
$ZipPath = $env:zippath
$ZipPrefix = $env:zipprefix
$NumberOfDays = $env:numberofdays
```

The Jenkins environmental variable should be all lowercase in your script. Once you have your parameters updated, it is time to create the job in Jenkins:

1 Open your web browser and log into your Jenkins instance.
2 Click *New Item*.
3 Enter a name for your project.
4 Select *Freestyle project*.
5 Click *OK*.
6 Check the box *This project is parameterized*.
7 Click the *Add Parameter* button and select *String* to bring up the screen shown in figure 3.4.

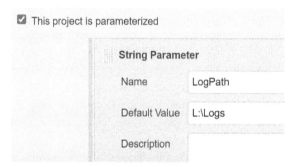

Figure 3.4   **Adding Jenkins parameters**

8   In the Name field, enter the name of your parameter: LogPath.
9   In the Default Value field, enter the path to the log files.
10 Repeat steps 7 to 9 for the ZipPath, ZipPrefix, and NumberOfDays parameters.
11 Scroll down to the Build Triggers section, shown in figure 3.5.

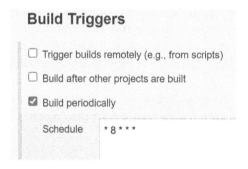

Figure 3.5   **Jenkins trigger**

12 Check the box *Build periodically*.
13 The syntax for the schedule is the same as Cron, so to run at 8 a.m. every day, enter * 8 * * *.

14 Scroll down to the Build section, shown in figure 3.6, and click the Add Build
Step button.

Figure 3.6   Jenkins script

15 Select PowerShell from the drop-down menu.
16 Copy and paste your Invoke-LogFileCleanup.ps1 script, with the replaced
parameters, into the Command block.
17 Click *Save.*
18 You can test your job right away by clicking the Build With Parameters button.
19 Click *Build.*
20 When your script is finished executing, you will see the job listed under the
Build History section.

If you click on any entry under Build History, you can view the console output of
your job.

3.3   *Watcher scripts*

A *watcher script* is a scheduled script that runs either continuously or at least every few
minutes. As a good rule of thumb, any script that needs to run every 15 minutes or less
should be considered a watcher. A typical example of this can be a file watcher, in
which you monitor a folder for new or updated files. Other examples are monitoring
a SharePoint list for new entries or checking a shared mailbox for new emails. Watcher
scripts can also be used for real-time monitoring, such as alerting on stopped services
or an unresponsive web application.

When creating a watcher script, you need to consider all the same things you do
with any unattended scripts (dealing with dependencies, making data dynamic, preventing user inputs, etc.). However, execution time needs to be at the forefront of
your mind during the designing and coding processes. For example, if you have a
script that executes once a minute and takes 2 minutes to run, you will encounter lots
of problems.

As you will see, one way to reduce your watcher script's run time is by having it use an *action script*. Think of it as a watcher script monitoring for a specific condition. Once that condition is met, the watcher script will invoke the action script. Since the action script runs in a separate process, your watcher script will not have to wait for the action script to finish executing. Also, you can invoke multiple action scripts from a single watcher, allowing them to run in parallel.

For example, consider a script that performs the following once a minute:

1 Check an FTP site for new files.
2 If files are found, download them locally.
3 Copy the files to different folders based on the names.

If written as a traditional PowerShell script, it will process the files one at a time, which means that you need to account for the time required for downloading the file, determining where to copy it, and copying it. In contrast, if you invoke an action script, shown in figure 3.7, multiple files can be processed at once, resulting in a much faster execution time and without the watcher waiting for each one.

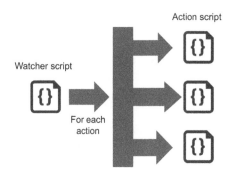

Figure 3.7   **A single watcher script can call multiple action scripts in parallel and run them in separate processes.**

Another advantage to using action scripts is that they execute as separate processes from the watcher script. So, any errors, delays, or problems they experience will not affect the action script.

The concept of watcher and action scripts is not inherent to the PowerShell framework. It is an automation process that I have used for years when building automations. The concepts behind it can be translated to any language or platform. There were attempts to build it into the PowerShell framework years ago when PowerShell Workflow was introduced as part of the SMA platform. And don't feel bad if you've never heard of PowerShell Workflow or SMA; most people haven't. The advantages that they brought in parallel processing and resuming can now all be achieved natively in PowerShell. The concepts you learn here can be made into building blocks that you can use with any automation you create.

3.3.1   *Designing watcher scripts*

Since watcher scripts tend to run every minute or so, the most important thing to consider is execution time. While the use of action scripts can help prevent your script from running too long, there is always the chance that an unforeseen situation will arise, causing your script to run longer than intended. However, through some good coding practices, you can prevent this from causing problems with your automations.

Before creating your watcher script, you must first know how often it will need to run. You need to do this to ensure that your watcher script executions will not overlap with each other. If there is a potential for overlap, you need to design a way for your script to gracefully exit before that happens. You also need to develop the watcher script to pick up where it last left off. We will walk through these concepts while building a folder watcher.

Consider the following scenario: you need to monitor a folder for new files. Once a file is added, it needs to be moved to another folder. This monitor needs to be as real-time as possible, so it will run once every minute. This is a common scenario that you could implement for multiple reasons, including monitoring an FTP folder for uploads from customers or monitoring a network share for exports from your ERP or payroll systems.

Before you begin, you need to break down the steps your automation will need to perform. Then, determine which functionality needs to be in the watcher script and which should go in the action script. Keep in mind that the goal is to have the watcher script run as efficiently as possible and pick up from where the last one left off.

The first thing you need to do is get the files in the folder. Then, every file found needs to be moved to another folder. Since you are dealing with data, you want to be careful not to overwrite or skip any files. To help address this concern, you can have the script check whether there is already a file with the same name in the destination folder. If there is, some of your choices are to

- Overwrite the file
- Skip moving the file
- Error out
- Rename the file

If you skip moving the file or error out, you will cause problems with subsequent executions because the script will keep picking up that same file again and again. Renaming the file would be the safest option. However, while you are preventing data loss, duplicating data can be a problem of its own. If the same file keeps getting added to the source folder, the script will just keep renaming and moving, causing massive duplicates in the destination folder. To prevent this from happening, you can implement a hybrid process to check whether the files with the same names are indeed the same file, as shown in figure 3.8.

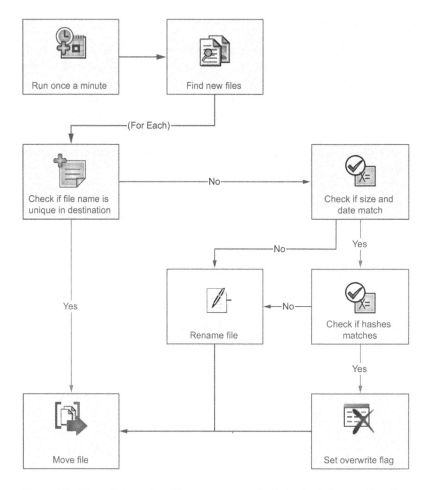

Figure 3.8   File watcher automation runs once a minute to check for new files. For each file found, it needs to confirm that the file is unique and, if not, determine if the hash matches or if it needs to be renamed.

You can check whether the file size is the same, the last write times match, and the file hash is the same. If all of these values match, it is safe to say that it is the same file and can be overwritten. If any one of those checks fails, it will be renamed and copied. This will help ensure that you don't overwrite any data, duplicate existing data, and remove all files from the source folder.

Next, you need to determine which steps will be in the watcher and which will be in the action script. Remember that you want as little processing done in the watcher as possible. So, it would make sense to have only the first step of finding the new files in the watcher. Then, let the action script handle everything else. This logic is illustrated in figure 3.9.

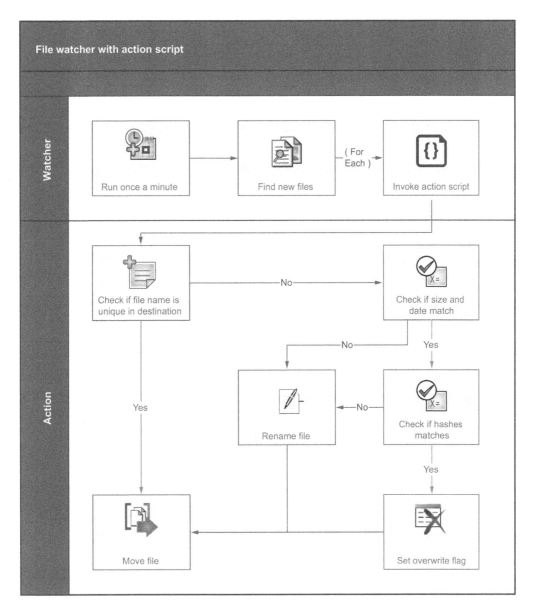

Figure 3.9   File watcher execution with the file actions of checking names and hashes is moved into an action script that runs in a separate process.

Now that you know what needs to go into the watcher script, you can start coding it, beginning with the command to find the new files in the folder. This can be done using the Get-ChildItem cmdlet. Since you want to ensure that your script runs as efficiently as possible, there are a few concepts you will want to follow regardless of the automation.

USE CMDLET-BASED FILTERS

When you need to filter your results, try to use the parameters provided by the cmdlets rather than using the Where-Object filtering whenever possible. In this case, you will be using the Get-ChildItem cmdlet, which has a filter parameter. So, if you only need to return XML files, you can use -Filter '*.xml' to limit your results. When you use the Where-Object after a pipe, the Get-ChildItem cmdlet will return all items, and then PowerShell will filter them, drastically increasing your run time.

AVOID RECURSION

It is always best to scope your scripts to only pull the data they need. If you have multiple subfolders or nested organizational units (OUs), parsing through all of them can be very time-consuming. It can often be quicker to run multiple get commands scoped to individual subfolders than to run one at the top level with recursion.

For example, if the folder watcher needs to look into multiple subfolders, it would be quicker to list the specific folders than to list the parent and have your script search through every child folder. You may also consider creating a separate watcher for each folder.

Another example of this is a watcher I created to monitor user accounts in Active Directory. The structure was that each office had its own OU. Inside each OU were separate OUs for computers, users, admins, printers, service accounts, etc. I only needed to monitor the user OU under each site OU. So, if I scoped the script to the top level and told it to recurse, it would find everything I needed, but it would also waste time searching through all of the other OUs. Instead, I had one command return all the OUs directly under the top level. Then I used a foreach to look directly in the User OU under each one. Doing this caused the script to execute in 10 seconds versus 90 seconds for the recursion command.

PROCESS IN ORDER

Since a watcher is time-sensitive, you always want to execute in the order received. In the folder-watch example, you will want the files sorted by the date and time they were created so that they will be processed in the order received. This helps to ensure that if the script stops for any reason, the subsequent execution will pick up right where the previous one left off. Following these practices, you can now build out the basic structure of your watcher, which will get the files in the folder, sort them by date, and then invoke the action script for each file.

LOG ACTIONS

Another thing to consider is what to do if the action script fails—for example, if something goes wrong and the action script is unable to complete. Every time the watcher runs, it may attempt to run the action script over and over. If the number of problem items grows larger than your concurrent job count, your entire automation could stop.

To protect against this, you can create a log to let your watcher know which actions have been invoked. Again, this will be different for every watcher, but the concept remains the same. For example, you can write the file's creation date before it invokes the action script for the folder watcher. Then, have the script filter on the last date from the log the next time it starts, preventing it from attempting to send the same files over and over.

AVOID UNNECESSARY COMMANDS

Adding additional checks or conditions to a watcher may be tempting to account for every situation, but you are sacrificing speed with every new command added. If you have multiple conditions, it may be best to break them into separate watchers or add them to the action script. This is especially true if you have more than one action that can be taken. A good rule to follow is one action per watcher. Not only will it speed up your execution, but it will also make your code easier to maintain in the long run.

3.3.2   Invoking action scripts

There are many ways you can invoke one PowerShell script from another. You can use the `Invoke-Command`, `Invoke-Expression`, `New-Job`, and `Start-Process` cmdlets. For action scripts, the best option is to use the `Start-Process`. Unlike the other cmdlets, the `Start-Process` cmdlet executes the script in a separate process from the watcher script. This means if the watcher script stops executing or has an error, the action scripts running are not affected, and vice versa.

To invoke the action script using the `Start-Process` cmdlet, you need to pass the script path and parameter values along with the path to the PowerShell executable. You can also pass the `-NoNewWindow` argument to keep from having a ton of windows pop up every time it runs. You will notice that the command argument is very similar to the arguments you used when creating a scheduled task earlier. That is because both are essentially the equivalent of running the command from a terminal or command prompt window.

When invoking your action script, you want to ensure that the parameters are primitive types (strings, int, Boolean, etc.) and not objects. This is because different object types can have different behavior when passed in this manner, and it is difficult to predict how they will react. For example, in the folder watcher, you want to pass the file's full path as a string versus the file object type from the `Get-ChildItem` cmdlet.

RESOURCE LIMITING

One thing to be cautious of when using the `Start-Process` cmdlet to invoke action scripts is overwhelming your system. This can happen easily since each action script is running as an independent process. So, in our example, if you suddenly have 100 files added to the folder you are monitoring, your watcher could end up trying to process all 100 at once.

To avoid this, you can add a limit to the number of action scripts a watcher can have running at once. This will prevent you from accidentally firing off more jobs than your system can handle. You can add the `-PassThru` switch to the `Start-Process` cmdlet to output the process ID (PID) of each action script and then save them to an array. Then have your script check how many of the processes are still running. Once the number of concurrently running jobs reaches the limit, have it wait until one has finished before continuing to the next.

3.3.3   *Graceful terminations*

As previously mentioned, you should aim for your script to complete in half the amount of the run interval. Therefore, you will want to monitor the execution time in your watcher script so you can terminate it if it runs for too long.

Most job scheduling platforms have settings for what to do if the previous task is still running and it is time for the next task to start. For example, in Task Scheduler, you can prevent the new task from starting, start it in parallel, queue it, or stop the existing instance. My recommendation here would be to choose to stop the existing instance. The main reason behind this is because if something goes wrong in the script, this would kill the process and start it fresh, hopefully resolving the issue.

Take, for example, an issue with authenticating to a network share. You all know it happens randomly from time to time. It would be much better to have the script start over and try to reauthenticate than to build all sorts of crazy logic into your script to try to handle this.

Having your script automatically terminate itself after a certain amount of time means you can ensure it executes at a point that will not affect the subsequent execution. Letting the task scheduler terminate it should only be used as a backup for unforeseen circumstances.

For your folder watcher script, we said it needs to run every 60 seconds, so you need to ensure that if it is still running after 30 seconds, you terminate it at a point of your choosing. An excellent tool to help you do this is the `System.Diagnostics` `.Stopwatch` .NET class.

The `Stopwatch` class provides you a quick and easy way to measure the execution times inside your script. You can create a new stopwatch instance by calling the class with the `StartNew` method. Once the stopwatch starts, the total time is in the `Elapsed` property. There are also different methods for stopping, restarting, and resetting the stopwatch. The following snippet shows how to start, get the elapsed time, and stop the stopwatch:

```
$Timer =  [system.diagnostics.stopwatch]::StartNew()
Start-Sleep -Seconds 3
$Timer.Elapsed
$Timer.Stop()
Days               : 0
Hours              : 0
Minutes            : 0
Seconds            : 2
Milliseconds       : 636
Ticks              : 26362390
TotalDays          : 3.0512025462963E-05
TotalHours         : 0.000732288611111111
TotalMinutes       : 0.0439373166666667
```

```
TotalSeconds      : 2.636239
TotalMilliseconds : 2636.239
```

To use this in the watcher script, add the following command where you want the timer to start:

```
$Timer = [system.diagnostics.stopwatch]::StartNew()
```

Then you can determine where the best place to stop the execution of your script will be.

Where you terminate will be different for every script, but typically, you want to terminate after the action script is called. If you terminate before, you run the risk of never making it to the action. You also want to avoid terminating before any of your logs are written. The best place to terminate in the folder watcher script is at the bottom of the `foreach` loop. This will ensure that the current file is sent to the action script before stopping or recording the next one.

3.3.4 *Folder watcher*

Now that we have gone through all the parts of a watcher, let's put it all together in the folder watcher script. Following the design recommendations, it will start by declaring the stopwatch. Then it will pick up the log with the last processed file's date in it. Since you don't want it to error out the first time it runs, or if something happens to the log, you can use the `Test-Path` cmdlet to confirm it exists before attempting to read it.

Now you are ready to query the files and sort them based on the creation date. Next, the script will write the creation time to the log for each file and then invoke the action script. After the action script is invoked, it will check whether the number of running jobs exceeds the limit. If it does, the script will wait until at least one of them finishes. Then it will confirm that the time limit is not exceeded. If not, it will continue to the next file. Once all files are sent to action scripts, the watcher script will exit. Figure 3.10 shows these steps, and the script is shown in the next listing.

Listing 3.4 Watch-Folder.ps1

```
param(
    [Parameter(Mandatory = $true)]
    [string]$Source,

    [Parameter(Mandatory = $true)]
    [string]$Destination,

    [Parameter(Mandatory = $true)]
    [string]$ActionScript,

    [Parameter(Mandatory = $true)]
    [int]$ConcurrentJobs,

    [Parameter(Mandatory = $true)]
    [string]$WatcherLog,
```

```
        [Parameter(Mandatory = $true)]
        [int]$TimeLimit
    )

    $Timer = [system.diagnostics.stopwatch]::StartNew()

    if (Test-Path $WatcherLog) {
        $logDate = Get-Content $WatcherLog -Raw
        try {
            $LastCreationTime = Get-Date $logDate -ErrorAction Stop
        }
        catch {
            $LastCreationTime = Get-Date 1970-01-01
        }
    }
    else {
        $LastCreationTime = Get-Date 1970-01-01
    }

    $files = Get-ChildItem -Path $Source |
        Where-Object { $_.CreationTimeUtc -gt $LastCreationTime }
    $sorted = $files | Sort-Object -Property CreationTime

    [int[]]$Pids = @()
    foreach ($file in $sorted) {
        Get-Date $file.CreationTimeUtc -Format o |
            Out-File $WatcherLog

        $Arguments = "-file ""$ActionScript""",
            "-FilePath ""$($file.FullName)""",
            "-Destination ""$($Destination)""",
            "-LogPath ""$($ActionLog)"""
        $jobParams = @{
            FilePath     = 'pwsh'
            ArgumentList = $Arguments
            NoNewWindow  = $true
        }
        $job = Start-Process @jobParams -PassThru
        $Pids += $job.Id

        while ($Pids.Count -ge $ConcurrentJobs) {
            Write-Host "Pausing PID count : $($Pids.Count)"
            Start-Sleep -Seconds 1
            $Pids = @(Get-Process -Id $Pids -ErrorAction SilentlyContinue |
                Select-Object -ExpandProperty Id)
        }

        if ($Timer.Elapsed.TotalSeconds -gt $TimeLimit) {
            Write-Host "Graceful terminating after $TimeLimit seconds"
            break
        }
    }
```

Start Stopwatch timer.

Check whether the log file exists, and set the filter date if it does.

Default time if no log file is found

Get all the files in the folder.

Sort the files based on creation time.

Create an array to hold the process IDs of the action scripts.

Record the files time to the log.

Set the arguments from the action script.

Invoke the action script with the PassThruswitch to pass the process id to a variable...

... and the id to the array.

If the number of process ids is greater than or equal to the number of current jobs, loop until it drops.

Check whether the total execution time is greater than the time limit.

The break command is used to exit the foreach loop, stopping the script since there is nothing after the loop.

Get-Process will only return running processes, so execute it to find the total number running.

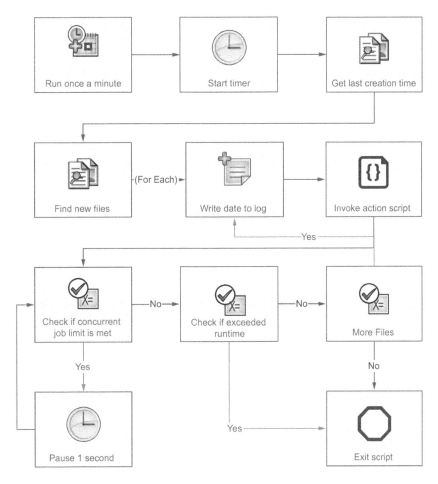

Figure 3.10 File watcher with action script invocation, concurrent job limiter, and execution timer

3.3.5 *Action scripts*

When it comes to creating the action script, there are not as many limits and things to consider. The process should follow all the standard PowerShell practices we've discussed regarding unattended scripts. Other than that, you may want to add some logging to your script.

Since the action script runs independently, the watcher is not aware of errors in it. This means it won't report them back to the invoking system or include them in its logs. Therefore, it is always a good idea to have some form of logging in your action scripts so that you can be aware of any issues or failures.

We will cover logging in more depth in later chapters. So, for now, we can add some simple text-file-based logging to the action script to record any errors. An excellent way to ensure that you adequately capture errors is by using a `try/catch/finally` block.

In the action script, you will create a function to perform all the duplicate checks and perform file moves. When you add the [CmdletBinding()] to the function, you can use the -ErrorAction argument and set it to Stop when you call the functions. During normal script execution, this would stop the script in the case of an error in the function. However, when used inside a try block, it will send the script to the catch block. If the function runs without any problems, the catch block is skipped. Thus, regardless of an error, the finally block will always run.

For the action script in our example, shown in figure 3.11, you can set a variable with a success message under the function call in the try block. Then, in the catch block, you can set that same variable to an error message. In the finally block, have it write that message to the log. If the function has an error, it will skip over the variable set in the try block and go right to the catch. Or, if there is no error, it will set the success message and skip the catch block. In either case, the log file will be updated.

> **NOTE** The variable $_ in a catch block will contain the error message. You can use this to record precisely what went wrong.

Taking what we now know and the tasks we identified at the beginning of this exercise, the task for this action script will be to test that the file exists. Then if it does, get the file object using the Get-Item cmdlet. This will allow you to get the item data you will need to use if a duplicate file is found. Remember, we are only passing in a string for the file path and not the file object.

Next, the action script will check whether a file with the same name already exists in the destination folder. If one does, it will check whether the files are the same. If they are, the script will overwrite the file to clear it out of the source folder. If not, it will rename the file with a unique name. Then the file is moved to the destination folder.

Getting a unique name

There are several ways to ensure that your file has a unique name. These include using GUIDs or creating an interval variable that you can increment until a unique one is found. But when it comes to file names, nothing beats the FileTime string in the DateTime object.

All DateTime objects contain the methods ToFileTime and ToFileTimeUtc. Invoking either of these methods will return a FileTime value. A FileTime value is the number of 100-nanosecond intervals since January 1, 1601. By getting the current time and converting it to FileTime, you are almost guaranteed a unique file name if you add it to the file name—that is, unless you have two files with the same name that are being moved within 100 nanoseconds of each other.

The FileTime value can also be parsed back into a standard DateTime format, giving you a record of when the file was renamed.

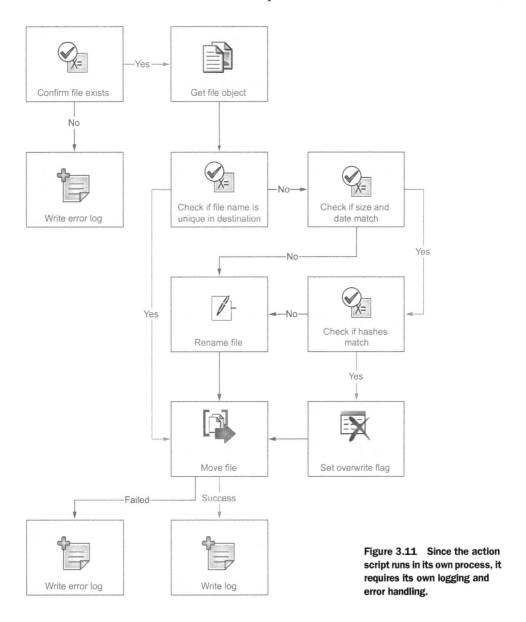

Figure 3.11 Since the action script runs in its own process, it requires its own logging and error handling.

Go ahead and create a second script named Move-WatcherFile.ps1. Then, build out the action script, as in the following listing.

Listing 3.5 Action script with logging and error handling

```
param(
    [Parameter(Mandatory = $true)]
    [string]$FilePath,
    [Parameter(Mandatory = $true)]
```

```
        [string]$Destination,
        [Parameter(Mandatory = $true)]
        [string]$LogPath
    )

    Function Move-ItemAdvanced {
        [CmdletBinding()]
        [OutputType()]
        param(
            [Parameter(Mandatory = $true)]
            [object]$File,
            [Parameter(Mandatory = $true)]
            [string]$Destination
        )

        $DestinationFile = Join-Path -Path $Destination -ChildPath $File.Name

        if (Test-Path $DestinationFile) {
            $FileMatch = $true
            $check = Get-Item $DestinationFile
            if ($check.Length -ne $file.Length) {
                $FileMatch = $false
            }
            if ($check.LastWriteTime -ne $file.LastWriteTime) {
                $FileMatch = $false
            }
            $SrcHash = Get-FileHash -Path $file.FullName
            $DstHash = Get-FileHash -Path $check.FullName
            if ($DstHash.Hash -ne $SrcHash.Hash) {
                $FileMatch = $false
            }

            if ($FileMatch -eq $false) {
                $ts = (Get-Date).ToFileTimeUtc()
                $name = $file.BaseName + "_" + $ts + $file.Extension
                $DestinationFile = Join-Path -Path $Destination -ChildPath $name
                Write-Verbose "File will be renamed '$($name)'"
            }
            else {
                Write-Verbose "File will be overwritten"
            }
        }
        else {
            $FileMatch = $false
        }

        $moveParams = @{
            Path        = $file.FullName
            Destination = $DestinationFile
        }
        if ($FileMatch -eq $true) {
            $moveParams.Add('Force', $true)
        }
        Move-Item @moveParams -PassThru
    }
```

Add a new function to perform file checks when a duplicate is found.

Check whether the file exists.

Get the matching file.

Check whether they have the same length.

Check whether they have the same last write time.

Check whether they have the same hash.

If they don't all match, create a unique filename with the timestamp.

If the two files matched, force an overwrite on the move.

```
if (-not (Test-Path $FilePath)) {
    "$(Get-Date) : File not found" | Out-File $LogPath -Append
    break
}

$file = Get-Item $FilePath

$Arguments = @{
    File        = $file
    Destination = $Destination
}

try {
    $moved = Move-ItemAdvanced @Arguments -ErrorAction Stop
    $message = "Moved '$($FilePath)' to '$($moved.FullName)'"
}
catch {
    $message = "Error moving '$($FilePath)' : $($_)"
}
finally {
    "$(Get-Date) : $message" | Out-File $LogPath -Append
}
```

Test that the file is found. If not, write to log and stop processing.

Get the file object.

Wrap the move command in a try/catch with an error action set to stop.

Create a custom message that includes the file path and the failure reason captured as $_.

Write to the log file using the finally block.

Catch will only run if an error is returned from within the try block.

Now your watcher and actions scripts are ready. As with all automations, there is no way to predict every situation, so chances are you will need to make some tweaks to either script. However, if you keep in mind execution time, concurrently running jobs, and logging, you will be in good shape.

3.4 Running watchers

A watcher script should be able to be executed the same way you execute any script. You just need to ensure that the watcher can access the action script and both can access the resources they need independently. This means you can use all the same tools for scheduling watchers as with any other PowerShell script.

3.4.1 Testing watcher execution

Before scheduling your watcher, you want to test it thoroughly. On top of your standard functionality testing, you need to measure the execution time. You can do this using the Measure-Command cmdlet.

The Measure-Command cmdlet allows you to measure the execution time of any command, expression, or script block. You can test the execution time of your watcher script by using it in conjunction with the Start-Process cmdlet. Similar to how you call the action script from the watcher, you can use the Start-Process cmdlet to call the watcher script from another PowerShell session. Doing this will ensure that it runs in a separate session, just like when started by Task Scheduler or any other job scheduler. The only difference here is that you are going to add the -Wait switch. This will ensure your script waits until the watcher has finished processing so you get an accurate measurement of the execution time. You can see in the following snippet how this looks when invoking the Invoke-LogFileCleanup.ps1 watcher script:

```
$Argument = '-File ' +
    '"C:\Scripts\Invoke-LogFileCleanup.ps1"' +
    ' -LogPath "L:\Logs\" -ZipPath "L:\Archives\"' +
    ' -ZipPrefix "LogArchive-" -NumberOfDays 30'
$jobParams = @{
    FilePath = "C:\Program Files\PowerShell\7\pwsh.exe"
    ArgumentList = $Argument
    NoNewWindow = $true
}
Measure-Command -Expression {
    $job = Start-Process @jobParams -Wait}
Days                 : 0
Hours                : 0
Minutes              : 0
Seconds              : 2
Milliseconds         : 17
Ticks                : 20173926
TotalDays            : 2.33494513888889E-05
TotalHours           : 0.000560386833333333
TotalMinutes         : 0.03362321
TotalSeconds         : 2.0173926
TotalMilliseconds    : 2017.3926
```

As you can see, TotalSeconds is well under the 30-second limit you wanted. But be sure to run multiple tests with different scenarios to ensure the time stays under the 30-second limit. For example, if I put 100 files in the watcher folder, my execution time jumps to 68 seconds, well over the 30-second limit. When this happens, there are two things you need to consider.

First and foremost, you need to ask if it is possible that 100 files could be added in one minute and, if so, for how long. If your script takes 68 seconds to process 100 files and 100 files are added every minute, you will have a massive backlog that will never clear. If this is the case, then you need to reconsider how your script is executing. It would help if you asked yourself questions such as the following:

- Could I increase the limit of currently running job action scripts?
- Is there a way I can increase the speed of execution of the watcher script?
- Can I split the load between two or more watchers, each grabbing a chunk of the files?

I cannot tell you the right answer because the answers will be different for every automation. Other automations may even have completely different questions. These are just examples to help you see what you need to think about when creating your automations.

For instance, if you discover that the average number of files added in 1 minute is around 10, you will know that your automation will handle the rare cases where 100 files are added. You may end up with a backlog for a few minutes, but it will quickly catch up. It becomes a balancing act that you will need to monitor and adjust over time.

Also, if you find your watchers are exceeding their run time on a regular basis, you can test the individual commands inside it using the `Measure-Command` cmdlet. This will help you determine where you can rewrite certain portions or commands to help speed things up.

3.4.2 *Scheduling watchers*

You can use all the same tools to schedule watcher scripts as you can to schedule monitor scripts. The only difference is that you need to consider the execution time and what happens if it is exceeded. Even though you built in a graceful termination, if the job scheduler has a setting for it, you should have it terminate the job if it is time for the next one to start as a backup. You should never have two instances of the same watcher running at the same time.

Also, each instance of the watcher running should be started by the job scheduler. It may be tempting to create a job that runs once a day with a loop built in to keep executing the same commands over and over for 24 hours. However, if something goes wrong during the execution—for example, if the script has a terminating error or the computer is rebooted—your automation will not run again until the next day.

Summary

- There are multiple different tools available that will allow you to schedule Power-Shell scripts, including Task Scheduler and Cron.
- When creating a watcher script, the time of execution is extremely important.
- A watcher script should only monitor for events. Any actions that need to be taken should be performed by an action script.
- You should know how long your script should execute and build a graceful termination if it runs too long.

Handling sensitive data 4

This chapter covers

- Basic security principles for automations
- PowerShell secure objects
- Securing sensitive data needed by your scripts
- Identifying and mitigating risk

In December 2020, one of the largest and most sophisticated cyberattacks ever was found to be taking place on systems across the globe. Security experts discovered that the SolarWinds Orion platform was the subject of a supply chain hack. Hackers were able to inject malware directly into the binaries of some Orion updates. This attack was a big deal because SolarWinds' Orion is a monitoring and automation platform. The company's motto, "One platform to rule your IT stack," makes it a very enticing target for bad actors.

More than 200 companies and federal agencies were impacted by this attack, including some big names such as Intel, Nvidia, Cisco, and the US Departments of Energy and Homeland Security. Experts suspect that this attack is responsible for other exploits found shortly after at Microsoft and VMware.

If someone is able to gain full access to an automation platform, not only are they able to perform any action that platform has permissions to perform, but they also have access to all the information and data stored inside that platform. So, if you have a script with full domain admin rights or full global administrator, the bad actors will have those same rights and privileges.

Even something that seems harmless, like an internal FTP address or public keys, can be exploited in ways you might never consider. In the examination of the Solar-Winds exploit, investigators discovered that the password for the SolarWinds update server was saved in plain text inside a script that was in a public GitHub repository. At the time of writing, it has not been confirmed that this is how the hackers were able to inject their malware directly into the Orion updates. However, it is not a far stretch to see how this mistake could have been the cause and a straightforward one to avoid. This attack serves as a great reminder of several fundamental IT and automation security principles, which we will cover in this chapter.

Throughout this chapter, we will use the SQL health check automation illustrated in figure 4.1 as an example, but the principles apply to any automation. In this automation, you will connect to a SQL instance using PowerShell and then check that the databases have their recovery model set to SIMPLE. If a database is not set to SIMPLE, it will send an email reporting the bad configuration. To run the SQL health check automation, you will need to retrieve secure data for both the SQL server connection and the SMTP connection.

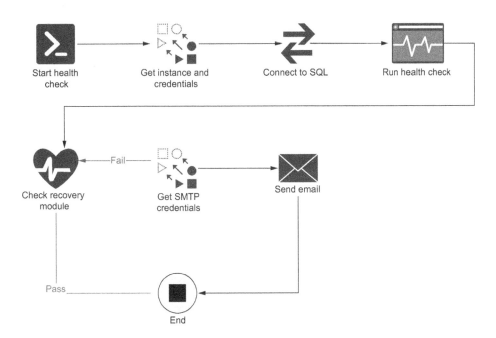

Figure 4.1   The SQL health check automation will send a notification if the recovery model is not set properly.

SQL health check prerequisites

To run the SQL health check, you need a SQL instance to test. I have provided a script in the chapter 4 Helper Scripts folder that will install and configure the latest version of SQL Server Express for you. I highly recommend that you use a virtual machine for this testing. If you set up the Jenkins server from the appendix, I recommend using that machine. Also, please note that this installation script must be run using Windows PowerShell 5.1.

If you choose to use an existing SQL instance, you will need to manually install the dbatools and Mailozaurr modules from the PowerShell gallery.

You will also need a SendGrid account to send the notification emails. You can sign up for a free account using a personal or work email address at sendgrid.com. The free account can send 100 emails per day.

Finally, you will need to install KeePass to use as a secret vault. The information necessary to set up the KeePass database is included later in this chapter. You can download and install KeePass from keepass.info or by using Chocolatey with the command `choco install keepass`.

4.1 Principles of automation security

Since every single company, platform, tool, and piece of software is different, someone could write an entire 500-page book on handling specific security situations and not come close to scratching the surface. However, we will cover some key concepts that you can apply across the board to any automation you are creating. To start, any time you are creating automations, you need to ask yourself the following questions:

- What are my risks if someone gains access to this automation?
- How can I limit the damage if someone does access it?

4.1.1 Do not store sensitive information in scripts

First and foremost, you should never, under any circumstance, include any sensitive data inside a script. While the SolarWinds hack in which someone gained access to the entire platform is an extreme example, the fact that a password saved in a script potentially started it all is not that unbelievable. Someone unwittingly sharing a script with a plain text password in it online, losing a thumb drive with a copy of a password, or sending the password over an unsecured email to a vendor is more common than most people would like to admit. To protect yourself from this and other possible breaches, you should never store sensitive data inside a script.

The question then becomes "What is sensitive data?" Some pretty obvious examples are

- Passwords and secrets
- API keys
- SSH keys

- Private certificates
- Certificate thumbprints
- PGP keys
- RSA tokens

Other sensitive information may not seem as obvious. For instance, in the example of a SQL health check, a SQL connection string may seem innocuous, especially if it uses a trusted connection and not a username and password. However, you are still giving someone a piece of the puzzle. Suppose a bad actor finds your script with the SQL connection string to the enterprise resource-planning database. In that case, they can quickly target their attacks, increasing the potential of gaining access to sensitive information before they are caught.

The same concern is valid for storing usernames in scripts. While the username itself is no good without the password, you have just given someone half of the information they need to gain access. Also, as you saw in the previous chapters, this makes your script less portable and harder to maintain.

Even when it isn't innocuous, people will often still put sensitive information in their scripts for a number of reasons. They might not know how to secure it properly, or they may be in a time crunch and intend to do it later—and, as we all know, later often never comes. However, as you will see in this chapter, setting up a secure store for passwords and other information is quick and easy. If you already have secure stores set up and available, you have no excuse for putting sensitive data in your scripts.

Remember to ask yourself whether this information would be of interest to an attacker. If the answer is yes, it should be considered sensitive data and stored securely outside of any scripts.

4.1.2 *Principle of least privilege*

Second only to not saving passwords in scripts is the principle of least privilege. This principle states that an account should only have the permissions it needs and nothing more. Unfortunately, people often do not want to spend the time figuring out permissions at a granular level, or even worse, some vendors will insist that an account needs full administrator access. Sure, it is easier to make an administrator account and move on. But, in doing so, you are creating an unacceptable level of risk.

In the case of our SQL health check script, you do not want to give the account database administrator rights because it only needs to read information about the database. If the account has database administrator rights and becomes compromised, the attacker not only can access all of your information, they can also create backdoors and separate accounts that you might not find for months or longer. For the health check script, you don't even need read permissions to the databases. You just need to be granted the view server state permissions. This means that even if the service account is compromised, it cannot be used to read the data in the database.

In another example, if you were part of an organization that used SolarWinds Orion, there would have been no way you could have prevented the attackers from gaining access. However, if you adhered to the principle of least privilege, you would not be as severely impacted as others who might do something like give a service account domain administrator access.

The principle of least privilege does not only apply to things like service account permissions. It can also include IP- or host-based restrictions. An excellent example of this is SMTP relays. I have heard of situations where the username and password of a service account with permission to impersonate any Exchange user gets leaked. Hackers can then use that account to send emails that appear to both people and data protection filters to come from a person inside the company. They can then submit payment requests to fake vendors.

In some cases, tens of thousands of dollars were stolen before anyone caught on. This could have all been avoided, or at least made much more difficult, if this account was only able to send these requests from a particular IP address or server. This is why I choose to use SendGrid in this automation example. Not only does it use an API key, so there is no user to compromise, but it also has IP-based restrictions and auditing to help prevent and detect unauthorized use.

4.1.3   Consider the context

An automation script intended to be run interactively versus one that is meant to be run unattended will have completely different security considerations. Suppose it is designed to run interactively. In that case, you can do things such as prompt for passwords, run under that user context, or use privileged access management solutions or delegated permissions.

However, suppose a script is going to run unattended. In that case, it will need a way to securely access sensitive data while preventing others from accessing the same data. Also, keep in mind that the solution to this may not involve passwords at all. Consider our SQL health check scenario. If the SQL server uses Windows domain authorization, there is no need to pass a username and password. You can use a job scheduler to run as that account and execute the script.

Another option is to set the job to run locally on the SQL server. This way, it can run under the system context without needing a password. If you limit the script to execute under the system context on the database server, the only way someone can exploit it is to gain access to your database server. And if that happened, you would have much more significant concerns than someone being able to see your script.

4.1.4   Create role-based service accounts

I cannot tell you how many times I have sent someone a list of required service accounts, and the first thing they ask is "Can these all use the same account?" Unfortunately, this has become a far too common practice, and it is a very dangerous one. On the other side, some will argue that managing hundreds of service accounts can, in itself, become a full-time job. This is why I like to use the concept of role-based access.

Let's take a look at the requirements for the SQL health check. First, we know we will need an account to authenticate with SQL and an account to send the email. In this case, I would recommend creating two separate accounts because they are interfacing with two completely different systems and performing different roles. Also, you will more than likely have more than one automation sending emails. So, instead of setting up every service account with a mailbox or other SMTP replay permissions, you can create one account to send emails and share it between automations.

Taking it a step further, if you decide to create an automation to perform automated SQL maintenance or backups, you can reuse the service account for the health check because they fall under the same role of SQL maintenance. However, if you create an automation to perform SQL extracts, I recommend creating a new account. Again, this is because the account serves a different function that does not fall under the role of SQL maintenance.

If an automation reaches out to different systems, especially ones outside of your network, it is always best to use separate accounts—even if they support single sign-on. This will help protect against situations where a vendor or a piece of software gets compromised. If that happens, you will have reduced the impact by limiting that service account to that specific platform.

It becomes a balancing act that you will get a feel for and adjust over time. Just follow the concept of one service account per role and system, and you will help to minimize the impact of any potential compromise.

4.1.5 Use logging and alerting

You will not be able to protect yourself against every threat out there. However, you can help to stop attacks as soon as possible through diligent logging and alerting. For example, if you have a service account that sends data from your on-premises data center to your cloud provider, and you suddenly start seeing logins from a foreign country, you will know something is up, and you can put a stop to it. Figure 4.2 shows an example of such an alert. The recent advancements in identity and threat protection solutions have been a very welcome addition to the automation community. The ability to see when and where an account is being used makes spotting these situations much more effortless.

Most enterprise-level password vaults have built-in logging that lets you see when and where passwords are accessed. Some even have AI behind them that can trigger alerts when anomalous activity occurs. Learn how to use and tune these alerts to your benefit.

Just as with the service accounts, it becomes a balancing act. Alert fatigue is a real thing. The quickest way to get your alerts ignored is by sending too many—especially if many of the alerts are false positives. For instance, the breach of Target Superstores in 2014 could have been stopped well before 40 million customers' credit and debit cards were leaked had someone not turned off a noisy alert.

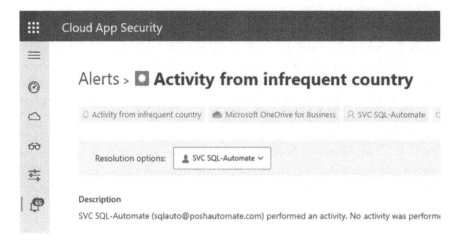

Figure 4.2   Alert on activity from an infrequent country from Microsoft Cloud App Security

4.1.6   *Do not rely on security through obscurity*

Security through obscurity (STO) is the reliance on secrecy or obscurity to protect yourself. While it may not seem like a bad idea on the surface, it should never be relied on as the only means of security. A typical scenario you will see is changing the default ports for SSH and RDP. This works against scanners looking for those particular ports, but once the secret that you changed the SSH port is discovered, an attacker will adjust. It is no different than locking all the doors to your house but leaving your house key under the doormat. Once someone knows it's there, they can get into your home with little to no problem.

That is not to say STO doesn't have its place. It should just never be relied on as the only means of security. One common and very insecure STO practice that I often see in PowerShell automations is the use of encoding to hide sensitive data in scripts. This is often done in situations where someone needs to run a script on an end user's device as an administrator. While the encoding does obfuscate the text, making it difficult for an end user to see, a bad actor can reverse it in seconds. Also, when it runs, the obfuscated values are decoded in memory as unsecured variables, making them easy to find.

Another example is compiling sensitive data into exe or dll files. While this may seem more secure than encoding, it is not challenging to decompile an exe or dll. Also, you run into the same vulnerability of having the data written as unsecured variables in memory.

As you will learn throughout this chapter, there are many ways you can secure the sensitive data that automations need to access. Both at rest and during execution, data will be more secure than only relying on STO.

4.1.7 Secure your scripts

Imagine you have an automation to collect health data from your servers. To avoid dealing with service accounts and permissions, you create a scheduled task on each server to execute the script. Then, to make your life even easier, you put the script on a network share. This way, if you need to update it, all machines will automatically get the new script the next time they run.

Now imagine that script was in an insecure share, and a bad actor updated it to create themselves a local administrator account on every single server. Since the script is running as the system account, the script will have no problems doing that. This is why you must maintain strict access to all production scripts, regardless of where they reside. If you are using a platform such as Jenkins or Azure Automation, you should set up at least two instances—one that people can access to develop and test their automations and a second to run production workloads that you have locked down, with access only given to a select few individuals.

Another way to prevent unauthorized script execution is by using coded signed scripts and setting your policies to block unsigned scripts from running. Code signing is a way to use a certificate to confirm the authenticity of a PowerShell script. The only way someone can swap out a script is if they also have access to your code signing certificate.

4.2 Credentials and secure strings in PowerShell

Back in the early days of PowerShell, when everything ran on-premises and was all connected to the same Active Directory domain, authentication was easy. You could use Task Scheduler or other job schedulers to run PowerShell scripts as a particular account. Nowadays, in your cross-platform hybrid environments, you can easily find yourself needing to authenticate across multiple environments for a single automation. In most cases, you will need to supply credentials, API keys, or other authentication data during the automation execution. To avoid storing these in plain text in both files and memory, you can use SecureString and Credential objects in PowerShell.

We will dig deeper into using these inside your scripts and with the SQL health check in section 4.3, but before we do, it is good to know precisely what these object types are and why they are more secure.

4.2.1 Secure strings

When you modify a standard string in PowerShell, it creates a copy of that string value in memory before changing it. Therefore, even if you delete the variable or set it to null, other copies of it might still exist in memory. Unlike a standard string object, when a SecureString is stored in memory, it is locked in place, so no copies are made, and it is encrypted. The fact that it is encrypted prevents memory dumps from being able to read the value. Also, because it gets pinned and not copied, you know the value will be deleted from memory when you delete the variable or your process ends.

NOTE   Before getting started with secure strings, be aware that they should be limited to Windows systems only. This is because the SecureString object relies on a .NET Framework API, not a .NET Core API, so while you can use SecureString on Linux and macOS, the values in memory are not encrypted.

There are two ways that you can create a SecureString in PowerShell. You can use the ConvertTo-SecureString cmdlet or the Read-Host cmdlet. To use the Read-Host cmdlet, you add the AsSecureString parameter to it. This will prompt the user to enter a value that is then saved as a secure string inside the script:

```
$SecureString = Read-Host -AsSecureString
$SecureString
System.Security.SecureString
```

The other method uses the ConvertTo-SecureString cmdlet, which converts an existing string to a secure string using the AsPlainText parameter. The thing to keep in mind here is that the plain text parameter will already be stored in memory, so it is not as secure as using the Read-Host method. If you included the plain text value anywhere in your script, it could be saved in the Event Logs and your PowerShell history. This is why it requires using the Force parameter to ensure you know the risks of using it:

```
$String = "password01"
$SecureString = ConvertTo-SecureString $String -AsPlainText -Force
$SecureString
System.Security.SecureString
```

You may be asking when you would use the ConvertTo-SecureString cmdlet. There are a few situations you will run into where you will need it, with the most common being a desire to make the scripts transportable. By default, SecureStrings are encrypted based on the user and the device. If you export the SecureString and try to import it to a different computer, it will fail. However, you can provide a custom key that you can use to perform the encryption. You can then use this key on other computers to import the secure string. Of course, this leads to the need to protect that key because if it gets leaked, all your SecureStrings could be decrypted. As you will see later in this chapter, the PowerShell team at Microsoft has created a new solution that utilizes password vaults instead of having to create custom encryption keys.

4.2.2   *Credential objects*

Credentials in PowerShell are stored as PSCredential objects. These are simply PowerShell objects that contain a standard string with the username and a SecureString property with the password. Like with SecureStrings, there are two ways you can create a PSCredential object.

The first way is to use the Get-Credential cmdlet and prompt the user for the credentials:

```
$Credential = Get-Credential
```

The other option is to manually create the PSCredential object by combing an existing unsecured string for the username and a SecureString for the password. If you are creating a PSCredential object using unsecured strings, those unsecured copies of the strings will still be in memory. However, they do have their uses, as you will see in section 4.4 when using the Jenkins built-in vault:

```
$Username = 'Contoso\BGates'
$Password = 'P@ssword'
$SecureString = ConvertTo-SecureString $Password -AsPlainText -Force
$Credential = New-Object System.Management.Automation.PSCredential $Username,
➥ $SecureString
```

PSCredentials can only be used by systems and commands that support PSCredentials, so passing them to other PowerShell cmdlets is not a problem. However, if you need to call external systems that do not support PSCredential objects, you can convert them to a .NET NetworkCredential object. An example of when you would use this is if you are building custom database connection strings or authenticating with a web application. In addition, you can use them for basic, digest, NTLM, and Kerberos authentication:

```
$Username = 'Contoso\BGates'
$Password = ConvertTo-SecureString 'Password' -AsPlainText -Force
$Credential = New-Object System.Management.Automation.PSCredential $Username,
➥ $Password
$NetCred = $Credential.GetNetworkCredential()
$NetCred
UserName    Domain
--------    ------
BGates      Contoso
```

> **NOTE**   The NetworkCredential object will contain the password in plain text. However, this is wiped from memory once the PowerShell session is closed.

4.3   *Storing credentials and secure strings in PowerShell*

There used to be no quicker way to trigger an argument in any PowerShell forum than by asking how to store a password for use by a PowerShell script. You would receive a dozen different opinions, each with others arguing why you should not use that approach. This became even more heated after the release of PowerShell Core and the discovery that the SecureString objects only exist in Windows.

Fortunately, the PowerShell team at Microsoft has been working diligently on this problem and has created the SecretManagement module. This module provides you with the ability to store and retrieve secrets and credentials from various password vaults. We will now set up the SecretManagement module for the SQL health check automation and any future automations you create.

4.3.1   *The SecretManagement module*

The SecretManagement module, which is shown in figure 4.3, is an engine that you can use to access different storage vaults. It allows you to use various vaults, including Azure Key Vault, KeePass, LastPass, and many others. The SecretManagement module enables you to interact with any of these storage vaults using a predefined set of commands. It allows you to swap out the backend storage vault seamlessly without needing to update your scripts. It also allows you to access multiple different vaults from within a single automation.

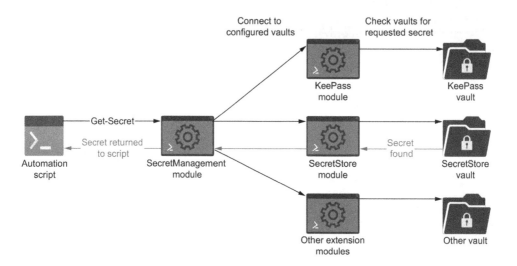

Figure 4.3   The SecretManagement module and how it can access multiple different vaults

In addition, the PowerShell team and Microsoft have released the SecretStore module, a storage vault built specifically for use with the SecretManagement module. The SecretStore module is not required to be able to use the SecretManagement module. You can use any other vault that has an extension built for it. To find a complete list of extensions, go to the PowerShell gallery and search for *SecretManagement*.

> **NOTE**   At this time, SecretManagement v1.0.0 is still only recommended for Windows environments as it relies on the SecureString object. It will work on Linux and macOS but will be less secure because the SecureString will be unencrypted in memory.

There is no required setup specific to the SecretManagement module aside from installing it. It just works as a translator for the different vaults. However, you will need to configure the various vaults and register them with the SecretManagement module so it knows how to access them.

4.3.2 Set up the SecretStore vault

Using the SecretStore module is a great way to familiarize yourself with the Secret-Management module. However, it does have one major drawback in that any vaults you create are tied to that specific user on that specific machine. This means that you cannot share the vault with others or easily move it to another system. However, the setup is easy, and you can get it up and running in a matter of minutes. To see how simple it is, we will set up the SecretManagement module, along with the SecretStore, to support the SQL health check automation.

INSTALL THE MODULES

The first step in the process is to install the two modules. They are both available from the PowerShell gallery, so you can install them by using `PowerShellGet`:

```
Install-Module Microsoft.PowerShell.SecretStore
Install-Module Microsoft.PowerShell.SecretManagement
```

CONFIGURE THE SECRETSTORE VAULT

Once you have the modules installed, you need to create a vault in the SecretStore. To do this, you will run the `Get-SecretStoreConfiguration` cmdlet. If this is your first time setting up the SecretStore, you will receive a prompt to provide a password. This is the password that you will use to access the vault:

```
Get-SecretStoreConfiguration
Creating a new Microsoft.PowerShell.SecretStore vault. A password is required
 by the current store configuration.
Enter password:
********
Enter password again for verification:
********
      Scope Authentication PasswordTimeout Interaction
      ----- -------------- --------------- -----------
CurrentUser       Password             900       Prompt
```

Before continuing, you should consider the implications of needing to enter a password to access the vault. While it is more secure to have a password, it does not work well for unattended automations because it requires user interaction. This is where the fact that the vault is tied to a machine and user comes in handy.

Since you want the SQL health check to run unattended, you will turn off the password requirement. When doing that, it is also a good idea to set the interaction to none to prevent scripts from hanging if the password requirement is turned back on for some reason. If the interaction is set to none and a password is required, an exception is thrown, causing the script to stop.

Go ahead and disable the password and the interaction using the `Set-SecretStore-Configuration` cmdlet:

```
Set-SecretStoreConfiguration -Authentication None -Interaction None
Confirm
Are you sure you want to perform this action?
```

```
Performing the operation "Changes local store configuration" on target "Secre
⇒tStore module local store".
[Y] Yes  [A] Yes to All  [N] No  [L] No to All  [S] Suspend  [?] Help (defaul
⇒t is "Y"): y
A password is no longer required for the local store configuration.
To complete the change please provide the current password.
Enter password:
********
```

By turning off the password requirement, your area of vulnerability is the account and machine that contains the vault. In this case, you will want to make sure that you take all the appropriate actions to secure this account, including using a strong password and auditing the logins made by this account and this machine.

REGISTER THE VAULT

The previous steps were all aimed at setting up the vault in the SecretStore module. Next, you need to register the vault with the SecretManagement module, so it knows where to look for the secret values. You do this by passing the name of the extension module and the vault's name to the `Register-SecretVault` cmdlet. The vault's name is what you will use to reference it in your scripts.

For the SQL health check, create a new vault named `SQLHealthCheck`:

```
Register-SecretVault -ModuleName Microsoft.PowerShell.SecretStore -Name SQLHe
⇒althCheck
```

The SecretStore module allows you to create multiple vaults under the same profile. Doing this can help with the management and organization of your secrets. Some vaults require that you provide information to `VaultParameters` parameters, but because SecretStore is tied to the machine and user, there are no additional configurations required.

> **Setting a default vault**
>
> The SecretManagement module allows you to set a default vault, so you do not have to specify a name when retrieving secrets. This is fine for personal use but should not be relied on for automations. You should always provide the vault name in automations to prevent failures if the default vault is changed.

4.3.3   *Set up a KeePass vault*

As previously mentioned, there are over a dozen different vaults that the SecretManagement module can use. We are now going to take a look at setting up a second vault with KeePass. If you are not familiar with KeePass, it is a free, open source password manager. Unlike other solutions vaults such as LastPass and Azure Key Vault, it is an entirely offline solution.

One major difference between a KeePass vault and a SecretStore vault is that KeePass uses a database file that you can move between machines and users or even store on a network share. Like SecretStore, it allows you to bypass entering a password, which works well for automations. However, KeePass can also use custom key files to provide an extra layer of security.

You do not need to install KeePass on a machine to use the KeePass extension. The extension module contains all the requirements to access the database file. However, you do need to have it installed to create a database file.

CREATE A KEEPASS DATABASE VAULT

When you create a KeePass database for use by the SecretManagement module, you need to consider the same things you do with SecretStore—that is, how it will run. If you are using it for unattended automations, you will want to exclude using a master password. However, it would be a good idea to use a key file.

KeePass uses a key file as an extra layer of security. Instead of providing a password, your automation can provide a key file. Since KeePass databases are not restricted to the machine that created them, the key file can help to protect you in situations in which a bad actor may get a copy of the database file. Without the key file, it will be useless to them. However, if a database file can be accessed using only the key file, you need to ensure that both the database file and the key file are appropriately stored and protected from unauthorized access and, most important, that they are never stored in the same place.

Go ahead and install KeePass and create a database file named SmtpKeePass.kdbx with a key file named SmtpKeePass.keyx. In the New Database Wizard, be sure to uncheck the Master Password box and then check Show Expert Options to create the key file. For more details, you can refer to https://keepass.info/.

INSTALL THE KEEPASS SECRETMANAGEMENT EXTENSION MODULE

Once you have KeePass installed and your database vault set up, you need to install the KeePass extension for the SecretManagement module so that you can use it through PowerShell:

```
Install-Module SecretManagement.KeePass
```

REGISTER KEEPASS WITH SECRETMANAGEMENT

Finally, you can register your KeePass database with the SecretManagement module using the `Register-SecretVault` cmdlet again. However, unlike with SecretStore, you will need to provide parameters for the vault. These are different for each vault type. For KeePass, you need to provide the path to the database file, if a master password is required, and the path to the key file.

For the SQL health check, run the `Register-SecretVault` cmdlet to register the SmtpKeePass database you just created. Set the `Path` to the full path of the SmtpKee-Pass.kdbx database file, `KeyPath` to the full path of the SmtpKeePass.keyx key file, and `UseMasterPassword` to false:

```
$ModuleName = 'SecretManagement.KeePass'
Register-SecretVault -Name 'SmtpKeePass' -ModuleName $ModuleName -VaultParame
ters @{
```

```
    Path = " \\ITShare\Automation\SmtpKeePass.kdbx"
    UseMasterPassword = $false
    KeyPath= "C:\Users\svcacct\SmtpKeePass.keyx"
}
```

Once registered, you can add and retrieve secrets using the same commands you use for SecretStore and any other vault attached to the SecretManagement module.

4.3.4   *Choosing the right vault*

The vault that you choose depends on your requirements. For example, SecretStore vaults are tied to a particular user and machine. While this does increase the security, it reduces the portability of your automation. In contrast, there is no such restriction on KeePass database files. However, since the KeePass file can be moved to a different machine, it is also more susceptible to being compromised if it is not properly stored and secured.

The nice thing about the SecretManagement module is that it can point to multiple vaults on the backend. So, you can use a combination of various vaults to meet your automation and security needs. Figure 4.4 shows an example.

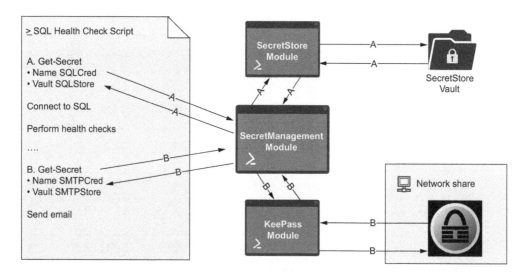

Figure 4.4   SecretManagement vault usage for the SQL health check automation

For example, in the SQL health check, you will use the KeePass vault to store the credentials needed to send the email via SendGrid and SecretStore to hold the secrets for connecting to the SQL instance. The reason for this is because you can have multiple automations that need to send emails.

If you create a new service account for each automation that needs to send an email, you will quickly run into a situation in which you have so many accounts that you cannot manage them. On the other hand, if you have a couple of service accounts for sending emails used by multiple automations, you need to make sure that all automations can be easily updated if anything changes. This is where shared vaults come in handy. If you put the credentials for the email into a shared vault, you can update all automations at once if anything ever changes while, at the same time, having a separate vault that contains the SQL connection information, providing you an extra layer of security. This way, if any one of your vaults gets compromised, the remaining automations will be unaffected.

4.3.5   Adding secrets to a vault

Once you have your vaults created and registered to the SecretManagement module, you can add your secrets to them. You use the `Set-Secret` cmdlet to add a secret to a vault. You need to specify the parameters:

- `Name`—The name for the secret. This will be used to retrieve the value later.
- `Vault`—The name of the vault to store the secret. If not specified, the default vault is used.
- `Secret`—The object containing the secret. The supported object types are
  - `byte[]`
  - `String`
  - `SecureString`
  - `PSCredential`
  - `Hashtable`

Table 4.1 lists these parameters for the SQL health check script. The value for the `Secret` parameter should be the only one that contains sensitive information. Also, if a secret already exists in the vault with the same name, the `Set-Secret` cmdlet will overwrite it unless you use the `NoClobber` switch.

You need to create secrets in both the SecretStore vault and the KeePass vault for the SQL health check automation. First, in the SecretStore vault, create a `PSCredential` object with the username and password for the SQL connection and a `SecureString` object with the name of the SQL server instance. Then, in the KeePass vault, you will create the entries for the SendGrid API.

Table 4.1   Secrets required for the SQL health check script using the SecretManagement module

Secret name	Vault	Secret object type	Notes
`TestSQL`	`SQLHealthCheck`	String	\<Your server name>\SQLEX-PRESS *
`TestSQLCredential`	`SQLHealthCheck`	Credentials	Username* : sqlhealth Password* : P@55w9rd
`SendGrid`	`SmtpKeePass`	Secure string	Your email address

Table 4.1   Secrets required for the SQL health check script using the SecretManagement module *(continued)*

Secret name	Vault	Secret object type	Notes
SendGridKey	SmtpKeePass	Credentials	When using SendGrid, the user-name will be apikey, and the password will be your API key.

These are the default values if you used the setup scripts provided in the GitHub repo.

Naming-related secrets

Whenever you have two or more secrets that are related to each other, as you do in the SQL health check, you should name them with the same prefix. Not only will it make it easier to keep track of, but it will also allow you to simplify your parameters by enabling you to pass one value that you can then append multiple suffixes to.

For example, to get the SQL secrets from table 4.1, you only need to pass the value 'TestSQL' Then, to get the credentials, you can simply append Credential to the name:

```
$SqlName  = 'TestSQL'
$SqlCred  = "$($SqlName)Credential"
```

The same can be done for the SendGrid secrets by adding Key to the end of the name.

Create the entries for the SecretStore vault:

```
$SQLServer = "$($env:COMPUTERNAME)\SQLEXPRESS"
Set-Secret -Name TestSQL -Secret $SQLServer -Vault SQLHealthCheck
$Credential = Get-Credential
Set-Secret -Name TestSQLCredential -Secret $Credential -Vault SQLHealthCheck
```

Create the entries for the KeePass vault:

```
$SmtpFrom = Read-Host -AsSecureString
Set-Secret -Name SendGrid -Secret $SmtpFrom -Vault SmtpKeePass
$Credential = Get-Credential
Set-Secret -Name SendGridKey -Secret $Credential -Vault SmtpKeePass
```

Now that you have the secrets stored in the vault, you are ready to set up your automation script to retrieve and use them.

4.4   *Using credentials and secure strings in your automations*

As you will see, using the SecretManagement module to retrieve sensitive data is a simple and easy process. However, there are still other viable options out there for storing and providing sensitive data to your scripts. Many popular automation and CD/CI platforms have ways of delivering credentials and other values to your scripts safely and securely. Using the SQL health check script, we will set up the automation first using the SecretManagement module and then using Jenkins with its built-in vault.

4.4.1 SecretManagement module

Once you have the vaults set up and registered to SecretManagement, you can start using them to retrieve secrets in your automations. Remember, the configurations are set to the user profile, so you need to be logged in as the user who will access the vault when configuring it. Then you need to ensure that your automation is running as that user. You can refer to chapter 3 to learn about scheduling automations to run as a particular user.

To retrieve a secret in your script, all you need to do is use the `Get-Secret` cmdlet. This cmdlet will return the first secret that matches the name you provided. This is why it is important to ensure that all of your secrets have unique names and why it is always good to include the `Vault` parameter. If you don't use the `Vault` parameter, the SecretManagement module searches through all vaults, starting with the default one.

By default, string secrets are returned as `SecureString` objects. However, if you need them returned as plain text, you can include the `AsPlainText` switch.

As you will see in the SQL health check script, you can use any combination of vaults and secrets you need inside your script. In this scenario, you need to retrieve the SQL server connection information from one vault and the SendGrid information from another. Also, when you retrieve the SQL server name and email address from the vault, these need to be converted into standard strings using the `AsPlainText` switch. Let's start by testing the SQL and SendGrid connections separately.

Starting with the SQL connection test in listing 4.1, you can retrieve the SQL connection information from the SecretStore vault and then run a simple SQL query using the `Invoke-DbaDiagnosticQuery` cmdlet. If the command output contains data in the `Results` property, you know it worked. If the `Results` property is empty, check the verbose output. If there is a permissions issue, it will be listed there. Try tweaking your SQL permissions and testing again until you receive the expected results.

Listing 4.1 Testing SQL connection information from the SecretStore vault

```
$Secret = @{                              Retrieve credentials
    Name  = 'TestSQLCredential'           for the SQL server
    Vault = 'SQLHealthCheck'              connection.
}
$SqlCredential = Get-Secret @Secret
$Secret = @{                              Retrieve the SQL server
    Name  = 'TestSQL'                     name and convert it to
    Vault = 'SQLHealthCheck'              plain text.
}
$SQLServer = Get-Secret @Secret -AsPlainText
```

```
$DbaDiagnosticQuery = @{                      ◁───────┐   Execute a diagnostic query
    SqlInstance   = $SQLServer                         │   against SQL to test the
    SqlCredential = $SqlCredential                     │   connection information
    QueryName     = 'Database Properties'              │   from the SecretStore vault.
}
Invoke-DbaDiagnosticQuery @DbaDiagnosticQuery -Verbose
```

Next, you can test sending an email through SendGrid using the `Send-EmailMessage` cmdlet, as shown in listing 4.2. In this case, you will retrieve this SendGrid API key and the email address from the KeePass vault. Then send a test email to the same email address. If you receive the email, you are ready to move forward with putting it all together in the SQL health check automation.

Listing 4.2 Testing the SendGrid connection information from the KeePass vault

```
$Secret = @{                        ◁──────┐   Get the email address
    Name  = 'SendGrid'                      │   for the "send from"
    Vault = 'SmtpKeePass'                   │   in plain text.
}
$From = Get-Secret @Secret -AsPlainText
$Secret = @{                        ◁──────┐   Get the API key
    Name  = 'SendGridKey'                   │   for SendGrid.
    Vault = 'SmtpKeePass'                   │
}
$EmailCredentials = Get-Secret @Secret      ┐   Send a test email with
                                            │   the SendGrid connection
$EmailMessage = @{                  ◁───────┤   information from the
    From       = $From                      │   KeePass vault.
    To         = $From
    Credential = $EmailCredentials
    Body       = 'This is a test of the SendGrid API'
    Priority   = 'High'
    Subject    = "Test SendGrid"
    SendGrid   = $true
}
Send-EmailMessage @EmailMessage
```

Now that you have confirmed you can run a health check query and send an email, it is time to put everything together into an automation script, starting with the parameters. You will want to set the names of the vaults and the names of the secret objects as parameters so you can easily use this script across different SQL instances. Since the related secrets are named with the same prefix, you only need to prompt for the prefix and then have the script append the suffix. So, instead of having a parameter for the SQL instance secret and a second one for the credential secret, you just need to create one to pass the prefix. Then, in your script, append `Credential` to the name. You can do the same for the SendGrid API key by appending `Key` to the variable. Finally, you will need a parameter for the email to send to in the case of a failed check.

Next, the script will get the SQL connection information from the vault and then execute the `'Database Properties'` query from the `Invoke-DbaDiagnosticQuery` cmdlet to return the recovery model information for all the databases. Next, it will confirm that all of them are set to SIMPLE. If any are not set to SIMPLE, it will gather the information to send an email notification by getting the SendGrid secrets. It will then create the email body by converting the PowerShell object containing the bad databases to an HTML table. Finally, it will send the email. The following listing shows the complete script.

Listing 4.3 SQL health check

```
param(
    [string]$SQLVault,
    [string]$SQLInstance,
    [string]$SmtpVault,
    [string]$FromSecret,
    [string]$SendTo
)
$Secret = @{
    Name  = "$($SQLInstance)Credential"
    Vault = $SQLVault
}
$SqlCredential = Get-Secret @Secret
$Secret = @{
    Name  = $SQLInstance
    Vault = $SQLVault
}
$SQLServer = Get-Secret @Secret -AsPlainText

$DbaDiagnosticQuery = @{
    SqlInstance   = $SQLServer
    SqlCredential = $SqlCredential
    QueryName     = 'Database Properties'
}
$HealthCheck = Invoke-DbaDiagnosticQuery @DbaDiagnosticQuery
$failedCheck = $HealthCheck.Result |
    Where-Object { $_.'Recovery Model' -ne 'SIMPLE' }

if ($failedCheck) {
    $Secret = @{
        Name  = $FromSecret
        Vault = $SmtpVault
    }
    $From = Get-Secret @Secret -AsPlainText
    $Secret = @{
        Name  = "$($FromSecret)Key"
        Vault = $SmtpVault
    }
    $EmailCredentials = Get-Secret @Secret

    $Body = $failedCheck | ConvertTo-Html -As List |
        Out-String

    $EmailMessage = @{
        From         = $From
```

Annotations:
- **Retrieve the credentials for the SQL server connection.**
- **Retrieve the SQL server name and convert it to plain text.**
- **Execute the Database Properties diagnostic query against SQL.**
- **Get the email address for the "send from" in plain text.**
- **Get the API key for SendGrid.**
- **Send a failure email notification.**
- **Create the email body by converting failed check results to an HTML table.**

```
        To        = $SendTo
        Credential = $EmailCredentials
        Body      = $Body
        Priority  = 'High'
        Subject   = "SQL Health Check Failed for $($SQLServer)"
        SendGrid  = $true
    }
    Send-EmailMessage @EmailMessage
}
```

4.4.2 *Using Jenkins credentials*

Before the SecretManagement module, the best way to store credentials was by using a third-party platform that has its own store. One of these platforms is Jenkins. So while you can use the SecretManagement module for scripts that run through Jenkins, you can also use the built-in Jenkins store.

One of the advantages of using the Jenkins credentials is that you do not need to worry about having the different secret vaults and module extensions installed on every Jenkins server. Instead, they will all be able to get credentials from one global store. Also, it provides a GUI interface and logging of which automations have used which objects.

By default, you will have a store named Jenkins, which we will use to store the SQL health check automation values. You can set up different vaults and even apply role-based access to them, but for now, we will use the global store.

In this example, we will update the SQL health check script to use Jenkins credentials and variables instead of the SecretManagement vaults.

To create credentials in Jenkins, you need to navigate to Manage Jenkins > Manage Credentials and then click the store you want to use. In this case, it will be the Jenkins store. Once in the store, click Global Credentials and create the credential objects listed in table 4.2.

Table 4.2 Secrets required for the SQL health check script using Jenkins

ID	Kind	Value
TestSQL	Secret text	<Your server name>\SQLEXPRESS *
TestSQLCredential	Username with password	Username* : sqlhealth Password* : P@55w9rd
SendGrid	Secret text	Your email address
SendGridKey	Username with password	When using SendGrid, the username will be apikey, and the password will be your API key.

* These are the default values if you used the setup scripts provided in the GitHub repo.

Now that you have the credentials and secrets created, you can use them in your scripts. But before you do, there are some things you need to know. Jenkins has its own methods for storing secret values and therefore does not have direct support for the `SecureString` and `PSCredential` objects in PowerShell. So, it loads the values into environment variables at the time of execution as standard unsecured strings. It has its own ways of preventing those variables from being written to the output logs or saved in memory. Therefore, when you need to use the values as `SecureString` or `PSCredential` objects, you need to convert them back from standard strings using the `ConvertTo-SecureString` cmdlet.

In the SQL health check script, you will need to recreate the credentials for the SQL connection and the SendGrid API key. The email address and SQL instance do not need to be converted because they are expected to be unsecured strings.

To get started, create a new Freestyle project in Jenkins. Then, under the Binding section, add two bindings for username and password (separated), and configure them to use the values in table 4.3.

Table 4.3 Credential bindings required for the SQL health check script in Jenkins build

Username variable	Password variable	Credentials
sqlusername	sqlpassword	TestSQLCredential
sendgridusername	sendgridpassword	SendGridKey

Next, add two binds for secret text and configure them to use the values in table 4.4.

Table 4.4 Secret text bindings required for the SQL health check script in Jenkins build

Variable	Credentials
sqlserver	TestSQL
sendgrid	SendGrid

Finally, you need to update the SQL health check script to replace the calls to the SecretManagement vaults with the environment variables for Jenkins, as shown in the following listing. Remember that you will need to recreate the credentials.

Listing 4.4 SQL health check through Jenkins

```
$secure = @{                                    Replace the Get-Secret call with Jenkins
    String = $ENV:sqlpassword                   environment variables and recreate the
    AsPlainText = $true                         credential object.
    Force = $true
}
$Password = ConvertTo-SecureString @secure
$SqlCredential = New-Object System.Management.Automation.PSCredential `
    ($ENV:sqlusername, $Password)
```

```
$SQLServer = $ENV:sqlserver

$DbaDiagnosticQuery = @{
    SqlInstance   = $SQLServer
    SqlCredential = $SqlCredential
    QueryName     = 'DatabaseProperties'
}
$HealthCheck = Invoke-DbaDiagnosticQuery @DbaDiagnosticQuery
$failedCheck = $HealthCheck.Result |
    Where-Object { $_.'Recovery Model' -ne 'SIMPLE' }

if ($failedCheck) {
    $From = $ENV:sendgrid
    $secure = @{
        String = $ENV:sendgridusername
        AsPlainText = $true
        Force = $true
    }
    $Password = ConvertTo-SecureString @secure
    $Credential = New-Object System.Management.Automation.PSCredential `
        ($ENV:sendgridpassword, $Password)

    $Body = $failedCheck | ConvertTo-Html -As List |
        Out-String

    $EmailMessage = @{
        From       = $From
        To         = $SendTo
        Credential = $EmailCredentials
        Body       = $Body
        Priority   = 'High'
        Subject    = "SQL Health Check Failed for $($SQLServer)"
        SendGrid   = $true
    }
    Send-EmailMessage @EmailMessage
}
```

Replace the Get-Secret call with Jenkins environment variables.

Replace the Get-Secret call with Jenkins environment variables and recreate the credential object.

If you want to make this build dynamic so you can run it against different SQL instances, all you need to do is change the bindings from specific credentials to parameter expressions. You can then enter the name of the secrets to use at run time.

4.5   *Know your risks*

Throughout this chapter, you have seen that there is always a potential vulnerability introduced when creating unattended automations. However, by knowing what they are, you can help mitigate them. Unfortunately, many companies can be so scared of automation from a security perspective that they make it impossible to get anything done. That is why it will be your job to understand the risks so that you can explain them and the steps you have taken to mitigate them.

In our example, with the SQL health check, we were able to reduce the risks using multiple techniques. First, we used an account specifically for running the health check, with the minimum required permissions, along with a separate API key to use SendGrid for sending notifications. We also prevented any sensitive data from being stored in the script by using the SecretManagement module and Jenkins credential stores.

However, even though we significantly reduced the vulnerabilities, there are still risks that you need to be aware of so you can take the steps to properly account for them. For example, the KeePass vault can be copied by a bad actor and used on a machine outside of your network. However, by using a key file and storing that key file in a separate secure location, that database would be worthless to them. You will also want to ensure that only authorized personnel can access either file through appropriate file and share permissions.

In addition, just using SendGrid, instead of an SMTP relay, provides you additional levels of security. For example, you can create IP-based restrictions, view audit logs, and create alerts for anomalous activity. Therefore, even if your KeePass database is copied and someone gets a copy of the key file, they may not be able to do anything with it.

Another potential vulnerability to consider is that Jenkins passes the secret values to PowerShell as unsecured strings. However, Jenkins has built-in security to prevent these values from being written out to any output stream, and the PowerShell runtime is terminated after execution, clearing the memory used. So, really, the only way someone could get the values would be to perform a memory dump during the script's execution, and if someone has access to your server and can perform a memory dump completely undetected, you have much bigger problems on your hands.

In all cases, we were able to reduce any risks added by introducing unattended automations. Of course, not even an air-gapped computer with an armed guard sitting next to it is 100% secure—and no security officer should ever expect that—but that doesn't mean you shouldn't do all you can to minimize risk. However, I can tell you from experience that being open and honest with your security team about the risks and the steps you have taken to reduce them can make getting your automations approved a much easier process.

Summary

- Following some basic principles such as using role-based access, assigning the least privilege, and not relying on security through obscurity can help to ensure that your automations are safe and secure.
- `SecureString` and `PSCredential` objects can be used natively in PowerShell to keep your sensitive data secure during execution and at rest.
- The SecretManagement module can be used with multiple password vaults to provide secure storage and access to sensitive data you need in your scripts.
- Many platforms have built-in vaults that you can use in place of the SecretManagement module.
- Knowing what your risks are is the only way that you can reduce them to an acceptable level.

PowerShell remote execution

This chapter covers

- Designing scripts for remote execution
- PowerShell-based remoting
- Hypervisor-based remoting
- Agent-based remoting

The ability to execute remote PowerShell commands is not only essential for recurring automations, but is also a powerful tool to have in your arsenal for ad-hoc situations. Just think back on your career and remember times when you needed to gather large-scale information about your environment or apply a change across multiple servers at once. You will quickly realize this is a common situation for any IT department. And, in some cases, especially security-related ones, time can be of the essence. Therefore, before these situations arise, you will want to have PowerShell remoting set up and know how to adapt your scripts for remote execution.

For instance, in May of 2021, security researchers identified vulnerabilities in several Visual Studio Code (VS Code) extensions. While discovering installed versions of VS Code may be simple, finding the installed extensions can present a significant challenge. This is because extensions are installed at the user level and not at the system level. Therefore, a lot of scanning tools will not pick them up. Fortunately, all VS Code extensions contain a vsixmanifest file, which we can search for and read to identify installed extensions.

We will use this scenario throughout this chapter to demonstrate the different ways that you can execute PowerShell remotely and how you will need to adjust your scripts depending on which type of remote execution you use. You can then apply these same fundamental principles to all remote execution automations. But before we get into that, let's quickly cover some of the basic concepts of PowerShell remoting.

5.1 PowerShell remoting

When discussing PowerShell remoting, there are two things you need to understand. One is the remote execution protocols, or how the machines talk to each other. The other is the remote execution context, or how the remote sessions behave.

For clarity, the machine you will be making the remote connects from is the *client*. Any devices you are connecting to are the *servers*.

5.1.1 Remote context

There are three main types of remote execution context:

- Remote commands
- Interactive sessions
- Imported sessions

A remote command is one in which you execute a predefined command or script against a remote server. Most commonly, you use the `Invoke-Command` cmdlet for this in automation scenarios. It not only allows you to execute the commands on the remote server, but it also allows you to return the results to the client machine.

In the VS Code extension scenario, this type of remote execution is the best choice. First, you can execute predefined scripts and commands, which you will have. Second, you can return all the results to a single session so you can view the results from all machines in a single place.

An interactive context is one in which you use the `Enter-PSSession` cmdlet to enter a remote session. This is the equivalent of opening a PowerShell prompt on the remote server. It is suitable for running one-off commands but does not lend itself very well to automation because the information from the commands is not returned to the local client.

The import context is one in which you use the `Import-PSSession` cmdlet to import the cmdlets and functions from a remote session into your local session. This allows you to use the commands without needing to install modules locally. It is most often used for Office 365 and Exchange-based automations. However, since the cmdlets are imported to the local client, it provides no way to interact with the remote server.

5.1.2   *Remote protocols*

When you look into PowerShell remoting protocols, it is easy to get overwhelmed. There are so many acronyms, initialisms, and abbreviations that it can be hard to tell what anything is. For instance, PowerShell 7 supports WMI, WS-Management (WSMan), Secure Shell Protocol (SSH), and RPC remoting. You will need to know which protocols to use based on the context required for the automation and the remote server's operating system.

WMI and RPC remoting have long been staples of PowerShell and Windows remoting in general—with the keyword here being *Windows*. If you have ever used a cmdlet that contains the `-ComputerName` parameter, chances are you have used either WMI or RPC. These protocols work great but can be very limiting. Not only are they restricted to Windows, but there are a limited number of cmdlets that contain the `-ComputerName` parameter. Therefore, to truly take full advantage of PowerShell remoting capabilities, you should use WSMan and SSH for executing remote commands.

The WSMan and SSH protocols create remote PowerShell sessions that let you run PowerShell under any remote context. Which one you use will depend on your particular environment. WSMan only works on Windows-based machines and can support local or Active Directory authentication. SSH can support both Windows and Linux but does not support Active Directory authentication.

> **NOTE** You will often hear the terms *WinRM* and *WSMan* used interchangeably. This is because WSMan is an open standard and WinRM is Microsoft's implementation of that standard.

Just as there are mixed environments nowadays, there is no reason you can't use a mixture of protocols. In most cases, if a machine is domain joined, I will use WSMan; otherwise, I'll use SSH. As you will see, you can easily adapt your scripts to support both.

5.1.3   *Persistent sessions*

When using the `Invoke-Command` and `Enter-PSSession` cmdlets, you have the option to either establish the session at the time of execution by using the `-ComputerName` argument or use an existing session, also known as a persistent session. You can create these persistent sessions using the `New-PSSession` cmdlet.

Persistent sessions allow you to connect to the same session multiple times. You can also use them to create connections to multiple remote servers and execute your commands against all of them at once, providing you parallel execution.

End-user devices and PowerShell remote execution

Remote PowerShell execution is generally limited to server devices and not end-user devices. The biggest reason for this is security. Allowing remote execution on end-user devices can leave you open to vulnerabilities if a device becomes compromised. And, as you know, the risk of an end-user device becoming compromised is exponentially larger than a server. Also, servers' network configurations remain relatively static compared to end-user devices. With the growing trend of work-anywhere, there is no guarantee that an end-user device will be reachable over your WAN. Therefore, it is best to use configuration management software or MDM for managing end-user devices with PowerShell. We will cover this in depth in chapter 11.

5.2 Script considerations for remote execution

There are two types of scripts we will talk about with regard to remote execution. The first are the scripts for execution on the remote server. In our scenario, it will be the script to find the VS Code extensions, but it can be any script you want to run remotely. The second is the control script. The control script runs on the local client and tells the remote servers to execute the script, as you can see in figure 5.1.

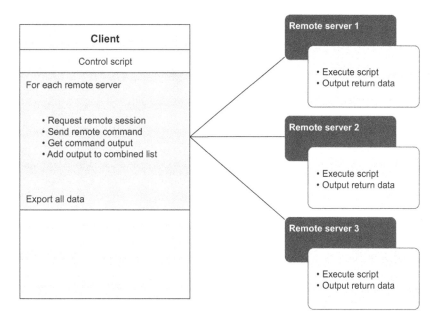

Figure 5.1 Control scripts are used to execute a PowerShell script or script block across multiple machines and return the data to a single place.

For the majority of this chapter, we will be discussing and working with control scripts. You will design these control scripts to be reusable for any script that you need to execute remotely. However, before we dive in, there are a few things you need to be mindful of when creating a script you know will be used for remote execution.

5.2.1 Remote execution scripts

All of the automation script fundamentals we've discussed in the other chapters still apply when designing a remote execution script. These include ensuring the remote server has any required modules installed and that the script does not contain any commands that would stop and wait for user interaction. In addition, you want to ensure that any information returned from a remote execution is appropriately formatted and that your script can work on the required operating systems and PowerShell versions. Again, we will use the VS Code extension example to help illustrate these points, as shown in figure 5.2, but keep in mind that these things apply to any remote PowerShell execution and not just to this specific scenario.

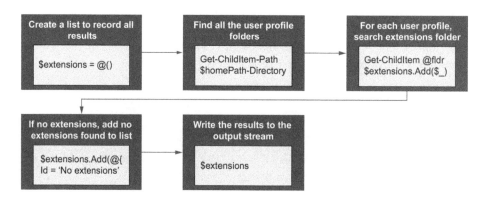

Figure 5.2   Search all user profiles for installed VS Code extensions and return the results.

Finding the installed VS Code extensions may seem like a reasonably simple task. You just need to search the VS Code extensions folder inside each user's home folders, gather the extensions found, and return the results or, if none are found, return a message stating that.

Since we know the cmdlets required to perform this task are built-in, we do not need to worry about module dependencies. We also know that they do not require user interactions. So, we can move on to the remote execution considerations.

The first thing you need to determine is what operating systems and PowerShell versions the remote machines are using. Ideally, you want to write one script that you can run on all devices. This way, if you need to change something, you only have to change it once.

In the VS Code extensions scenario, you are searching in user home folders, and different operating systems have different home paths. In other scenarios, there could be different environmental variables, services, system paths, or any other number of things. Luckily, PowerShell has built-in variables to help you deal with this. The variables $IsLinux, $IsWindows, and $IsMacOS will return True or False depending on the operating system. Using these variables allows you to set your own variables for the specific operating system while leaving the rest of the script universal. For our scenario, you can create an if/else condition to set the home path based on the operating system and leave the rest of the script the same.

Ideally, all servers would be running PowerShell 7 or greater, but in reality, that is not always the case. There are plenty of situations where you need to ensure that your scripts can run in Windows PowerShell and PowerShell 7. While the majority of PowerShell commands remained the same, there are some breaking changes between the two versions. It is also easy to fall into the habits of the newer versions. For example, the $IsLinux, $IsWindows, and $IsMacOS variables were introduced with PowerShell 6. To account for this, you could build some logic into your scripts to check PowerShell versions and end up with multiple different nested if/else conditions, or you could use your knowledge of PowerShell to your advantage. You know that prior to PowerShell 6, PowerShell only ran on Windows. Therefore, it doesn't have the $IsLinux, $IsWindows, or $IsMacOS variables. This means you can use a simple if $IsLinux use the Linux path, else if $IsMacOS use the macOS path, else use the Windows path. Since the $IsLinux and $IsMacOS variables don't exist in Windows PowerShell, a Windows device will always use the else path:

```
if ($IsLinux) {
    # set Linux specific variables
}
elseif ($IsMacOS) {
    # set macOS specific variables
}
else {
    # set Windows specific variables
}
```

The next item to consider is how to structure any data you need to return from remote execution. Similar to executing a function, everything written to the output stream by the script will be returned to the control script. Therefore, you need to know what commands write to the output stream and only return the information you need.

Another item that seems obvious but is often overlooked is adding the machine's name to the information returned. If you run a script against 10 machines and they all return data, it doesn't do any good unless you know which machine returned it. While some remote protocols will automatically add the remote machine's name to the return data, others do not. So, it is best to have the script return the machine name in the output. This will guarantee that you will know which machine it was, regardless of the remote method used.

> **NOTE** The environment variable to return the machine name $env:COMPUTER-NAME doesn't work in Linux, but the .NET Core call [system.environment] ::MachineName works in Linux and Windows.

Also, it is good practice to add the date and time to the output, especially if you plan to execute the script multiple times.

One last thing to consider is what to do if there is no data to return. For example, if no extensions are found with the VS Code extension script, there is nothing to return. However, that also means you don't have a record that it ran. Therefore, you want to include a check in your code when designing remote execution scripts to return something, even if the conditions are not met. In addition, you want to ensure that this return is formatted the same way as if results were found, so your results can be stored together. You will see why this is important in the next section when we cover the control scripts. The following listing shows the completed script.

Listing 5.1   Get-VSCodeExtensions.ps1

```powershell
[System.Collections.Generic.List[PSObject]] $extensions = @()
if ($IsLinux) {                          Set the home folder
    $homePath = '/home/'                 path based on the
}                                        operating system.
else {
    $homePath = "$($env:HOMEDRIVE)\Users"
}
                                                            Get the subfolders
                                                            under the home
$homeDirs = Get-ChildItem -Path $homePath -Directory        path.

foreach ($dir in $homeDirs) {
    $vscPath = Join-Path $dir.FullName '.vscode\extensions'
    if (Test-Path -Path $vscPath) {              If the VS Code extension
        $ChildItem = @{                          folder is present, search
            Path    = $vscPath                   it for vsixmanifest files.
            Recurse = $true
            Filter  = '.vsixmanifest'
            Force   = $true                                Get the contents of
        }                                                  the vsixmanifest
        $manifests = Get-ChildItem @ChildItem              file and convert it
        foreach ($m in $manifests) {                       to a PowerShell
            [xml]$vsix = Get-Content -Path $m.FullName      XML object.
            $vsix.PackageManifest.Metadata.Identity |
            Select-Object -Property Id, Version, Publisher,
            @{l = 'Folder'; e = { $m.FullName } },
            @{l = 'ComputerName'; e = {[system.environment]::MachineName}},
            @{l = 'Date'; e = { Get-Date } } |
            ForEach-Object { $extensions.Add($_) }
        }
    }
}
if ($extensions.Count -eq 0) {              If no extensions are found,
    $extensions.Add([pscustomobject]@{     return a PowerShell object
        Id        = 'No extension found'    with the same properties
        Version   = $null                   stating nothing was found.
        Publisher = $null
        Folder    = $null
```

Annotations:
- Set the home folder path based on the operating system.
- Get the subfolders under the home path.
- **Parse through each folder and check for VS Code extensions.**
- If the VS Code extension folder is present, search it for vsixmanifest files.
- Get the contents of the vsixmanifest file and convert it to a PowerShell XML object.
- **Get the details from the manifest and add them to the extensions list.**
- **Add the folder path, computer name, and date to the output.**
- If no extensions are found, return a PowerShell object with the same properties stating nothing was found.

```
                ComputerName = [system.environment]::MachineName
                Date         = Get-Date
        })
}
$extensions
```

Just like an extension, include the output at the end.

Once you have created this script, save it to your local machine with the name Get-VSCodeExtensions.ps1. This is the script you will be using to test your control scripts.

5.2.2 Remote execution control scripts

When executing a script against multiple remote servers, you will want to have a control script. The control script will create the remote connection, run the remote command, and gather any information returned, as shown in figure 5.3. Based on the type of remote execution you are performing, the cmdlets used will differ, but the overall process remains the same.

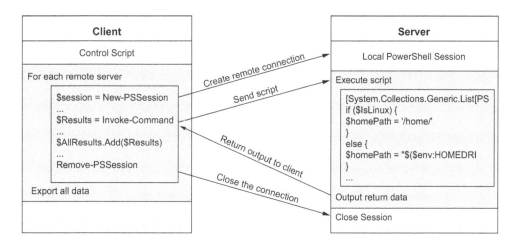

Figure 5.3 Control scripts are used to initiate PowerShell sessions across multiple machines and return the data to a single place.

When designing your control scripts, one of the first things to consider is the execution time. For example, you can use a foreach to loop through each remote device and run the script on it. However, these will not run in parallel. So, if your script takes 30 seconds to execute and you check 20 servers, it will take 10 minutes to complete. On the other hand, if you run the command on multiple servers at once, you can dramatically reduce execution time.

PowerShell offers multiple ways to run remote commands sequentially. For example, some remote execution cmdlets, like the Invoke-Command, allow you to pass an array of computers. However, you need to be careful with this because if one computer fails, it could cause the others not to run. A better way to handle this is by using persistent connections.

Persistent connections allow you to establish the remote session before executing the command and will keep it active until you tell it to close. This enables you to create an entire group of connections in a matter of seconds and execute the remote script against them all at once. It also allows you to account for failed connections so the rest of the remote devices are not affected. As you can see in figure 5.4, even if creating the persistent connection takes around 1 second, you will end up saving time in the long run—and that is just with 10 servers.

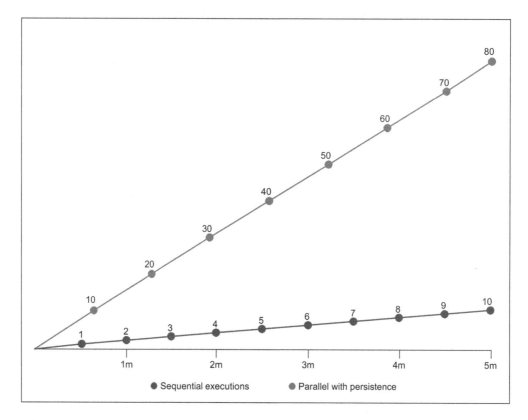

Figure 5.4   Comparison of the number of executions in a 5-minute window when using persistent connections for parallel execution versus individual executions

As with most things in automation, there is always a balancing act. You do not want to create so many connections at once that your computer and network slow to a crawl. PowerShell remoting is limited to 32 persistent connections per session by default, but that number can be changed. The amount of memory and bandwidth needed will depend on what commands you are using and how much data the script collects. You will have to test and figure out what works best for you and your environment.

As with most things in PowerShell, there is always more than one way to accomplish something. In this chapter, you will see four different ways of executing remote scripts. In addition, there are other ways to run PowerShell processes in parallel, such as foreach parallel loops or using jobs, which both present their unique challenges and advantages. However, from my experiences, persistent connections are the way to go when dealing with remote execution.

Aside from making the remote connections, the next most important thing is handling the data returned from each machine. If you run this script against 5 or 10 computers, you can probably run them all at once and just save the output to a single variable. However, if you are executing against 50, 100, 1,000, or more computers, you must combine the executions' data. For example, if you have 50 machines to check, you can break them into five groups of 10. Then, use an array to add the data together after each group finishes.

Consider a situation where you processed through half of the machines, and your network connection drops or your PowerShell console closes. If you restart your script, it will resume from the beginning and check all of the devices again. This may not be a big deal if you are checking 50 machines, but what if you are checking 500 or 1,000 machines? Starting over will be a colossal waste of time. This is where saving your return data outside of PowerShell comes in handy. The easiest way to do this is by exporting it to a CSV file. PowerShell natively supports importing and exporting of objects to CSV using the cmdlets Import-Csv and Export-Csv. In addition, CSV data is easily human-readable.

> **Formatting data for Export-Csv**
>
> When using the Export-Csv cmdlet to append to an existing CSV file, you need to be aware that it will only include the fields that are currently in the header row. This is why it is crucial to return all data from your script using the same format.

If you export your results after each remote execution, you can reimport them if you need to restart the script. Then, you simply need to check whether the CSV file exists. If it does, load the data into a variable and use it to filter your machine list to exclude those that have already been checked.

When filtering, you want to ensure that you use the value your script used to connect to create the remote session and not the name returned from the return data. For example, when using the Invoke-Command cmdlet, the PSComputerName property is automatically added to the output. By filtering on this, you will prevent duplicate submissions due to things like your control script using the FQDN and your script returning the NetBIOS or using DNS aliases.

One last thing to consider is creating a separate CSV export for any machines that fail to connect. This way, they are not stored in the same CSV as the actual results you want, and the file provides you with an excellent list to use for troubleshooting and fixing the failed connections.

Now, it is time to look into how you can execute your scripts on different remote systems and build your control scripts. We will start with the native capabilities in PowerShell.

5.3 PowerShell remoting over WSMan

When using PowerShell in an Active Directory environment, WSMan is your best option. Not only does it support Active Directory authentication, but it is also enabled by default on Windows server operating systems. You can also use Group Policy Objects (GPOs) to enable WSMan remoting, making your setup almost effortless.

5.3.1 Enable WSMan PowerShell remoting

Unfortunately, at this time, only Windows PowerShell can be controlled via GPOs and not PowerShell Core. Therefore, if you want to execute remote command using Power-Shell 6 or above, you will need to run the `Enable-PSRemoting` cmdlet on each server. You can add the `-Force` switch to prevent prompts when enabling:

```
Enable-PSRemoting -Force
```

If you run the `Enable-PSRemoting` cmdlet and receive an error that one or more network connections are public, you can include the `-SkipNetworkProfileCheck` switch or make the connection private.

Also, the `Enable-PSRemoting` cmdlet will only enable remote PowerShell for the version you run the command in. So, for example, if you run the `Enable-PSRemoting` cmdlet in a PowerShell 7 session, it will not enable remoting in Windows PowerShell or the other way around.

5.3.2 Permissions for WSMan PowerShell remoting

By default, members of the Administrators and the Remote Management Users groups have permission to connect via PowerShell remoting to the server. Users in the Remote Management Users group have the same rights as a standard user unless they have additional permissions on the server.

For your VS Code extension scenario, you want to give the user administrator privileges because they need to read the files inside each user profile. You can add the user using the Computer Management console or by running the following command in an administrative PowerShell prompt:

```
Add-LocalGroupMember -Group "Administrators" -Member "<YourUser>"
```

5.3.3 *Execute commands with WSMan PowerShell remoting*

Now that your remote servers are set up, you are ready to start executing your remote commands. The next step is determining how to perform the remote executions and recording the results. You do this using a control script to invoke the Get-VSCodeExtensions.ps1 script you made earlier, but keep in mind that this control script is designed for use with any other script you need to execute across multiple different systems.

When using the Invoke-Command cmdlet, the script file only needs to be accessible to the local client and not the remote servers. You can also pass just a script block instead, which works well for one-line or two-line commands. But when you are passing a complex script, it is best to save it as a separate script file. This will also allow you to make your control script reusable by not having the commands hardcoded.

Next, you need to provide the Invoke-Command cmdlet with the remote servers. As discussed earlier, you want to create persistent sessions for each machine using the New-PSSession cmdlet. Then pass all the sessions to the Invoke-Command as an array to the -Session argument. Doing this will also allow you to isolate specific machines that failed to make the connection so that you can fix them separately.

When creating the array of remote sessions, you need to be careful to only add successful connections to the array. If you add a session that did not connect to your array and then pass that array to the Invoke-Command, it will error, and no commands will run on the remote server. To prevent this, you can wrap the New-PSSession command in a try/catch and set the -ErrorAction argument to Stop. Then, if there is an error in the New-PSSession, your script will automatically jump to the catch block, skipping all other lines inside the try block. You can see this in the following snippet. If the New-PSSession has an error, it will skip the line to add it to the array, thus ensuring your array only contains successful sessions:

```
$s = "localhost"
try{
    $session = New-PSSession -ComputerName $s -ErrorAction Stop
    $Sessions.Add($session)
}
catch{
    Write-Host "$($s) failed to connect: $($_)"
}
```

To finish out the structure of your control script, you just need to add the list to collect all the returned data and the CSV import and export. Figure 5.5 illustrates the logic.

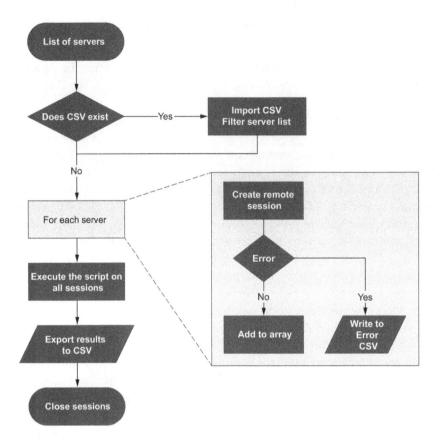

Figure 5.5   WSMan control script for remote script execution with persistent connections

The final step in the process is closing the remote sessions. When you create a session using the New-PSSession cmdlet, that session remains active on the local client and the remote server. To close it, you use the Remove-PSSession cmdlet as in listing 5.2. This cmdlet will close the session, releasing the resources back to the remote server and closing the connection between the two machines. If you do not close your sessions, you can quickly run into issues with running out of memory or hitting concurrent session limits.

Listing 5.2   Executing local script against remote computers using WSMan remoting

Another CSV file to record
connection errors

Array of servers
to connect to

Path to save
results to

```
$servers = 'Svr01', 'Svr02', 'Svr03'
$CsvFile = 'P:\Scripts\VSCodeExtensions.csv'
$ScriptFile = 'P:\Scripts\Get-VSCodeExtensions.ps1'
$ConnectionErrors = "P:\Scripts\VSCodeErrors.csv"
```

The script
file from
listing 5.1

```
if (Test-Path -Path $CsvFile) {                    <------------------         Test whether the
    $csvData = Import-Csv -Path $CsvFile |                                      CSV file exists; if
        Select-Object -ExpandProperty PSComputerName -Unique                   it does, exclude
    $servers = $servers | Where-Object { $_ -notin $csvData }                  the servers
}                                                                              already scanned.

[System.Collections.Generic.List[PSObject]] $Sessions = @()
foreach ($s in $servers) {                  <------
    $PSSession = @{                                       Connect to each server
        ComputerName = $s                                and add the session to
    }                                                    the $Sessions array list.
    try {
        $session = New-PSSession @PSSession -ErrorAction Stop
        $Sessions.Add($session)
    }                                             Add any errors to
    catch {                                       the connection
        [pscustomobject]@{              <------   error CSV file.
            ComputerName = $s
            Date         = Get-Date
            ErrorMsg     = $_
        } | Export-Csv -Path $ConnectionErrors -Append
    }
}
                                          Execute the script
$Command = @{                  <------    on all remote
    Session  = $Sessions                  sessions at once.
    FilePath = $ScriptFile
}
$Results = Invoke-Command @Command
                                                          Export the
                                                          results to CSV.
$Results | Export-Csv -Path $CsvFile -Append    <------

                                                 Close and remove the
Remove-PSSession -Session $Sessions   <------    remote sessions.
```

5.3.4   Connect to the desired version of PowerShell

Before PowerShell 6, running the New-PSSession cmdlet, like you did in listing 5.2, is all you would need to do to execute a remote command. However, since PowerShell 6 and 7 are separate from Windows PowerShell, you may need to include the -ConfigurationName argument. If you don't specify this argument, the cmdlet will default to the value in the $PSSessionConfigurationName preference variable. Unless you expressly set this variable, it will default to using Windows PowerShell 5.1. Therefore, to use PowerShell 7 remotely, you need to specify PowerShell.7 to the -ConfigurationName argument or set the value in the $PSSessionConfigurationName variable.

The introduction of the -ConfigurationName argument means you have some additional items to consider in your automation. For example, if you use the Power-Shell 7 configuration, your command will fail to connect to machines that don't have PowerShell 7 installed.

If you use the default of Windows PowerShell 5.1, you will need to ensure that your script can run in Windows PowerShell 5.1. Plus, as you will see in the next section, SSH connections use the default on the remote machine. Since SSH is only supported in PowerShell 6 and later, you need to ensure that your script will run in both Power-Shell 7 and Windows PowerShell.

As discussed earlier, most commands work the same in PowerShell 7 and Windows PowerShell, but there are some breaking changes between them. Also, you are introducing complexity to your automation by trying to support both. In the long run, it is better to use the `-ConfigurationName` argument and fix any servers that are not configured correctly. Not only will it be cleaner this way, but you will also be setting yourself up for future automations. But, to keep things simple in this example, we will skip using this argument because the script can work in both versions.

5.4   PowerShell remoting over SSH

Secure Shell Protocol (SSH) has been in use for Unix/Linux systems for over 25 years. However, in recent years, Microsoft has started to introduce it in the Windows ecosystem. Starting with PowerShell 6, SSH remoting can be done natively using OpenSSH. PowerShell can use SSH for remote connections between any combination of Windows, Linux, and macOS devices.

There are a few differences between SSH and WSMan remoting that you need to be aware of. The first is that SSH does not support Active Directory domain authentication. So, the accounts used for remote execution have to be local accounts on the remote server. Also, SSH remoting does not support remote configuration. This means that you cannot specify the version of PowerShell to use on the remote server. Instead, Power-Shell will automatically connect to the default version set on the remote server. There are also a few differences in the way you connect, which we will cover now.

5.4.1   Enable SSH PowerShell remoting

Unlike with WSMan, there is no command to enable SSH remoting for PowerShell. All of the configuration for SSH is done in the sshd_config file. Also, OpenSSH is not included in the PowerShell binaries, so you must install it separately. There are two components in OpenSSH: the client and the server. The client is for connecting to remote servers, and the server component accepts those connection requests. To enable SSH PowerShell remoting, you need to perform the following steps:

1 Install OpenSSH.
2 Enable the OpenSSH services.
3 Set authentication methods.
4 Add PowerShell to the SSH subsystem.

To get started, you need to install OpenSSH on the Windows device. If you are using Windows 10 build 1809 or later or Windows 2019 or later, OpenSSH is included as a feature. You can install it using the following command as an administrator:

```
Get-WindowsCapability -Online |
Where-Object{ $_.Name -like 'OpenSSH*' -and $_.State -ne 'Installed' } |
ForEach-Object{ Add-WindowsCapability -Online -Name $_.Name }
```

If you are running an older version of Windows, you can install a portable version of OpenSSH made for PowerShell. It is available on the PowerShell GitHub repository (https://github.com/PowerShell/OpenSSH-Portable).

Next, you want to ensure that the sshd and ssh-agent services are set to start automatically and are running:

```
Get-Service -Name sshd,ssh-agent |
    Set-Service -StartupType Automatic
Start-Service sshd,ssh-agent
```

On the client machine, you are only making outbound connections, so this is all that needs to be done for now. For remote servers, you need to configure OpenSSH to allow remote connections and to use PowerShell. To do this, open the sshd_config file on the remote server. For Windows, the path to the configuration file is typically %ProgramData%\ssh and for Linux, /etc/ssh.

To get started, you can enable password-based authentication by setting the line with PasswordAuthentication to yes or leaving it commented out because its default is yes. You also want to uncomment the key-based authentication setting, PubkeyAuthentication and set it to yes:

```
PasswordAuthentication yes
PubkeyAuthentication yes
```

You will eventually disable password-based authentication, but you need to leave it on until you configure key-based authentication in the next section.

Next, you need to add a subsystem entry to let SSH know where the PowerShell binaries are:

```
# Windows
Subsystem powershell c:/progra~1/powershell/7/pwsh.exe -sshs -NoLogo

# Linux with Snap
Subsystem powershell /snap/powershell/160/opt/powershell/pwsh -sshs -NoLogo

# Other Linux
Subsystem powershell /opt/microsoft/powershell/7/pwsh -sshs -NoLogo
Subsystem powershell /usr/bin/pwsh -sshs -NoLogo
```

Note that the Windows path uses the 8.3 short name for the path. There is a bug in OpenSSH for Windows that does not allow paths with spaces in them.

5.4.2 Authenticating with PowerShell and SSH

As you just saw, there are two methods to authenticating with SSH, passwords and keys. The big difference between these two, besides security, is that passwords cannot be passed to the New-PSSession or Invoke-Command cmdlets. Instead, they must be typed at the time of execution. So, as far as automations go, you want to use key-based authentication, illustrated in figure 5.6.

For those unfamiliar with SSH, key-based authentication works by using key pairs. There is a private key and a public key. The private key is maintained on the local client initiating the connection. It is the equivalent of a password, so access to the private key must be strictly controlled. The public key is copied to the remote servers you want to access. You can generate a key pair using the ssh-keygen command. For our example of connecting from Windows to Linux, the Windows client will have the private key, and the public key is copied to the Linux server.

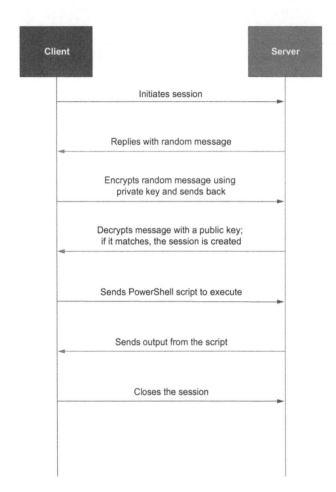

Figure 5.6   How SSH remote execution works with key pair authentication

After generating a key pair, you can store the private key using the ssh-agent for extra security. The agent will associate the private key with the user account on that system. You can then move the private key file to a secure storage location.

Another concept of SSH that you need to be familiar with is the known host. When you connect to a remote SSH server, it will provide a host key. This key is different from the authentication key pair. This key is unique to the host and used to identify it.

It is helpful to prevent attacks using DNS redirects or other similar tactics. The first time you connect to a remote server, it will prompt you to confirm the server's key. If you select yes, the server and its key are added to the known_hosts file on the local client. From then on, you will be able to connect without being prompted.

As you can tell, there is a lot more that goes into setting up SSH remoting. But once you have everything configured, it will be smooth sailing. To illustrate this, we will walk through the steps to set up a Windows client to use SSH to connect to a Linux server:

1 Generate a key pair on the Windows client.
2 Add the private key to the Windows ssh-agent.
3 Enable password authentication on the Linux server.
4 Copy the public key to the Linux server.
5 Enable key-based authentication on the Linux server.
6 Disable password authentication on the Linux server.
7 Test the connection from Windows to Linux.

On the Windows client, open a PowerShell 7 prompt. First, you'll run the command ssh-keygen to generate your key pair. If you leave everything set to the defaults, it will create the private key file (id_rsa) and the public key file (id_rsa.pub) in the .ssh folder of your profile. Then, you want to import the private key to the ssh-agent so you don't need to leave the private key file sitting around on your machine:

```
ssh-keygen
ssh-add "$($env:USERPROFILE)\.ssh\id_rsa"
```

After running the ssh-add, you can move the private key file to a more secure storage location.

Now, you need to copy the public key to the remote servers. The best way to do this is by using ssh to copy it.

On the Linux server, ensure that password- and key-based authentication are set to yes in the sshd_config file. Then, run the following command from the Windows client to copy the key to the user's profile on the remote Linux server. Replace username with the account's name on the remote server and hostname with the name or IP address of the server. If this is your first time connecting, you will be prompted to add the machine to the trusted hosts and provide the password:

```
type "$($env:USERPROFILE)\.ssh\id_rsa.pub" | ssh username@hostname "mkdir -p
➥~/.ssh && touch ~/.ssh/authorized_keys && chmod -R go= ~/.ssh && cat >> ~/.ss
➥h/authorized_keys"
```

Now you can disable password authentication in the sshd_config file on the remote machine. To disable password-based authentication, you must uncomment the PasswordAuthentication attribute and set it to no. The default behavior is to accept password-based authentication, so having a hash sign (#) at the beginning of this line is the same as having it set to yes.

```
PasswordAuthentication no
PubkeyAuthentication yes
```

You should now be able to connect to the remote machine without being prompted. You can test this using the following command from your Windows client:

```
Invoke-Command -HostName 'remotemachine' -UserName 'user' -ScriptBlock{$psver
➥ siontable}
```

5.4.3   SSH environment considerations

Most individuals who use PowerShell regularly are used to working in Active Directory environments, where a lot of the authentication and account management is taken care of for you. However, since SSH only works on local accounts, you need to pay extra attention to your configurations.

For example, when using WSMan with a domain account, it is pretty much a given that you can authenticate to all the devices with the same username and password combination. However, when using SSH connections, this is not always the case. When copying the public key to the remote devices, you can place the key under any user profile you have access to on that device. But if you use different account names during this process, it can cause you issues with your automation.

Therefore, you need to ensure that you either copy the public key to the same-named account on all servers or maintain a list of servers and the accounts associated with them. I prefer to use the same-named account because it makes automations easier and keeps your environment cleaner and easier to manage.

5.4.4   Execute commands with SSH PowerShell remoting

You execute commands with SSH remoting the same way you execute them with WSMan remoting. The only difference is that you need to use the -HostName and -UserName arguments instead of the -ComputerName and -Credential arguments.

Since you are using the New-PSSession cmdlet to create the sessions, you do not need to change the Invoke-Command or any other commands in the script. You just need to update the New-PSSession to handle SSH connections. The only problem now is figuring out how to deal with the fact that there are different parameters for SSH and WSMan connections.

You could use the try/catch block in the script to attempt the SSH connection if the WSMan connection fails. The downside is that the New-PSSession cmdlet can sometimes take 20–30 seconds to return an error. If you are checking a large number of servers, this could drastically increase your execution time. To prevent this, you can add a simple port check to the script using the Test-NetConnection cmdlet. You can first test whether a device is listening on port 5985, the default WSMan port. If that fails, you can test to see whether it is listening on the SSH port of 22. Based on the results of the port test, your script will pick the appropriate connection to use, as shown in figure 5.7.

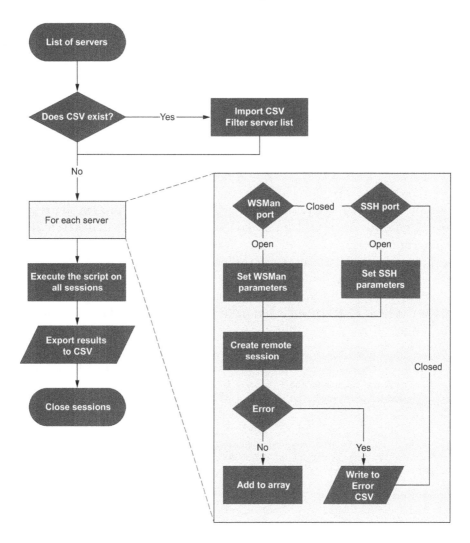

Figure 5.7   Control script for remote script execution with persistent connections using both WSMan and SSH protocols

Another issue you need to consider is that, by default, in certain scenarios SSH has prompts that rely on user interactions. The first is when the device you are connecting to is not in the known_hosts file in your local profile. The second is when key-based authentication fails, and password-based authentication is enabled on the remote server. If you run into these situations during the script execution, the script will hang waiting for input.

To resolve this, you can create a profile-specific config file on the client initiating the remote connections and configure it to fail in these situations. Then, by using a try/catch, you can record the reasons for the failures and address them afterward.

To do this, simply create a file named config in the .ssh folder in your profile and add the following lines:

```
PasswordAuthentication no
StrictHostKeyChecking yes
```

You can also achieve this by using a one-line PowerShell command:

```
"PasswordAuthentication no\r\nStrictHostKeyChecking yes" |
Out-File "$($env:USERPROFILE)/.ssh/config"
```

Now, you do not have to worry about your automations hanging, and there is nothing else you need to change in your script to support it. So, all you need to do is add the logic for the Test-NetConnection and the New-PSSession parameters to support SSH connections.

Since the Test-NetConnection cmdlet returns true or false Boolean values, you can use it directly inside an if/else conditional statement and build the parameters based on the successful connection. Then, if it is false on both, have it throw an error so the catch block is triggered and the error is recorded. The following listing shows the script.

Listing 5.3   Remote execution using WSMan and SSH

```
                Added variable for the
              default ssh username to use                    Remaining
                                                             variables are
$SshUser = 'posh'        ◄──────┘                            unchanged.
$servers = 'Svr01', 'Svr02', 'Svr03'    ◄────┘
$CsvFile = 'P:\Scripts\VSCodeExtensions.csv'
$ScriptFile = 'P:\Scripts\Get-VSCodeExtensions.ps1'
$ConnectionErrors = "P:\Scripts\VSCodeErrors.csv"

if (Test-Path -Path $CsvFile) {
    $csvData = Import-Csv -Path $CsvFile |
    Select-Object -ExpandProperty PSComputerName -Unique
    $servers = $servers | Where-Object { $_ -notin $csvData }
}

[System.Collections.Generic.List[PSObject]] $Sessions = @()
foreach ($s in $servers) {
    $test = @{                          ◄───   Set the parameters for the
        ComputerName     = $s                  Test-NetConnection calls.
        InformationLevel = 'Quiet'
        WarningAction    = 'SilentlyContinue'
    }
    try {
        $PSSession = @{                 ◄───   Create a hashtable for
            ErrorAction = 'Stop'                New-PSSession parameters.
        }
        if (Test-NetConnection @test -Port 5985) {
            $PSSession.Add('ComputerName', $s)
        }
    }
```

If listening on the WSMan port ─┤►

```
        elseif (Test-NetConnection @test -Port 22) {          ◁──── If listening on
            $PSSession.Add('HostName', $s)                            the SSH port
            $PSSession.Add('UserName', $SshUser)
        }
If neither,  else {
throw to the  ├──▷ 
catch block.      throw "connection test failed"
        }
        $session = New-PSSession @PSSession          ◁──┐ Create a remote session
        $Sessions.Add($session)                           using the parameters set
    }                                                     based on the results of
    catch {                                               the Test-NetConnection
        [pscustomobject]@{                                commands.
            ComputerName = $s
            Date         = Get-Date
            ErrorMsg     = $_
        } | Export-Csv -Path $ConnectionErrors -Append
    }
}                              ┌ Remainder of the
                               │ script is unchanged
$Command = @{          ◁──────┘ from listing 5.2
    Session  = $Sessions
    FilePath = $ScriptFile
}
$Results = Invoke-Command @Command

$Results | Export-Csv -Path $CsvFile -Append

Remove-PSSession -Session $Sessions
```

If you convert the variable at the beginning of this listing to parameters, it can be reused for any automation that requires you to connect to multiple remote machines and makes a great building block to keep around.

5.5   *Hypervisor-based remoting*

Unlike PowerShell native remoting, hypervisor-based remoting relies on an intermediary to execute PowerShell on a remote machine. However, like with native PowerShell remoting, you can use a control script to make these connections. This method uses a hypervisor to initiate the remote session. For example, Microsoft Hyper-V can use PowerShell Direct, and VMware uses the Invoke-VMScript cmdlet, which is part of their PowerCLI module. Even most cloud providers, including Azure and Amazon Web Services, have this functionality available to their virtual machines.

The most significant advantage to hypervisor-based remoting over native PowerShell remoting is that you do not need to have direct network communication with the virtual machine itself, as you can see in figure 5.8. Instead, you only need to be able to communicate with the host. From there, you can let the hypervisor integration tools take over. This can be indispensable for things like initial machine configurations or even enabling native PowerShell remoting.

This can also come in handy when dealing with machines in a DMZ and especially in the cloud. Another great example is the Azure Virtual Machine Run Command

Figure 5.8   Remote script execution using hypervisor-based remoting

functionality. It allows you to run a command on an Azure virtual machine, and you only need port 443 access to Azure. You do not need any network access to the virtual machine itself.

As with all remote connections, hypervisor-based remoting has its own unique considerations and caveats. One big issue to be mindful of is that a virtual machine's name may not always be the same as the name in the guest operating system. So, you need to be aware of this when passing in the list of computers. In most cases, it will need to be the name of the virtual machine.

A huge advantage that hypervisor-based connections have is the ability to have your control script turn on virtual machines that may be off. Then, after it runs the script on them, it can turn them back off. However, using this approach can present other problems. For example, a host may not be able to support turning on every virtual machine at once. Therefore, your best option would be to check each server individually, even though it will take longer to run in those situations.

In the previous example, you used a list of servers to create remote connections using either WSMan or SSH. Then, PowerShell used those sessions to run the VS Code extension script on the remote servers. In this scenario, you will substitute the server list with a command to return all the virtual machines on a Hyper-V host and then use PowerShell Direct to connect to each virtual machine.

As mentioned, many of these hypervisor-based remoting solutions have their own specific caveats, and Hyper-V PowerShell Direct is no exception. Your host and guest operating systems must all be Windows 10, Windows Server 2016, or later for this to work. Also, the control script must run on the host machine with administrator privileges. As you can imagine, in clustered environments, this could pose a problem.

However, PowerShell Direct is supported using the same cmdlets as native PowerShell remoting. Since you will be processing each machine individually, there is no need to use the New-PSSession cmdlet. Therefore, your script can simply create the connection at the time of execution in the Invoke-Command cmdlet.

So, the script will get all the virtual machines on the host. Then for each one, it will turn on if required and wait for the operating system to respond. Next, it will run the remote command, write the results to the CSV file, and turn the virtual machine off if it started it. These steps are illustrated in figure 5.9.

Before you put everything together in the script, there are a few additional items to take into account. First, if you cannot authenticate to the virtual machine operating system using your current credentials, you will be prompted to provide a username

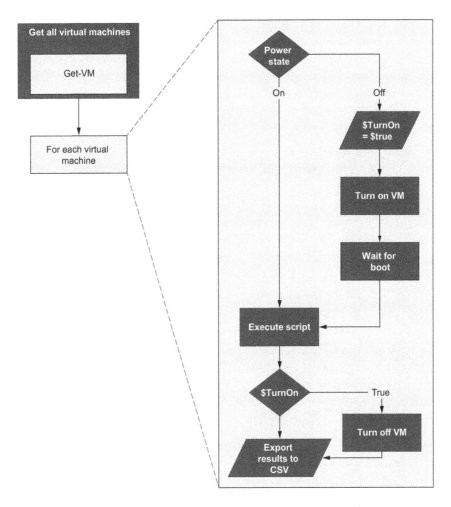

Figure 5.9   Control script for remote script execution using PowerShell Direct on Hyper-V

and password. Just like with the SSH connections, this causes the script to hang wait-ing for the credentials. However, if you pass credentials to the machine and they fail, it will simply error out, which is the behavior you want in an automated script. So, you can create the credential object using the Get-Credential cmdlet or the Secret-Management module. Even though Get-Credential requires user interaction, it is only once when the script starts, and for ease of the example, we will use it here.

The other item to consider is what happens if the virtual machine fails to turn on or the operating system does not properly boot. Addressing the issue of the virtual machine failing to start can be handled the same way you dealt with the New-PSSession: by using a try/catch and having the catch use a continue to skip the rest of the loop.

The trickier issue is dealing with the operating system not booting properly. You can determine whether the operating system has started by the Heartbeat property of the virtual machine returning either OkApplicationsHealthy or OkApplications-Unknown. So, how do you tell if a server is still booting or if the boot failed? Unfortunately, there is no perfect way. However, to prevent your automation from just sitting there waiting for a machine that may never boot, you can use a stopwatch to stop waiting after a predetermined amount of time. In this case, you can use an if statement to check whether the allotted amount of time has elapsed and, if so, use a break command to quit the loop.

Listing 5.4   Connecting to all virtual machines from a Hyper-V host

```
$Credential = Get-Credential              ←— Prompt for credentials.
$CsvFile = 'P:\Scripts\VSCodeExtensions.csv'          ←— Path to save results to
$ScriptFile = 'P:\Scripts\Get-VSCodeExtensions.ps1'   ←— The script file from listing 5.1
$ConnectionErrors = "P:\Scripts\VSCodeErrors.csv"     ←— Another CSV file to record connection errors

$servers = Get-VM                  ←— Get all the virtual machines on the host.
foreach ($VM in $servers) {
    $TurnOff = $false
    if ($VM.State -ne 'Running') {     ←— Check whether the virtual machine is running.
        try {
            $VM | Start-VM -ErrorAction Stop    ←— Start the virtual machine.
        }
        catch {
            [pscustomobject]@{
                ComputerName = $s
                Date         = Get-Date
                ErrorMsg     = $_
            } | Export-Csv -Path $ConnectionErrors -Append
            continue                   ←— If the start command fails, continue to the next virtual machine.
        }
        $TurnOff = $true
        $timer = [system.diagnostics.stopwatch]::StartNew()
        while ($VM.Heartbeat -notmatch '^OK') {    ←— Wait for the heartbeat to equal a value that starts with OK, letting you know the OS has booted.
            if ($timer.Elapsed.TotalSeconds -gt 5) {
                break              ←— If the operating system does not boot, break the loop and continue to the connection.
            }
        }
    }

    $Command = @{                  ←— Set the parameters using the virtual machine ID
        VMId        = $Vm.Id
        FilePath    = $ScriptFile
        Credential  = $Credential
        ErrorAction = 'Stop'
    }
    try {
        $Results = Invoke-Command @Command    ←— Execute the script on the virtual machine.
        $Results | Export-Csv -Path $CsvFile -Append
    }
    catch {
        [pscustomobject]@{          ←— If execution fails, record the error.
            ComputerName = $s
```

```
            Date          = Get-Date
            ErrorMsg      = $_
    } | Export-Csv -Path $ConnectionErrors -Append
}

if ($TurnOff -eq $true) {
    $VM | Stop-VM
}
}
```

If the virtual machine was not running to start with, turn it back off.

There is no disconnect needed because you did not create a persistent connection.

If you use VMware, Citrix, Azure, Amazon Web Services, or any other hypervisor or cloud provider, the cmdlets used will be different, but the concept remains the same.

5.6 Agent-based remoting

Like hypervisor-based remoting, agent-based remoting relies on an intermediate tool to execute this script. However, in this case, it is usually a third-party platform. There are numerous platforms that support agent-based remote execution. These include Jenkins nodes, Azure Automation Hybrid Runbook Workers, HPE Operations Agents, and System Center Orchestrator Runbook Workers, to name a few.

These connections use a locally installed agent to execute the script directly on the remote device. They offer an advantage over PowerShell remoting because the agent will typically handle all the permissions and authentication.

We will not delve down into the nitty-gritty on setting these up, as each platform is unique. But we are going to discuss how you need to adapt your scripts when using these agents. These concepts can also apply to other scenarios, such as running a script via group policy or configuration management software.

The most significant difference with this form of remote execution is that there is no control script. This means that if your script is gathering information to return, you need to figure out how you will collect that data. Even if your script performs an action and not data collection, you will want to log its execution and results. Therefore, you want to adjust your script to return data to one centralized location.

Depending on your environment, this location could be any number of things. Typically, in a domain environment, a file share would be a safe bet. However, when using mixed environments, all servers may not have access to a single file share. In these cases, you can use an FTP site or cloud-based storage option to store the data. No matter which option you choose, the concepts you will learn here will remain the same. In all cases, you need to write the data to a centralized location while protecting against potential conflicts from multiple machines writing data simultaneously.

For example, if you decide to go the network share route, you can simply put an `Export-Csv` command at the end of the script pointing to a predetermined CSV file on a network share. Then, to prevent accidentally overwriting the data from other devices, you can include the `-Append` switch. However, having multiple machines simultaneously writing to the same file can cause conflict and write errors. To prevent that from happening, your best option is to have each system write to its own file, as shown in figure 5.10. Then, on your end, you can write a script that will gather all the files at once and import them to a single object.

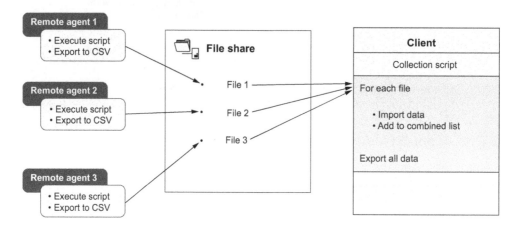

Figure 5.10   Example workflow for collecting data returned by remote agent executions to a central location

Now you need to consider how you will ensure that each server creates a unique file because you do not want to have two or more servers constantly overwriting the same file. Depending on your environment, you may be able to get away with just using the system name to make your file name unique. However, in large or multiple domain environments, this may not always be the case. You can't even guarantee that using something like the device SID will produce unique values. Even the trick you used in chapter 3 of adding the timestamp to the file may not work because there is a chance that two computers with the same name will run the script simultaneously. It is a very small chance, but not one that would be out of the realm of possibility.

While there is no 100% foolproof way to ensure a unique value, you can get pretty close by using a globally unique identifier, more commonly referred to as a GUID. A GUID is made up of 32 hexadecimal values split into five groups. Thus, there are 2^{128} different possible GUID combinations. This is more than the number of stars in the known universe, and the best part is that you can create all the GUIDs you want by simply using the `New-Guid` cmdlet. So, if you append the system name and a randomly generated GUID to the file name and you still end up with a duplicate name, you better run straight out and buy a lottery ticket.

Using these concepts, you can update the `Get-VSCodeExtensions.ps1` as in the following listing to write the results to a network share with a unique name with just a couple of extra lines added to the bottom.

Listing 5.5 Remote execution with output results to network share

```
$CsvPath = '\\Srv01\IT\Automations\VSCode'                      ◄──
[System.Collections.Generic.List[PSObject]] $extensions = @()
if ($IsLinux) {
    $homePath = '/home/'                              Add a variable with the
}                                                     path to the network share.
else {
    $homePath = "$($env:HOMEDRIVE)\Users"
}


$homeDirs = Get-ChildItem -Path $homePath -Directory

foreach ($dir in $homeDirs) {
    $vscPath = Join-Path $dir.FullName '.vscode\extensions'
    if (Test-Path -Path $vscPath) {
        $ChildItem = @{
            Path    = $vscPath
            Recurse = $true
            Filter  = '.vsixmanifest'
            Force   = $true
        }
        $manifests = Get-ChildItem @ChildItem
        foreach ($m in $manifests) {
            [xml]$vsix = Get-Content -Path $m.FullName
            $vsix.PackageManifest.Metadata.Identity |
            Select-Object -Property Id, Version, Publisher,
            @{l = 'Folder'; e = { $m.FullName } },
            @{l = 'ComputerName'; e = {[system.environment]::MachineName}},
            @{l = 'Date'; e = { Get-Date } } |
            ForEach-Object { $extensions.Add($_) }
        }
    }
}


if ($extensions.Count -eq 0) {
    $extensions.Add([pscustomobject]@{
            Id           = 'No extension found'
            Version      = $null
            Publisher    = $null
            Folder       = $null
            ComputerName = [system.environment]::MachineName
            Date         = Get-Date
        })
}
$fileName = [system.environment]::MachineName +                 ◄──
    '-' + (New-Guid).ToString() + '.csv'
$File = Join-Path -Path $CsvPath -ChildPath $fileName
$extensions | Export-Csv -Path $File -Append                    ◄──
```

Create a unique file name by combining the machine name with a randomly generate GUID.

Combine the file name with the path of the network share.

Export the results to the CSV file.

5.7 Setting yourself up for success with PowerShell remoting

I cannot emphasize strongly enough that you should know how to remotely connect to all systems in your environment and have them preconfigured. As you saw, there is no need to use a single remote connection type. You can certainly use a combination that makes sense for your environment. However, by having everything set up and your control script built, you can be ready for whatever situations may arise. And the concepts we covered with the VS Code extensions can apply to any script you need to run remotely.

To give a real-world example, I once had a customer call me in a panic because a bad update had been automatically pushed to their antivirus software. This bad update had not only stopped a number of their business applications but had also broken its own updating mechanism. The only resolution was to reinstall the application manually on 150+ servers.

The customer called looking for extra hands to help with all the manual reinstalls. However, I informed them that we had already written a control script to install an agent a few weeks before. After changing a few lines of code, we were able to reinstall the antivirus software on every server in under an hour.

The most remarkable thing about this is that we could handle it from one central location, even though they had a very disjointed network. They had a mixture of Windows, Linux, on-premises, and cloud servers. They also had to deal with remote offices that were not always in a trusted domain.

We used a combination of WSMan and SSH PowerShell remoting for all the servers in their data center and then used the Azure Virtual Machine Run Command for some machines in Azure. Finally, since we had set up the servers in their remote offices as Azure Automation Hybrid Workers, we were able to update all of those using the agent.

Through the use of PowerShell remoting, we saved this company many person-hours of manually connecting to and reinstalling an application. But, more important, we were able to get their business applications back online faster, saving them untold thousands in potential lost revenue.

Summary

- WSMan remoting works well in Windows Active Directory environments.
- For non–Active Directory environments or ones with Linux and macOS, you need to use SSH remoting.
- Control scripts are used to execute a remote command against multiple servers and can be designed to use a mixture of remoting protocols.
- When using agent-based remoting, you need to account for not having a control script.
- Hypervisor-based remoting works well for situations in which other remoting is not an option; however, it may not be a viable option for recurring automations.

Making adaptable automations

This chapter covers

- Using event handling to account for known errors
- Creating dynamic functions
- Using external data in your scripts

One of the toughest challenges you will face with automation is figuring out how to make things as efficient and maintainable as possible. The best way to achieve that is by making your code as smart and adaptable as possible. As you will see, adaptable scripting can mean many different things. For example, something as simple as adding parameters to a function makes your code more adaptable. But in this chapter, we will take it to the next level by making functions that can account for potential known errors and resolve them and make a function that can create dynamic if/else statements on the fly. And, at the end, you will see how you can tie all these functions together into a dynamic automation.

To demonstrate this, we will build an automation to perform some basic server setup tasks. This automation will perform the following steps:

1 Install Windows Features and Roles
2 Stop and disable unneeded services
3 Configure the security baseline setting
4 Configure the Windows firewall

We will start with stopping and disabling unneeded services, which will provide a great example of using error handling in your script to do more than just report a problem or halt execution. Next, we will configure security baselines by providing the script with a list of registry keys to check and update. Then, we will see how you can tie together all four steps listed previously into a single automation using a configuration data file.

Since the scenarios in this chapter deal with changing system settings, I suggest creating a new virtual machine with Windows Server 2016 or newer for your testing. Also, since we are dealing with a new server, all code will work in Windows PowerShell and PowerShell 7.

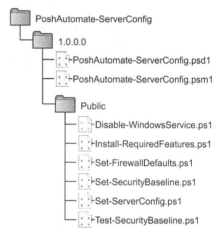

Figure 6.1   PoshAutomate-ServerConfig module file structure

We will be putting all the code created into a module named PoshAutomate-ServerConfig, shown in the next listing. You can quickly generate the base structure you will need using the New-ModuleTemplate function from chapter 2. The file structure is shown in figure 6.1.

Listing 6.1   Creating the PoshAutomate-ServerConfig module

```
Function New-ModuleTemplate {          ◁──   This is the same
    [CmdletBinding()]                         function as in
    [OutputType()]                            listing 2.5.
    param(
        [Parameter(Mandatory = $true)]
        [string]$ModuleName,
        [Parameter(Mandatory = $true)]
        [string]$ModuleVersion,
        [Parameter(Mandatory = $true)]
        [string]$Author,
        [Parameter(Mandatory = $true)]
        [string]$PSVersion,
        [Parameter(Mandatory = $false)]
        [string[]]$Functions
    )
    $ModulePath = Join-Path .\ "$($ModuleName)\$($ModuleVersion)"
    New-Item -Path $ModulePath -ItemType Directory
```

```
Set-Location $ModulePath
New-Item -Path .\Public -ItemType Directory

$ManifestParameters = @{
    ModuleVersion     = $ModuleVersion
    Author            = $Author
    Path              = ".\$($ModuleName).psd1"
    RootModule        = ".\$($ModuleName).psm1"
    PowerShellVersion = $PSVersion
}
New-ModuleManifest @ManifestParameters

$File = @{
    FilePath = ".\$($ModuleName).psm1"
    Encoding = 'utf8'
}
Out-File @File

$Functions | ForEach-Object {
    Out-File -Path ".\Public\$($_).ps1" -Encoding utf8
}
}
```

The version of your module → `$module = @{` ← **Set the parameters to pass to the function.**

The name of your module →

`    ModuleName    = 'PoshAutomate-ServerConfig'` ←

Your name →

```
    ModuleVersion = "1.0.0.0"
    Author        = "YourNameHere"
    PSVersion     = '5.1'
```
← **The minimum PowerShell version this module supports**

```
    Functions     = 'Disable-WindowsService',
        'Install-RequiredFeatures', 'Set-FirewallDefaults',
        'Set-SecurityBaseline', 'Set-ServerConfig',
        'Test-SecurityBaseline'
}
New-ModuleTemplate @module
```

The functions to create blank files for in the Public folder

Execute the function to create the new module.

Once you get the file structure created, you can add the following code to the Posh-Automate-ServerConfig.psm1 to automatically import the functions from the Public folder.

Listing 6.2 PoshAutomate-ServerConfig.psm1

```
$Path = Join-Path $PSScriptRoot 'Public'
$Functions = Get-ChildItem -Path $Path -Filter '*.ps1'
```
← **Get all the ps1 files in the Public folder.**

```
Foreach ($import in $Functions) {
```
← **Loop through each ps1 file.**

```
    Try {
        Write-Verbose "dot-sourcing file '$($import.fullname)'"
        . $import.fullname
```
← **Execute each ps1 file to load the function into memory.**

```
    }
    Catch {
        Write-Error -Message "Failed to import function $($import.name)"
    }
}
```

6.1   Event handling

To see the true potential and cost savings of automation, you must be able to build event handling into your scripts. Any time you have to go in after an automation runs and fix something, make a note of it. If you see something that happens on a regular basis, there is a good chance you need to add some event handling to your script.

Take, for example, the first scenario in our automation of stopping and disabling services. Anyone who has worked with Windows knows that you can do this with a few lines of code:

```
Get-Service -Name Spooler |
    Set-Service -StartupType Disabled -PassThru |
    Stop-Service -PassThru
```

Now think about what happens if the service is not found. For example, if you pass the name of a service that does not exist to the Get-Service cmdlet, it will return an error. But if the service does not exist, there is nothing to stop or disable. So, is it really an error? I would say it is not an error, but it is something that you should record.

To prevent your script from throwing an error, you can choose to suppress errors on that command using the parameter -ErrorAction SilentlyContinue. However, when you do this, there is no way for you to know for sure that the service does not exist. You are just assuming that the reason for the error was that the service did not exist. But when you suppress the error message, there is no way to know for sure. For example, it could also throw an error if you do not have the appropriate permissions. The only way to know for sure is to capture and evaluate the error message using a try/catch block.

6.1.1   Using try/catch blocks for event handling

By default, a PowerShell script will stop executing when a command throws a terminating error, except for when that error happens inside of a try block. When there is a terminating error inside a try block, the script will skip the remainder of the code inside the try block and go to the catch block. If there are no errors, the script will skip the code in the catch block. You can also add a finally block, as in figure 6.2, that will execute last in all cases. So, let's see how we can use this with our services function.

If you open a PowerShell command and enter Get-Service -Name xyz, you will see an error stating it cannot find the service. If you run that command again but wrap in a try/catch, you will still see the same error. That is because this particular error is not a terminating error. Therefore, the catch block is not triggered. So, to ensure the catch block is triggered, you can add -ErrorAction Stop to the end of the command to turn all error messages into terminating errors, ensuring that the catch block will be triggered:

```
try{
    Get-Service -Name xyz -ErrorAction Stop
}
catch{
    $_
}
```

When you run this command in Windows PowerShell, you will still see the error message, but notice that the output is now white instead of red. This is because of the $_ in the catch block. When a catch block is triggered, the error that caused it is automatically saved to the variable $_. We can use this to test that the error we received was the expected one.

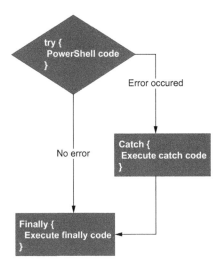

Figure 6.2 **When code in a try block throws an error, the catch block is run, and then the finally block is run. If there is no error, the catch block is skipped, and the finally block is run after the try block finishes.**

In PowerShell 7, the error displays in red as typical errors do, but the functionality is the same. The error is saved to the $_ variable, and the error does not cause the script to terminate.

Inside the catch block, you can use an if/else conditional statement to check the error message. If it does not match the expected error, it will call the Write-Error cmdlet to let PowerShell error handling report the error but not terminate the execution. You should use nonterminating errors in situations where the subsequent steps can still process even though an error has occurred.

For example, you do not need to stop processing the other services in this scenario if one of them fails. The other services can still be stopped and disabled. Then, you can go back and address the failures:

```
$Name = 'xyz'
try{
    $Service = Get-Service -Name $Name -ErrorAction Stop
}
catch{
    if($_.FullyQualifiedErrorId -ne 'NoServiceFoundForGivenName,Microsoft
    .PowerShell.Commands.GetServiceCommand'){
        Write-Error $_
    }
}
```

However, if an error on a particular step would cause subsequent failures, you will want to terminate the execution—for instance, if you are setting up a web server and IIS failed to install. There would be no need to continue with the steps to configure IIS because it would not be there. In these situations, you could simply replace the Write-Error command with throw:

```
$Name = 'xyz'
try{
    $Service = Get-Service -Name $Name -ErrorAction Stop
}
catch{

    if($_.FullyQualifiedErrorId -ne 'NoServiceFoundForGivenName,Microsoft.Pow
erShell.Commands.GetServiceCommand'){
        throw $_
    }
}
```

In the next step, we want to set the service startup type to disabled. You do not need to stop a service before you disable it. And since we want to ensure they are disabled, it makes sense to put that command before the stop command. This way, if the function runs into an unexpected error in the stop process, we will have guaranteed that the service is at least disabled.

In this situation, we can put the Set-Service cmdlet directly under the Get-Service cmdlet because the Get-Service cmdlet has the error action set to stop. Thus, if there is an error in the Get-Service command, it will jump to the catch block, skipping the Set-Service command.

6.1.2 *Creating custom event handles*

Now that we have disabled the service, it is time to stop it. I am almost positive that everyone reading this book has run into a situation in which you tell a service to stop running, and it just hangs. If you've ever experienced this through PowerShell, you have most likely seen your console fill with warning after warning stating, "Waiting for service 'xyz' to stop." And PowerShell will continue to repeat that message until the service stops or you manually kill the execution—neither of which is an ideal situation in an automation scenario. So, let's take a look at how we can avoid this through some parallel processing.

Most cmdlets that act upon an outside resource and wait for a particular state will have an option to bypass that wait. In this scenario, the Stop-Service cmdlet has a -NoWait switch. This switch tells the cmdlet to send the stop command but not wait for it to stop. Doing this will allow you to send multiple stop commands one after another without waiting for one to finish stopping. It will also allow you to create your own event handling to kill the process after a predetermined amount of time. So, we need to make the functionality to do the following:

1 Send the stop command to multiple services without waiting
2 Check the status of the services to ensure they have all stopped

 3 If any have not stopped after 60 seconds, attempt to kill the process
 4 If any have not stopped after 90 seconds, notify that a reboot is required

Unlike with the `Get-Service` cmdlet, we do not care whether the `Stop-Service` cmdlet throws an error. This is because regardless of what happens on the stop, the service has already been disabled. So, even if there is an error or it does not stop in the time we allotted, a reboot will be requested, which will ensure that the service does not come back up. Therefore, there is no problem adding the `-ErrorAction SilentlyContinue` argument to the command in this situation.

Using jobs to bypass waits

Some cmdlets that you may want to run in parallel do not have a no-wait option—for example, downloading multiple files using the `Invoke-WebRequest` cmdlet. In these situations, you can use PowerShell jobs to run the command as background processes. You can see this in the following snippet, where two files are downloaded simultaneously as jobs. Then, `Get-Job` followed by `Wait-Job` will pause the script until both jobs are complete:

```
Start-Job -ScriptBlock {
    Invoke-WebRequest -Uri $UrlA -OutFile $FileA
}
Start-Job -ScriptBlock {
    Invoke-WebRequest -Uri $UrlB -OutFile $FileB
}
Get-Job | Wait-Job
```

Once the jobs are complete, you can continue with your script. You can also get the return information from the jobs by using the `Receive-Job` cmdlet.

Since we will be checking multiple services for multiple conditions, it is a good idea to create a custom PowerShell object to keep track of the status and startup type for every service. Then, when you can create a `while` loop to check that the services have stopped, you do not need to check ones you know have stopped or were not found.

   The `while` loop will need to run as long as services are running but should also contain a timer to terminate after a set amount of time, even if all the services do not stop. You will also want to add the ability to perform a hard kill of the running process if it does not stop on its own. You can do this by using the `Get-CimInstance` cmdlet to get the process ID of the service and then using the `Stop-Process` cmdlet to force it to stop. Since you do not want to run the `Stop-Process` repeatedly, you can add a property to the object to record that there was an attempt to stop it. Therefore, the custom PowerShell object will need the following properties:

- `Service`—Service name
- `Status`—The status of the service

- `Startup`—The startup type of the service
- `HardKill`—A Boolean value set to true after the `Stop-Process` command

Once you put everything together, the process should look like figure 6.3. You can see the script in listing 6.3.

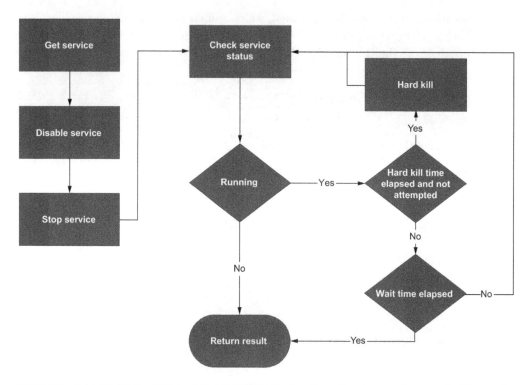

Figure 6.3   For each service that needs to be stopped, the function will wait a certain amount of time, and if it does not stop, then a hard kill will be issued.

Listing 6.3 `Disable-WindowsService`

```
Function Disable-WindowsService {
    [CmdletBinding()]
    [OutputType([object])]
    param(
        [Parameter(Mandatory = $true)]
        [string[]]$Services,
        [Parameter(Mandatory = $true)]
        [int]$HardKillSeconds,
        [Parameter(Mandatory = $true)]
        [int]$SecondsToWait
    )

    [System.Collections.Generic.List[PSObject]] $ServiceStatus = @()
    foreach ($Name in $Services) {
```

```
                    $ServiceStatus.Add([pscustomobject]@{
                         Service  = $Name
                         HardKill = $false
                         Status   = $null
                         Startup  = $null
                    })
                try {
                    $Get = @{
                         Name        = $Name
                         ErrorAction = 'Stop'
                    }
                    $Service = Get-Service @Get
                    $Set = @{
                         InputObject = $Service
                         StartupType = 'Disabled'
                    }
                    Set-Service @Set
                    $Stop = @{
                         InputObject = $Service
                         Force       = $true
                         NoWait      = $true
                         ErrorAction = 'SilentlyContinue'
                    }
                    Stop-Service @Stop
                    Get-Service -Name $Name | ForEach-Object {
                         $ServiceStatus[-1].Status = $_.Status.ToString()
                         $ServiceStatus[-1].Startup = $_.StartType.ToString()
                    }
                }
                catch {
                    $msg = 'NoServiceFoundForGivenName,Microsoft.PowerShell' +
                        '.Commands.GetServiceCommand'
                    if ($_.FullyQualifiedErrorId -eq $msg) {
                         $ServiceStatus[-1].Status = 'Stopped'
                    }
                    else {
                         Write-Error $_
                    }
                }
            }

            $timer = [system.diagnostics.stopwatch]::StartNew()
            do {
                $ServiceStatus | Where-Object { $_.Status -ne 'Stopped' } |
                ForEach-Object {
                    $_.Status = (Get-Service $_.Service).Status.ToString()

                    if ($_.HardKill -eq $false -and
                        $timer.Elapsed.TotalSeconds -gt $HardKillSeconds) {
                        Write-Verbose "Attempting hard kill on $($_.Service)"
                        $query = "SELECT * from Win32_Service WHERE name = '{0}'"
                        $query = $query -f $_.Service
                        $svcProcess = Get-CimInstance -Query $query
                        $Process = @{
                             Id          = $svcProcess.ProcessId
```

Create a custom PowerShell object to track the status of each service.

Attempt to find the service and then disable and stop it.

If the service doesn't exist, there is nothing to stop, so consider that a success.

Monitor the stopping of each service.

If any services have not stopped in the predetermined amount of time, kill the process.

```
                              Force       = $true
                              ErrorAction = 'SilentlyContinue'
```
Set the   `}`
reboot   `Stop-Process @Process`
required if   `$_.HardKill = $true`
any services   `}`
did not stop.   `}`
```
            $Running = $ServiceStatus | Where-Object { $_.Status -ne 'Stopped' }
        } while ( $Running -and $timer.Elapsed.TotalSeconds -lt $SecondsToWait )
        $ServiceStatus |
            Where-Object { $_.Status -ne 'Stopped' } |
            ForEach-Object { $_.Status = 'Reboot Required' }
```

`    $ServiceStatus`   ◁——| **Return the**
`}`   **results.**

Like many things in this book, event handling could be a book, or at least several chapters, on its own. This section was intended to give you an overview of some different ways that you can use it in your automations. There are many other ways to achieve event handling, some of which we will cover in subsequent chapters. I also encourage you to explore more resources on it because good event handling can really make your automations shine.

The next step in the automation will be checking and setting security baseline registry values. This will present a new concept of adaptable automation, which uses configuration data to control your script's execution.

6.2   *Building data-driven functions*

The Don't Repeat Yourself (DRY) principle is key to creating efficient and manageable automations. Even if you are not familiar with the term, you should be familiar with the concept of not repeating code over and over again in your scripts. This is the fundamental concept behind functions, modules, and the building blocks we talked about in the first half of this book. However, as you will see here, you can extend this concept beyond those and use external data to drive your automation.

The first and most crucial step in building a data-driven function is figuring out your data structure. Once you have your data structure figured out, you need to write the code to handle it and decide how and where to store it. To demonstrate how to do this, we will build the step in the automation to configure the security baseline setting for your server. This will be done by checking and setting different registry keys.

You can easily return registry keys with the `Get-ItemProperty` cmdlet and change or add them with the `New-ItemProperty` cmdlet. If you build a couple of functions that can do this, you only need one or two lines per registry key to check. But if you have ever looked at the list of registry keys required for security hardening, you will see this could quickly grow into a 500+ line script. In fact, if you do a quick search on GitHub or the PowerShell Gallery for security hardening scripts, you will find dozens of scripts over 1,000 lines long. Now imagine you have to maintain different copies for different operating system versions and different server roles. It would become a nightmare.

To prevent this from happening to you, we will create a function that can use external serialized data to provide the registry keys and values to your script. This data can be stored in external files that are human-readable, easy to update, and easy to use in PowerShell.

6.2.1 Determining your data structure

Checking and setting hundreds of registry keys may sound like an extremely tedious task that can have all sorts of different requirements. However, as with many things, the best approach is to break it up into different scenarios.

For example, I reviewed the Windows security baseline (http://mng.bz/DDaR) recommendations for an Azure virtual machine and found 135 registry settings. Out of those 135 different registry settings, the script needs to meet only four different types of conditions (equals, greater than or equal to, between two numbers, and equals or does not exist). Therefore, I can narrow my scope to concentrate on these four conditions. I know if the script can handle those, it can handle all 135.

I have selected an entry from each of these four to test with and listed them in table 6.1.

Table 6.1   Registry key values to check

Key path	Key name	Expected value
LanManServer\Parameters\	EnableSecuritySignature	= 1
EventLog\Security\	MaxSize	≥ 32768
LanManServer\Parameters\	AutoDisconnect	Between 1 and 15
LanManServer\Parameters\	EnableForcedLogoff	= 1 or does not exist

All key paths start in HKLM:\SYSTEM\CurrentControlSet\Services\

Based on this table, we know our function will have to check whether the value of a key is equal to a number, greater than or equal to a number, between two numbers, or does not exist. Knowing this, we can start to build the data structure.

Table 6.1 shows that you will need the Key Path, the Key Name, the expected value, and how to evaluate that value. You can convert those evaluations to comparison operators in PowerShell.

The first two conditions you need to test for are pretty straightforward. Equal is -eq, and greater than or equal to is -ge. The third one makes things a little more complicated because it checks between two numbers. But this can be achieved by creating an array and using the -in operator. So, just considering these, your data structure might look something like figure 6.4.

However, things get a little more complicated with the fourth condition because it can be one of two

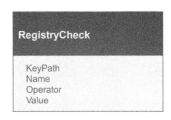

Figure 6.4   Initial data structure for the registry check

conditions, and one of those conditions is that it does not exist. However, when you think about it, "does not exist" is the equivalent of saying "is equal to null." So, now the only tricky part is handling the two different conditions. You can take the value and operator properties, put them in their own class, and add them as an array to the registry check class, as in figure 6.5. Then, you can have your script evaluate as many as you need. As long as one of them evaluates to true, the check will pass.

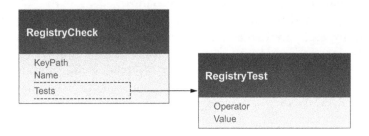

Figure 6.5   Updated data structure for the registry check to include the test operator and value as a nested array

If you were to build this out as a hashtable in PowerShell, it would be something like the following snippet:

```
@{
    KeyPath = 'HKLM:\SYSTEM\Path\Example'
    Name    = 'SecurityKey'
    Tests   = @(
        @{operator = 'eq'; value = '1' }
        @{operator = 'eq'; value = $null }
    )
}
```

6.2.2 *Storing your data*

Once you have your basic structure, it is time to think about how to store that data. There are numerous data serialization formats out there, and many have native support in PowerShell. These include XML, CSV, JSON, and PowerShell Data Files. The format you choose for your automations depends on your needs, but my recommendation is to use JSON unless you have a specific reason not to. JSON consists of key-value pairs and supports strings, numbers, dates, Boolean, arrays, and nested objects. It is versatile and human-readable. You can also convert any JSON string to a PowerShell object using the ConvertFrom-Json cmdlet and back into JSON using the ConvertTo-Json cmdlet. You can see the results of this conversion in figure 6.6.

```
@{                                  {
  KeyPath = 'HKLM:\...'               "KeyPath": "HKLM:\\...",
  Name = 'Enabled'                    "Name": "Enabled",
  Test = @(                           "Test": [
    @{                                  {
      operator = 'eq'                     "operator": "eq",
      value = '1'                         "value": "1"
    }                                   },
    @{                                  {
      operator = 'eq'                     "operator": "eq",
      value = $null                       "value": null
    }                                   }
  )                                   ]
}                                   }
```

Figure 6.6   Side-by-side comparison of PowerShell hashtable and the hashtable converted to JSON

By taking the data structure we just determined, you can build a PowerShell object with your checks, convert it to a JSON string, then export the JSON to a file. The following listing shows the execution.

Listing 6.4   Creating JSON

```
[System.Collections.Generic.List[PSObject]] $JsonBuilder = @()
$JsonBuilder.Add(@{
    KeyPath =
    'HKLM:\SYSTEM\CurrentControlSet\Services\LanManServer\Parameters'
    Name    = 'EnableSecuritySignature'
    Tests   = @(
        @{operator = 'eq'; value = '1' }
    )
})
$JsonBuilder.Add(@{
    KeyPath =
    'HKLM:\SYSTEM\CurrentControlSet\Services\EventLog\Security'
    Name    = 'MaxSize'
    Tests   = @(
        @{operator = 'ge'; value = '32768' }
    )
})
$JsonBuilder.Add(@{
    KeyPath =
    'HKLM:\SYSTEM\CurrentControlSet\Services\LanManServer\Parameters'
    Name    = 'AutoDisconnect'
    Tests   = @(
        @{operator = 'in'; value = '1..15' }
    )
})
$JsonBuilder.Add(@{
    KeyPath =
    'HKLM:\SYSTEM\CurrentControlSet\Services\LanManServer\Parameters'
    Name    = 'EnableForcedLogoff'
    Tests   = @(
```

Add an entry for each registry key to check.

```
        @{operator = 'eq'; value = '1' }
        @{operator = 'eq'; value = '$null' }
    )
})                                          Convert the PowerShell
                                            object to JSON and
                                            export it to a file.
$JsonBuilder |
    ConvertTo-Json -Depth 3 |      ⟵
    Out-File .\RegistryChecks.json -Encoding UTF8
```

As you can see in listing 6.4, the ConvertTo-Json only creates a JSON string. Similarly, the ConvertFrom-Json cmdlet only accepts strings. Since neither of these cmdlets can read or write to a file or any other external source, you need to use them in conjunction with other cmdlets.

The fact that the JSON cmdlets accept strings is actually a huge advantage. It means you can get your string from anywhere and convert it from JSON. For our purposes, we are going to read and write to the local file system. For this, we are going to use the Out-File cmdlet to write to a file and the Get-Content cmdlet to read from it. But in other situations, you could receive JSON from a web request, a SQL database, or even passed in as parameters. Anywhere you can get a string value from, you can use JSON.

That is not to say that JSON is the end-all, be-all for automations and PowerShell. Other formats also have their pros and cons.

XML is a tried-and-true format that has been around for over 20 years and is used by many applications. It is exceptionally versatile, like JSON, but has the advantage of schemas to aid in data validation. While JSON does have schema support, that functionality does not exist natively in PowerShell. Instead, PowerShell just makes its best guess as to the data type based on how it is structured in the string. This gives XML an advantage when it needs to be transferred between different applications. However, JSON is much easier to read and define. For example, in figure 6.7, I took the same PowerShell object for a single registry check and exported it to JSON (left) and XML (right).

CSV is excellent when you need to share the information with someone else—especially nontechnical people since you can use Excel to read and edit it. However, CSVs are flat files, so you can't have nest objects or arrays. Plus, PowerShell natively treats every item in a CSV as a string.

A PowerShell Data File (PSD1) contains key–value pairs very similar to JSON, except PowerShell treats them as hashtables instead of PowerShell objects. You are most likely familiar with these as module manifest files, but they can also be used to store data that you import into your script. They look very similar to JSON and support many of the same data types. However, one considerable disadvantage to PSD1 files is they require a physical file, whereas JSON is converted from a string variable. Also, as the name implies, PowerShell Data Files are unique to PowerShell and cannot be used in other applications. Therefore, PSD1 files are best left for use inside modules with relatively static data.

```json
1  {
2     "KeyPath": "HKLM:\\SYSTEM\\CurrentControlSet\\Services\\LanManServ
3     "Name": "EnableForcedLogoff",
4     "Tests": [
5        {
6           "operator": "eq",
7           "value": "1"
8        },
9        {
10          "operator": "eq",
11          "value": null
12       }
13    ]
14 }
15
```

```xml
1  <Objs Version="1.1.0.1" xmlns="http://schemas.microsoft.com/powershell/200
2    <Obj RefId="0">
3      <TN RefId="0">
4        <T>System.Collections.Specialized.OrderedDictionary</T>
5        <T>System.Object</T>
6      </TN>
7      <DCT>
8        <En>
9          <S N="key">KeyPath</S>
10         <S N="Value">HKLM:\SYSTEM\CurrentControlSet\Services\LanManServer\
11       </En>
12       <En>
13         <S N="key">Name</S>
14         <S N="Value">EnableForcedLogoff</S>
15       </En>
16       <En>
17         <S N="key">Tests</S>
18         <Obj N="Value" RefId="1">
19           <TN RefId="1">
20             <T>System.Object[]</T>
21             <T>System.Array</T>
22             <T>System.Object</T>
23           </TN>
24           <LST>
25             <Obj RefId="2">
26               <TN RefId="2">
27                 <T>System.Collections.Hashtable</T>
28                 <T>System.Object</T>
29               </TN>
30               <DCT>
31                 <En>
32                   <S N="Key">operator</S>
33                   <S N="Value">eq</S>
34                 </En>
35                 <En>
36                   <S N="Key">value</S>
37                   <S N="Value">1</S>
38                 </En>
39               </DCT>
40             </Obj>
41             <Obj RefId="3">
42               <TNRef RefId="2" />
43               <DCT>
44                 <En>
45                   <S N="Key">operator</S>
46                   <S N="Value">eq</S>
47                 </En>
48                 <En>
49                   <S N="Key">value</S>
50                   <Nil N="Value" />
51                 </En>
52               </DCT>
53             </Obj>
54           </LST>
55         </Obj>
56       </En>
57     </DCT>
58   </Obj>
59 </Objs>
```

Figure 6.7   The same PowerShell object converted to JSON and XML

JSON validation

Unless you are familiar enough with JSON to know which characters to escape and which are not supported, it is always a good idea to use PowerShell or some other JSON editor to update your JSON files. Also, if you ever have problems importing your JSON, you can use the website jsonlint.com to evaluate it and let you know precisely where the issues are. There are also numerous JSON validation extensions for VS Code.

6.2.3   *Updating your data structure*

Now that you have your test data defined and exported to JSON, it is time to consider the data you need to resolve the failed checks. Since the tests are not always a one-for-one type comparison (i.e., EnableForcedLogoff can either be 1 or null), you cannot use the test value as the value to set. Therefore, you will need to add a new property to the JSON. This new property will tell the script what value to set when a check fails. You will also want to note the type of value it should be (e.g., DWORD, String, Binary, etc.).

To add these new fields to your JSON, you have two options. You can open the JSON in VS Code and manually copy and paste the fields into every entry in the file, all the while hoping you don't miss one or accidentally enter an illegal character. Or use the preferred method of having PowerShell help you update all the entries.

You can quickly and easily add a new property to a PowerShell object using the Select-Object cmdlet. This cmdlet lets you specify the properties you want to return from a PowerShell object and allows you to create custom properties on the fly by passing a hashtable as a property. The hashtable only needs two key pairs: Label for the name of the property and Expression for the expression to evaluate. You will often see these written simply as l and e for short in scripts.

So, let's add some new properties to the JSON file. The first one we want is the data type named Type. We know most of them are of the type DWORD, so we can just hard-code DWORD into the property. You can then manually change any you need to. We'll name the second property Data and default its value to the first value in our test array. The data structure with these properties is shown in figure 6.8. Again, you can manually update afterward, but this gives you a good head start instead of just writing blank values.

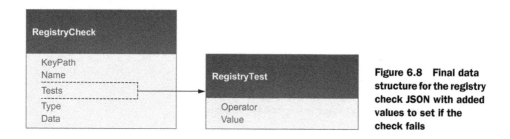

Figure 6.8   Final data structure for the registry check JSON with added values to set if the check fails

You can use the snippet in the following listing to add these fields to your JSON and export it as a new file.

Listing 6.5   Adding new data to JSON using PowerShell

```
$checks = Get-Content .\RegistryChecks.json -Raw |      ← Import the JSON file
    ConvertFrom-Json                                        and convert it to a
                                                            PowerShell object.

$updated = $checks |                                     ← Use Select-Object to
    Select-Object -Property *, @{l='Type';e={'DWORD'}},    add new properties to
        @{l='Data';e={$_.Tests[0].Value}}                  the object.
```

```
ConvertTo-Json -InputObject $updated -Depth 3 |
    Out-File -FilePath .\RegistryChecksAndResolves.json -Encoding utf8
```

**Convert the updated object with the new
properties back to JSON and export it.**

Now that we have the data structure, it is time to look at how to import it into the automation. To save you the trouble of filling out the JSON file, I have included a copy in the Helper Scripts for this chapter.

6.2.4 Creating classes

One of the great things about using serialized data is that it can be dynamic. For example, when you query a REST API that returns JSON, you do not need to know the data structure beforehand. PowerShell will automatically convert it to a PowerShell object. However, this can also be a bad thing when a script is expecting a specifically formatted object. In these cases, your best option is to create a custom class to define the properties your object needs.

As we see in our example here, we know what properties need to exist for the registry check. So, to prevent unexpected data from causing problems in your function, you will want to create a class. In fact, you will need to create two classes because your JSON has a nested object with the `Tests` property. Classes can exist inside their own files, or you can declare them in the psm1 for the module. For our purposes, we will create these in the PoshAutomate-ServerConfig.psm1 file. Also, you will want to be sure that your classes are located before the `import function` code, as it can cause errors if a function tries to reference a class before it is loaded.

Starting with the class for the `Tests` objects, you will need two string properties: the operator and value. When you build a class, you can create custom constructors inside of it. These allow you to convert objects or perform data validations or other types of data manipulation to ensure your object has the correct values. Since the JSON import creates a generic object, we will create a constructor to accept a single object and then have it assign the appropriate properties. We will also include a constructor with no parameters that will allow you to create an empty version of this call.

To define a class, you need to include the `class` keyword followed by the name of the class and curly brackets, as shown in the next listing. Inside the brackets, you will define the properties of the class, followed by the constructors. The constructors must have the same name as the class.

Listing 6.6 Registry test class

```
class RegistryTest {
    [string]$operator
    [string]$Value
    RegistryTest(){
    }
    RegistryTest(
        [object]$object
```

**Method to create a
blank instance of
this class**

**Method to create an instance of this
class populated with data from a
generic PowerShell object**

```
) {
    $this.operator = $object.Operator
    $this.Value = $object.Value
  }
}
```

Now we can create the class for the main registry check object. It will be similar to the other class, except for the Tests property. In this case, we want to make it an array by adding square brackets inside the data type declaration. Then, in our constructor, we will add a foreach to loop through each test and add it to the array. These methods are shown in the following listing.

Listing 6.7 Registry check class

```
class RegistryCheck {
    [string]$KeyPath
    [string]$Name
    [string]$Type
    [string]$Data
    [string]$SetValue
    [Boolean]$Success          Method to create a
    [RegistryTest[]]$Tests      blank instance of
    RegistryCheck(){            this class
        $this.Tests += [RegistryTest]::new()
        $this.Success = $false
    }
    RegistryCheck(            Method to create an instance of this
        [object]$object       class populated with data from a
    ){                        generic PowerShell object
        $this.KeyPath = $object.KeyPath
        $this.Name = $object.Name
        $this.Type = $object.Type
        $this.Data = $object.Data
        $this.Success = $false
        $this.SetValue = $object.SetValue

        $object.Tests | Foreach-Object {
            $this.Tests += [RegistryTest]::new($_)
        }
    }
}
```

Finally, we can add two additional properties, shown in the data structure in figure 6.9, to help with debugging and to confirm your script is getting the correct data. First, add a blank object of SetValue so you can record the value that the script is checking. It is set to object because you do not know what type of data may be returned from the different registry keys. Next, add a Boolean value named Success and set it to false. You will have the script flip this to true if the check passes. These do not need to be in the JSON because their values are not predefined.

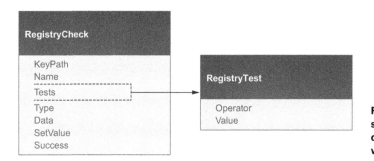

Figure 6.9   Final data structure for the registry check class with added values recording results

6.2.5   Building the function

Since we only have four conditions to check for, it may be tempting to create an if/else conditional statement to test against each. However, there is the possibility that you could have different conditions in the future. In that case, you could build an if/else that will handle all 14 different comparison operators in PowerShell, but that would make a huge nested mess of if/else statements, which would be a nightmare to troubleshoot. Plus, it goes against the DRY principle because you are repeating the same thing. Instead, we will look at how we can build a function to accept dynamic conditions. However, first, we need to get the value to check.

As mentioned previously, the Get-ItemProperty cmdlet can return the value of a registry key. However, if the key or the key path does not exist, it will throw an error. Since a key not existing can be an expected result, you do not want this. You also will not want to use a try/catch here because there could be other reasons why a value is not returned. For example, if access is denied, you could end up with a false positive using a try/catch. Instead, you can use the Test-Path cmdlet to test that the path exists. Then, if it does, use the Get-Item cmdlet to return all the subkeys and confirm the one you want is present. If both of these conditions are met, you can be assured that the key exists, and you can get the value from it. Figure 6.10 shows the process.

Now that you have the value, it is time to build the logic to confirm that it matches the expected value. The Invoke-Expression cmdlet allows you to take a string and execute it as PowerShell code. Let's take, for example, our first registry key that should equal 1. A simple test for this may look something like this:

```
if($Data -eq 1){
    $true
}
```

You can quickly turn this into a string to swap the operator and the value on using some simple string formatting and pass it to the Invoke-Expression cmdlet:

```
'if($Data -{0} {1}){{$true}}' -f 'eq', 1
```

The best thing about Invoke-Expression is that it treats everything just like you typed it out in your script. This means it will easily be able to handle arrays for checking

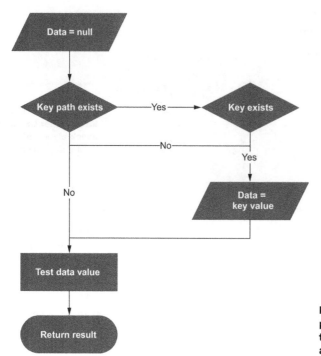

Figure 6.10   Confirming that the path to the registry key exists and that the key itself exists before attempting to get the value from it

between values. For example, in the following snippet, the value passed in is a string set to `1..15`. If you type `1..15` into PowerShell, it will create an array from 1 to 15. When this string is passed to the `Invoke-Expression`, it will be evaluated as an array, thus making it easy for you to determine whether a value is between two numbers. When you run the following snippet, it should output `true`. You can then experiment with switching around the values for the first three variables to see how it works:

```
$Data = 3
$Operator = 'in'
$Expected = '1..15'
$cmd = 'if($Data -{0} {1}){{$true}}' -f $Operator, $Expected
Invoke-Expression $cmd
```

Now, all you have to do is loop through each test from your JSON, and if any of them return `true`, you know the value is correct, as shown in figure 6.11. Another advantage to this is that you can output the expression string to the Verbose stream to aid in testing and troubleshooting.

One more thing to consider when building the logic of this function is how you want to pass the parameters. You can pass an object and reference the properties or list each property as a separate parameter. Passing the individual properties can make things easier for reusability and testing when you cannot guarantee you will always have your data formatted in a consistent manner. However, in this case, since we have

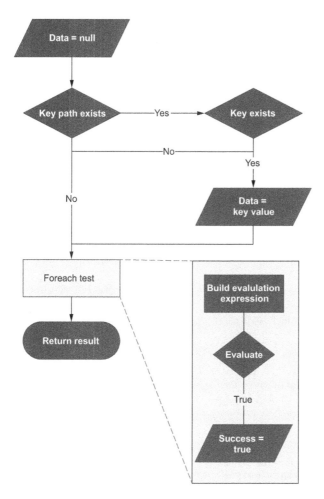

Figure 6.11 The registry check workflow with the dynamic expression builder

built a custom class object, you can guarantee that. Also, regardless of which method you choose, the tests will need to be specifically formatted objects. So, since you have already declared the class and can create the required object whenever you need to, you can simply have it pass the object. Let's make the Test-SecurityBaseline function in the following listing.

Listing 6.8 Test-SecurityBaseline

```
Function Test-SecurityBaseline {
    [CmdletBinding()]
    [OutputType([object])]
    param(
        [Parameter(Mandatory = $true)]
        [RegistryCheck]$Check
    )
    $Data = $null
    if (-not (Test-Path -Path $Check.KeyPath)) {
```

Set the initial value of $Data to null.

```
                Write-Verbose "Path not found"
        }
        else {
            $SubKeys = Get-Item -LiteralPath $Check.KeyPath
            if ($SubKeys.Property -notcontains $Check.Name) {
                Write-Verbose "Name not found"
            }
            else {
                try {
                    $ItemProperty = @{
                        Path = $Check.KeyPath
                        Name = $Check.Name
                    }
                    $Data = Get-ItemProperty @ItemProperty |
                        Select-Object -ExpandProperty $Check.Name
                }
                catch {
                    $Data = $null
                }
            }
        }
    }

    foreach ($test in $Check.Tests) {
        $filter = 'if($Data -{0} {1}){{$true}}'
        $filter = $filter -f $test.operator, $test.Value
        Write-Verbose $filter
        if (Invoke-Expression $filter) {
            $Check.Success = $true
        }
    }

    $Check.SetValue = $Data
    $Check
}
```

Get the keys that exist in the key path and confirm that the key you want is present.

If the key is found, get the value and update the $Data variable with the value.

If the path is not found, there is nothing to do because $Data is already set to null.

If the key is not found, there is nothing to do because $Data is already set to null.

Run through each test for this registry key.

Build the string to create the If statement to test the value of the $Data variable.

If the statement returns true, you know a test passed, so update the Success property.

Add the value of the key for your records and debugging.

To handle the updating of the failed checks, you will want to create a separate function. This will allow you to run and test the checks and the updates separately.

This function will be named `Set-SecurityBaseline`, as in listing 6.9, and it can use the same object from the `Test-SecurityBaseline` function in listing 6.8 to update the failed checks. This function will be pretty standard PowerShell. It just needs to ensure that the key path exists and create it if it doesn't. Then, set the key to the value defined in the JSON. We will also force `-ErrorAction` to `Continue` so one failed entry does not stop the processing of the others.

Listing 6.9　`Set-SecurityBaseline`

```
Function Set-SecurityBaseline{
    [CmdletBinding()]
    [OutputType([object])]
    param(
        [Parameter(Mandatory = $true)]
```

```
                    [RegistryCheck]$Check
                )
```

Create the
registry key
path if it does
not exist.

```
                if(-not (Test-Path -Path $Check.KeyPath)){
                    New-Item -Path $Check.KeyPath -Force -ErrorAction Stop
                }

                $ItemProperty = @{
                    Path         = $Check.KeyPath
                    Name         = $Check.Name
                    Value        = $Check.Data
                    PropertyType = $Check.Type
                    Force        = $true
                    ErrorAction  = 'Continue'
                }
                New-ItemProperty @ItemProperty
            }
```

Create or Update the
registry key with the
predetermined value.

6.3   *Controlling scripts with configuration data*

In the previous sections, we saw how you can use event handling and serialized data to control the actions of a function. Now, we can take it a step further and build a genuinely dynamic automation that can stitch together all of these functions. This is where the fundamentals of the building blocks concept from chapter 1 come into their own.

We started with a function to stop and disable services. Then, we built a second function to check registry values based on a JSON input and a third function to automatically set the registry value for those that did not meet the requirements. Finally, let's finish our automation with a few more simple examples that will help demonstrate the concepts here. First, in the following listing, we will create a function to pass a string array to install Windows Features.

Listing 6.10   `Install-RequiredFeatures`

```
Function Install-RequiredFeatures {
    [CmdletBinding()]
    [OutputType([object])]
    param(
        [Parameter(Mandatory = $true)]
        [string[]]$Features
    )
    [System.Collections.Generic.List[PSObject]] $FeatureInstalls = @()
    foreach ($Name in $Features) {
        Install-WindowsFeature -Name $Name -ErrorAction SilentlyContinue |
            Select-Object -Property @{l='Name';e={$Name}}, * |
                ForEach-Object{ $FeatureInstalls.Add($_) }
    }

    $FeatureInstalls
}
```

Loops
through
each
feature and
install it

Then you can use the following listing to configure the internal firewall logging.

Listing 6.11 Set-FirewallDefaults

```
Function Set-FirewallDefaults {
    [CmdletBinding()]
    [OutputType([object])]
    param(
        [Parameter(Mandatory = $true)]
        [UInt64]$LogSize
    )
    $FirewallSettings = [pscustomobject]@{
        Enabled       = $false
        PublicBlocked = $false
        LogFileSet    = $false
        Errors        = $null
    }

    try {
        $NetFirewallProfile = @{
            Profile     = 'Domain', 'Public', 'Private'
            Enabled     = 'True'
            ErrorAction = 'Stop'
        }
        Set-NetFirewallProfile @NetFirewallProfile
        $FirewallSettings.Enabled = $true

        $NetFirewallProfile = @{
            Name                 = 'Public'
            DefaultInboundAction = 'Block'
            ErrorAction          = 'Stop'
        }
        Set-NetFirewallProfile @NetFirewallProfile
        $FirewallSettings.PublicBlocked = $true

        $log = '%windir%\system32\logfiles\firewall\pfirewall.log'
        $NetFirewallProfile = @{
            Name                = 'Domain', 'Public', 'Private'
            LogFileName         = $log
            LogBlocked          = 'True'
            LogMaxSizeKilobytes = $LogSize
            ErrorAction         = 'Stop'
        }
        Set-NetFirewallProfile @NetFirewallProfile
        $FirewallSettings.LogFileSet = $true
    }
    catch {
        $FirewallSettings.Errors = $_
    }

    $FirewallSettings
}
```

Create a custom object to record and output the results of the commands.

Enable all firewall profiles.

Block all inbound public traffic.

Set the firewall log settings, including the size.

These functions can go on and on as you think of other things to add or your requirements change.

Now comes the next challenge—determining how to string all of these functions together and provide the correct parameters for them. This is where dynamic-based configuration data comes into play.

Similar to how you controlled the conditional statements in the previous example, you can perform similar tasks at the script level. For instance, you can generate a configuration file for each of the previously listed steps based on the parameters of the functions and then have a single script to call each function with the appropriate parameters.

6.3.1 Organizing your data

We now have five separate functions for this automation, each with its own parameters. The values provided to those parameters can change between operating system versions and server roles, which once again leaves us with one of those fine balancing acts of automation. Do you put everything into one massive JSON file and have the script parse it? Do you create a separate JSON file for each operating system version? Then, would you need separate files for each role that a server would need for each operating system? As you can see, it is as easy to end up with a massive mess of files as it is to end up with a few gigantic unmanageable files. The best thing to do in these situations is to write it out.

Look at each step of your automation and think about the parameter requirements across versions and roles. Doing this will help you determine the best way to structure your data:

- Step 1 of installing roles and features is relatively consistent across operating system versions but wildly different between server roles.
- Step 2 is stopping and disabling services. These can change slightly between operating system versions and based on the server role.
- Step 3 of setting security baselines remains fairly consistent across roles but differs between operating system versions.
- Step 4 of setting the internal firewall settings is consistent across operating systems but not server roles.

As you can see, there is no clear winner between operating system or server role, which, again, is where the beauty of this model comes into play. Technically, you don't have to choose. What you can do is combine them.

For instance, you can create a Windows Server 2019 baseline configuration file with the settings all servers will have regardless of their role. Then, you can make smaller role-specific configurations just to apply the deltas. You can even create new functions that could, for example, turn services back on.

For our purposes, we will build a simple configuration file that can be used on any Windows Server 2016 or later operating system. Taking a look at the different steps, we know we will need the following parameters, shown in figure 6.12:

1 Features—Default features and roles to install
2 Services—List of services to stop and disable

3 `SecurityBaseline`—Security baseline registry keys

4 `FirewallLogSize`—Firewall log size

The tricky one here is the security baseline registry keys. There could be hundreds of entries in this list. To keep things cleaner, you can store these in a separate file and just reference them in the control JSON. But you risk inadvertently causing issues if you don't remain vigilant about ensuring that those references are not broken. The safe approach would be to combine them into one JSON.

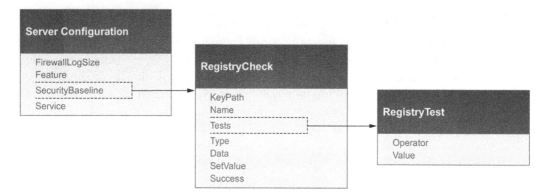

Figure 6.12   The SecurityBaseline property for the Server Configuration class uses the custom class RegistryCheck, which, in turn, uses the custom class RegistryTest.

And, once again, you can create a class in the PoshAutomate-ServerConfig.psm1. This class, shown in the following listing, consists of the four previously discussed parameters.

Listing 6.12   `ServerConfig` class

```
class ServerConfig {
    [string[]]$Features
    [string[]]$Services
    [RegistryCheck[]]$SecurityBaseline            Method to create
    [UInt64]$FirewallLogSize                      a blank instance of
    ServerConfig(){                               this class
        $this.SecurityBaseline += [RegistryCheck]::new()
    }
    ServerConfig(                                 Method to create an instance of this
        [object]$object                          class populated with data from a
    ){                                           generic PowerShell object
        $this.Features = $object.Features
        $this.Services = $object.Services
        $this.FirewallLogSize = $object.FirewallLogSize
        $object.SecurityBaseline | Foreach-Object {
            $this.SecurityBaseline += [RegistryCheck]::new($_)
        }
    }
}
```

Another significant advantage of using classes is that you can quickly and easily create your configuration JSON. You can add another function to the PoshAutomate-Server-Config.psm1 named `New-ServerConfig`, as in the following listing, and have it create a blank version of the `ServerConfig` class.

Listing 6.13   `New-ServerConfig`

```
Function New-ServerConfig{
    [ServerConfig]::new()
}
```

To keep from having a 140-line long listing here, I have included a copy of the complete PoshAutomate-ServerConfig.psm1 in the Helper Scripts folder for this chapter. Once you have the PoshAutomate-ServerConfig.psm1, you use the `New-ServerConfig` function to create a JSON template:

```
Import-Module .\PoshAutomate-ServerConfig.psd1 -Force
New-ServerConfig | ConvertTo-Json -Depth 4

{
    "Features": null,
    "Service": null,
    "SecurityBaseline": [
        {
            "KeyPath": null,
            "Name": null,
            "Type": null,
            "Data": null,
            "SetValue": null,
            "Tests": [
                {
                    "operator": null,
                    "Value": null
                }
            ]
        }
    ],
    "FirewallLogSize": 0
}
```

Now that we have all our data defined, it is time to build the final part of the automation.

6.3.2   *Using your configuration data*

The final step in this process is to tie everything together nicely with one script. This last script will get the required configuration information from the JSON file. Then, use that data to run each of the functions you have created.

   It is also a good idea for a script like this to add some logging output to record what was done. In this case, we can just create a function that will output the returned data to a table view and write it to a text file on the local machine. This means the script will need a parameter for the JSON file and one for the log file.

You can use the combination of the `Get-Content` and `ConvertFrom-Json` cmdlets that we used before to import your configuration data. Then, convert that object to the `ServerConfig` class you defined. Now all you need to do is call each function in the order you want to execute them. Since each function has error handling built in, you do not have to worry about it here. Just run the function and write the results to the log. After the execution completes, you can review the log for any potential errors or issues.

The only exception here is the security baseline functions. Since there are two separate functions, you can have the script run the check once. Then, fix any noncompliant registry keys. Finally, run the check once more to confirm everything is compliant. Putting it all together, the script will follow the flow shown in figure 6.13.

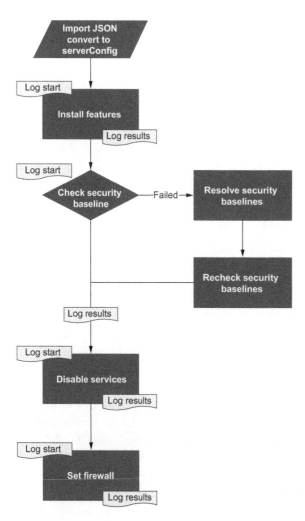

Figure 6.13   Workflow to set server configurations based on a JSON template

To include this function as part of the module, add a new file under the Public folder named Set-ServerConfig.ps1 and enter the code from the following listing.

Listing 6.14 Set-ServerConfig

```
Function Set-ServerConfig {
    [CmdletBinding()]
    [OutputType([object])]
    param(
        [Parameter(Mandatory = $true)]
        [object]$ConfigJson,
        [Parameter(Mandatory = $true)]
        [object]$LogFile
    )
    $JsonObject = Get-Content $ConfigJson -Raw |
        ConvertFrom-Json
    $Config = [ServerConfig]::new($JsonObject)

    Function Write-StartLog {
        param(
            $Message
        )
        "`n$('#' * 50)`n# $($Message)`n" | Out-File $LogFile -Append
        Write-Host $Message
    }

    Function Write-OutputLog {
        param(
            $Object
        )
        $output = $Object | Format-Table | Out-String
        if ([string]::IsNullOrEmpty($output)) {
            $output = 'No data'
        }
        "$($output.Trim())`n$('#' * 50)" | Out-File $LogFile -Append
        Write-Host $output
    }
    $msg = "Start Server Setup - $(Get-Date)`nFrom JSON $($ConfigJson)"
    Write-StartLog -Message $msg

    Write-StartLog -Message "Set Features"
    $Features = Install-RequiredFeatures -Features $Config.Features
    Write-OutputLog -Object $Features

    Write-StartLog -Message "Set Services"
    $WindowsService = @{
        Services        = $Config.Services
        HardKillSeconds = 60
        SecondsToWait   = 90
    }
    $Services = Disable-WindowsService @WindowsService
    Write-OutputLog -Object $Services

    Write-StartLog -Message "Set Security Baseline"
    foreach ($sbl in $Config.SecurityBaseline) {
```

Import the configuration data from the JSON file.

Convert the JSON data to the class you defined.

A small function to ensure consistent logs are written for an activity starting

A small function to ensure consistent logs are written for an activity completing

Set Windows Features first.

Set the services.

Check each registry key in the Security Baseline.

```
        $sbl = Test-SecurityBaseline $sbl
    }

    foreach ($sbl in $Config.SecurityBaseline |        ◄────  Fix any that did
        Where-Object { $_.Success -ne $true }) {              not pass the test.
        Set-SecurityBaseline $sbl
        $sbl = Test-SecurityBaseline $sbl
    }
    $SecLog = $SecBaseline |
        Select-Object -Property KeyPath, Name, Data, Result, SetValue
    Write-OutputLog -Object $SecLog

                                                        ┃  Set the firewall.
    Write-StartLog -Message "Set Firewall"        ◄────┘
    $Firewall = Set-FirewallDefaults -LogSize $Config.FirewallLogSize
    Write-OutputLog -Object $Firewall

    Write-Host "Server configuration is complete."
    Write-Host "All logs written to $($LogFile)"
}
```

6.3.3 Storing your configuration data

Where you store your configuration, data can change from automation to automation, but it makes sense to store the configuration data within the module in most cases. Doing this will not only ensure that your data is there when you need it, but if you implement version control on your modules, you will be able to track changes to the configuration files as well.

Another bonus to storing your configuration files within the module is that you can create a wrapper function to help you select the files. This way, you do not have to look up the full path to the JSON file every time you want to run it. You can do this in a similar fashion to how you load the module functions from the different ps1 files.

To set this up, add a folder named Configurations to the module directory and place your configuration JSON files in there, as in the following listing.

Listing 6.15   Creating Server Configuration JSON

```
Import-Module .\PoshAutomate-ServerConfig.psd1 -Force    ◄────  Import the
                                                                 module.
$Config = New-ServerConfig          ◄────  Create a blank
                                           configuration item.

$Content = @{                                      ◄────  Import security
    Path = '.\RegistryChecksAndResolves.json'             baseline registry
    Raw  = $true                                          keys.
}
$Data = (Get-Content @Content | ConvertFrom-Json)
$Config.SecurityBaseline = $Data

$Config.FirewallLogSize = 4096      ◄────  Set the default
                                           firewall log size.

$Config.Features = @(      ◄────  Set roles and
    "RSAT-AD-PowerShell"          features to install.
    "RSAT-AD-AdminCenter"
```

```
        "RSAT-ADDS-Toolsf"
)

$Config.Services = @(          ◄──┐  Set services
    "PrintNotify",                 │  to disable.
    "Spooler",
    "lltdsvc",
    "SharedAccess",
    "wisvc"                                     Create the
)                                               Configurations
                                                folder.
if(-not (Test-Path ".\Configurations")){   ◄──┘
    New-Item -Path ".\Configurations" -ItemType Directory
}                                                    Export
                                                     the security
$Config | ConvertTo-Json -Depth 4 |                  baseline.
    Out-File ".\Configurations\SecurityBaseline.json" -Encoding UTF8  ◄──
```

In the PoshAutomate-ServerConfig.psm1 file, add a command to query this folder for the different JSON files. Then, add a function named `Invoke-ServerConfig` that will display the JSON files for you to select. Once you make your selection, it will automatically execute the `Set-ServerConfig` function for you.

You can even use the `Out-GridView` to make a pop-up to make selections, or you can just pass in the name if you know it. Also, it can have multiple selections allowing you to run the operating system and role-based configurations one after the other. The following listing shows the updated script.

Listing 6.16   `Invoke-ServerConfig`

```
Function Invoke-ServerConfig{
    [CmdletBinding()]
    [OutputType([object])]
    param(
        [string[]]$Config = $null
    )
    [System.Collections.Generic.List[PSObject]]$selection = @()
    $Path = @{                          ◄──┐  Get the
        Path      = $PSScriptRoot           │  Configurations
        ChildPath = 'Configurations'        │  folder.
    }
    $ConfigPath = Join-Path @Path

                               ┌── Get all the JSON files
    $ChildItem = @{        ◄───┤   in the Configurations
        Path   = $ConfigPath       │   folder.
        Filter = '*.JSON'
    }
    $Configurations = Get-ChildItem @ChildItem      If a config name is
                                                    passed, attempt to
    if(-not [string]::IsNullOrEmpty($Config)){  ◄── find the file.
        foreach($c in $Config){
            $Configurations | Where-Object{ $_.BaseName -eq $Config } |
                ForEach-Object { $selection.Add($_) }
```

```
        }
    }

    if($selection.Count -eq 0){
        $Configurations | Select-Object BaseName, FullName |
            Out-GridView -PassThru | ForEach-Object { $selection.Add($_) }
    }

    $Log = "$($env:COMPUTERNAME)-Config.log"
    $LogFile = Join-Path -Path $($env:SystemDrive) -ChildPath $Log

    foreach($json in $selection){
        Set-ServerConfig -ConfigJson $json.FullName -LogFile $LogFile
    }
}
```

Set the default log file path.

Run the Set-ServerConfig for each JSON file.

If a config name is not passed or a name is not found, prompt for a file to use.

Once you have everything put together, you can copy the module files over to your new server, import it, and run the configuration:

```
Import-Module .\PoshAutomate-ServerConfig.psd1 -Force
Invoke-ServerConfig
```

6.3.4 *Do not put cmdlets into your configuration data*

One final thing to remember when using configuration data is that you never want to put any actual commands in your data. The values in your data should be static. Putting commands in your configuration data will not only make troubleshooting and testing a nightmare but can cause unexpected conditions in your code that could have dire consequences. While this may seem contradictory to the last section, it is not. In that section, we passed in values and conditional operators but not actual commands. Those values and operators will return the same result every single time you run them.

An excellent example of this is dealing with dates. Say you need to check that a date is over *X* number of years from now. The best way to handle that would be to have your script create the DateTime object. Then, you can include a property in your configuration that holds the number of years. Finally, this property can be passed to the AddYears() method of the DateTime to have the script set the date value for you:

```
$AddYears = 1
$Data = Get-Date 1/21/2035
$DateFromConfig = (Get-Date).AddYears($AddYears)
$cmd = 'if($Data -{0} {1}){{$true}}' -f 'gt', '$DateFromConfig'
Invoke-Expression $cmd
```

A bad example would be to pass in a string set to (Get-Date).AddYears(1) and use the Invoke-Expression to evaluate it. While it would have the same results as the previous example, it is also more prone to error and more difficult to troubleshoot, and it opens you up to potential injection attacks:

```
$Data = Get-Date 1/21/2035
$cmd = 'if($Data -{0} {1}){{$true}}' -f 'gt', '(Get-Date).AddYears(1)'
Invoke-Expression $cmd
```

The critical thing to remember here is that you should test all of your functions independently without running any external commands. The configuration data import is just a way for you to provide a list of parameters to your scripts.

Summary

- You can use `try/catch` blocks to capture specific errors and take actions based on them.
- Remember the DRY principle: don't repeat the same code over and over. Instead, use your data to help drive your scripts.
- JSON is a versatile data-serialization format that supports most of the same data types you find natively in PowerShell.
- If you have a defined data structure, you should create a class to help maintain its integrity.
- You can use external data to create data-driven functions and to control the execution of your scripts.
- Data files should be stored with the scripts when they are directly related to each other.

Working with SQL

7

This chapter covers

- Building SQL databases and tables
- Inserting and updating data
- Retrieving data
- Using data validation before writing to SQL

Anyone who has worked in IT long enough has inevitably received a call from a panicked department head saying that the Excel spreadsheet or Access database the entire department is reliant on has broken. As you investigate, you discover a mess of spaghetti code macros that have been cobbled together over the years. As you are racking your brain trying to reverse engineer it, you keep thinking to yourself, how did this happen?

I have found that these are often the result of one person taking some initiative to try to improve their job—in much the same way an automator thinks. However, before they realized what was happening, the entire department became dependent on what they threw together in their spare time. I am here to tell you this is not just a problem in "other" departments. It happens with IT and with automations as well. And I am also here to show you how not to fall into this trap by learning to use a proper database.

In the last chapter, we saw how you can use data to help drive your scripts and automations, and the data we used was stored in local JSON files. This is fine when the data is relatively static and you have tight control over who can update it. However, a local or even shared file will not cut it when you have data that needs to be shared with multiple people who can update it. In these cases, you will want to use a relational database.

There are multiple different database engines available that you can use with PowerShell, but we will work with Microsoft SQL Server for this chapter. However, many of the items discussed here are database agnostic, so you could easily implement the same automations using your database of choice.

At the end of chapter 5, I told the story of how I used PowerShell remoting across various systems in different environments to resolve an issue with a bad definition update. What I failed to mention was how I knew where all the systems resided. With today's hybrid environments, it is increasingly difficult to track whether a server is physical, a VMware VM, a Hyper-V VM, an Azure or AWS VM, etc.

To help solve this problem, we will be creating a PowerShell module you and your team can use to track your server assets across all your different environments. This module will store the data about your servers in a SQL database, and you will build the functionality to

1 Add a server to the database
2 Search the database for servers
3 Update the information for one or more servers

You can use Microsoft SQL Server Express for this automation, which you can download and use for free. If you already installed SQL Express in chapter 4 for the database health checks, you can use the same one here. Otherwise, I've included a script in the Helper Scripts folder for this chapter to install and set up a SQL Express instance.

We will also be using the dbatools PowerShell module to perform all the interactions with SQL, including creating the database objects, which we will start with right now in listing 7.1 by using the `New-DbaDatabase` cmdlet. To create the database, all you need to do is provide the SQL instance and the database name. We will also set the Recovery Mode to `Simple`. Without delving deep into DBA territory, a simple recovery model is acceptable unless you are designing mission-critical, highly available, zero data loss systems. You can still create full and differential backups with simple logs, so there is no need to require the resources that full logs will take.

If you are running PowerShell on the same machine as the SQL Express install, you can run the following listing, as written, to create the database. However, if you are on a remote machine or using your own SQL instance, be sure to update the `$SqlInstance` variable for your environment.

Listing 7.1   Creating PoshAssetMgmt database

```
$SqlInstance = "$($env:COMPUTERNAME)\SQLEXPRESS"
$DatabaseName = 'PoshAssetMgmt'
$DbaDatabase = @{
    SqlInstance   = $SqlInstance
    Name          = $DatabaseName
    RecoveryModel = 'Simple'
}
New-DbaDatabase @DbaDatabase
```

One last note before we get started—this chapter does not expect you to be a DBA, nor will it teach you how to be one. We will only use simple queries in the functions to provide examples of interacting with SQL. There are plenty of resources out there to help you learn how to create complex queries, backup your databases, and perform preventive maintenance. For now, we are just going to focus on getting data in and out of a database.

7.1   Setting your schema

As we have now seen with almost every automation, the most crucial step in the automation process is defining the data you will need. In this case, you will need to create a table to hold your server information. For the SQL table, you can start with some fairly standard columns like

- *Name*—The name of the asset
- *Operating System Type*—Linux or Windows
- *Operating System Version*—The name of the operating system version
- *Status*—Whether it is in service, being repaired, or retired
- *Remote Method*—The method of remote connection to use for this server (SSH, WSMan, Power CLI, etc.)

Next, you will need to add some additional columns that will allow you to create references to the external systems. When creating references to external systems, it is best to avoid using values that are subject to change, like display names. Most hypervisors have a unique internal identifier for their virtual machines. For instance, VMware has the Managed Object Reference ID for every VM. Azure VMs all have a universally unique identifier (UUID). No matter what systems you use, you should be able to find a way to uniquely identify the different servers:

- *UUID*—The unique identifier from the source systems.
- *Source*—The system that you are referencing (Hyper-V, VMware, Azure, AWS, etc.).
- *Source Instance*—The instance of the source environment. This can be the vSphere cluster, Azure subscription, etc.—anything to let you know where that data came from.

Along with the previously listed items, you will want to create an identity column. An identity column is a column that is automatically populated by the database. This will allow you to automatically assign an ID to every entry without having to write any code to do it. This will come in handy when you need to reference items between tables. Also, when updating items, you can use the ID instead of trying to match on other fields.

You can add additional fields for tracking cost centers, IP address, subnet, or whatever would make your job easier. Keep in mind that the ultimate goal here is to create one place to see all servers and quickly identify where they live. Be careful you are not just duplicating the data from other systems.

7.1.1 Data types

Much like when building a PowerShell function, you need to consider the data types when determining your table schema. However, it is not always as simple as an int equals an int. This is especially true when it comes to string.

In SQL, as well as other database engines, there are multiple types of strings, and we could spend the entire rest of the chapter discussing the different types and when and why to use each. But the most common one used is the nvarchar type.

A nvarchar column can hold 1–4,000 byte pairs, and, most important, it can support Unicode characters. Since there is such a size range, when you declare a nvarchar, you also need to set a maximum character length.

> **NOTE** There is a nvarchar max in which you can store approximately 1 billion characters. However, using this is very inefficient on the SQL backend and, in most cases, is just unnecessary.

For most other fields, the decisions between SQL and PowerShell data types are straightforward. Based on the size of a number you need, you can choose an int, float, double, real, decimal, etc. And there are some data types with different names. For example, a GUID in SQL is a uniqueidentifier and a Boolean is a bit.

The last thing you need to consider is whether or not to allow null values. In our example, we want to ensure that all fields are populated because the data would not be helpful if any data is missing. However, if you added a column for the cost center, you could allow it to be null. This is because there could be servers without a cost center, so requiring it could prevent you from being able to add a server. On the other hand, having a blank UUID would make the entry worthless because you cannot reference it back to the source system.

So now we can map our data needed to their SQL data types. Table 7.1 shows the values.

Now that you have the data defined, you can use the New-DbaDbTable cmdlet to create the table. Start by defining each column in a hashtable and then adding the different hashtables into an array for each table. This array is then passed to the -ColumnMap

Table 7.1   Servers

Name	Type	MaxLength	Nullable	Identity
ID	int	N/A	No	Yes
Name	nvarchar	50	No	No
OSType	nvarchar	15	No	No
OSVersion	nvarchar	50	No	No
Status	nvarchar	15	No	No
RemoteMethod	nvarchar	25	No	No
UUID*	nvarchar	255	No	No
Source	nvarchar	15	No	No
SourceInstance	nvarchar	255	No	No

*UUID is not a unique identifier because it will not always be a GUID.

parameter to set schema information for each column. Finally, you can translate the information from the table directly into the hashtables:

```
$ID = @{
    Name = 'ID';
    Type = 'int';
    MaxLength = $null;
    Nullable = $false;
    Identity = $true;
}
```

Now that you have your table schema defined, you can create the table by supplying the SQL instance, the database to create it, and a name for the table, as shown in the following listing.

Listing 7.2   Creating a Servers table in SQL

```
$SqlInstance = "$($env:COMPUTERNAME)\SQLEXPRESS"
$DatabaseName = 'PoshAssetMgmt'
$ServersTable = 'Servers'
$ServersColumns = @(
    @{Name = 'ID';                        ⟵─┐ Create the ID
        Type = 'int'; MaxLength = $null;    │ column as an
        Nullable = $false; Identity = $true; │ identity column.
    }
    @{Name = 'Name';                      ⟵─┐ Create the Name column
        Type = 'nvarchar'; MaxLength = 50;  │ as a string with a max
        Nullable = $false; Identity = $false;│ length of 50 characters.
    }
    @{Name = 'OSType';                    ⟵─┐ Create the OSType column
        Type = 'nvarchar'; MaxLength = 15;  │ as a string with a max
                                             │ length of 15 characters.
```

```
                    Nullable = $false; Identity = $false;
    }
    @{Name = 'OSVersion';                          <────
        Type = 'nvarchar'; MaxLength = 50;
        Nullable = $false; Identity = $false;
    }
    @{Name = 'Status';                             <────
        Type = 'nvarchar'; MaxLength = 15;
        Nullable = $false; Identity = $false;
    }
    @{Name = 'RemoteMethod';                       <────
        Type = 'nvarchar'; MaxLength = 25;
        Nullable = $false; Identity = $false;
    }
    @{Name = 'UUID';                               <────
        Type = 'nvarchar'; MaxLength = 255;
        Nullable = $false; Identity = $false;
    }
    @{Name = 'Source';                             <────
        Type = 'nvarchar'; MaxLength = 15;
        Nullable = $false; Identity = $false;
    }
    @{Name = 'SourceInstance';                     <────
        Type = 'nvarchar'; MaxLength = 255;
        Nullable = $false; Identity = $false;
    }
)
$DbaDbTable = @{
    SqlInstance = $SqlInstance
    Database    = $DatabaseName
    Name        = $ServersTable
    ColumnMap   = $ServersColumns
}
New-DbaDbTable @DbaDbTable
```

Create the OSVersion column as a string with a max length of 50 characters.

Create the a Status column as a string with a max length of 15 characters.

Create the RemoteMethod column as a string with a max length of 25 characters.

Create the UUID column as a string with a max length of 255 characters.

Create the Source column as a string with a max length of 15 characters.

Create the SourceInstance column as a string with a max length of 255 characters.

Once you have your table created, it is time to create the module and functions to interact with them.

7.2 Connecting to SQL

Throughout this chapter, you will be making calls to a single SQL instance and database. To keep from having to pass these as parameters to your functions each and every time, you can set them as variables in the module's psm1 file. Then, just reference these variables in your functions.

When you do this, it is always good to make the variables with a name that will be unique to your module. I tend to also include an underscore at the beginning of the variable name to help identify it as a module variable.

For things like connection information, it makes sense to create it as a single PowerShell object, with properties for the individual values, like the SQL server instance, the database, and any table name. This can make things cleaner and more manageable by only having one variable. But before you can do that, you need to create the module files.

We will be putting all the code created into a module named PoshAssetMgmt. You can quickly generate the base structure in the following listing by using the New-ModuleTemplate function from chapter 2.

Listing 7.3   Creating the PoshAssetMgmt module

```
Function New-ModuleTemplate {              ◄─── This is the same
    [CmdletBinding()]                           function as in
    [OutputType()]                              listing 2.5.
    param(
        [Parameter(Mandatory = $true)]
        [string]$ModuleName,
        [Parameter(Mandatory = $true)]
        [string]$ModuleVersion,
        [Parameter(Mandatory = $true)]
        [string]$Author,
        [Parameter(Mandatory = $true)]
        [string]$PSVersion,
        [Parameter(Mandatory = $false)]
        [string[]]$Functions
    )
    $ModulePath = Join-Path .\ "$($ModuleName)\$($ModuleVersion)"
    New-Item -Path $ModulePath -ItemType Directory
    Set-Location $ModulePath
    New-Item -Path .\Public -ItemType Directory

    $ManifestParameters = @{
        ModuleVersion     = $ModuleVersion
        Author            = $Author
        Path              = ".\$($ModuleName).psd1"
        RootModule        = ".\$($ModuleName).psm1"
        PowerShellVersion = $PSVersion
    }
    New-ModuleManifest @ManifestParameters

    $File = @{
        Path     = ".\$($ModuleName).psm1"
        Encoding = 'utf8'
    }
    Out-File @File

    $Functions | ForEach-Object {
        Out-File -Path ".\Public\$($_).ps1" -Encoding utf8
    }
}
```

Set the parameters to pass to the function.

The version of your module

The name of your module

```
$module = @{              ◄───
    ModuleName    = 'PoshAssetMgmt'
    ModuleVersion = "1.0.0.0"              ◄───
    Author        = "YourNameHere"
    PSVersion     = '7.1'                  ◄───
    Functions     = 'Connect-PoshAssetMgmt',
    'New-PoshServer', 'Get-PoshServer', 'Set-PoshServer'
}
New-ModuleTemplate @module              ◄───
```

The minimum PowerShell version this module supports

Your name

The functions to create blank files for in the Public folder

Execute the function to create the new module.

Once the files have been created, open the PoshAssetMgmt.psm1 file and create a variable named $_PoshAssetMgmt to hold the connection information about your database. Since this variable is declared inside the psm1 file, it will automatically be scoped so all functions inside the module can access it. Therefore, you don't need to add it as a parameter or set it globally. You will also add the same functionality we used in previous modules to import ps1 files and check for the dbatools module, as in the following listing.

Listing 7.4   `PoshAutomate-AssetMgmt`

```
$_PoshAssetMgmt = [pscustomobject]@{
    SqlInstance = 'YourSqlSrv\SQLEXPRESS'      ◁──┐   Update SqlInstance
    Database    = 'PoshAssetMgmt'                  │   to match your server
    ServerTable = 'Servers'                        │   name.
}


$Path = Join-Path $PSScriptRoot 'Public'              ┐   Get all the ps1 files
$Functions = Get-ChildItem -Path $Path -Filter '*.ps1'  ◁──┘   in the Public folder.


Foreach ($import in $Functions) {        ◁──── Loop through each ps1 file.
    Try {
        Write-Verbose "dot-sourcing file '$($import.fullname)'"
        . $import.fullname                   ◁──┐   Execute each ps1 file to load
    }                                           │   the function into memory.
    Catch {
        Write-Error -Message "Failed to import function $($import.name)"
    }
}


[System.Collections.Generic.List[PSObject]]$RequiredModules = @()
$RequiredModules.Add([pscustomobject]@{      ◁──┐   Create an object for
    Name = 'dbatools'                            │   each module to check.
    Version = '1.1.5'
})


foreach($module in $RequiredModules){               ◁──┐   Check whether the
    $Check = Get-Module $module.Name -ListAvailable     │   module is installed
                                                         │   on the local machine.
    if(-not $check){
        throw "Module $($module.Name) not found"
    }

    $VersionCheck = $Check |
        Where-Object{ $_.Version -ge $module.Version }

    if(-not $VersionCheck){
        Write-Error "Module $($module.Name) running older version"
    }

    Import-Module -Name $module.Name
}
```

7.2.1 *Permissions*

One of the best advantages of using SQL is the built-in permission handling. Microsoft SQL has so many different levels of permissions that it is sure to fit your needs. It goes way deeper than simple read and write permissions. SQL can even support permissions down to the row and column levels.

You may have noticed that the first listing in the chapter where you created the database did not include a credential parameter. That is because the dbatools module will use the logged-in user if no other credentials are supplied. This makes things super simple to implement in an Active Directory domain environment. However, not everyone is running in a domain, and there are times where you may want to run as a different user. To account for these situations, you can build a connection function using the `Connect-DbaInstance` cmdlet. This will allow you to set a default connection that all the other functions can use.

To do this, you create the `Connect-PoshAssetMgmt` function. The parameters of this function will allow you to pass in a SQL instance, database, and credentials. If the SQL instance or database is not provided, it can use the default values set in the `$_PoshAssetMgmt` variable.

Creating a connection function like this is pointless if you still have to pass it to every function. Therefore, you can save the connection information to a variable that the other functions can reference—similar to what you just did with the `$_PoshAsset-Mgmt` variable in the psm1. The only difference here is that this variable is inside of a function and not in the psm1.

When a variable is set inside the psm1, it is automatically scoped to the script level. This allows all the other functions in the module to read that variable. However, when you set a variable inside a function, it only exists in the scope of that function—that is, unless you scope to the script level by adding `$script:` to the variable name. As you can see in the next listing, the variable for the connection information is set using `$script:_SqlInstance` to ensure that it is scoped to the script level.

Listing 7.5 `Connect-PoshAssetMgmt`

```
Function Connect-PoshAssetMgmt {
    [CmdletBinding()]
    [OutputType([object])]
    param(
        [Parameter(Mandatory = $false)]
        [string]$SqlInstance = $_PoshAssetMgmt.SqlInstance,

        [Parameter(Mandatory = $false)]
        [string]$Database = $_PoshAssetMgmt.Database,

        [Parameter(Mandatory = $false)]
        [PSCredential]$Credential
    )

    $connection = @{                        ⟵——  Set the default
        SqlInstance = $SqlInstance                connection parameters.
```

```
    Database     = $Database
}
                                              Add the credential
if ($Credential) {                        ◄┘ object if passed.
    $connection.Add('SqlCredential', $Credential)
}

$Script:_SqlInstance = Connect-DbaInstance @connection

                                     Output the result so the person
$Script:_SqlInstance           ◄─┤   running it can confirm the
}                                    connection information.
```

You can test it by importing the module and running the `Connect-PoshAssetMgmt` function:

```
Import-Module '.\PoshAssetMgmt.psd1' -Force
Connect-PoshAssetMgmt
ComputerName Name                 ConnectedAs
------------ ----                 -----------
SRV01        SRV01\SQLEXPRESS SRV01\Administrator
```

7.3 Adding data to a table

Now that you have the connection defined and the database created, the next step is to import the data into the tables. To do this, we will create a new function named `New-PoshServer`. This function will use the `Write-DbaDataTable` cmdlet to add an entry to the `Servers` table in SQL.

You can define the data to import by mapping the parameters to the table columns, thus ensuring you receive the correct data. However, that is just a small part of the equation. To ensure that you are inserting properly formatted data, you need to validate it before inserting it.

7.3.1 String validation

To ensure that the `New-PoshServer` function can insert the data into the table, you must confirm that you have the correct data and that it matches the data types and lengths set in the table. Luckily for us, a lot of this validation can be done using the PowerShell parameter validation functionality.

For example, you want to ensure that you do not pass any null or blank values. You can quickly achieve this by setting the `Mandatory` parameter attribute to `True` for all the parameters. By default, PowerShell sets them to not required.

You will also need to check the length for all string parameters to ensure they do not exceed the max length for the column. To confirm a string does not exceed the max length, you can use the parameter validation attribute `ValidateScript`. The `ValidateScript` attribute allows you to define a script block that can validate a parameter's value. If your script block returns `true`, the value is considered valid. For instance, to confirm the name is under the 50-character limit, you can have a simple conditional statement that checks the length of the string:

```
Function New-PoshServer {
    param(
        [Parameter(Mandatory=$true)]
        [ValidateScript({$_.Length -le 50 })]
        [string]$Name
    )
    $PSBoundParameters
}
New-PoshServer -Name 'Srv01'
New-PoshServer -Name
    'ThisIsAReallyLongServerNameThatWillCertainlyExceed50Characters'
```

You can then repeat this same pattern with the OSVersion, UUID, and SourceInstance parameters, ensuring you enter the maximum length for each.

You will want to take a different approach for the Status, OSType, RemoteMethod, and Source parameters because these columns will have predefined values. For these, you can use the ValidateSet parameter attribute to control which values can be passed to this parameter:

```
[Parameter(Mandatory=$true)]
[ValidateSet('Active','Depot','Retired')]
[string]$Status,

[Parameter(Mandatory=$true)]
[ValidateSet('Windows','Linux')]
[string]$OSType,

[Parameter(Mandatory=$true)]
[ValidateSet('WSMan','SSH','PowerCLI','HyperV','AzureRemote')]
[string]$RemoteMethod,

[Parameter(Mandatory=$true)]
[ValidateSet('Physical','VMware','Hyper-V','Azure','AWS')]
[string]$Source,
```

You can update these validation sets to fit your individual needs. The great thing about them is that they prevent situations where you can have misspellings or different abbreviations skewing your data. For instance, I've seen situations where half the VMs are listed as being in HyperV and the other half as being in Hyper-V, making searching for all Hyper-V VMs a tedious and error-prone task.

In more advanced applications, you can use enumeration sets that contain a list of named constants with an underlying integral value. These are invaluable when building APIs or bringing data in from multiple locations. But for a simple PowerShell function, they can be overkill.

7.3.2 *Inserting data to a table*

Once you have all your data validated, it is time to write it to the SQL table following the process shown in figure 7.1. To do this, you can write a T-SQL Insert statement and have it passed to a query, but the dbatools module has a cmdlet to make it even easier

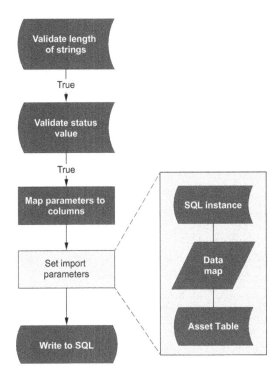

Figure 7.1 `New-PoshServer` function with validation and SQL instance information to add a new entry into the SQL database

for you. You can perform single or bulk data uploads to a SQL table using the Write-DbaDataTable cmdlet, with no SQL commands required.

To use the Write-DbaDataTable cmdlet, you need to provide a PowerShell object where the properties match the columns in the table and then provide the SQL instance and the table, and the cmdlet will handle the rest of the insert process for you. Putting this all together in the following listing, we can create our first function, New-PoshServer.

Listing 7.6 `New-PoshServer`

```
Function New-PoshServer {
    [CmdletBinding()]
    [OutputType([object])]
    param(
        [Parameter(Mandatory = $true)]
        [ValidateScript( { $_.Length -le 50 })]
        [string]$Name,

        [Parameter(Mandatory = $true)]
        [ValidateSet('Windows', 'Linux')]
        [string]$OSType,

        [Parameter(Mandatory = $true)]
        [ValidateScript( { $_.Length -le 50 })]
        [string]$OSVersion,
```

Validate that the server name is less than or equal to 50 characters.

Validate that the OSType is one of the predefined values.

Validate that the OSVersion is less than or equal to 50 characters.

Validate that the Status is one of the predefined values.

```
[Parameter(Mandatory = $true)]
[ValidateSet('Active', 'Depot', 'Retired')]
[string]$Status,
```

Validate that the RemoteMethod is one of the predefined values.

```
[Parameter(Mandatory = $true)]
[ValidateSet('WSMan', 'SSH', 'PowerCLI', 'HyperV', 'AzureRemote')]
[string]$RemoteMethod,
```

Validate that the UUID is less than or equal to 255 characters.

```
[Parameter(Mandatory = $false)]
[ValidateScript( { $_.Length -le 255 })]
[string]$UUID,
```

Validate that the Source is one of the predefined values.

```
[Parameter(Mandatory = $true)]
[ValidateSet('Physical', 'VMware', 'Hyper-V', 'Azure', 'AWS')]
[string]$Source,
```

Validate that the SourceInstance is less than or equal to 255 characters.

```
    [Parameter(Mandatory = $false)]
    [ValidateScript( { $_.Length -le 255 })]
    [string]$SourceInstance
)
```

Build the data mapping for the SQL columns.

```
$Data = [pscustomobject]@{
    Name            = $Name
    OSType          = $OSType
    OSVersion       = $OSVersion
    Status          = $Status
    RemoteMethod    = $RemoteMethod
    UUID            = $UUID
    Source          = $Source
    SourceInstance  = $SourceInstance
}
```

Write the data to the table.

```
$DbaDataTable = @{
    SqlInstance = $_SqlInstance
    Database    = $_PoshAssetMgmt.Database
    InputObject = $Data
    Table       = $_PoshAssetMgmt.ServerTable
}
Write-DbaDataTable @DbaDataTable

    Write-Output $Data
}
```

Since Write-DbaDataTable doesn't have any output the data object, you know which ones were added.

Once you have the function created, you can test it by creating a few test servers:

```
Import-Module '.\PoshAssetMgmt.psd1' -Force
Connect-PoshAssetMgmt | Out-Null

$testData = @{
    OSType          = 'Windows'
    Status          = 'Active'
    RemoteMethod    = 'WSMan'
    Source          = 'VMware'
    OSVersion       = 'Microsoft Windows Server 2019 Standard'
    SourceInstance  = 'Cluster1'
}
```

```
New-PoshServer -Name 'Srv01' -UUID '001' @testData
New-PoshServer -Name 'Srv02' -UUID '002' @testData
New-PoshServer -Name 'Srv03' -UUID '003' @testData
```

Now that there is data in the database, let's look at how you can retrieve it.

7.4   Getting data from a table

The `Invoke-DbaQuery` cmdlet from the dbatools module returns the results of a T-SQL query to PowerShell. All you need to do is pass the information about the connection (that is, SQL instance, database, credentials, etc.) along with the query. So, for example, running the following snippet will return all the servers you just added to the table:

```
$DbaQuery = @{
    SqlInstance = "$($env:COMPUTERNAME)\SQLEXPRESS"
    Database = 'PoshAssetMgmt'
    Query = 'SELECT * FROM Servers'
}
Invoke-DbaQuery @DbaQuery
```

This query works fine for now because you only have a few entries in your table. But as you add more servers to it, it will quickly become very resource-intensive. This is because the query will return every single record from the table to PowerShell. This will require you to use the `Where-Object` cmdlet to filter the data if you only want specific servers—and doing that is horribly inefficient.

By filtering your results before they get returned to PowerShell, you will not only save on memory consumption by not having unneeded records sitting there waiting to be filtered out, but it will also be exponentially faster. This is due to SQL's ability to optimize data retrieval. Through the use of query execution plans, indexes, and statistics, SQL can note the queries you run, which it can use in the future to retrieve those results again, much faster. Some more modern versions even have automatic indexing and optimization.

When you use the `Where-Object` cmdlet, PowerShell loops through each record one at a time to determine whether it needs to be filtered or not. This occurs at a much slower and more resource-intensive rate. So, let's look at how to filter the data before it ever gets to PowerShell.

7.4.1   SQL where clause

To filter your data in a SQL query, you can add a `where` clause to it. `Where` clauses in SQL allow you to filter on any column in the table. For example, if I want to get the server named Srv01, I can use the following SQL query:

```
SELECT * FROM Servers WHERE Name = 'Srv01'
```

However, like with most things we deal with, you will want to make it dynamic. You can do this by replacing the value `'Srv01'` with a SQL variable. A SQL variable is declared using the at symbol (`@`) in your query. You can then create a hashtable mapping the actual values to the variables. You then pass this hashtable to the `-SqlParameter` argument in the `Invoke-DbaQuery` cmdlet. This will then swap your variables for the values when it executes in SQL:

```
$DbaQuery = @{
    SqlInstance = "$($env:COMPUTERNAME)\SQLEXPRESS"
    Database = 'PoshAssetMgmt'
    Query = 'SELECT * FROM Servers WHERE Name = @name'
    SqlParameter = @{name = 'Srv01'}
}
Invoke-DbaQuery @DbaQuery
```

While swapping the values for variables and then creating a hashtable with the values may seem like a lot of extra steps, there are several very good reasons to do it this way:

- It checks that the correct data types are passed.
- It will automatically escape characters in your values that may cause issues in a standard SQL string.
- It automatically converts data types, like `DateTime`, from PowerShell to SQL format.
- It allows SQL to use the same query plan even with different values, making things faster.
- It can prevent SQL injection attacks.

SQL injection attacks

A SQL injection attack is when an attacker is able to insert unwanted code into your SQL queries. For example, you could dynamically build the SQL where clause by joining strings together:

```
$query = "SELECT * FROM Servers WHERE Name = '$($Server)'"
```

If the value of the `$Server` variable is `'Srv01'`, it would create the query string:

```
SELECT * FROM Servers WHERE Name = 'Srv01'
```

The problem with this method is that it leaves you vulnerable. A person could inject any value they wanted into the `$Server` variable, including malicious code, and your SQL server would not know any different—for instance, if someone set the value of `$Server` to `"';Truncate table xyz;select '"`. In this case, your automation would execute the following query, erasing all data from the table XYZ:

```
SELECT * FROM Servers WHERE Name = '';Truncate table xyz;select ''
```

By parameterizing the values, you prevent this. So, if someone happened to pass the value `"';Truncate table xyz;select '"` as the name of a server, SQL would only recognize it as a string with that value and not actually execute the malicious code.

Since there are eight columns in the table, there may be dozens of different where clause combinations you could want. So, in lieu of trying to guess the different where clauses a person could want, you can use PowerShell to build it dynamically.

Just like with the insert function, you need to start by determining your parameters. And once again, you can create a one-for-one mapping between the columns and the parameters.

We can also make a couple of assumptions about the behavior of the where clause. For instance, we will want to use -and, not -or, if multiple parameters are passed. You will also want to allow it to be run without a where clause.

Now that you know your parameters and how you want them to act, you can build the logic shown in figure 7.2 to create and append your where clause to the SQL query. One of the best ways to do this is by creating a string array that you populate based on the parameters passed. The trick here is to only add the items to the where clause if a value is passed to the parameter. You can do this by using the $PSBound-Parameters variable.

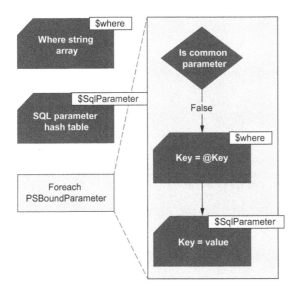

Figure 7.2   Create a string array for the where clause and a hashtable for the parameter values, allowing you to dynamically create your SQL queries at run time.

The $PSBoundParameters variable is populated inside of every function by PowerShell and is a hashtable of the parameters and the values you passed. If a parameter is not used, there is no entry in the $PSBoundParameters variable. Therefore, you can loop through the items in the $PSBoundParameters variable to build the where clause.

However, there is one catch to using the $PSBoundParameters variable in this manner. When you add the CmdletBinding to your function, it adds the common parameters to it. So, for instance, if you added the Verbose switch to your command, $PSBoundParameters would contain a key with the name Verbose. This would cause your code to add an entry in the where clause for Verbose. To prevent this, you can filter out any parameters added by the CmdletBinding by filtering names listed in the [System.Management.Automation.Cmdlet]::CommonParameters property list. This will ensure that only your defined parameters are used.

By using the GetEnumerator() method on the $PSBoundParameters, you can loop through each key pair in the hashtable and add the text for that column's filter. The text will be in the format "column operator variable" and added to a string array.

You do not need to add the -and between the different clauses at this point. That will be added at the end by using a join on the string array.

As you loop through each item, you will also need to build a hashtable with the key and the value for each parameter. For example, if you passed the parameter Name with the value of 'Srv02', the where argument would look like Name = @Name. Then, the hashtable entry would have the key Name with the value 'Srv02'.

Once you have the where clause string built, it is time to add it to the query, keeping in mind that you could run it without any filters. Therefore, you'll need to check whether there are any values to filter. Again, this can be done with a simple if condition to check the count of the where array, shown in figure 7.3. If it is greater than

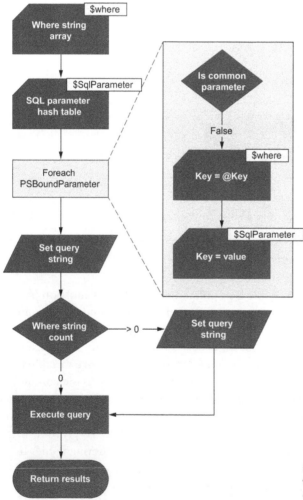

Figure 7.3 Get-PoshServer function with dynamic where clause for SQL side filtering

zero, then add the `where` clause. Finally, you can execute the `Invoke-DbaQuery` cmdlet to run the query and return the results, as in the following listing.

Listing 7.7   Get-PoshServer

```
Function Get-PoshServer {
    [CmdletBinding()]
    [OutputType([object])]
    param(
        [Parameter(Mandatory = $false)]
        [int]$ID,

        [Parameter(Mandatory = $false)]
        [string]$Name,

        [Parameter(Mandatory = $false)]
        [string]$OSType,

        [Parameter(Mandatory = $false)]
        [string]$OSVersion,

        [Parameter(Mandatory = $false)]
        [string]$Status,

        [Parameter(Mandatory = $false)]
        [string]$RemoteMethod,

        [Parameter(Mandatory = $false)]
        [string]$UUID,

        [Parameter(Mandatory = $false)]
        [string]$Source,

        [Parameter(Mandatory = $false)]
        [string]$SourceInstance
    )

    [System.Collections.Generic.List[string]] $where = @()
    $SqlParameter = @{}
    $PSBoundParameters.GetEnumerator() |              ⟵──────  Loop through each item in
    Where-Object { $_.Key -notin                              the $PSBoundParameters
        [System.Management.Automation.Cmdlet]::CommonParameters } |   to create the where clause
    ForEach-Object {                                          while filtering out common
        $where.Add("$($_.Key) = @$($_.Key)")                 parameters.
        $SqlParameter.Add($_.Key, $_.Value)
    }

    $Query = "SELECT * FROM " +      ◁── Set the default query.
        $_PoshAssetMgmt.ServerTable
                                              If the where clause
    if ($where.Count -gt 0) {        ⟵──┘   is needed, add it
        $Query += " Where " + ($where -join (' and '))   to the query.
    }
```

```
Write-Verbose $Query

$DbaQuery = @{
    SqlInstance  = $_SqlInstance
    Database     = $_PoshAssetMgmt.Database
    Query        = $Query
    SqlParameter = $SqlParameter
}

Invoke-DbaQuery @DbaQuery
}
```

Execute the query and output the results.

Go ahead and test it out with a few different combinations:

```
Import-Module '.\PoshAssetMgmt.psd1' -Force
Connect-PoshAssetMgmt
Get-PoshServer | Format-Table
Get-PoshServer -Id 1 | Format-Table
Get-PoshServer -Name 'Srv02' | Format-Table
Get-PoshServer -Source 'VMware' -Status 'Active' | Format-Table
```

7.5   *Updating records*

Now that you can insert and retrieve values, it is time to look at updating records. You can update data using the Invoke-DbaQuery cmdlet, but unlike with retrieving data, you will use an Update SQL statement. This new function, Set-PoshServer, will be a combination of the Get and the New functions.

To start with, you already built all the data validation into the New-PoshServer function, all of which you can reuse in the Set-PoshServer function, except this time, you are going to add two additional parameters: InputObject and ID. The ID parameter is for the ID of an existing server entry, and the InputObject parameter will use pipeline values from the Get-PoshServer function.

Since the function will need either the ID or the InputObject to update a record, you will need to ensure that at least one of them is included but not both at the same time. To keep PowerShell from requiring both, you can use the ParameterSetName attribute and assign different names for the InputObject and ID parameters. This way, when the pipeline is used, it will not see the ID parameter as mandatory, and vice versa. It will also keep someone from using both at the same time:

```
[Parameter(ValueFromPipeline = $true,ParameterSetName="Pipeline")]
[object]$InputObject,
[Parameter(Mandatory = $true,ParameterSetName="Id")]
[int]$ID,
```

All other parameters not defined with a parameter set can be used regardless of whether the pipeline or the ID parameter is used.

7.5.1 Passing pipeline data

Allowing values from pipelines is a great way to update multiple servers at once. For example, say you changed the name of your VMware cluster. You can use the Get-PoshServer function to get all the entries with the old cluster name and update them to the new name in a single line. However, to ensure you properly process the pipeline values, there is more required than just adding ValueFromPipeline to the parameter.

When using pipeline data, you must add the begin, process, and end blocks to your function, as shown in figure 7.4. When you pass values from the pipeline, the begin and end blocks execute once, but the process block executes once for each value passed. Without it, only the last value passed to the pipeline will process.

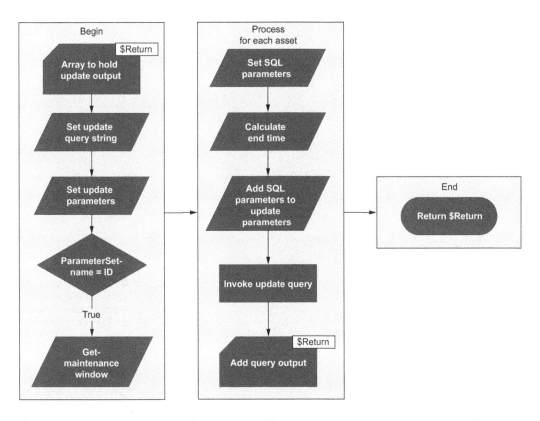

Figure 7.4 Set-PoshServer **function with the ability to use a pipeline or an ID number to identify which item to update**

When the function in listing 7.8 executes, the begin block executes once, regardless of how many items are in the pipeline. So, you use the begin block to set any variables or logic that only needs to run once. Then, the process block is executed once for each item in the pipeline. Once all the values in the process block finish, the end block runs once. This can be used to create return data, close connections, etc.

Listing 7.8   `Set-PoshServer`

```
Function Set-PoshServer {
    [CmdletBinding()]
    [OutputType([object])]
    param
    (
        [Parameter(ValueFromPipeline = $true,
            ParameterSetName = "Pipeline")]
        [object]$InputObject,
        [Parameter(Mandatory = $true,
            ParameterSetName = "ID")]
        [int]$ID,

        [Parameter(Mandatory = $false)]
        [ValidateScript( { $_.Length -le 50 })]
        [string]$Name,

        [Parameter(Mandatory = $false)]
        [ValidateSet('Windows', 'Linux')]
        [string]$OSType,

        [Parameter(Mandatory = $false)]
        [ValidateScript( { $_.Length -le 50 })]
        [string]$OSVersion,

        [Parameter(Mandatory = $false)]
        [ValidateSet('Active', 'Depot', 'Retired')]
        [string]$Status,

        [Parameter(Mandatory = $false)]
        [ValidateSet('WSMan', 'SSH', 'PowerCLI', 'HyperV', 'AzureRemote')]
        [string]$RemoteMethod,
                                                    Loop through each item in the
        [Parameter(Mandatory = $false)]            $PSBoundParameters to create
        [ValidateScript( { $_.Length -le 255 })]   the where clause while filtering
        [string]$UUID,                             out common parameters and the
                                                    ID and InputObject parameters.
        [Parameter(Mandatory = $false)]
        [ValidateSet('Physical', 'VMware', 'Hyper-V', 'Azure', 'AWS')]
        [string]$Source,
                                                         Create the SQL
        [Parameter(Mandatory = $false)]              Parameters hashtable to
        [ValidateScript( { $_.Length -le 255 })]     hold the values for the SQL
        [string]$SourceInstance                      variables, starting with
    )                                                 a null value for the ID.
    begin {
        [System.Collections.Generic.List[object]] $Return = @()
        [System.Collections.Generic.List[string]] $Set = @()
        [System.Collections.Generic.List[string]] $Output = @()
        $SqlParameter = @{ID = $null}                      ◄────────┐

        $PSBoundParameters.GetEnumerator() |               ◄──────
        Where-Object { $_.Key -notin @('ID', 'InputObject') +
            [System.Management.Automation.Cmdlet]::CommonParameters  } |
```

```
                        ForEach-Object {
                            $set.Add("$($_.Key) = @$($_.Key)")
                            $Output.Add("deleted.$($_.Key) AS Prev_$($_.Key),
                                inserted.$($_.Key) AS $($_.Key)")
                            $SqlParameter.Add($_.Key, $_.Value)
                        }

                        $query = 'UPDATE [dbo].' +
                        "[$($_PoshAssetMgmt.ServerTable)] " +
                        'SET ' +
                        ($set -join (', ')) +
                        ' OUTPUT @ID AS ID, ' +
                        ($Output -join (', ')) +
                        ' WHERE ID = @ID'

                        Write-Verbose $query

                        $Parameters = @{
                            SqlInstance  = $_SqlInstance
                            Database     = $_PoshAssetMgmt.Database
                            Query        = $query
                            SqlParameter = @{}
                        }

                    if ($PSCmdlet.ParameterSetName -eq 'ID') {
                        $InputObject = Get-PoshServer -Id $Id
                        if (-not $InputObject) {
                            throw "No server object was found for id '$Id'"
                        }
                    }
                }
            }
            process {
                $SqlParameter['ID'] = $InputObject.ID

                $Parameters['SqlParameter'] = $SqlParameter
                Invoke-DbaQuery @Parameters | ForEach-Object { $Return.Add($_) }
            }
            end {
                $Return
            }
        }
```

Set the query with the output of the changed items.

Add parameters other than the ID or InputObject to the Set clause array and SqlParameters.

Set the parameters for the database update command.

If the ID was passed, check that it matches an existing server.

Update the ID for this InputObject.

Return the changes.

Update SQL parameters and execute the update.

Starting with the begin block, you can declare an array to store the results from each update and set the string for the query. Just like with the Get-PoshServer function, you will build your query dynamically, except this time, instead of building the where clause, you are building the SET values. You can also include a second string array to build an OUTPUT clause on the update query to return the values and compare the field before and after. For example, to update the Source column for a server, your query should look like the following snippet:

```
UPDATE [dbo].[Server]
SET Source = @Source
```

```
OUTPUT @ID AS ID, deleted.Source AS Prev_Source,
    inserted.Source AS Source
WHERE ID = @ID
```

When building the query, you will also want to ensure that you exclude the ID and InputObject parameters from being added to the query and hashtable, just like you do with the common parameters.

Next, you can set the parameters for the Invoke-DbaQuery command since these will be the same for each update. Finally, if the ID parameter is passed and not the Input-Object, you will want to check that it is a valid ID number before trying to update it.

There are a few ways to test whether the invoking command included the ID parameter or the pipeline. But the best way is by check the value of the Parameter-SetName property on the $PSCmdlet variable. The $PSCmdlet variable is automatically created when a function is executed and contains the information about the invocation. If the property is equal to ID, you can guarantee the ID parameter was used. If you simply check for the existence of the $ID variable, you could run into a false positive if someone has set a global variable with that same name.

Next, in the process block, you can execute the update query for each Input-Object. Here all you need to do is add the value for the ID to the SQL parameters and then add the SQL parameters to the Invoke-DbaQuery parameters.

Now that you have all the values set for the update statement, you can pass it to the Invoke-DbaQuery cmdlet and add the output to the $Return array. Finally, in the end block, you can write the $Return to the output stream.

Now you can test using both an ID and the pipeline:

```
Import-Module '.\PoshAssetMgmt.psd1' -Force
Connect-PoshAssetMgmt
Set-PoshServer -Id 1 -Status 'Retired' -Verbose
Get-PoshServer -SourceInstance 'Cluster1' | Set-PoshServer -SourceInstance
    'Cluster2'
```

7.6   *Keeping data in sync*

One of the biggest challenges with any list, spreadsheet, or database is keeping data up to date. Unfortunately, since every environment is different, I cannot give you one fool-proof way to keep all your data update to date, but I can provide some tips.

The first and most important tip is to create a schedule for syncing your data. The more often you do this, the better your data will be, and it will be much easier to spot errors or omissions. If you can, the best way is to set up a scheduled job to run daily to check and confirm your data.

The second tip is that you should only remove data when absolutely necessary. You may have noticed that we did not create a Remove-PoshServer function. This is because the removal of asset information should be carefully controlled. This is why there is a retired status for servers. You should only remove items after a predetermined amount of time or if bad data gets entered.

Right up there with the other tips is to watch out for duplicate data. Because of the way the `New-PoshServer` function is written, it will allow you to add the same server in the system over and over. Again, this is by design because you could very well have two servers with the same name or even the same UUID. (Trust me, I've seen enough cloned VMs in my days not to doubt this.) So, when you are building your automation to sync the data, you will want to build in checks to ensure the data is unique to your environment.

7.6.1 Getting server data

The way you retrieve your server information will depend very much on the type of servers and hypervisors you have. For example, VMware PowerCLI will return the guest operating system from the `Get-VM` cmdlet. However, the `Get-VM` cmdlet for Hyper-V does not, but you can get the VM ID within the running VM. Again, this is another topic that could be a chapter on its own. But to get you started, I have included a couple of samples in the Helper Scripts folder for this chapter for different hypervisors and clouds.

Another option is to gather the data from external sources and export it to a CSV or JSON file. Then, import that file into PowerShell and run the update sync. This method works well for disconnected networks. You can test this method out for yourself with the following listing and the SampleData.CSV file from the Helper Scripts folder.

Listing 7.9 Sync from external CSV

```
$ServerData = Import-Csv ".\SampleData.CSV"        ⟵  Import the data
                                                       from the CSV.
$ServerData | ForEach-Object {
    $values = @{                            ⟵
        Name            = $_.Name                 Get the values for all
        OSType          = $_.OSType               items and map them to
        OSVersion       = $_.OSVersion            the parameters for the
        Status          = 'Active'                Set-PoshServer and New-
        RemoteMethod    = 'PowerCLI'              PoshServer functions.
        UUID            = $_.UUID
        Source          = 'VMware'
        SourceInstance  = $_.SourceInstance            Run the Get-PoshServer
    }                                                  to see whether a record
                                                       exists with a matching
    $record = Get-PoshServer -UUID $_.UUID    ⟵       UUID.

    if($record){                        ⟵
        $record | Set-PoshServer @values      If the record exists,
    }                                         update it; otherwise,
    else{                                     add a new record.
        New-PoshServer @values
    }
}
```

Get all the VMs.

7.7   *Setting a solid foundation*

Building your solutions using a relational database has several advantages. Not only is it set up with better backup and recovery, speed, and reliability, but it also makes things easier on you. For example, you do not need to worry about building anything into your code to deal with permissions. Just let SQL handle it.

Also, your functions will run much more smoothly because you can filter results before they ever get to PowerShell. Imagine if this was all in a CSV file. You would need to import all the data into PowerShell, convert everything that is not a string back to its indented data type, and rely on pipeline filtering. Finally, as you will see in the next few chapters, having data stored in a relational database will set you up nicely for future growth by allowing you to create interactions with the database outside of a standard module like this.

Summary

- Using a relational database is more reliable than shared files.
- Most relational databases can handle permissions on their own without you needing to code anything specific for it.
- You always want to validate your data before writing it to a database.
- Setting variables as parameters in a SQL script helps with data type conversions, escape characters, and preventing SQL injection attacks.
- When using pipelines, include the process block so each item in the pipeline is processed.

Cloud-based automation

This chapter covers

- Setting up Azure Automation
- Creating PowerShell runbooks in Azure Automation
- Executing runbooks from Azure to on-premises environments

With most companies embracing, at the very least, a hybrid approach to cloud-based computing, a lot of IT professionals have had to quickly adapt to keep up. However, at the same time, it has opened up an entirely new set of tools that you can use to perform your automations.

When you hear the words *cloud-based automation*, that can refer to two different things. One is the automation of cloud-based assets such as virtual machines (VMs) or PaaS services. The other, and the one we will be focusing on, is using a cloud-based tool to perform automations. And, as you will learn in this chapter, those automations are not limited to just cloud-based resources.

You may remember that way back in chapter 2, we created a script to clean up log files by adding them to a ZIP archive. I mentioned that you could then copy those archives to a cloud-based storage container. You also saw in chapter 3 how you can use tools like Task Scheduler and Jenkins to schedule jobs like this. In this chapter, we will take it a step further and use Azure Automation to copy those archive files from your on-premises server to Azure Blob storage.

Azure Automation is a cloud-based automation platform that allows you to run serverless PowerShell scripts directly in Azure. However, it is not just limited to Azure-based executions. It can use *hybrid runbook workers* to execute these scripts, known as *runbooks*, on individual servers or groups of servers. This allows you to store and schedule scripts in Azure to run on servers in your on-premises environment or even in other clouds.

8.1   Chapter resources

This chapter is divided into three parts. First, you will create the Azure resources required to support the automation. Then, you will set up a local server as a hybrid runbook worker. The final part will be the creation of the automation in Azure.

If you do not have an Azure subscription, you can sign up for a free 30-day trial. Since Azure Automation is a cloud-based service, there are fees associated with job run times. At the time of this writing, and ever since Azure Automation was introduced, it provides 500 minutes a month for free. After you use the 500 minutes, the cost is a fraction of a cent per minute. In September of 2021, it is US$0.002, which comes out to just under $90 a month if you have an automation that runs 24/7. For the purposes of this chapter, we will stay well under 500 minutes.

In addition to the Azure subscription, you will also need a server running Windows Server 2012 R2 or greater with TCP port 443 access to the internet. This server will execute scripts from Azure in your on-premises environment.

Since this chapter deals with hybrid scenarios, there will be different places where you will need to execute different code snippets and scripts. Also, some of it will require PowerShell 5.1 as Azure Automation does not fully support PowerShell 7 yet.

To help keep everything straight, I will include callouts for which environment and version of PowerShell to use. For this chapter, there will be three different environments:

- Any device with PowerShell 7 installed. Most likely, the one you have used throughout this book.
- The server that you will connect to Azure for the hybrid scenario. All snippets for this will use PowerShell 5.1 and ISE.
- The script editor in the Azure Automation portal.

The first two can be the same device, but make sure to pay attention to when you need to use Windows PowerShell 5.1 versus PowerShell 7.

8.2   Setting up Azure Automation

Setting up an Azure Automation account can be as simple as going to the Azure portal, clicking Create Resource, and then running through the wizard to create a new automation account. This approach will work if you plan on only doing cloud-based automations. However, if you want to create hybrid runbook workers, you need to do a few more things.

The basic organizational structure, for those not familiar with Azure, is a single Azure Active Directory (Azure AD) Tenant, with subscriptions and resources underneath it. The tenant is where all your user accounts, groups, and service principal are stored.

Subscriptions are where you create Azure resources. All Azure consumption is billed at the Subscription level. You can have multiple subscriptions under one tenant.

Next are the Resource Groups, shown in figure 8.1. Resources like Azure Automation accounts or VMs cannot be added directly to a subscription. Instead, they are added to Resource Groups. Resource Groups allow you to group your individual resources into logical collections. They also help with setting permissions since all Azure resources inherit permissions down, and there is no way to block inheritance or create deny permissions.

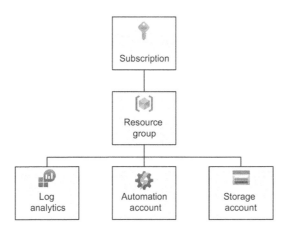

Figure 8.1 Azure resources required for the storage upload automation. All resources are grouped into a single Resource Group, which resides under a subscription.

For this chapter, we will create a brand-new Resource Group so you can keep everything separate from any other Azure resources you may have. Then, you will create the required Azure resources. For this automation, we will create the following resources:

- *Azure Automation account*—This is the automation platform that will hold and execute your scripts.
- *Log Analytics Workspace*—This provides the agent for creating a hybrid runbook worker for executing Azure Automation scripts in your on-premises environment.
- *Storage Account*—This will be used to store the files uploaded from the automation.

8.2.1 Azure Automation

As mentioned previously, Azure Automation is a cloud-based automation platform with the ability to run automations in the cloud, on-premises, or in other clouds. The automations are created as runbooks. A runbook can be a script written in PowerShell 5.1, PowerShell Workflow, Python 2, or Python 3. In addition, there are also graphical runbooks that allow you to drag and drop different actions. For our automation, we will be creating a PowerShell runbook.

PowerShell 7

While I was writing this book, Microsoft added PowerShell 7 as a preview feature in Azure Automation. So, while all the PowerShell runbooks in this chapter were written and tested in PowerShell 5.1, you should be able to run them in either version. As of April 2022, there is an additional prompt to select the PowerShell version when creating a new runbook.

When you execute a runbook in Azure Automation, you can choose to execute it in Azure or on a hybrid runbook worker, as you can see in figure 8.2. The hybrid runbook worker is what allows Azure Automation to access resources in your on-premises environment. When you execute a runbook on a hybrid runbook worker, the runbook is delivered to the machine for execution. This gives you one central place to store and maintain your scripts, regardless of where they need to run.

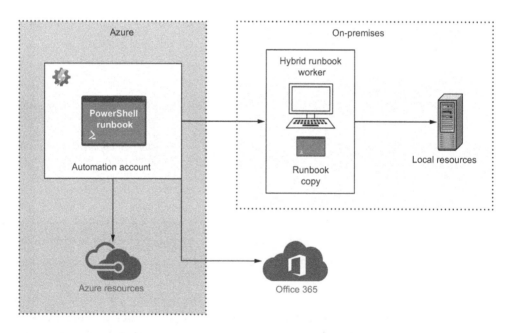

Figure 8.2   Automation account hybrid runbook worker automation flow, showing how runbooks can be executed either in the cloud or directly in your on-premises environment

Azure Automation also has the ability to store different assets for your runbooks to use. These include modules, variables, credentials, and certificates.

8.2.2 Log Analytics

A lot of the functionality in Azure Automation is tightly integrated with Log Analytics, including the hybrid runbook workers. To make a server a hybrid runbook worker, the Microsoft Monitoring Agent (MMA) must be installed and set to a Log Analytics workspace with the Azure Automation solution added.

Log Analytics is a monitoring and data collection tool in Azure. Most services in Azure have the ability to send diagnostic and metric logs to Log Analytics. You can then search these logs using Kusto queries and create alerts based on query results. (Kusto is an Azure-based query similar to SQL but designed for ad hoc big data queries.) You can also send logs from on-premises or VMs in other clouds via MMA. When MMA communicates with a Log Analytics workspace with the Automation solution added, it will download the files you need to make the server a hybrid runbook worker.

The process to set up Azure Automation and add a server as a hybrid runbook worker is as follows:

1 Create an Azure Automation account.
2 Create a Log Analytics workspace.
3 Add the Automation Solution to the workspace.
4 Install the MMA on an on-premises server.
5 Connect the MMA to the Log Analytics workspace.
6 The MMA will download the hybrid runbook worker files and PowerShell module.
7 Use the hybrid runbook worker module to connect to the Azure Automation account.

Even if you are not planning to use hybrid runbook workers, setting a Log Analytics workspace is a good idea because you can forward the logs from your automations to it. This will give you the ability to search your job executions, outputs, and errors easily. Plus, it will allow you to create alerts for failed jobs or errors.

8.2.3 Creating Azure resources

Before you can do anything, you must first install the Azure PowerShell modules and connect to your Azure subscription.

There are several methods for connecting to Azure via PowerShell. You can have it prompt you to authenticate. You can pass a credential object to the command or use a service principal and certificate. For now, we just want to install the Azure modules and connect by having it prompt you.

To support this automation, you will need to create a Resource Group, Azure Automation account, Log Analytics workspace, and an Azure Storage account. Different resources have different naming requirements. For most Azure resources, the name can contain only letters, numbers, and hyphens. In addition, the name must start with a letter, and it must end with a letter or a number. And most have a length limit. For example, Log Analytics must be between 4 and 63 characters, and Azure Automation is 6–50. However, storage accounts present their own unique naming requirements.

A storage account's name must be 3–24 characters long and contain only lowercase letters and numbers. And, most important, the name must be unique across all existing storage account names in Azure—not *your* Azure but *all* of Azure. So, a little trick I've developed is to add a timestamp to the end of the name. Also, since all of these resources are being used for the same automation, you can give them all the same name—that is, as long as the name meets the requirements of the resource with the strictest standard. For the most current version of the Azure naming rules, refer to the Microsoft Docs page Naming Rules And Restrictions For Azure Resources (http://mng.bz/JV0Q).

You will also need to choose a region when setting up Azure resources. Some resources are only available in certain regions, and some have regional dependencies when interacting with other resources. For example, to link your Azure Automation account to a Log Analytics workspace, they need to be in compatible regions. Generally, this means that they are in the same region, but there are exceptions to this rule. For instance, you can only link Log Analytics in EastUS to Azure Automation in EastUS2. You can see a listing of compatible regions in table 8.1.

Table 8.1   Supported regions for linked Automation accounts and Log Analytics workspaces

Log Analytics workspace region	Azure Automation region
AustraliaEast	AustraliaEast
AustraliaSoutheast	AustraliaSoutheast
BrazilSouth	BrazilSouth
CanadaCentral	CanadaCentral
CentralIndia	CentralIndia
CentralUS	CentralUS
ChinaEast2	ChinaEast2
EastAsia	EastAsia
EastUS2	EastUS
EastUS	EastUS2
FranceCentral	FranceCentral
JapanEast	JapanEast
KoreaCentral	KoreaCentral
NorthCentralUS	NorthCentralUS
NorthEurope	NorthEurope
NorwayEast	NorwayEast
SouthCentralUS	SouthCentralUS
SoutheastAsia	SoutheastAsia

Table 8.1   Supported regions for linked Automation accounts and Log Analytics workspaces *(continued)*

Log Analytics workspace region	Azure Automation region
SwitzerlandNorth	SwitzerlandNorth
UAENorth	UAENorth
UKSouth	UKSouth
USGovArizona	USGovArizona
USGovVirginia	USGovVirginia
WestCentralUS	WestCentralUS
WestEurope	WestEurope
WestUS	WestUS
WestUS2	WestUS2

For the complete list of supported mappings, refer to the Microsoft Docs (http://mng .bz/wy6g).

NOTE   All code snippets in this section use PowerShell 7.

Go ahead and open a PowerShell console or VS Code, install the required Azure PowerShell modules, and import them to your local session:

```
Install-Module -Name Az
Install-Module -Name Az.MonitoringSolutions
Import-Module -Name Az,Az.MonitoringSolutions
```

Next, set the variables to use throughout this section. Feel free to change the values to whatever naming conventions you would like to use:

```
$SubscriptionId = 'The GUID of your Azure subscription'
$DateString = (Get-Date).ToString('yyMMddHHmm')
$ResourceGroupName = 'PoshAutomate'
$WorkspaceName = 'poshauto' + $DateString
$AutomationAccountName = 'poshauto' + $DateString
$StorageAccountName = 'poshauto' + $DateString
$AutomationLocation = 'SouthCentralUS'
$WorkspaceLocation = 'SouthCentralUS'
```

Then connect to your subscription:

```
Connect-AzAccount -Subscription $SubscriptionId
```

Now that you are connected to your Azure subscription, you can create your resources, starting with the resource group:

```
New-AzResourceGroup -Name $ResourceGroupName -Location $AutomationLocation
```

Then you can create the Log Analytics workspace, Azure Automation account, and Storage account inside the resource group:

```
$WorkspaceParams = @{
    ResourceGroupName = $ResourceGroupName
    Name              = $WorkspaceName
    Location          = $WorkspaceLocation
}
New-AzOperationalInsightsWorkspace @WorkspaceParams

$AzAutomationAccount = @{
    ResourceGroupName = $ResourceGroupName
    Name              = $AutomationAccountName
    Location          = $AutomationLocation
    Plan              = 'Basic'
}
New-AzAutomationAccount @AzAutomationAccount

$AzStorageAccount = @{
    ResourceGroupName = $ResourceGroupName
    AccountName       = $StorageAccountName
    Location          = $AutomationLocation
    SkuName           = 'Standard_LRS'
    AccessTier        = 'Cool'
}
New-AzStorageAccount @AzStorageAccount
```

You will also need to add the Azure Automation solution to the Log Analytics workspace. This is what will allow you to create hybrid runbook workers:

```
$WorkspaceParams = @{
    ResourceGroupName = $ResourceGroupName
    Name              = $WorkspaceName
}
$workspace = Get-AzOperationalInsightsWorkspace @WorkspaceParams

$AzMonitorLogAnalyticsSolution = @{
    Type                = 'AzureAutomation'
    ResourceGroupName   = $ResourceGroupName
    Location            = $workspace.Location
    WorkspaceResourceId = $workspace.ResourceId
}
New-AzMonitorLogAnalyticsSolution @AzMonitorLogAnalyticsSolution
```

8.2.4 *Authentication from Automation runbooks*

When you execute a runbook in Azure Automation, it does not by default have access to any other Azure resources. When Azure Automation executes the runbook on a hybrid runbook worker, it has access to the local system, but that is it. If you need your runbook to connect to different Azure resources or other local systems, you must set it up to do so.

To access Azure-based resources, you can create a managed identity. A managed identity is an Azure AD object that you can assign to the Automation account. Then, when your automation executes, it can run under the context of this managed identity. You can think of this as the equivalent to setting the run as account in a scheduled task or Cron job from chapter 3.

You can then give this identity permissions to any Azure resources just as you would with any user account. The best part about it is that there are no passwords or secrets required. You just assign it to the Automation account, and your runbooks can use it. We will discuss the security implications of this later in this chapter.

We will create a system-assigned managed identity for our automation and give it contributor access to the storage account:

```
$AzStorageAccount = @{
    ResourceGroupName = $ResourceGroupName
    AccountName       = $StorageAccountName
}
$storage = Get-AzStorageAccount @AzStorageAccount

$AzAutomationAccount = @{
    ResourceGroupName     = $ResourceGroupName
    AutomationAccountName = $AutomationAccountName
    AssignSystemIdentity  = $true
}
$Identity = Set-AzAutomationAccount @AzAutomationAccount

$AzRoleAssignment = @{
    ObjectId           = $Identity.Identity.PrincipalId
    Scope              = $storage.Id
    RoleDefinitionName = "Contributor"
}
New-AzRoleAssignment @AzRoleAssignment
```

8.2.5 Resource keys

Now that you have all the resources created, you need to get the variable and keys required to connect your local server to the Log Analytics workspace and Azure Automation account to make it a hybrid runbook worker. You will need the Log Analytics workspace ID and key and the Automation account's URL and key. Luckily, this is something we can get via PowerShell. After running this command, save the output, as you will need it to set up the hybrid runbook worker in the next section:

```
$InsightsWorkspace = @{
    ResourceGroupName = $ResourceGroupName
    Name              = $WorkspaceName
}
$Workspace = Get-AzOperationalInsightsWorkspace @InsightsWorkspace

$WorkspaceSharedKey = @{
    ResourceGroupName = $ResourceGroupName
    Name              = $WorkspaceName
}
$WorspaceKeys = Get-AzOperationalInsightsWorkspaceSharedKey
    @WorkspaceSharedKey
```

```
$AzAutomationRegistrationInfo = @{
    ResourceGroupName      = $ResourceGroupName
    AutomationAccountName = $AutomationAccountName
}
$AutomationReg = Get-AzAutomationRegistrationInfo
    @AzAutomationRegistrationInfo
@"
`$WorkspaceID = '$($Workspace.CustomerId)'
`$WorkSpaceKey = '$($WorspaceKeys.PrimarySharedKey)'
`$AutoURL = '$($AutomationReg.Endpoint)'
`$AutoKey = '$($AutomationReg.PrimaryKey)'
"@
```

8.3   *Creating a hybrid runbook worker*

Now that you have all the Azure resources created, you can create a hybrid runbook worker that will allow you to execute runbooks locally. To do this, you need to install MMA, link it to the Log Analytics workspace, and then link it to the Automation account.

Hybrid runbook workers can be Linux or Windows servers, but the following instructions are for a Windows-based server to not overcomplicate things. For Linux, the process is the same but with shell commands.

> **NOTE**   All code listings in this section must be run on the server on which you are making a hybrid runbook worker and will use Windows PowerShell 5.1.

On the server on which you want to make a hybrid runbook worker, open PowerShell ISE as an administrator. Then, add the workspace ID and key to the following listing to install the Log Analytics agent using PowerShell.

Listing 8.1   Install Microsoft Monitoring Agent

```
$WorkspaceID = 'YourId'              ⟵  Set the parameters for
$WorkSpaceKey = 'YourKey'                your workspace.

                                                          URL for the
                                                          agent installer
$agentURL = 'https://download.microsoft.com/download' +  ⟵
    '/3/c/d/3cd6f5b3-3fbe-43c0-88e0-8256d02db5b7/MMASetup-AMD64.exe'


$FileName = Split-Path $agentURL -Leaf                 ⟵
$MMAFile = Join-Path -Path $env:Temp -ChildPath $FileName   Download
Invoke-WebRequest -Uri $agentURL -OutFile $MMAFile | Out-Null   the agent.


$ArgumentList = '/C:"setup.exe /qn ' +     ⟵   Install the
    'ADD_OPINSIGHTS_WORKSPACE=0 ' +              agent.
    'AcceptEndUserLicenseAgreement=1"'
$Install = @{
    FilePath      = $MMAFile
    ArgumentList = $ArgumentList
    ErrorAction  = 'Stop'
}
Start-Process @Install -Wait | Out-Null
```

Load the agent config com object.

```
$Object = @{
    ComObject = 'AgentConfigManager.MgmtSvcCfg'
}
$AgentCfg = New-Object @Object

$AgentCfg.AddCloudWorkspace($WorkspaceID,
    $WorkspaceKey)

Restart-Service HealthService
```

Set the workspace ID and key.

Restart the agent for the changes to take effect.

Once the install completes, you will need to wait a couple of minutes for it to perform the initial sync. This initial sync will download the hybrid runbook worker files, allowing you to connect the local server to Azure Automation.

When creating hybrid runbook workers, you need to include a group name. The group allows you to create a pool of workers for load balancing and high availability. However, you have no control over which individual server in that group will execute a script. Therefore, if you need to execute a script on a specific server, you can use PowerShell remoting or put it in a hybrid worker group on its own.

In our scenario where we are copying a file from the local system to the cloud, it would make sense to create a single hybrid runbook worker so it can just go from the local system to the cloud. However, suppose the files are saved to a network share. In that case, you could create multiple hybrid runbooks workers in a single group where anyone could execute the runbook.

To create your hybrid runbook worker, add the Automation URL and key you retrieved earlier and run the following listing to link the local server with your Automation account.

Listing 8.2   Create a hybrid runbook worker

```
$AutoUrl = ''
$AutoKey = ''
$Group   = $env:COMPUTERNAME

$Path = 'HKLM:\SOFTWARE\Microsoft\System Center ' +
    'Operations Manager\12\Setup\Agent'
$installPath = Get-ItemProperty -Path $Path |
    Select-Object -ExpandProperty InstallDirectory
$AutomationFolder = Join-Path $installPath 'AzureAutomation'

$ChildItem = @{
    Path    = $AutomationFolder
    Recurse = $true
    Include = 'HybridRegistration.psd1'
}
$modulePath = Get-ChildItem @ChildItem |
    Select-Object -ExpandProperty FullName


Import-Module $modulePath
```

Set the parameters for your Automation account.

Find the directory the agent was installed in.

Search the folder for the HybridRegistration module.

Import the HybridRegistration module.

```
$HybridRunbookWorker = @{          ◄──┐   Register the local
    Url       = $AutoUrl              │   machine with the
    key       = $AutoKey              │   Automation account.
    GroupName = $Group                │
}
Add-HybridRunbookWorker @HybridRunbookWorker
```

8.3.1   *PowerShell modules on hybrid runbook workers*

When building your runbooks for use in Azure Automation, you have to be mindful of your module dependencies, especially when executing on a hybrid runbook worker. You can import modules to your automation account directly from the PowerShell gallery and even upload your own custom ones. These modules are automatically imported when your runbook executes in Azure. However, these modules do not transfer to your hybrid runbook workers. Therefore, you need to manually ensure that you have the correct module versions installed on the hybrid runbook workers.

For this automation, you will be uploading a file from the local file system to Azure Blob. Therefore, you will need the Az.Storage module installed on the hybrid runbook worker. This module is part of the default Az PowerShell module installation.

Also, when installing modules on the hybrid runbook worker, you must scope them to install for all users. Otherwise, your automation may not be able to find them:

```
Install-Module -Name Az -Scope AllUsers
```

8.4   *Creating a PowerShell runbook*

When creating a PowerShell runbook, you have two options. You can write the script locally using an IDE like VS Code or ISE and import it to the Automation account, or you can write it directly in the portal using the runbook editor. The advantage of the local development is that testing is much easier and quicker. The disadvantage is that there are some commands unique to Azure Automation for importing assets like credentials and variables. For this reason, I recommend using a hybrid approach. You can develop the script locally to get all the functionality working, then transfer it to Azure Automation, and update it to use any assets you need.

To see how this works, you will build the script for uploading the archive files to Azure Blob storage locally. Then, you will import it to the Automation account and update it to use the managed identity.

Since the purpose of this chapter is to show you how to use Azure Automation and not all the ins and outs of Azure Blob storage, the script I provide in listing 8.3 is relatively simple. It will check a folder for ZIP files, upload them to the Azure Blob, and then delete them from the local system. Figure 8.3 illustrates the process. I have also included the script New-TestArchiveFile.ps1 in the Helper Scripts for this chapter that you can use to make some test ZIP files.

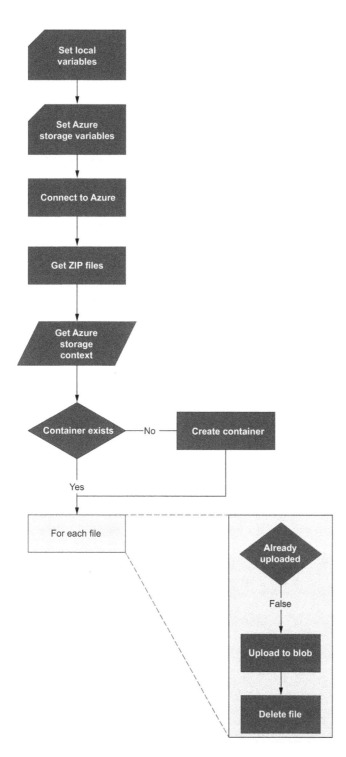

Figure 8.3 ZIP file upload
process when running locally

As with any cloud-based automation, the first thing we need to do is connect to the account. For testing, you can use the `Connect-AzAccount` cmdlet without any credentials or other authentication parameters. This will cause it to prompt you to authenticate manually. You will change this to automate the authentication once it is imported as a runbook.

To upload to Azure Storage, you must create a context object using a storage account key. The Azure Storage cmdlets use this context to authenticate with the storage account. You can create all sorts of different keys with different permissions. By default, there will be two keys with full permissions. We will use one of these for this automation.

Next, you need a container to put the files in, similar to a folder on the local file system. You can use different containers for organizing files and also for controlling access for different files. Then, finally, the script will check whether the file already exists in Azure, and if not, it will upload it and then delete it.

You may notice here that we are not doing any checks before deleting the file. That is because the `Set-AzStorageBlobContent` cmdlet has built-in hash checks. Therefore, if something goes wrong during the upload process, it will return an error. You can then stop the removal by having the execution terminate if there is an error.

NOTE Listing 8.3 should be created and tested on the hybrid runbook worker using Windows PowerShell 5.1.

Listing 8.3   Upload ZIP files to Azure Blob

```
$FolderPath = 'L:\Archives'    ⟵──── Set the local variables.
$Container = 'devtest'

$ResourceGroupName = 'PoshAutomate'    ⟵─┐ Set the Azure
$StorageAccountName = ''                   │ Storage variables.
$SubscriptionID = ''

Connect-AzAccount    ⟵──────────┐ Connect to Azure.
Set-AzContext -Subscription $SubscriptionID

$ChildItem = @{    ⟵──────┐ Get all the ZIP
    Path   = $FolderPath   │ files in the folder.
    Filter = '*.zip'
}
$ZipFiles = Get-ChildItem @ChildItem

$AzStorageAccountKey = @{    ⟵──────────┐ Get the storage keys and
    ResourceGroupName = $ResourceGroupName │ create a context object that
    Name              = $StorageAccountName │ will be used to authenticate
}                                            │ with the storage account.
$Keys = Get-AzStorageAccountKey @AzStorageAccountKey
$AzStorageContext = @{
    StorageAccountName = $StorageAccountName
    StorageAccountKey  = $Keys[0].Value
```

```
}
$Context = New-AzStorageContext @AzStorageContext

$AzStorageContainer = @{
    Name        = $Container
    Context     = $Context
    ErrorAction = 'SilentlyContinue'
}
$containerCheck = Get-AzStorageContainer @AzStorageContainer
if(-not $containerCheck){
    $AzStorageContainer = @{
        Name        = $Container
        Context     = $Context
        ErrorAction = 'Stop'
    }
    New-AzStorageContainer @AzStorageContainer| Out-Null
}

foreach($file in $ZipFiles){
    $AzStorageBlob = @{
        Container   = $container
        Blob        = $file.Name
        Context     = $Context
        ErrorAction = 'SilentlyContinue'
    }
    $blobCheck = Get-AzStorageBlob @AzStorageBlob
    if (-not $blobCheck) {
        $AzStorageBlobContent = @{
            File        = $file.FullName
            Container   = $Container
            Blob        = $file.Name
            Context     = $Context
            Force       = $true
            ErrorAction = 'Stop'
        }
        Set-AzStorageBlobContent @AzStorageBlobContent
        Remove-Item -Path $file.FullName -Force
    }
}
```

Check to see whether the container exists. If it does not, create it.

Check whether the file already exists in the container. If not, upload it, and then delete it from the local server.

Upload the file to Azure storage.

After successfully testing the script, you can save it as a ps1 file and upload it to Azure Automation:

```
$AzAutomationRunbook = @{
    Path                  = 'C:\Path\Upload-ZipToBlob.ps1'
    ResourceGroupName     = $ResourceGroupName
    AutomationAccountName = $AutomationAccountName
    Type                  = 'PowerShell'
    Name                  = 'Upload-ZipToBlob'
    Force                 = $true
}
$import = Import-AzAutomationRunbook @AzAutomationRunbook
```

Go ahead and run the New-TestArchiveFile.ps1 script again on the hybrid runbook worker to make a new ZIP file for testing through Azure.

8.4.1 Automation assets

When testing the ZIP file upload script, we hardcoded the values required for connecting to the storage account. Instead of hardcoding those values into the script, you can convert them to variables in the Azure Automation account.

Making them variables gives you the ability to share them among other runbooks in the same account. This is great for things like the storage account and subscription IDs where you could have multiple different automations using the same resource. Then, if you later change the storage account or want to reuse this same runbook in another subscription, all you need to do is update the variables. But, at the same time, this can be a double-edged sword because changing one variable can affect multiple different runbooks.

Also, don't be afraid of using descriptive names for your variable. It will save you a lot of guessing in the long run. For example, for this automation, instead of making a variable named `ResourceGroup`, make it descriptive, like `ZipStorage_Resource-Group`. This way, you know it is the resource group for the Zip Storage automation.

Azure Automation also provides the ability to encrypt your variables. You can do this in the portal or through PowerShell by setting the `Encrypted` argument to `true`. As we will discuss later with the security considerations, there are different permission levels in Azure Automation. Therefore, if someone has read access to the Automation account, they can see the value of unencrypted variables in plain text. While variables may not be as sensitive as passwords, they can hold sensitive data like connection strings or API keys. So, to prevent accidentally having sensitive data in plain text, I recommend encrypting all variables. Go ahead and create variables for the subscription, resource group, and storage account:

```
$AutoAcct = @{
    ResourceGroupName     = $ResourceGroupName
    AutomationAccountName = $AutomationAccountName
    Encrypted             = $true
}
$Variable = @{
    Name  = 'ZipStorage_AccountName'
    Value = $StorageAccountName
}
New-AzAutomationVariable @AutoAcct @Variable

$Variable = @{
    Name  = 'ZipStorage_SubscriptionID'
    Value = $SubscriptionID
}
New-AzAutomationVariable @AutoAcct @Variable

$Variable = @{
    Name  = 'ZipStorage_ResourceGroup'
    Value = $ResourceGroupName
}
New-AzAutomationVariable @AutoAcct @Variable
```

8.4.2   Runbook Editor

Now that you have your variables created, you need to tell your script about them. To do this, navigate to the Azure portal and your Automation account. Select Runbooks from the left menu and then click on the runbook named Upload-ZipToBlob. When the runbook loads, click the Edit button to open the runbook editor.

This runbook editor works just like any other IDE or development editor. It has autocomplete suggestions and syntax highlighting. But on top of that, it can insert assets stored in the Automation account. If you expand Assets > Variables in the left menu, you will see the variables you just created.

> **NOTE**   All remaining code snippets and listings are using the Runbook Editor in Azure Automation.

Starting with the $SubscriptionID variable, remove the value set in the script so that the line is just $SubscriptionID =. Place the cursor after the equals sign, click the ellipsis next to ZipStorage_SubscriptionID, and select Add Get Variable to Canvas. The line should now look like this:

```
$SubscriptionID = Get-AutomationVariable -Name 'ZipStorage_SubscriptionID'
```

Repeat this same process with the resource group and storage account name variables, as shown in figure 8.4. Next, you can convert the $FolderPath and $Container variables to parameters.

One final thing to do is to have the script authenticate with Azure. Since you are using a managed identity, there is no need to add credential assets or pass secrets to the runbook. Instead, you can connect to Azure as the managed identity by adding the -Identity switch to the Connect-AzAccount cmdlet.

Now, the final version of the runbook should look like the following listing.

Listing 8.4   Upload-ZipToBlob

```
param(
    [Parameter(Mandatory = $true)]
    [string]$FolderPath,
    [Parameter(Mandatory = $true)]
    [string]$Container
)
                                                        Get the Azure
                                                        Storage variables.
$SubscriptionID = Get-AutomationVariable `        ⟵┘
    -Name 'ZipStorage_SubscriptionID'
$ResourceGroupName = Get-AutomationVariable -Name 'ZipStorage_ResourceGroup'
$StorageAccountName = Get-AutomationVariable -Name 'ZipStorage_AccountName'

Connect-AzAccount -Identity              ⟵————— Connect to Azure.
Set-AzContext -Subscription $SubscriptionID
```

```
$ChildItem = @{                          ◄────┐  Get all the ZIP files
    Path   = $FolderPath                       │  in the folder.
    Filter = '*.zip'
}
$ZipFiles = Get-ChildItem @ChildItem
                                             ┌─────  Get the storage keys and
$AzStorageAccountKey = @{            ◄───────┤       create a context object that
    ResourceGroupName = $ResourceGroupName    │       will be used to authenticate
    Name              = $StorageAccountName   │       with the storage account.
}
$Keys = Get-AzStorageAccountKey @AzStorageAccountKey
$AzStorageContext = @{
    StorageAccountName = $StorageAccountName
    StorageAccountKey  = $Keys[0].Value
}
$Context = New-AzStorageContext @AzStorageContext


$AzStorageContainer = @{      ◄──────┐  Check to see whether
    Name        = $Container          │  the container exists. If
    Context     = $Context            │  it does not, create it.
    ErrorAction = 'SilentlyContinue'
}
$containerCheck = Get-AzStorageContainer @AzStorageContainer
if(-not $containerCheck){
    $AzStorageContainer = @{
        Name        = $Container
        Context     = $Context
        ErrorAction = 'Stop'
    }
    New-AzStorageContainer @AzStorageContainer| Out-Null
}
                                     ┌──  Check whether the file
                                     │    already exists in the
foreach($file in $ZipFiles){         │    container. If not, upload
    $AzStorageBlob = @{      ◄────────┤    it, and then delete it
        Container   = $container      │    from the local server.
        Blob        = $file.Name
        Context     = $Context
        ErrorAction = 'SilentlyContinue'
    }
    $blobCheck = Get-AzStorageBlob @AzStorageBlob
    if (-not $blobCheck) {
        $AzStorageBlobContent = @{    ◄────┐  Upload the file
            File        = $file.FullName    │  to Azure Storage.
            Container   = $Container
            Blob        = $file.Name
            Context     = $Context
            Force       = $true
            ErrorAction = 'Stop'
        }
        Set-AzStorageBlobContent @AzStorageBlobContent
        Remove-Item -Path $file.FullName -Force
    }
}
```

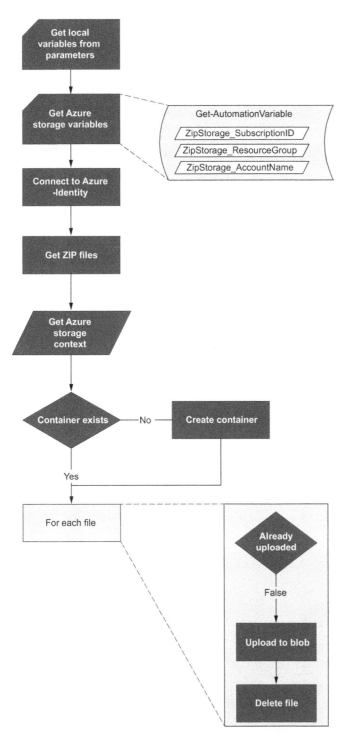

Figure 8.4   ZIP file upload process when running through Automation hybrid worker runbook

Once you have the updates done to the script, it is time to test it. Click the Test Pane button. In the test pane, you can test the execution of the script. First, enter the values for the folder path and container name parameters. Then, under Run Settings, select Hybrid Worker and select the server you set up earlier. Then, click Start.

Since you selected the hybrid runbook worker, it will execute on that server and should behave just as it did when you ran it earlier. If the test runs successfully, check the storage account to confirm the file was uploaded.

Then, back in the runbook editor, close the test pane, and click Publish. When you do this, your runbook is available to anyone with permission to execute it. From this main runbook screen, you can manually execute a runbook or create a recurring schedule for it. You can also make additional edits and use the tester without affecting the published version until you click the Publish button again.

Go ahead and run the New-TestArchiveFile.ps1 on the hybrid runbook worker server to make a new test file. Then, from the Upload-ZipToBlob runbook in the Azure portal, click Start. You will see the input fields shown in figure 8.5. Enter the same parameter values, select your hybrid worker, and click OK.

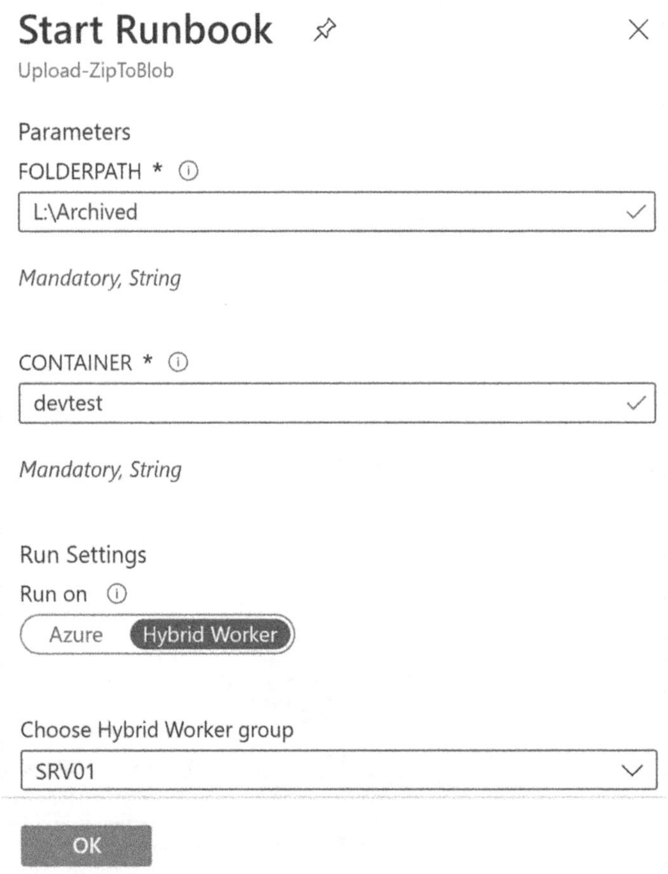

Start Runbook 📌   ✕

Upload-ZipToBlob

Parameters

FOLDERPATH * ⓘ

| L:\Archived | ✓ |

Mandatory, String

CONTAINER * ⓘ

| devtest | ✓ |

Mandatory, String

Run Settings

Run on ⓘ

(Azure **Hybrid Worker**)

Choose Hybrid Worker group

| SRV01 | ⌄ |

OK

Figure 8.5   Starting an Azure Automation runbook with parameters and on a hybrid runbook worker

This will execute the runbook and open the job screen. From the job screen, you can view all the execution details, including the hybrid worker used, the parameters, the output, and any errors or warnings. This data is retained in the portal for 30 days after execution.

8.4.3   Runbook output

I mentioned earlier that you can take any PowerShell script and import it to Azure Automation as a runbook. While this is true, there are a few commands that do not work in Azure Automation runbooks. Two of the most common ones are `Write-Host` and `Write-Progress`.

You can still include `Write-Host` and `Write-Progress` in your scripts; just know that since there is no console, they will not produce any output. To show data in the Output section of the runbook, it must be written to the output stream using `Write-Output`. Therefore, it is usually best to convert any `Write-Host` commands to `Write-Output` when making a runbook. Since there is no other equivalent to `Write-Progress`, it would be best to remove this command from the script.

Also, verbose logging is off by default. So, if you have any `Write-Verbose` commands in your script, it will not display in the logs unless you specifically turn on verbose logging in the runbook settings, as shown in figure 8.6.

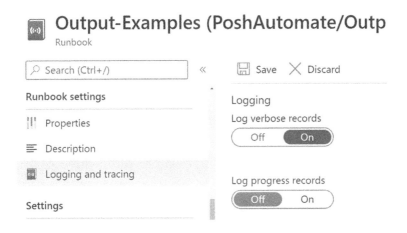

Figure 8.6   Enable verbose logging for an Azure Automation runbook.

Once you do this, the verbose logs will show in the All Logs section of the runbook job. But be careful because verbose logging can slow down the execution of your runbooks, so only use it when needed, and then turn it back off.

You can see how the different outputs work by importing the Output-Examples.ps1 script from the Helper Scripts folder as a runbook and executing it. Figure 8.7 shows an example.

Output-Examples 7/15/2022, 8:45 AM ···
Job   ● Directory:

▷ Resume   ☐ Stop || Suspend   ○ Refresh

Errors   Warnings

1 ●   1 ⚠

Type : **Any**

🔍 Search logs...

Time	Type	Details
7/15/2022, 8:45:57 AM	▷ Output	Write-Output shows in the All Logs and Output tabs
7/15/2022, 8:45:57 AM	● Verbose	Write-Verbose only shows in All Logs when it is turned on
7/15/2022, 8:45:57 AM	⚠ Warning	Write-Warning shows in the All Logs and Warnings tabs
7/15/2022, 8:45:57 AM	✗ Error	Write-Error does shows in the All Logs and Errors tabs
7/15/2022, 8:45:58 AM	▷ Output	Writing directly to the stream works, but can be unreliable. It is best to use Write-Output

Figure 8.7   Azure Automation runbook output example

8.4.4   Interactive Cmdlets

As with most automation situations, you cannot have cmdlets that require interactive input in your runbooks. For example, Read-Host will not work because there is no way to interact with the runbook other than entering parameters.

You can also run into issues with cmdlets that have interactive logins. For example, the Add-AzAccount cmdlet will prompt for credentials if none are provided. The runbooks can often detect these and terminate the execution rather than hang and wait for input that will never come. However, this does not work all the time. So, to be safe, if you have a cmdlet that could prompt for user interaction, it is best to test and confirm that the way you are using it will not cause a user prompt to appear.

8.5   Security considerations

Like with any other automation platform, you need to be aware of the security implications of both what the automations can do and what data is stored in it. For instance, you just created a managed identity and assigned it permissions to a storage account. Now, any person with permissions to create runbooks in that Automation account can use that managed identity in their scripts. The same goes for any variables, credentials, and certificates you store in that account. However, there are a few things you can do to help protect your environment.

In Azure Automation, there are multiple different levels of permissions that you can assign to users. One of these is the Automation Operator. This role will allow someone to execute a runbook, but they cannot create, edit, or delete one. A good use case for this is a runbook that performs maintenance tasks on a VM that requires elevated permissions. You can assign those permissions to the managed identity and then give the people who need to execute it the Automation Operator role. They will now only be able to perform what your runbook can perform and not edit or create any custom automations. Also, they don't even need permissions to the individual VMs as it will run as the managed identity.

The cloud offers the awesome ability to create new instances of items in seconds. Therefore, you should create a separate development Automation account that you can point to other development resources. Have your team build and test their runbooks there. Then, once you are ready, you can move them to your production account with stricter controls and permissions.

Summary

- Azure Automation can execute PowerShell scripts serverless in Azure or on a hybrid runbook worker in your local environment.
- Log Analytics with the Automation solution is required to support hybrid runbook workers.
- You can securely store variables, credentials, and certificates in Azure Automation.
- You can develop and test your PowerShell scripts outside of Azure Automation and then import the ps1 file as a runbook.
- If someone has permission to create a runbook in an Automation account, they have access to all the assets, including credentials and managed identities stored in that account.

Working outside
of PowerShell

While PowerShell is a very robust language with multiple different integrations and custom modules, there are still some situations in which you need to work with something outside of PowerShell. This can range from calling separate executables to remote API calls and interacting directly with Component Object Module (COM) objects and Dynamic Link Library (DLL) files. As you will see, PowerShell has specially built cmdlets to deal with each one of these situations.

In this chapter, you will learn how to interact with different resources to solve one of the biggest problems in IT: system documentation (or the lack thereof). You will create a script that will populate a Word document using the Word COM object. You will then use PowerShell to gather information about your local computer and enter that data in the Word document.

Then, taking it further, you will use a remote REST API to get your external IP address and location information for the document. Then, finally, you will call a Python script to create a time-series graph that you can insert into the document. The process is illustrated in figure 9.1.

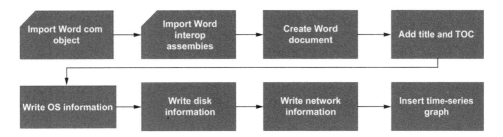

Figure 9.1   Write computer information to a Word document automation flow

Having good documentation of your systems is critical for a business. Not only does it help with accountability, but it also helps with disaster recovery. By utilizing Power-Shell, you can ensure that you have good documentation that all follows the same formatting and is easy to generate and maintain. It could save you days' worth of work if you ever need to rebuild an environment. Also, the things shown here aren't only for documenting system builds. They can be used for any data that you want to put into a defined and clean format.

> **NOTE**   The code in this chapter requires that you have Microsoft Office Word installed locally. You will also need Python 3.8 with the pandas and Matplotlib libraries for section 9.4 (Python 3.9 or newer should work as well but has not been tested). There is a script in the Helper Script folder for setting up Python if you do not have it installed.

9.1   *Using COM objects and .NET Framework*

As you have already seen numerous times throughout this book, you can call native .NET classes directly in PowerShell. However, we will now look at how you can use nonnative frameworks and objects in PowerShell using the `New-Object` cmdlet.

The `New-Object` cmdlet allows you to create a PowerShell object using a .NET Framework class (often stored in DLL files) or a ProgID (Programmatic Identifier) of a COM object. When you output this command to a PowerShell variable, it creates an instance of that object that you can use in your script. Typically, this is done using the methods associated with the object.

> **ProgID**
>
> The ProgID, or Programmatic Identifier, of a COM object is not the same as a process ID. The ProgID is a string that represents the CLSID (Class ID) of an application. This allows you to use a simple name instead of looking up or memorizing the GUID of the CLSID. For example, Outlook has a ProgID `Outlook.Application` which represents the CLSID of {0006F03A-0000-0000-C000-000000000046}.

.NET and, by extension, PowerShell objects contain different members. The two you are probably most familiar with are properties and methods. Properties represent the data associated with the object, and methods are the actions the object can perform. Thus, you can think of methods as similar to functions, just with a different syntax for invoking.

9.1.1   Importing Word objects

In this automation, you want to interact with Microsoft Word. The COM object ProgID for Microsoft Word is `Word.Application`. You can create an instance of this in PowerShell by using the `New-Object` cmdlet and the ProgID:

```
$Word = New-Object -ComObject Word.Application
```

In some cases, this is all you will need to do. However, in addition to the Word COM object, you will want to import the Microsoft Office Interop object for Word. Using the Office interop object helps to simplify some of the interactions with the Word COM object. The Office interop is installed by default when you install Office, and it is stored in the Global Assembly Cache (GAC).

   If you are using Windows PowerShell 5.1, these can be called using just the name of the interop, as in the previous snippet. However, with PowerShell 7 using .NET Core, you need to supply the full path to the DLLs. Fortunately, you can use the `Get-ChildItem` cmdlet to search the GAC to find the assemblies you need and then load them into your current session using the `Add-Type` cmdlet:

```
$GAC = Join-Path $env:WINDIR 'assembly\GAC_MSIL'
Get-ChildItem -Path $GAC -Recurse -Include
➥ 'Microsoft.Office.Interop.Word.dll','office.dll' |
Foreach-Object{
    Add-Type -Path $_.FullName
}
```

9.1.2   Creating a Word document

Now that you have the Word objects imported into your current session, you can create your document. To do that, you first need to determine which methods and properties are needed. And, fortunately, PowerShell has a great way to help you do that. If you pipe the Word COM object in PowerShell to the `Get-Member` cmdlet, you will be able to see all the different properties and methods available:

```
$Word | Get-Member
Name                           MemberType           Definition
----                           ----------           ----------
Activate                       Method               void Activate ()
AddAddress                     Method               void AddAddress ()
AutomaticChange                Method               void AutomaticChange ()
BuildKeyCode                   Method               int BuildKeyCode (WdKey..
CentimetersToPoints            Method               float CentimetersToPoints ()
ChangeFileOpenDirectory        Method               void ChangeFileOpenDirectory
CheckGrammar                   Method               bool CheckGrammar (string..
...
ActiveDocument                 Property             Document ActiveDocument ()
ActiveEncryptionSession        Property             int ActiveEncryptionSession
ActivePrinter                  Property             string ActivePrinter (){get}
ActiveWindow                   Property             Window ActiveWindow () {get}
AddIns                         Property             AddIns AddIns () {get}
...
```

Right now, we are only concerned with three properties: Visible, Documents, and Selection. Visible is whether the Word application is actually open on your local screen. If you set Visible to true, you will see the data being written to the document as we go along. However, you need to create or open a document before you can see anything.

Since you are creating a new document, you can simply use the Add method on the Document property. This will create a new document instance in the Word COM object that you will reference in your code.

Then, finally, setting the Selection property will let the code know where to put the data you want to insert. Think of it as where the cursor is. If you run the following snippet, you should see Word open and a new document created. It will also set the selection area to the top of the document since it is a blank document:

```
$Word = New-Object -ComObject Word.Application
$Word.Visible = $True
$Document = $Word.Documents.Add()
$Selection = $Word.Selection
```

9.1.3   Writing to a Word document

Now that you have a Word document created and the selection set to a variable, you can use the properties and methods to add data to your document. To start, you can use the Style property to set the style of the paragraph. Then, use the TypeText() method to add your text, followed by the TypeParagraph() method to start the next paragraph. As you saw in the Get-Member output, most of the methods in this object are named with logical names. You can find the parameters required for each method by using the Get-Member cmdlet again and examining the output:

```
$Selection | Get-Member -Name TypeText, TypeParagraph
   TypeName: System.__ComObject#{00020975-0000-0000-c000-000000000046}
```

```
Name             MemberType  Definition
----             ----------  ----------
TypeText         Method      void TypeText (string Text)
TypeParagraph    Method      void TypeParagraph ()
```

For the `TypeText()` method, you just need to pass in any string value. This string can be a hardcoded string, a string returned from a command, or a variable. The `Type-Paragraph()` method does not require any input and is the equivalent of pressing Enter while typing in a document. You can test this yourself by using the following snippet to enter a title for the document:

```
$Selection.Style = 'Title'
$Selection.TypeText("$([system.environment]::MachineName) - System Document")
$Selection.TypeParagraph()
```

When each method in the previous snippet executes, it updates the selection variable with the location of the cursor. Similar to how your cursor moves as you type, this works just fine when you are adding text line by line. However, there are times when you will want to use a range. A range can represent any part of the document, unlike the selection, which is only the cursor's current position. Ranges work well because they allow you to select multiple spots simultaneously and are not affected by the cursor location. For instance, if I moved the cursor back to the top of the document and used the `TypeText()` method again, it would enter the text before the title. However, if I set the range to the selection and then move the cursor, the range location will not change. Also, methods that create objects will require ranges and not selection—for example, adding a table of contents or a table.

9.1.4 *Adding tables to a Word document*

To add a table to a selection or range, you can use the `Add()` method on the `Tables` property. First, however, you need to know what parameters are required for the `Add()` method. Unfortunately, if you use the `Get-Member` cmdlet to list the methods or the `Table` property, it will give you an error saying, "You must specify an object for the Get-Member cmdlet." This is because there is no table yet, and the `Get-Member` cmdlet cannot be used with `null` properties. So, how can you figure out what properties you need to supply the `Add()` method?

The first method is to read the documentation. For instance, you can find all the information you need at the Microsoft Doc site for the Word object model (https://mng.bz/qoDz). However, not all objects are as well documented as products like Microsoft Office are. In those cases, you can view the `PSObject` property, which exists for all PowerShell objects. The `PSObject` property lists all the methods and properties, similar to `Get-Member`, but without needing the object to contain any data. If you run the following command, you can see the parameters required for the `Add()` method:

```
$Selection.Tables.psobject.methods

OverloadDefinitions
-------------------
Table Item (int Index)
Table AddOld (Range Range, int NumRows, int NumColumns)
Table Add (Range Range, int NumRows, int NumColumns, Variant
  DefaultTableBehavior, Variant AutoFitBehavior)
```

As you can see, the `Add()` method requires a range, which we already discussed, and then the number of rows and columns. The next two arguments, `DefaultTable-Behavior` and `AutoFitBehavior`, are listed as variants. Since a variant can represent any other data type, you will need to refer to the documentation to see what these object types need to be. In this case, both are enumerators, or Enums. An Enum is a set of named constants with an associated integer. For instance, the `AutoFitBehavior` Enum has three different options, as shown in table 9.1.

Table 9.1 `WdAutoFitBehavior` **Enum**

Enum	Int	Description
wdAutoFitContent	1	The table is automatically sized to fit the content contained in the table.
wdAutoFitFixed	0	The table is set to a fixed size, regardless of the content, and is not automatically sized.
wdAutoFitWindow	2	The table is automatically sized to the width of the active window.

On the back end, the computer only cares about the integer value. However, using Enums creates a level of abstraction, allowing you to use easily identifiable names instead of remembering which value is associated with which integer. So, now all you need to do is identify the corresponding Enum and add it to your command.

All the Enums for Office are in the Office Interop DLLs you imported earlier. Therefore, you can enter the full path of the Enum class between square brackets, followed by two colons and then the name of the Enum value. For example, to use the `wdAutoFit-Fixed` Enum in the `WdAutoFitBehavior` Enum, you would enter the following:

```
[Microsoft.Office.Interop.Word.WdAutoFitBehavior]::wdAutoFitContent
```

The best part about using the Enums like this is that you do not have to memorize them or look them up if you want to change the behavior. Instead, you can simply call the `GetEnumValues()` method on the Enum object to get a list of the values you can use:

```
[Microsoft.Office.Interop.Word.WdAutoFitBehavior].GetEnumValues() |
    Select-Object @{l='Name';e={$_}}, @{l='value';e={$_.value__}}
          Name Value
          ---- -----
    wdAutoFitFixed       0
  wdAutoFitContent       1
  wdAutoFitWindow        2
```

> ### WdAutoFitBehavior vs AutoFitBehavior
>
> You may have noticed that the Add method on the Table property showed the fields as `AutoFitBehavior` and `DefaultTableBehavior`. However, the Enums themselves start with a `Wd` prefix, which stands for Word. You will see similar naming conventions with the other Office products, like `Xl` for Excel or `Ol` for Outlook. Unfortunately, there is no standard across the industry, so you will need to check the documentation for any other products you are interfacing with.

Now, you can put it all together and create a table at the current selection position:

```
$Table = $Selection.Tables.add($Word.Selection.Range, 3, 2,
   [Microsoft.Office.Interop.Word.WdDefaultTableBehavior]::wdWord9TableBehavior,
   [Microsoft.Office.Interop.Word.WdAutoFitBehavior]::wdAutoFitContent)
```

Then, to fill in the data for the table, you call the `Cell()` method and supply the row and column you want to update. Go ahead and test it out with the table you just created:

```
$Table.Cell(1,1).Range.Text = 'First Cell'
$Table.Cell(3,2).Range.Text = 'Last Cell'
```

9.2   *Building tables from a PowerShell object*

Now that you know how to make tables, let's look at how we can automatically fill one out using the data from a PowerShell object, as shown in figure 9.2.

```
PS C:\> Get-CimInstance -ClassName Win32_OperatingSystem | Select-Object Caption,
InstallDate, ServicePackMajorVersion, OSArchitecture, BootDevice, BuildNumber,
CSName, @{l='Total Memory';e={[math]::Round($_.TotalVisibleMemorySize/1MB)}} |
Format-List


Caption                 : Microsoft Windows 11 Enterprise
InstallDate             : 10/21/2021 5:09:00 PM
ServicePackMajorVersion : 0
OSArchitecture          : 64-bit
BootDevice              : \Device\HarddiskVolume3
BuildNumber             : 22000
CSName                  : MYPC
Total Memory            : 32
```

Caption	Microsoft Windows 11 Enterprise
InstallDate	10/21/2021 5:09:00 PM
ServicePackMajorVersion	0
OSArchitecture	64-bit
BootDevice	\Device\HarddiskVolume3
BuildNumber	22000
CSName	MYPC
Total Memory	32

Figure 9.2   Operating system data displayed in a two-column table

First, we can gather information about the operating system and write the results to a single table with two columns. The first column will be the property name, and the second column will be the value. This is similar to the output you would see when you pipe to the Format-List cmdlet at the end of a PowerShell command.

Then, create another table with the disk space information for the computer. Since there can be multiple disks on any given machine, we need to make this dynamic so the correct number of rows is added. As you can see in figure 9.3, this is similar to the output you would see when you pipe to the Format-Table cmdlet at the end of a Power-Shell command.

```
PS C:\> Get-CimInstance -Class Win32_LogicalDisk | Select-Object
DeviceId, @{l='Size';e={[Math]::Round($_.Size / 1GB, 2)}}, @
{l='FreeSpace';e={[Math]::Round($_.FreeSpace / 1GB, 2)}} |
Format-Table

DeviceId   Size FreeSpace
--------   ---- ---------

C:        930.9    747.35
D:         1863    720.74
E:       931.51    114.38
```

DeviceId	Size	FreeSpace
C:	930.9	747.35
D:	1863	720.74
E:	931.51	114.38

Figure 9.3 Disk space data displayed in a dynamically created table

To accomplish this, we will make two different functions. One, named New-WordTableFromObject, will create the two-column table with the properties and values. The other function, New-WordTableFromArray, will be able to handle a dynamic range of columns and rows.

9.2.1 Converting PowerShell objects to tables

Let's start with getting the data to send to the New-WordTableFromObject function by gathering data from the Win32_OperatingSystem WMI class:

```
$OperatingSystem = Get-CimInstance -ClassName Win32_OperatingSystem |
Select-Object Caption, InstallDate, ServicePackMajorVersion, OSArchitecture,
  BootDevice,  BuildNumber, CSName,
  @{l='Total Memory';e={[math]::Round($_.TotalVisibleMemorySize/1MB)}}
```

To help build and populate the data in Word, we will again use the PsObject property—except this time, you are going to use the subproperty of Properties. If you save the value of $object.PsObject.Properties to a variable, you can then use that variable to determine the number of rows and the value of the first column. The nice thing about using the PsObject properties as opposed to the Get-Member is that the PsObject is in the order that you see on the screen, whereas the Get-Member will automatically alphabetize the properties.

Once you have the properties, you can create the table by setting the rows to the count of the properties. Then, use a for statement to loop through each property to populate the first column with the name and the second column with the value, as shown in figure 9.4. Finally, once your table is populated, add a paragraph break at the end so that you can start the next part of your document.

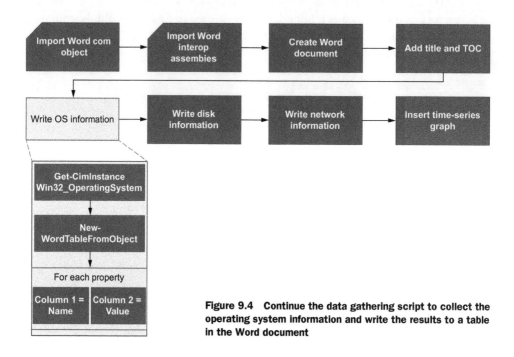

Figure 9.4   Continue the data gathering script to collect the operating system information and write the results to a table in the Word document

Listing 9.1   New-WordTableFromObject

```
Function New-WordTableFromObject {
    [CmdletBinding()]
    [OutputType()]
    param(
        [Parameter(Mandatory = $true)]
        [object]$object
    )

    $Properties = @($object.psobject.Properties)          Get the
                                                          properties of
                                                          the object.

    $Table = $Selection.Tables.add(        Create
    $Word.Selection.Range,                 the table.
    $Properties.Count,
    2,
[Microsoft.Office.Interop.Word.WdDefaultTableBehavior]::wdWord9TableBehavior
    , [Microsoft.Office.Interop.Word.WdAutoFitBehavior]::wdAutoFitContent
    )
```

```
    for ($r = 0; $r -lt $Properties.Count; $r++) {
        $Table.Cell($r + 1, 1).Range.Text =
        $Properties[$r].Name.ToString()
        $Table.Cell($r + 1, 2).Range.Text =
        $Properties[$r].Value.ToString()
    }

    $Word.Selection.Start = $Document.Content.End
    $Selection.TypeParagraph()
}
```

Loop through each
property, adding it
and the value to
the table.

Add a paragraph
after the table.

You can test this using the following command to collect the operating system data and send it to the function:

```
$OperatingSystem = Get-CimInstance -Class Win32_OperatingSystem |
    Select-Object Caption, InstallDate, ServicePackMajorVersion,
    OSArchitecture, BootDevice, BuildNumber, CSName,
    @{l='Total Memory';e={[math]::Round($_.TotalVisibleMemorySize/1MB)}}
New-WordTableFromObject $OperatingSystem
```

9.2.2 Converting PowerShell arrays to tables

The next table will be structured in a more traditional manner with a header row followed by data rows. You will need to build the function to use a dynamic value for the rows and the columns to do this.

Once again, you are going to create a variable with the values from the PsObject .Properties—except this time, you are going to use the count to set the number of columns. The number of rows will be the number of objects in your array, plus 1 for the header.

You will also need to take into consideration that the object, in this case, is an array. This means that if you simply put $object.psobject.Properties like before, you will get the properties for each and every iteration in the array. So, if you have three iterations in the array, you will end up with three of each header. To prevent this, you can use the Select-Object with the argument -First 1 to only return the properties from the first entry in the array.

After the table is created, use a single for statement to populate the header. Then, you will need to create another for statement to populate the data for each row. This second for statement will need to have a third nested for statement inside it to loop through each column in the row. Think about it like you are moving one cell at a time across and then going to the start of the next line and moving across. Figure 9.5 illustrates the process.

Then, just like before, you'll add a paragraph break at the end to continue your document.

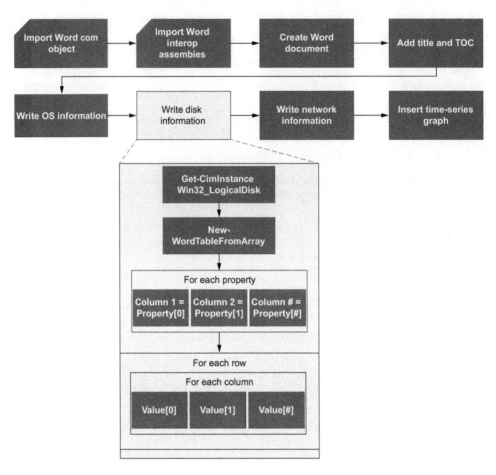

Figure 9.5   Continue the data gathering script to get disk information and write to a table in the Word document.

Listing 9.2 `New-WordTableFromArray`

```
Function New-WordTableFromArray{
    [CmdletBinding()]
    [OutputType()]
    param(
        [Parameter(Mandatory = $true)]
        [object]$object
    )

    $columns = $object | Select-Object -First 1 |           ⮜  Get the name of
    Select-Object -Property @{l='Name';e={$_.psobject.Properties.Name}} |   the columns.
    Select-Object -ExpandProperty Name

    $Table = $Selection.Tables.add(        ⮜  Create
    $Word.Selection.Range,                     the table.
```

```
        $Object.Count + 1,
        $columns.Count,
[Microsoft.Office.Interop.Word.WdDefaultTableBehavior]::wdWord9TableBehavior
        ,[Microsoft.Office.Interop.Word.WdAutoFitBehavior]::wdAutoFitContent
        )
```

Set the table style.

```
        $Table.Style = 'Grid Table 1 Light'
```

Add the header row.

```
        for($c = 0; $c -lt $columns.Count; $c++){
            $Table.Cell(1,$c+1).Range.Text = $columns[$c]
        }
```

Loop through each item in the array row, adding the data to the correct row.

Loop through each column, adding the data to the correct cell.

```
        for($r = 0; $r -lt $object.Count; $r++){
            for($c = 0; $c -lt $columns.Count; $c++){
                $Table.Cell($r+2,$c+1).Range.Text =
                    $object[$r].psobject.Properties.Value[$c].ToString()
            }
        }

        $Word.Selection.Start= $Document.Content.End
        $Selection.TypeParagraph()
}
```

Add a paragraph after the table.

You can test this function using the disk space data:

```
$DiskInfo = Get-CimInstance -Class Win32_LogicalDisk |
    Select-Object DeviceId,
    @{l='Size';e={[Math]::Round($_.Size / 1GB, 2)}},
    @{l='FreeSpace';e={[Math]::Round($_.FreeSpace / 1GB, 2)}}
New-WordTableFromArray $DiskInfo
```

9.3   Getting web data

When I started working as a sysadmin oh so many years ago, web APIs were something I thought only developers would have to deal with. However, with the shift in the industry to Platform as a Service (PaaS), many system administrators are finding themselves needing to interact with web-based applications.

One of the most common types of web APIs is representational state transfer, or REST. A typical REST request is made up of a URI, method, body, and header. The URI is similar to a URL but can contain parameters that are passed to the receiving server. The method tells the remote system what to do with the request. For instance, GET will return data, POST and PUT will often update an existing object or create new ones, etc. The body will often contain the information for the POST or PUT type methods. And, finally, the header will contain information related to the authentication and content types. The most common context types used by REST are JSON and XML, both of which have native PowerShell support.

To interact with a REST API through PowerShell, you can use the Invoke-RestMethod cmdlet. This cmdlet is excellent because it automatically formats the response from your web request to a PowerShell object. Therefore, you don't need to build any custom classes or parse a bunch of output data. Instead, you simply save the output from the `Invoke-RestMethod` to a variable in PowerShell, and you can use it in your script just like you would any other object.

What is a REST API?

REST is an architectural style for submitting HTTP requests, not a protocol or a standard. For an API to be considered REST, it must conform to specific criteria. These include a client-server architecture, stateless communication, cacheable, a layered system, and a uniform interface between components. However, since it is not a protocol or standard, developers can create their own patterns, headers, and responses. Therefore, you will need to refer to the developer documentation on the best ways to interface with their API.

Also, not all HTTP requests are REST. There are other architectures out there. However, the way you communicate with them is the same. So, you can use the `Invoke-WebRequest` instead of the `Invoke-RestMethod` for other types of communication. In fact, under the hood, the `Invoke-RestMethod` cmdlet uses the `Invoke-WebRequest` to perform the communication. The `Invoke-RestMethod` cmdlet just contains some additional functionality to automatically convert the response data into a PowerShell object. The `Invoke-WebRequest` cmdlet returns the raw results; it is up to you to parse and convert them.

To show you how easy it can be, let's call the ipify API to find your public IP address:

```
$IP = Invoke-RestMethod -Uri 'https://api.ipify.org?format=json'
$IP

ip
--
48.52.216.180
```

Now that you have the external IP address, it is time to get the geolocation for it. However, in order to get this information, you will need to obtain an API key from ipify.org.

9.3.1   API keys

It is very rare to come across an open API that just lets you call it without some form of authentication. The most common form of authentication is via API keys. API keys allow the server to verify who is sending the request, preventing abuse and ensuring that it is not someone trying to impersonate someone else.

Unfortunately, every API is different, so there is no way I could cover all the ways of generating and passing API keys. However, most APIs have documentation on how to authenticate with them. We will use the geolocation API from geo.ipify.org to return the city, region, and country from your public IP address.

Go ahead and sign up for a free account at geo.ipify.org. Once you have signed in, you will receive an API key for 1,000 free geolocation lookups (more than enough for our needs). Like with most public APIs, they have a section on their website with code samples on how to use the API.

Passing data to an API is usually done in a key/value format. You can think of the key as the parameter, which, like in PowerShell, is a predetermined string. For example, the geolocation API has two parameters, apiKey and ipAddress.

To pass the required information to the API, we will build a hashtable that you will pass to the -Body parameter. The hashtable will contain the values for the IP address to look up and the API key:

```
$apiKey = "your_API_key"
$ApiUrl = "https://geo.ipify.org/api/v2/country,city"
$Body = @{
    apiKey    = $apiKey
    ipAddress = $IP.ip
}
$geoData = $null
$geoData = Invoke-RestMethod -Uri $ApiUrl -Body $Body
$geoData.location
country    : US
region     : Illinois
city       : Chicago
lat        : 41.94756
lng        : -87.65650
postalCode : 60613
timezone   : -05:00
```

Now you can put this all together and use these API results to populate data in your Word document, as shown in figure 9.6:

```
$IP = Invoke-RestMethod -Uri 'https://api.ipify.org?format=json'
$Selection.TypeText("IP Address  : $($IP.ip)")
$Selection.TypeText([char]11)

$apiKey = "your_API_key"
$ApiUrl = "https://geo.ipify.org/api/v2/country,city"
$Body = @{
    apiKey = $apiKey
    ipAddress = $IP.ip
}
$geoData = $null
$geoData = Invoke-RestMethod -Uri $ApiUrl -Body $Body
$Selection.TypeText("IP Location : $($geoData.location.city),
➥ $($geoData.location.country)")
$Selection.TypeParagraph()
```

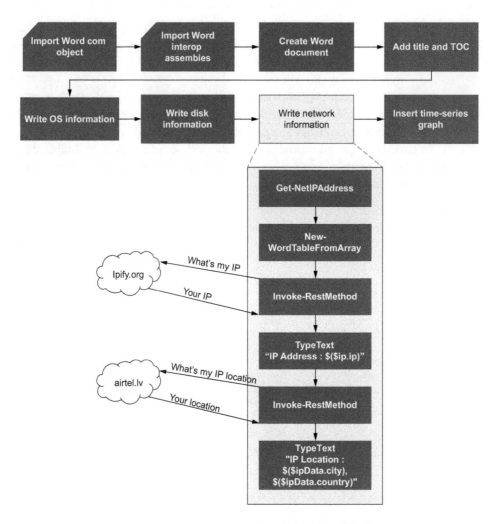

Figure 9.6   Getting data from an external REST API and writing it to Word

9.4   *Using external applications*

As useful as PowerShell is, like any other language out there, it cannot do everything. So, there are times when you need to interact with applications outside of PowerShell. These are often command-line applications that do not have PowerShell-equivalent commands. But, as you are about to see, PowerShell can also interact with scripts from other languages.

When it comes to creating data visualizations, the Matplotlib library is much more advanced than anything in PowerShell. If you are not familiar with Python, don't worry; you don't need to be to use this script. But you do need to have Python installed and the Matplotlib and pandas library installed. As always, there is a PowerShell script in the Helper Scripts for this chapter to install and configure these for you.

Regardless of the application you are using, the process shown here remains the same. There are several ways to call an external application from PowerShell, but the most consistent and easy-to-use way is by using the `Start-Process` cmdlet. Not only does this cmdlet provide the functionality to execute external applications and provide command-line arguments, but it also provides a mechanism to capture the output and errors from the command.

9.4.1   Calling an external executable

To get started with the `Start-Process` cmdlet, you need to start with the arguments `FilePath` and `ArgumentList`. The `FilePath` is the path to the executable. It can either be the full path (e.g. `C:\Windows\System32\PING.EXE`), use environment variables (e.g. `$env:SystemRoot\System32\PING.EXE`), or simply the name of the executable, assuming the path of the file is in the PATH environmental variable (e.g. `PING.EXE`).

The `ArgumentList` is the parameters and values that you want to pass to the executable. It can either be a single string, written as you would inside a command prompt, or an array of strings that PowerShell will combine into a single string for you. You can try this out yourself using `PING.EXE` to ping a remote host. First, use a single argument of the remote host, and then two arguments specify the number of pings:

```
Start-Process -FilePath 'ping.exe' -ArgumentList 'google.com'
Start-Process -FilePath 'ping.exe' -ArgumentList 'google.com','-n 10'
```

9.4.2   Monitoring execution

When you use the `Start-Process` cmdlet, the default behavior is to start the process and continue with the script. Therefore, it will not wait for the execution to finish unless you include the `-Wait` switch. However, when talking about automations, especially ones that run without interactions, you never want to rely on a `wait` argument that does not have a timeout argument. This is because there are situations where an executable can hang, and your script will continue to run indefinitely. To prevent this, you can use a `while` loop with a counter or timer to automatically exit or kill the process if it exceeds a certain threshold.

To monitor the status, you add the `-PassThru` switch to the `Start-Process` command. This will return the information about the running process to PowerShell. You can then use the `HasExited` inside a `while` loop to pause your script while the process is still active. Then, you can use a `stopwatch` timer to check that the process has not exceeded the allowed run time. If it does exceed the run time, you can use the `Stop-Process` to kill it and use a `throw` or `Write-Error` to let the PowerShell script know the process failed to complete:

```
$RuntimeSeconds = 2
$ping = Start-Process -FilePath 'ping.exe' -ArgumentList
    'google.com','-n 10' -PassThru
$timer = [system.diagnostics.stopwatch]::StartNew()
```

```
while($ping.HasExited -eq $false){
    if($timer.Elapsed.TotalSeconds -gt $RuntimeSeconds){
        $ping | Stop-Process -Force
        throw "The application did not exit in time"
    }
}
$timer.Elapsed.TotalSeconds
$timer.Stop()
```

9.4.3   Getting the output

When you run these commands, you will notice that they open in a new window, and nothing is returned to the PowerShell window. If you include the switch -NoNewWindow, the results will return to the same window as the Start-Process command. However, they will not always be returned to the output stream. As you most likely know, not all command-line applications are built the same. Not only does the output vary wildly from application to application, but some will interpret the output as error streams. For a good example of this, try the Start-Process cmdlet with git.exe. It thinks all outputs are errors. To prevent this from causing problems in your script, you can capture and parse the outputs and errors from the command.

The parameters -RedirectStandardOutput and -RedirectStandardError will send the outputs and errors to text files. You can then parse these files to get the data you need. You can test this out by using Driverquery.exe with the -RedirectStandardOutput and -RedirectStandardError arguments. With this command, the file StdOutput.txt should contain the results of the command, and the ErrorOutput.txt should be empty:

```
$Process = @{
    FilePath               = 'Driverquery.exe'
    ArgumentList           = '/NH'
    RedirectStandardOutput = 'StdOutput.txt'
    RedirectStandardError  = 'ErrorOutput.txt'
    NoNewWindow            = $true
    Wait                   = $true
}
Start-Process @Process
Get-Content 'ErrorOutput.txt'
Get-Content 'StdOutput.txt'
1394ohci     1394 OHCI Compliant Ho Kernel
3ware        3ware                  Kernel   5/18/2015 5:28:03 PM
ACPI         Microsoft ACPI Driver  Kernel
AcpiDev      ACPI Devices driver    Kernel
acpiex       Microsoft ACPIEx Drive Kernel
acpipagr     ACPI Processor Aggrega Kernel
AcpiPmi      ACPI Power Meter Drive Kernel
acpitime     ACPI Wake Alarm Driver Kernel
Acx01000     Acx01000               Kernel
ADP80XX      ADP80XX                Kernel   4/9/2015 3:49:48 PM
...
```

Now let's try it again, but this time, we will add /FO List to the argument list. This will cause an error because the list output is incompatible with the /NH argument. This

time, the StdOutput.txt is blank, and the ErrorOutput.txt contains the error message
from the command:

```
$Process = @{
    FilePath              = 'Driverquery.exe'
    ArgumentList          = '/FO List /NH'
    RedirectStandardOutput = 'StdOutput.txt'
    RedirectStandardError  = 'ErrorOutput.txt'
    NoNewWindow           = $true
    Wait                  = $true
}
Start-Process @Process
Get-Content 'ErrorOutput.txt'
Get-Content 'StdOutput.txt'
ERROR: Invalid syntax. /NH option is valid only for "TABLE" and "CSV" format.
Type "DRIVERQUERY /?" for usage.
```

As mentioned earlier, not all applications work as nicely as this one. Therefore, you
will want to test each executable individually to ensure that your output matches what
is expected. For example, if you use PING.EXE with a bad hostname, it will not return
anything to the error file, but the output file will contain the message letting you know
the host wasn't found. It will be up to you to parse these files and have your script take
appropriate actions based on the results.

9.4.4   Creating Start-Process wrapper function

For the Word document automation, we want to insert a time-series graph of the per-
centage of processor time counter. Since there may be other counters you will want to
add down the line, building a wrapper function to create this graph makes sense. This
function will take the counter values, convert them to the appropriate JSON format,
and then call the timeseries.py script to create an image file of the graph. This image
can then be inserted into your Word document.

   If you have not already done so, please use the Install-Python.ps1 in the Helper
Scripts for this chapter to set up Python. The timeseries.py script requires three
arguments. These are the path to save the output PNG image, a title for the graph,
and a JSON object of the time-series. We'll start by getting some data to test with,
using the Get-Counter cmdlet to get the % Processor Time counter:

```
$sampleData = Get-Counter -Counter "\Processor(_Total)\% Processor Time"
  -SampleInterval 2 -MaxSamples 10
```

Now we can start building out the structure of the function, starting with the parameters. The parameters of the script we are invoking are the PNG path, title, and JSON.
The timeseries.py script expects the JSON to be an array with two keys: timestamp and
value. Therefore, instead of converting the counter to JSON before calling the function, it would be best to have the function convert it. This way, you can ensure that the
data passed is appropriately formatted.

For the PNG path, you can write it to the Temp directory since we will only need it long enough to insert it into the Word document. You will also need to know the path to the Python executable and to the timeseries.py script itself. Therefore, the parameters will be

- `PyPath`—The path to the Python executable. If you do not know this, use the command `py -0p` to display the installed versions of Python. We are using version 3.8 for this.
- `ScriptPath`—The path to the timeseries.py script.
- `Title`—The title to display at the top of the graph.
- `CounterData`—The output from the `Get-Counter` cmdlet. You can ensure the correct data is sent by setting the type on the parameter to `[PerformanceCounter-SampleSet]`.

Now you need to determine the arguments to use with the `Start-Process` cmdlet. You know you will need the `-FilePath` and `-ArgumentList`. When building the arguments string, you need to ensure you take into consideration spaces and escape characters. For Python, any value with a space in it needs to be wrapped in double quotes. You can ensure that this happens by wrapping the value in quotes in the argument list—for example, `"""$($Title)"""`.

Then, with the JSON, you need to escape the double quotes inside it to keep Python from thinking it is multiple arguments. You can do this with a simple replace to place a slash before each double quote.

You will also want to include the `-NoNewWindow` and `-PassThru` switches to allow you to monitor the execution process. Finally, you will want to include the `-Redirect-StandardOutput` and `-RedirectStandardError` arguments to capture the outputs.

You will need to ensure that the file names you use when redirecting the output and creating the PNG are unique each time you run them. This will prevent issues where multiple scripts may be running and conflicting with each other. As we saw way back in chapter 2, the best way to get a unique name is by using a GUID. So, you can create a GUID using the `New-Guid` cmdlet. Then, use that GUID to name the output files and the PNG.

Next, you can create a `while` loop to monitor the execution of the process. Then, once the process completes, you can parse the contents of the output files and return the appropriate information to the main script. Figure 9.7 illustrates the logic.

In this case, we know that the script executed successfully when the output states "File saved to :" followed by the path to the PNG, and the error output is blank. Therefore, you can build an `if/else` statement to check for this and return the path to the PNG file back to the main script. Finally, you will want to ensure that you clean up the output files to prevent them from using unneeded disk space. Listing 9.3 provides the script.

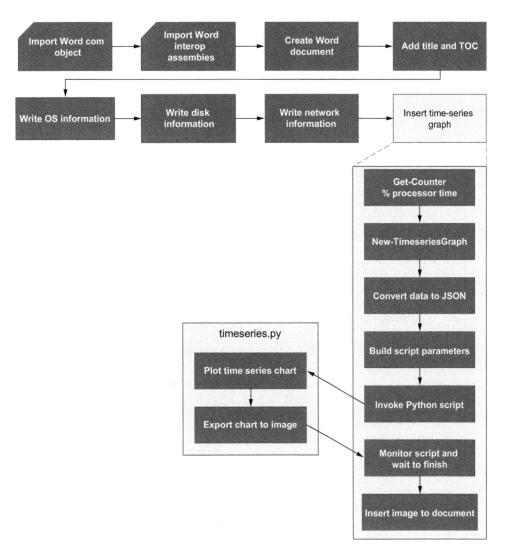

Figure 9.7 Invoke Python script from PowerShell and pass parameters as a JSON string. The Python script will execute, while PowerShell waits for it to finish.

Listing 9.3 New-TimeseriesGraph

```
Function New-TimeseriesGraph {
    [CmdletBinding()]
    [OutputType()]
    param(
        [Parameter(Mandatory = $true)]
        [string]$PyPath,
        [Parameter(Mandatory = $true)]
        [string]$ScriptPath,
```

```
    [Parameter(Mandatory = $true)]
    [string]$Title,
    [Parameter(Mandatory = $true)]
[Microsoft.PowerShell.Commands.GetCounter.PerformanceCounterSampleSet[]]
    $CounterData
)

$CounterJson = $CounterData |
    Select-Object Timestamp,
    @{l = 'Value'; e = { $_.CounterSamples.CookedValue } } |
    ConvertTo-Json -Compress

$Guid = New-Guid

$path = @{
    Path = $env:TEMP
}
$picture = Join-Path @Path -ChildPath "$($Guid).PNG"
$StandardOutput = Join-Path @Path -ChildPath "$($Guid)-Output.txt"
$StandardError = Join-Path @Path -ChildPath "$($Guid)-Error.txt"

$ArgumentList = @(
    """$($ScriptPath)"""
    """$($picture)"""
    """$($Title)"""
    $CounterJson.Replace('"', '\"')
)
$Process = @{
    FilePath               = $PyPath
    ArgumentList           = $ArgumentList
    RedirectStandardOutput = $StandardOutput
    RedirectStandardError  = $StandardError
    NoNewWindow            = $true
    PassThru               = $true
}
$graph = Start-Process @Process

$RuntimeSeconds = 30
$timer = [system.diagnostics.stopwatch]::StartNew()
while ($graph.HasExited -eq $false) {
    if ($timer.Elapsed.TotalSeconds -gt $RuntimeSeconds) {
        $graph | Stop-Process -Force
        throw "The application did not exit in time"
    }
}
$timer.Stop()

$OutputContent = Get-Content -Path $StandardOutput
$ErrorContent = Get-Content -Path $StandardError
if ($ErrorContent) {
    Write-Error $ErrorContent
}
```

Convert the counter data into a JSON string.

Generate a random GUID to use with the file names.

Set the name and path of the picture and output file.

Set the arguments for the timeseries.py script. Wrap the parameters in double quotes to account for potential spaces.

Set the arguments for the Start-Process command.

Start the timer and wait for the process to exit.

Get the content from the output and error files.

If there is anything in the error file, write it as an error in the PowerShell console.

```
    elseif ($OutputContent | Where-Object { $_ -match 'File saved to :' }) {
        $output = $OutputContent |
            Where-Object { $_ -match 'File saved to :' }
        $Return = $output.Substring($output.IndexOf(':') + 1).Trim()
    }
    else {
        Write-Error "Unknown error occurred"          ◁──────────
    }

    Remove-Item -LiteralPath $StandardOutput -Force   ◁──────
    Remove-Item -LiteralPath $StandardError -Force

    $Return
}
```

If there was no error and no output, then something else went wrong, so you will want to notify the person running the script.

Delete the output files.

If the output has the expected data, parse it to return what you need in PowerShell.

9.5 Putting It all together

Now that we have all of our functionality to write to Word, get the external IP information, and use an external application to create a time-series graph, you can put it all together into one script. Start with the three functions you created:

- New-WordTableFromObject
- New-WordTableFromArray
- New-TimeseriesGraph

Then, you can create a new function to create the section headers for each section in the Word document. This function will take the three commands needed to set the heading style, enter the heading text, and create the paragraph break in a single command.

After the functions, you will first need the commands to load the Word COM object and create your new document, followed by the commands to load the Word interop assemblies from the GAC into PowerShell. Now it is time to start populating the Word document.

First, start by creating a title using the name of the computer. You can also add a table of contents by using the Add() method on the TableOfContents property of the document.

Next, you can add the system information starting with a heading, followed by the tables for the operating system information and the disk usage, with the operating system information using the New-WordTableFromObject function and the disk usage using the New-WordTableFromArray. After this, you can create a new heading for Network Data. Then, use the Get-NetIpAddress cmdlet to get the internal IP address information and write it to a table once again using the New-WordTableFromArray function. Once you have that, you can use the Invoke-RestMethod cmdlet with the ipify APIs to get the external IP information and write that to the document.

Next, go ahead and collect some sample data from the % Processor Time counter using the Get-Counter cmdlet and pass it to the New-TimeseriesGraph function to create the PNG image. You can then add this image to the document using the method `$Document.InlineShapes.AddPicture($pathtoPicture)`.

Then, once you are done populating all the information into the document, you can update the table of contents to refresh it with the headings you just created. Then, save it to your local system.

You will also want to clean up any picture files and close the Word objects in Power-Shell to release them from memory. Due to the length of this final snippet, I have chosen to omit it from the text. A copy of it can be found with the accompanying files or on GitHub at http://mng.bz/neda.

Summary

- .NET classes and COM objects can be loaded and interacted with directly in PowerShell.
- Assemblies in the Global Assembly Cache (GAC) are not automatically loaded in PowerShell 7, so you may need to update scripts if moving from Windows PowerShell 5.1.
- REST is a common HTTP request architecture used across industries, but it does not define the structure of the data. You will need to refer to each API's documentation for specifics of interacting with it.
- How an external application outputs data or error messages depends on that application. So, you will want to capture and examine both in your scripts.

Automation coding best practices

This chapter covers

- Building a full automation from start to finish
- How to write and comment your code so others can understand it
- Best practices around building robust and resumable automations

One of the biggest challenges most IT professionals face today is the speed at which things change. It used to be that you upgraded your operating systems and applications every three to five years. However, the subscription- and cloud-based models have drastically increased the frequency of upgrades. As a result, it is not uncommon to see multiple major upgrades in a single year now. One of the best ways to help yourself keep up with these trends is through automation. In this chapter, you will learn how you can ensure that your automations will grow with you by applying some best practices to your code.

Back in 2015, when Microsoft first released Windows 10, they introduced the concept of feature updates, where twice a year a new version of Windows is released. And this trend will continue with Windows 11. Even many Linux distros will have multiple versions. For instance, Ubuntu has some with long-term support (LTS) versions and some short-term support (STS) versions. Some distros have even moved to a continuous delivery model. All this means that you can end up with an assortment of different operating systems in your environment.

One of the most challenging things for administrators to keep up with is the security and management enhancements in all these different versions. You will find that some support Mobile Device Management (MDM), some can support autopilot or Trusted Platform Module (TPM), and the list can go on. The point is you may need to test any given operating system at any time. At the same time, it would not make sense to leave a bunch of different virtual machines lying around just in case you need to test something. To solve this problem, we will create a zero-touch Windows ISO that you can use to quickly deploy a new virtual machine with a click of a button.

Typically, in the past, you would have downloaded and installed the Windows Assessment and Deployment Kit (Windows ADK), and then built out an auto-unattended file and manually created a custom ISO. But with releases every six months, you can save yourself a lot of time by automating the creation of the zero-touch ISO image.

So, this automation will contain two parts. The first part will be creating the zero-touch ISO image from the original source ISO. The second part will be creating a virtual machine and installing the operating system without needing to interact with it.

While creating this automation, we will look at how you can use some best practices to ensure that it will be adaptable for future releases and that others will be able to use it. I have personally been using and updating this automation since 2015.

While I take great care throughout this book to make the automations as universal as possible, when it comes to creating virtual machines, there is no way to create a single script that would work for every hypervisor. Therefore, I have chosen Hyper-V because it is built into Windows 10 and 11. There is also a free version of the Hyper-V server that you can download.

I completed all the automations in this chapter using Hyper-V on my Windows 11 desktop and Windows 10 laptop. You will need the following items to complete all the scripts in this chapter:

- *Windows Server 2022 ISO*—If you do not have a copy of this ISO handy, you can download a 180-day trial from the Microsoft Evaluation Center (http://mng.bz/vXR7).
- *Oscdimg command-line tool*—This tool is part of the Windows ADK and is used to create customized Windows ISOs. I have included a copy of it in the Helper Scripts folder for this chapter.

Oscdimg and Windows ADK

I completely understand that some of you may not feel comfortable using an executable downloaded from a third-party. So, if you prefer, you can obtain a copy of the oscdimg.exe by installing the Windows ADK for Windows 10 or above (http://mng.bz/49Xw). When installing the Windows ADK, you only need to install the Deployment Tools feature. This will include the oscdimg.exe directly from Microsoft.

While this chapter is written to work with Hyper-V, its lessons apply to any hypervisor and, really, any automation.

10.1 Defining the full automation

As we talked about way back in chapter 1, the first thing you need to do when starting a new automation project is to clearly define the steps and the goals. Of course, you will not be able to figure out every detail before you begin, but having a general outline and the end goal is paramount to successful automation. An excellent way to do this is by defining your goal and then expanding upon that.

For this chapter, the goal is to build an automation that can create a Windows Server 2022 virtual machine with little to no interaction required. Then, building on that, you can define the high-level steps it takes to create a virtual machine and install Windows Server 2022:

1 Create a virtual machine.
2 Attach Windows Server 2022 ISO.
3 Run through the installation wizard.
4 Attach a second virtual hard drive.
5 Add the disk to the operating system

Steps 1, 2, and 4 should be straightforward to automate. Since we are using Hyper-V, all of this can be done in PowerShell. The same can be said for pretty much every hypervisor out there. I guarantee if you search your preferred search engine for "Create VM PowerShell," you will find all sorts of examples. You can also say the same thing about step 5. Again, there are plenty of examples of attaching a new disk inside of Windows.

So, let's flesh out these tasks a little further with some more details:

1 Create a virtual machine.
    a Give it a name.
    b Find the path to create it.
    c Determine which network to connect to.
    d Create the operating system disk.
    e Set memory and processor requirements.
2 Attach Windows Server 2022 ISO.
3 Run through the installation wizard.
4 Attach a second virtual hard drive.
    a Create a disk in the same location as the operating system disk.
    b Attach the disk to the virtual machine.
5 Add the second disk to the operating system.
    a Initialize the disk.
    b Create partitions and format.
    c Assign a drive letter.

This leaves you to figure out step 3 of automating the installation of the operating system. To do this, you need to create a zero-touch ISO. By zero touch, I mean you can attach the ISO to a virtual machine, turn it on, and have the operating system install without you needing to interact with it. To do this, you will need to make some changes to the files in the ISO and include an auto-unattended answer file.

To keep things focused on PowerShell automation and not get sucked into the weeds of creating an auto-unattended answer file, I have provided a copy of a basic one for Windows Server 2022 with the source code for this chapter. It is the file named Autounattend.xml in the Helper Script folder. The process to create these can be quite involved. I would recommend the blog post "How to create an automated install for Windows Server 2016" by Mischa Taylor (https://mng.bz/7Z24) if you are interested in creating your own. Most of the items carry over to Windows Server 2019 and 2022.

10.1.1 Structuring your automation

It used to be that you would need to make a new ISO file every few years when a new operating system was released. But with releases coming as often as every six months, you can save yourself a lot of time by automating the creation of the zero-touch ISO. This will allow you to quickly and easily keep your files up to date. The steps to create a zero-touch ISO are shown in figure 10.1.

The big thing here is that this process does not fit into the larger automation. There is no need to recreate the ISO every time you create a virtual machine. Therefore, this part should be considered separate automation and stored in a separate file. You could put it all in one giant script, but then you would need to include all sorts of additional logic, and it could be a nightmare to update and test.

There is no set limit, like that scripts should only be 1,000 or fewer lines. It is more of a logical choice to determine whether they fit together. For instance, say you want to automate the setup of a WordPress server. For this, you will need to install Apache, PHP, MySQL, and WordPress itself. Then, you will need to configure the WordPress site. At a minimum, each installation should be a single function. You don't want to have to search through thousands of lines of code to make a tweak to one of the components.

Similarly, with the configuration, you could have a hosted WordPress site that you don't need to install, just configure. Therefore, the configuration should be in a completely separate script to run separately from the setup. In short, if multiple steps will always be run together, they can be in the same script but should be in stand-alone functions. If there is a chance they will run separately, they should be in separate scripts.

So, for this automation, you will create two scripts. You need one to create the ISO and another to create the virtual machine with that ISO. Let's start with creating the zero-touch ISO.

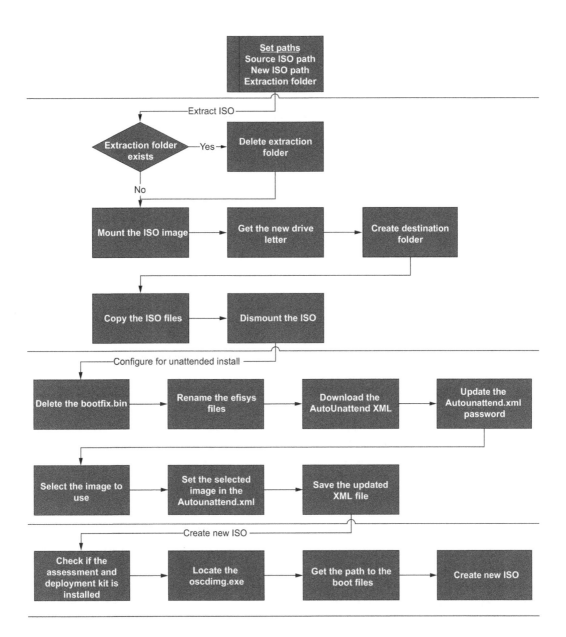

Figure 10.1   Mount the ISO and extract the contents to your local machine, configure the image for unattended install suppressing the "Press Any Key to Boot from CD or DVD" prompt and adding the Autounattend.xml, set the default password, select which version of the OS you want, and, finally, package all this together in a new ISO file.

10.2 *Converting a manual task to an automated one*

Converting a manual task to automation is not always a one-to-one translation. When performing a manual task, you often do things that you may not realize you are doing. Therefore, you might not even think to consider them before building your automation.

For instance, there is no native PowerShell cmdlet to extract an ISO, but there is native support to mount an ISO. So, instead of extracting, you can mount the ISO using the `Mount-DiskImage` cmdlet and then copy the files to the local computer using the `Copy-Item` cmdlet.

On the surface, that sounds simple enough, but when you try to script it, you will quickly discover another issue. The `Mount-DiskImage` cmdlet does not tell you what drive letter it mounts the ISO to. When you are doing things manually, you don't often pay attention to something like the drive letter. You just mount it, open the drive, and copy the files. However, you need to know exactly where the files are when automating. So, you will need to perform a look-up for the drive letter. Luckily, you can do this by piping the results of the `Mount-DiskImage` cmdlet to the `Get-Volume` cmdlet. But it is an extra step you may not have considered when building your automation.

Another thing you might not consider is whether the destination folder already has files from another ISO in it. The `Copy-Item` cmdlet can overwrite files with the `-Force` switch, but it will not remove files that do not exist in the source location. So, if you run this script multiple times for different ISOs, you could end up with all sorts of extra files. These extra files may be harmless, or they may not be. Either way, they should not be there. So, your best course of action is to check if there are files in the directory first and then remove them before copying the new files.

Finally, you may discover during your testing that you cannot overwrite some of the ISO files. This is because the copy process will sometimes make them read-only files. Luckily, once again, this can be quickly resolved using PowerShell, as shown in the script in the next listing. Just get all the files and folders you copied using the `Get-ChildItem` cmdlet. Then, use a `foreach` to loop through each one and set the `IsReadOnly` flag to `false` using the `Set-ItemProperty` cmdlet.

Listing 10.1 Extracting the ISO

```
$ExtractTo = 'C:\Temp'
$SourceISOPath = 'C:\ISO\WindowsSrv2022.iso'
if (test-path $ExtractTo) {                    ⮜    Check if the folder
    Remove-Item -Path $ExtractTo -Recurse -Force        exists and delete it
}                                                       if it does.

$DiskImage = @{                    ⮜    Mount the
    ImagePath = $SourceISOPath          ISO image.
    PassThru  = $true
}
$image = Mount-DiskImage @DiskImage
```

```
$drive = $image |                    ◄─────────────┐  Get the new
    Get-Volume |                                   │  drive letter.
    Select-Object -ExpandProperty DriveLetter

New-Item -type directory -Path $ExtractTo    ◄─┐  Create
                                               │  destination folder.
Get-ChildItem -Path "$($drive):" |
    Copy-Item -Destination $ExtractTo -recurse -Force

Get-ChildItem -Path $ExtractTo -Recurse |   ◄─┤  Remove the read-only flag
    ForEach-Object {                          │  for all files and folders.
        Set-ItemProperty -Path $_.FullName -Name IsReadOnly -Value $false
    }
                                  ┌  Dismount
$image | Dismount-DiskImage    ◄──┘  the ISO.
```

**Copy the
ISO files.**

Now that you have the ISO files extracted, it is time to set it up as a zero-touch image
and customize the Autounattend.xml for the particular image you are using.

10.3   *Updating structured data*

To create a zero-touch ISO, you must delete the bootfix.bin and rename the efisys_
noprompt.bin to efisys.bin. Doing this will bypass the "Press Any Key to Boot from CD
or DVD…" and take you directly to the installation wizard. To bypass the installation
wizard, you need to provide it with the answers it needs. This is where the Autounat-
tend.xml comes in. However, since not every environment is the same, you will need
to make slight adjustments to this XML file to meet your needs.

When it comes to updating files with structured data, your best course of action is
to load the data into a PowerShell object. Then, make the changes in PowerShell and
export the changes back to the original format. You can do this for any data type that
has support in PowerShell like JSON and, in this case, XML. Using this method is
more straightforward and safer than trying to write some regular expressions or wildcard look-up to perform a find and replace inside the file.

For instance, in the following XML snippet, you can see the entry to the administrator's password:

```
<UserAccounts>
  <AdministratorPassword>
    <Value>pasword</Value>
    <PlainText>false</PlainText>
  </AdministratorPassword>
</UserAccounts>
```

If you perform a simple find and replace on the word *password*, it could cause you to
update the lines with AdministratorPassword unintentionally. Even if you used a regular expression to find the line <Value>password</Value>, there is no guarantee that
this is the only line that matches that value.

However, if you import the XML to a PowerShell object, then you can change the
value of the property directly in PowerShell by finding the correct path:

```
$object = $Autounattend.unattend.settings |
    Where-Object { $_.pass -eq "oobeSystem" }
$object.component.UserAccounts.AdministratorPassword.Value = $NewPassword
```

Also, since the password is a Base64 encoded string, you can have PowerShell encode it, then write it for you. One thing to note is that you must add the string `Administrator-Password` to the end of the password before encoding it. That's just a requirement of the Autounattend.xml:

```
$NewPassword = 'P@ssw0rd'
$pass = $NewPassword + 'AdministratorPassword'
$bytes = [System.Text.Encoding]::Unicode.GetBytes($pass)
$base64Password = [system.convert]::ToBase64String($bytes)
```

Your final output should look similar to the following example:

```
<UserAccounts>
  <AdministratorPassword>
    <Value>UABAAHMAcwB3ADAAcgBkAEEAZABtAGkAbgAA==</Value>
    <PlainText>false</PlainText>
  </AdministratorPassword>
</UserAccounts>
```

Finally, you will need to select which operating system image to use. Most ISO files will contain multiple versions of the operating system. For example, a Windows Server 2022 contains the following installation images:

- Windows Server 2022 Standard
- Windows Server 2022 Standard (Desktop Experience)
- Windows Server 2022 Datacenter
- Windows Server 2022 Datacenter (Desktop Experience)

Since this list will be different for each operating system, you need to prompt the person running the automation to select which one to use. You can do this by passing the `install.wim` from the extracted ISO to the `Get-WindowsImage` cmdlet. Then, pipe those results to the `Out-GridView` cmdlet.

The `Out-GridView` cmdlet will automatically create a pop-up window with the values piped to it. By including the `-PassThru` switch, you can allow the user to select one or more of the values in the window and pass that back to the PowerShell session.

> **WARNING**   Only use `Out-GridView` when you know someone will be running an automation manually. If you try to schedule a script with an `Out-GridView` cmdlet, your automation will become hung waiting for the input.

Once you have the image to use, you can update the `Autounattend` PowerShell object with the image number, similar to how you updated the administrator password. Then, you can save all your changes back to the original Autounattend.XML file using the `Save` method on the Autounattend PowerShell object. The script is shown in the following listing.

Listing 10.2   Create a Windows zero-touch ISO

```
$ExtractTo = 'C:\Temp'
$password = 'P@55word'                                              Delete the
$bootFix = Join-Path $ExtractTo "boot\bootfix.bin"    ←┘           bootfix.bin.
Remove-Item -Path $bootFix -Force


$ChildItem = @{                    ←──┐   Rename the
    Path    = $ExtractTo             │   efisys files.
    Filter  = "efisys.bin"
    Recurse = $true
}
Get-ChildItem @ChildItem | Rename-Item -NewName "efisys_prompt.bin"
$ChildItem['Filter'] = "efisys_noprompt.bin"
Get-ChildItem @ChildItem | Rename-Item -NewName "efisys.bin"


$Path = @{                         ←──────┐   Download the
    Path      = $ExtractTo               │    AutoUnattend XML.
    ChildPath = "Autounattend.xml"
}
$AutounattendXML = Join-Path @Path
$Uri = 'https://gist.githubusercontent.com/mdowst/3826e74507e0d0188e13b8' +
  'c1be453cf1/raw/0f018ec04d583b63c8cb98a52ad9f500be4ece75/Autounattend.xml'
Invoke-WebRequest -Uri $Uri -OutFile $AutounattendXML
                                                          Load the
                                                          Autounattend.xml.
[xml]$Autounattend = Get-Content $AutounattendXML     ←──┘


$passStr = $password + 'AdministratorPassword'            ←──────┐  Update
$bytes = [System.Text.Encoding]::Unicode.GetBytes($passStr)    │   the values.
$passEncoded = [system.convert]::ToBase64String($bytes)
$setting = $Autounattend.unattend.settings |
    Where-Object{$_.pass -eq 'oobeSystem'}
$setting.component.UserAccounts.AdministratorPassword.Value = $passEncoded


$ChildItem = @{                    ←──┐   Select the
    Path    = $ExtractTo             │   image to use.
    Include = "install.wim"
    Recurse = $true
}
$ImageWim = Get-ChildItem @ChildItem
$WinImage = Get-WindowsImage -ImagePath $ImageWim.FullName |
    Out-GridView -Title 'Select the image to use' -PassThru
$image = $WinImage.ImageIndex.ToString()


$setup = $Autounattend.unattend.settings |        ←──┐  Set the selected image in
    Where-Object{$_.pass -eq 'windowsPE'} |          │   the Autounattend.xml.
    Select-Object -ExpandProperty component |
    Where-Object{ $_.name -eq "Microsoft-Windows-Setup"}
$setup.ImageInstall.OSImage.InstallFrom.MetaData.Value = $image


$Autounattend.Save($AutounattendXML)     ←──┐   Save the updated
                                            │   XML file.
```

AutoUnattend Product Keys

If you downloaded the trial ISO for Windows Server, it does not require a product key during installation. However, if you are using a volume license, Microsoft Developer Network, or other ISO, it may require a product key to allow full zero-touch. In these cases, you can add the product key to the AutoUnattend.xml file under UserData\ProductKey:

```
<UserData>
  <ProductKey>
    <Key>12345-12345-12345-12345-12345</Key>
    <WillShowUI>Never</WillShowUI>
  </ProductKey>
</UserData>
```

10.4   Using external tools

Unfortunately, not everything can be achieved directly in PowerShell. There are instances where you need to call external tools. For instance, creating a new Windows ISO file with the Autounattend.XML requires the use of a specific executable oscdimg.

The oscdimg executable is included in the Windows ADK. Unfortunately, the Windows ADK is not included in Windows, so you must download and install it manually. This means that you cannot guarantee that the oscdimg executable will be in the same location on every machine. Therefore, you will need to locate it first.

If the application is a stand-alone executable, your best option is to include it with the automation script. This way, you can always ensure it is there. But if an application needs to be installed on the machine, you will need to include some additional logic to find it.

10.4.1 Finding installed applications

Since not all programs are installed in the same manner, even on the same operating system, you will need to adjust your automation based on the specific one you need. However, there are a few standard options you can use to locate an application. Of course, these are dependent on the operating system. And since Windows ADK is only supported on Windows, we will look at those options.

First, you can try checking the Uninstall keys in the registry. These keys are where the items listed in Add/Remove Programs come from. You can usually search under these keys to find the installation information for the application. Keep in mind that there are two Uninstall keys because of support for x86 programs:

```
HKLM:\SOFTWARE\Microsoft\Windows\CurrentVersion\Uninstall
HKLM:\SOFTWARE\WOW6432Node\Microsoft\Windows\CurrentVersion\Uninstall
```

Once again, this is something PowerShell can do. You can use the Get-ChildItem cmdlet to search the DisplayName value for each key under the Uninstall registry key. Then check if the value matches your search string. The following snippet should return data if you have the Windows ADK installed:

```
$SearchFor = '*Windows Assessment and Deployment Kit*'
$Path =  'HKLM:\SOFTWARE\WOW6432Node\Microsoft\Windows\CurrentVersion\Uninstall'
Get-ChildItem -Path $Path | ForEach-Object{
    if($_.GetValue('DisplayName') -like $SearchFor){
        $_
    }
}
}
```

If you are lucky, the entry in the Uninstall key will contain the path to the Install directory. However, that is not always the case, like with the Windows ADK. So, you'll need to find a different way to locate it.

The next thing I'll usually try is to open File Explorer and locate the installation path manually. Then, I'll open the Registry Editor and search for that path, starting under HKEY_LOCAL_MACHINE\SOFTWARE and working my way up. If you are lucky, the application may have stored the installation path in the registry.

With the Windows ADK, you are in luck because you should find the installation path in the value KitsRoot10 under the key HKLM:\SOFTWARE\WOW6432Node\Microsoft\ Windows Kits\Installed Roots. Therefore, you can use the following snippet to get the install path in your script:

```
$Path = 'HKLM:\SOFTWARE\WOW6432Node\Microsoft\Windows Kits\Installed Roots'
$DevTools = Get-ItemProperty -Path $Path
$DevTools.KitsRoot10
```

If you cannot locate the installation path in the registry, your next option is to search the file system. However, since installers can install programs anywhere, you need to build logic into the search. Your goal should be to make the search process as efficient as possible. Therefore, you will want to build a tiered search.

You can start first by searching standard directories where applications are often installed. And remember, you cannot count on the folders to be in the same spot on every computer. So, you will want to use environmental variables to locate these folders. Table 10.1 lists standard directories for application installs and their environment variable names.

Table 10.1   Common install directories and their environment variable (Windows)

Directory	Environment variable
Program Files	`$env:ProgramFiles`
Program Files (x86)	`${env:ProgramFiles(x86)}`
ProgramData	`$env:ProgramData`
AppData\Local	`$env:LOCALAPPDATA`

The goal here is to be as efficient as possible. So, you can search each of these folders in order and stop if you find the executable you want. If you do not find it, you can move to a broader search of the system drives.

To achieve this in a script, you can build a list of the folders you want to check first. Then use the `Get-Volume` cmdlet to return the different drives for the local computer, filtering out removable and temporary storage. Then, use a `foreach` loop to check each location and check for the installation files using the `Get-ChildItem` cmdlet. Then, if the file is found, break the loop because there is no need to check any further. You can also include an `if` statement after the `foreach` to check that the file was found and, if not, throw an error to stop the execution.

Before you carry on with your script, you must consider one more situation. What happens if multiple copies of the same file are found? This can happen when there are multiple versions of an application installed. In this case, you can use the `-First 1` argument with the `Select-Object` cmdlet to return only the first one found. This will prevent you from accidentally executing the command multiple times because you found multiple copies. You can see this in the following listing where the script searches for the oscdimg.exe file.

Listing 10.3   Find the oscdimg.exe file

Check if the Assessment and Deployment Kit is installed.

```
$FileName = 'oscdimg.exe'
[System.Collections.Generic.List[PSObject]] $SearchFolders = @()

$ItemProperty = @{
    Path = 'HKLM:\SOFTWARE\WOW6432Node\Microsoft\Windows Kits\Installed
    Roots'
}
$DevTools = Get-ItemProperty @ItemProperty

if(-not [string]::IsNullOrEmpty($DevTools.KitsRoot10)){    ⬅  If ADK is found,
    $SearchFolders.Add($DevTools.KitsRoot10)                  add the path to the
}                                                              folder search list.

$SearchFolders.Add($env:ProgramFiles)         ⬅
$SearchFolders.Add(${env:ProgramFiles(x86)})     Add the other common
$SearchFolders.Add($env:ProgramData)             installation locations to
$SearchFolders.Add($env:LOCALAPPDATA)            the folder search list.

Get-Volume |                                                      ⬅
    Where-Object { $_.FileSystemLabel -ne 'Temporary Storage' -and
    $_.DriveType -ne 'Removable' -and $_.DriveLetter } |          Add the
    Sort-Object DriveLetter -Descending | Foreach-Object {        system disks
        $SearchFolders.Add("$($_.DriveLetter):\")                 to the folder
}                                                                 search list.

foreach ($path in $SearchFolders) {      ⬅   Loop through each
    $ChildItem = @{                          folder and break if the
        Path        = $path                  executable is found.
        Filter      = $FileName
        Recurse     = $true
        ErrorAction = 'SilentlyContinue'
    }
```

```
    $filePath = Get-ChildItem @ChildItem |
        Select-Object -ExpandProperty FullName -First 1
    if($filePath){
        break
    }
}

if(-not $filePath){
    throw "$FileName not found"
}

$filePath
```

10.4.2 Call operators

Fortunately for us, the oscdimg executable is a stand-alone application, so I included a copy of it in the Helper Script folder for this chapter. So, all you need to do is put it in the same folder as the script, and you can create the path to it by combining the `$PSScriptRoot` variable with the name of the executable. Then, if it is not found in the directory, you can search the system for it.

To finish the ISO build, you will build the command-line arguments and call the oscdimg executable by placing the call operator `&` at the beginning of the line. The `&` tells PowerShell that the variable is a command to execute. You can see this at work in the following listing.

Listing 10.4 Running the oscdimg.exe

```
$NewIsoPath = 'C:\ISO\WindowsSrv2022_zerotouch.iso'
$filePath = ".\Chapter10\Helper Scripts\oscdimg.exe"
$Path = @{                            ◁──┐  Get the path to the
    Path      = $ExtractTo               │  etfsboot.com file.
    ChildPath = 'boot\etfsboot.com'
}
$etfsboot = Join-Path @Path      ◁──┐  Get the path to
$Path = @{                           │  the efisys.bin file.
    Path      = $ExtractTo
    ChildPath = 'efi\microsoft\boot\efisys.bin'
}
$efisys = Join-Path @Path
$arguments = @(              ◁──┐  Build an array with
    '-m'                        │  the arguments for
    '-o'                        │  the oscdimg.exe.
    '-u2'
    '-udfver102'
    "-bootdata:2#p0,e,b$($etfsboot)#pEF,e,b$($efisys)"
    $ExtractTo
    $NewIsoPath
)                            ┌  Execute the oscdimg.exe
                             │  with the arguments using
& $filePath $arguments    ◁──┘  the call operator.
```

Since the oscdimg executable runs in a child scope of the main script, the output will be returned directly to the PowerShell console. One downside is that PowerShell often interprets the output as an error message. There are a couple of ways to handle this. You can use the `Start-Process` cmdlet, but that requires capturing and reading multiple output files. Also, you will need to know what will be written in those files to determine if an error occurred. The easier way to check is by using the `$LASTEXITCODE` variable. This variable returns the exit code of the last call operation. If it equals zero, the command completed successfully. The following listing puts the entire zero-touch automation script together.

Listing 10.5   Create a Windows zero-touch ISO—final

```
$SourceISOPath = "C:\ISO\Windows_Server_2022.iso"
$NewIsoPath = 'D:\ISO\Windows_Server_2022_ZeroTouch.iso'
$ExtractTo = 'D:\Win_ISO'
$password = 'P@55word'

$Uri = 'https://gist.githubusercontent.com/mdowst/3826e74507e0d0188e13b8' +
    'c1be453cf1/raw/0f018ec04d583b63c8cb98a52ad9f500be4ece75/Autounattend.xml'
$FileName = 'oscdimg.exe'
[System.Collections.Generic.List[PSObject]] $SearchFolders = @()

if(test-path $ExtractTo){                         ⟵   Check if the folder
    Remove-Item -Path $ExtractTo -Recurse -Force       exists and delete it
}                                                       if it does.

$DiskImage = @{
    ImagePath = $SourceISOPath
    PassThru  = $true
}
$image = Mount-DiskImage @DiskImage

$drive = $image |          ⟵|  Get the new
    Get-Volume |               drive letter.
    Select-Object -ExpandProperty DriveLetter

                                               Create the
New-Item -type directory -Path $ExtractTo  ⟵|  destination
                                               folder.
Get-ChildItem -Path "$($drive):" |
    Copy-Item -Destination $ExtractTo -recurse -Force

$image | Dismount-DiskImage    ⟵——— Dismount the ISO.

$bootFix = Join-Path $ExtractTo "boot\bootfix.bin"   ⟵|  Delete the
Remove-Item -Path $bootFix -Force                        bootfix.bin.

$ChildItem = @{          ⟵|  Rename the
    Path    = $ExtractTo     efisys files.
    Filter  = "efisys.bin"
    Recurse = $true
}
Get-ChildItem @ChildItem | Rename-Item -NewName "efisys_prompt.bin"
```

Mount the ISO image. → (points to `$DiskImage` block)

Copy the ISO files. → (points to `Get-ChildItem -Path` block)

```
$ChildItem['Filter'] = "efisys_noprompt.bin"
Get-ChildItem @ChildItem | Rename-Item -NewName "efisys.bin"

$Path = @{                          ←────────┐  Download the
    Path      = $ExtractTo                   │  AutoUnattend XML.
    ChildPath = "Autounattend.xml"
}
$AutounattendXML = Join-Path @Path
Invoke-WebRequest -Uri $Uri -OutFile $AutounattendXML
                                                    ┌─ Load the
                                                    │  Autounattend.xml.
[xml]$Autounattend = Get-Content $AutounattendXML  ←┘

$passStr = $password + 'AdministratorPassword'         ←──┐  Update the
$bytes = [System.Text.Encoding]::Unicode.GetBytes($passStr) │  values.
$passEncoded = [system.convert]::ToBase64String($bytes)
$setting = $Autounattend.unattend.settings |
    Where-Object{$_.pass -eq 'oobeSystem'}
$setting.component.UserAccounts.AdministratorPassword.Value = $passEncoded

$ChildItem = @{            ←────────┐  Select the
    Path    = $ExtractTo            │  image to use.
    Include = "install.wim"
    Recurse = $true
}
$ImageWim = Get-ChildItem @ChildItem
$WinImage = Get-WindowsImage -ImagePath $ImageWim.FullName |
    Out-GridView -Title 'Select the image to use' -PassThru
$image = $WinImage.ImageIndex.ToString()

$setup = $Autounattend.unattend.settings |      ←──┐ Set the selected image in
    Where-Object{$_.pass -eq 'windowsPE'} |        │ the Autounattend.xml.
    Select-Object -ExpandProperty component |
    Where-Object{ $_.name -eq "Microsoft-Windows-Setup"}
$setup.ImageInstall.OSImage.InstallFrom.MetaData.Value = $image

$Autounattend.Save($AutounattendXML)    ←──┐ Save the updated
                                           │ XML file.

$ItemProperty = @{                                          ←────────┐
    Path = 'HKLM:\SOFTWARE\WOW6432Node\Microsoft\Windows Kits\Installed
     Roots'                                                          │
}                                        Check if the Assessment and
$DevTools = Get-ItemProperty @ItemProperty  Deployment Kit is installed.

if(-not [string]::IsNullOrEmpty($DevTools.KitsRoot10)){   ←──┐ If the ADK is found,
    $SearchFolders.Add($DevTools.KitsRoot10)                │ add the path to the
}                                                           │ folder search list.

$SearchFolders.Add($env:ProgramFiles)        ←──┐ Add the other common installation
$SearchFolders.Add(${env:ProgramFiles(x86)})    │ locations to the folder search list.
$SearchFolders.Add($env:ProgramData)
$SearchFolders.Add($env:LOCALAPPDATA)
                                          ┌─ Add the system disks to
                                          │  the folder search list.
Get-Volume |
    Where-Object { $_.FileSystemLabel -ne 'Temporary Storage' -and
    $_.DriveType -ne 'Removable' -and $_.DriveLetter } |
```

```
    Sort-Object DriveLetter -Descending | Foreach-Object {
        $SearchFolders.Add("$($_.DriveLetter):\")
}


foreach ($path in $SearchFolders) {           ◁──┐ Loop through each
    $ChildItem = @{                                │ folder and break if the
        Path        = $path                        │ executable is found.
        Filter      = $FileName
        Recurse     = $true
        ErrorAction = 'SilentlyContinue'
    }
    $filePath = Get-ChildItem @ChildItem |
        Select-Object -ExpandProperty FullName -First 1
    if($filePath){
        break
    }
}


if(-not $filePath){
    throw "$FileName not found"
}
                                        ┌── Get the path to the
$Path = @{                          ◁───┘   etfsboot.com file.
    Path      = $ExtractTo
    ChildPath = 'boot\etfsboot.com'
}
$etfsboot = Join-Path @Path          ◁──┐ Get the path to
$Path = @{                              │ the efisys.bin file.
    Path      = $ExtractTo
    ChildPath = 'efi\microsoft\boot\efisys.bin'
}
$efisys = Join-Path @Path
$arguments = @(              ◁──┐ Build an array with
    '-m'                         │ the arguments for
    '-o'                         │ the oscdimg.exe.
    '-u2'
    '-udfver102'
    "-bootdata:2#p0,e,b$($etfsboot)#pEF,e,b$($efisys)"
    $ExtractTo
    $NewIsoPath
)                             ┌── Execute the oscdimg.exe
                              │   with the arguments using
& $filePath $arguments    ◁───┘   the call operator.


if($LASTEXITCODE -ne 0){    ◁──┐ Confirm the last
    throw "ISO creation failed"  │ exit code is zero.
}
```

Go ahead and run this script to create your zero-touch ISO to complete the first script in the automation. Then you will be ready for the next script, where you will automate the virtual machine creation.

10.5 Defining parameters

In my opinion, one of the toughest yet least talked about aspects of creating an automation script is defining the parameters. If you hardcode too many variables in your script, your automation may not be flexible enough. On the other hand, if you make too many parameters and choices, you could end up making an automation process that is more difficult than the manual process. Therefore, you will want to try and find a balance between the two.

An excellent example of this is a project I was assigned to a few years ago to automate the installation of System Center products. The goal was to provide a simple interface that consultants could use to deploy products like Configuration Manager and Service Manager for customers. This also had the added bonus of creating standardized installations, making it simple for consultants to pick up where another left off.

I started with the Service Manager installation. Service Manager typically consists of two servers: a management server and a data warehouse server. Additional management servers may be deployed for large companies, but the installation is always the same.

I created a script to generate an answer file to perform a silent installation. The consultant had to provide about six or seven parameters, and it would go off and perform the installations. It would download and install all the prerequisites and even install the SQL backend for them. The script worked great, so I moved on to doing the same for Configuration Manager.

I started by talking to consultants who regularly set up Configuration Manager for clients. Unlike Service Manager, Configuration Manager has numerous different roles that can spread across multiple machines—and that doesn't even include the remote distribution points at client sites.

As I talked to more and more of the consultants, I discovered more scenarios. As I took notes, I quickly realized that if I built a script to accommodate all the different scenarios, I would essentially be remaking the installation wizard. So, we decided that it wasn't worth scripting the entire installation, but we could script portions to help consultants save time and standardize where possible.

I bring this up because I don't want you to fall down the rabbit hole of trying to accommodate every situation through parameters, because you may end up just reinventing the wheel/wizard/GUI. But, at the same time, that doesn't mean your automation should not consider different scenarios or environments because some can be handled by your code.

Let's start by looking at what values are required to create a new virtual machine:

- Which Hyper-V host to create it on
- The name of the virtual machine
- Where to store the virtual machine configuration and disks
- The sizes of the operating system disk
- The number and size of secondary disks
- The virtual switch

- How much memory to assign
- The location of the ISO
- If you want automatic checkpoints
- Which virtual machine generation to use
- What the boot order should be

As you can see, there are many things to consider, but as you think through these things, remember that your automation does not have to fit every single scenario. However, there are four buckets a potential parameter can fall into:

- *Mandatory*—The parameter must be supplied by the person or script initiating the automation.
- *Fixed*—A predetermined value that cannot be changed.
- *Optional*—A parameter that the person can choose to supply or not, but keep in mind that optional parameters should have a fixed value they default to if not supplied.
- *Logical*—Parameters that can use logic to determine their value. Like with optional parameters, logical parameters should have a fallback plan if they cannot determine a value.

For example, when it comes to automatic checkpoints, you know that you never want to use them. So, you can just set it as a fixed value to disable them in your script. Then, if there is ever a time when you want them, you can just turn them back on manually after the creation process.

An example of an optional parameter is the virtual hard disk (VHD) space. Most operating systems require 30–40 GB of space to install. Knowing that you can increase the disk size after installation, you could fix it to 50 GB or make it an optional parameter. This way, you can provide another size if you want.

A parameter you can use a logical value for is the virtual switch. Here, you can have your script attempt to locate the switch for you. You can have it check for an external switch and, if it doesn't find it, try to find the default switch. If for some reason it is unable to find a switch, you can leave it off since you can still install the operating system without it.

Another logical parameter can be the path for the virtual machine configuration and disks. Hyper-V has a default location to store virtual machines. So, you can have your script get this location and then just append a folder with the virtual machine name to it. If there is some reason you don't want to use the default path, then chances are you are doing something out of the ordinary, in which case using the wizard might be your best bet.

So, looking back at the original list of parameters, you can now determine which ones to make into input parameters that the person running the script will need to provide, which ones you create logic for, and which ones you have set in the script, as shown in figure 10.2. Also, be sure to remember that unless it is a mandatory parameter, there needs to be a default value.

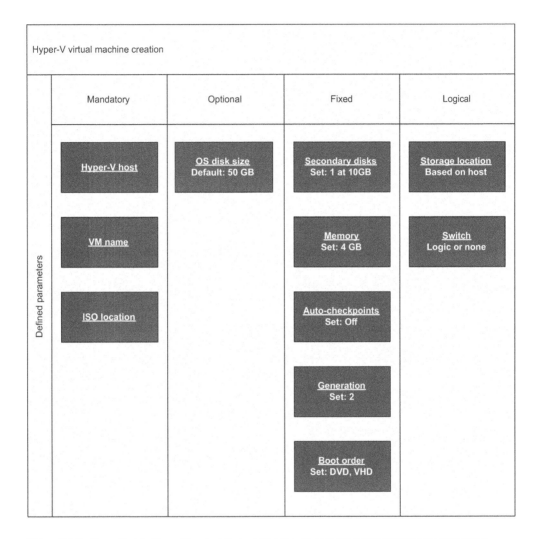

Figure 10.2 Hyper-V virtual machine creation parameters broken down into buckets for mandatory (values that must be supplied), optional (values that have a default value but can be overwritten by the user), fixed (values that are hardcoded), and logical (values that are determined by logic in the script)

Obviously, you can adapt these parameters to meet your needs and requirements. This is just a thought experiment to give you an idea of how to think about requirements and parameters. But once you have your parameters defined, it is time to move on with the automation process.

10.6 *Making resumable automations*

One of the most overlooked concepts I've seen in automation scripts is the concept of resuming. When building multistage automations, you need to think about the following things:

- What can go wrong at each stage?
- Can the automation continue if it fails?
- Can you rerun the stage?

For instance, in the first part of the virtual machine creation automation, you will collect the information for the logical parameters, disk paths, and the virtual switch. Then, you will create the virtual machine using the New-VM cmdlet. Once the virtual machine is created, you need to set the memory values and the automatic snapshots, add the ISO file, set the boot order, and then turn on the virtual machine. Each one of those is a separate command, as you can see in figure 10.3.

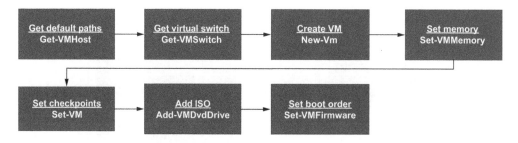

Figure 10.3   Virtual machine creation script process that includes determining the host and switch, creating the virtual machine, setting the memory and check-points, adding the ISO, and setting the boot order

Now you need to consider what would happen if an error occurred at any one of these steps. And if it did, how would restarting the script affect the automation, and how can you prevent any adverse conditions?

Start with the first commands to collect the information about the storage location. If this fails, the virtual machine creation will fail because it won't have a path. So, you can write a few extra lines of code to check that the path exists and is accessible. But that might be unnecessary because you know that when you run the New-VM cmdlet with a blank path, it will fail and tell you exactly why.

However, this is dependent on you knowing the exact behavior of the cmdlet and assuming this behavior will not change between versions. For example, if the behavior of the New-VM cmdlet changes to create a virtual machine in a potentially unwanted location, you would need to check first. Therefore, it would be in your best interest to include a quick Test-Path check to confirm that the script can access the location.

The next step to get the virtual switch is similar, except that you can create a virtual machine without a switch. But if a switch is not found and you pass a `null` value for the parameter to the `New-VM` cmdlet, it will fail. So, in this case, you can include some logic to only add the parameter if a switch is found, as shown in the following listing.

Listing 10.6   Getting the path and external switch

```
$VmHost = Get-VMHost -ComputerName $VMHostName          ⟵  Get the VM host to
                                                           determine the VM path.

$TestPath = Test-Path -Path $VmHost.VirtualMachinePath      ⟵
if($TestPath -eq $false){                                       Confirm the
    throw "Unable to access path '$($VmHost.VirtualMachinePath)'"   script can access
}                                                               the VM path.

$Path = @{                          ⟵  Set the path for the
    Path      = $VmHost.VirtualMachinePath    VM's virtual hard disk
    ChildPath = "$VMName\$VMName.vhdx"
}
$NewVHDPath = Join-Path @Path

$VMParams = @{                      ⟵  Set the new VM
    Name            = $VMName           parameters.
    NewVHDPath      = $NewVHDPath
    NewVHDSizeBytes = 40GB
    Path            = $VmHost.VirtualMachinePath
    Generation      = 2
}
                                                    Determine the
$VmSwitch = Get-VMSwitch -SwitchType External |   ⟵ switch to use.
    Select-Object -First 1
if (-not $VmSwitch) {
    $VmSwitch = Get-VMSwitch -Name 'Default Switch'
}
                                            If the switch is
if ($VmSwitch) {                        ⟵  found, add it to the
    $VMParams.Add('SwitchName',$VmSwitch.Name)   VM parameters.
}
```

With both of these steps, you know you can run them every time the script restarts without causing any issue because they are just gathering information. But the next command—to create the virtual machine—will need to be treated differently.

  If the command to create the new virtual machine fails, the script cannot continue. So, you can easily handle that using the argument `-ErrorAction Stop` on the command to create the virtual machine to stop the execution if there is an error. But now, consider what would happen if there was an error later in the script. Looking at the following listing, consider what would happen if you restarted the automation.

Listing 10.7   Create a virtual machine

```
$VMParams = @{
    Name             = $VMName
    NewVHDPath       = $NewVHDPath
    NewVHDSizeBytes  = 40GB
    SwitchName       = $VmSwitch.Name
    Path             = $VmHost.VirtualMachinePath
    Generation       = 2
    ErrorAction      = 'Stop'
}
$VM = New-VM @VMParams
```

As is, if you were to restart the script, the virtual machine creation would fail because a machine with that name already exists. This would prevent the rest of the automation from continuing because you included the argument -ErrorAction Stop on the machine creation command. However, it is not truly an error because the virtual machine does exist.

So, before you create the virtual machine, you can check if it already exists using the Get-VM cmdlet and create it if it doesn't—except now, there is one more problem. If you run the Get-VM cmdlet and the virtual machine doesn't exist, it will return an error. Of course, you can suppress the error, but how do you know if it failed because the virtual machine was not found or because of some other problem? So, instead of suppressing the error, you can use a try/catch and check the error message, as in listing 10.8. If it is due to the virtual machine not existing, then carry on. If not, then throw a terminating error. Figure 10.4 illustrates the process.

Listing 10.8   Check if the VM exists before creating it

```
try {                          ◁── Attempt to see if the
    $VM = Get-VM -Name $VMName -ErrorAction Stop      VM already exists.
}
catch {            ◁── If the catch is triggered, then set        If the error is not the
    $VM = $null        $VM to null to ensure that any             expected one for a VM not
                       previous data is cleared out.              being there, then throw a
                                                                  terminating error.
    if ($_.FullyQualifiedErrorId -ne          ◁──
        'InvalidParameter,Microsoft.HyperV.PowerShell.Commands.GetVM') {
        throw $_
    }
}
                               If the VM is not
if ($null -eq $VM) {    ◁──    found, then
    $VMParams = @{             create it.
        Name             = $VMName   ◁──  Create the VM.
        NewVHDPath       = $NewVHDPath
        NewVHDSizeBytes  = 40GB
        SwitchName       = $VmSwitch.Name
        Path             = $VmHost.VirtualMachinePath
        Generation       = 2
```

```
        ErrorAction    = 'Stop'
    }
    $VM = New-VM @VMParams
}
```

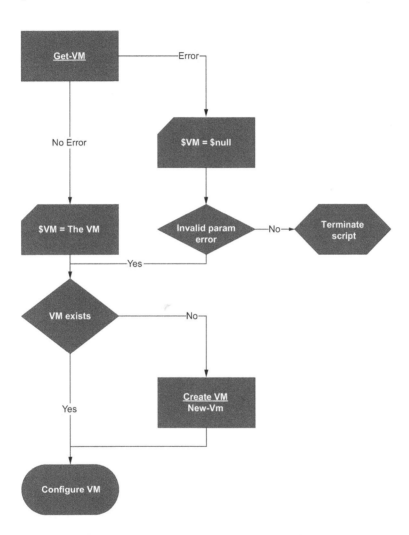

Figure 10.4   Test if a virtual machine exists before attempting to create it. If it exists, skip the creation, but continue with the rest of the script.

Now, consider the steps to set the memory values and the automatic snapshots, add the ISO file, set the boot order, and turn on the virtual machine. Think about what would happen if any of these steps failed or if the script had to restart.

For example, say the cmdlet to set the ISO file, Add-VMDvdDrive, fails because you entered the wrong path in the parameters. You already built the logic, so you know the virtual machine will not be recreated, but what about the setting memory and checkpoints commands? If you rerun either of those, it won't make much difference because it will just set the same values again. However, if setting the boot order with `Set-VMFirmware` fails and you need to restart, the `Add-VMDvdDrive` cmdlet will run again. If that happens, a second DVD drive will be attached to the virtual machine. It might not hurt anything, but it really is not what you would want either. So, for this particular command, you will want to check whether a drive is already attached, and, if it is, just add the ISO file to it using a script like the one in the following listing.

Listing 10.9   Updating virtual machine settings

```
$VMMemory = @{                              ◁────  Set the VM
    DynamicMemoryEnabled = $true                   memory.
    MinimumBytes         = 512MB
    MaximumBytes         = 2048MB
    Buffer               = 20
    StartupBytes         = 1024MB
}
$VM | Set-VMMemory @VMMemory
                                                   Disable automatic
$VM | Set-VM -AutomaticCheckpointsEnabled $false  ◁──  checkpoints.

if(-not $VM.DVDDrives){                      ◁────  Add the Windows
    $VM | Add-VMDvdDrive -Path $ISO                installation ISO.
}
else{
    $VM | Set-VMDvdDrive -Path $ISO
}
                                       Set the boot
$BootOrder = @(      ◁───────          order to use the
    $VM.DVDDrives[0]                   DVD drive first.
    $VM.HardDrives[0]
)
$VM | Set-VMFirmware -BootOrder $BootOrder
```

You cannot change the boot order or change some memory allocation settings when a virtual machine is running. Therefore, you will check to see if the virtual machine is running before executing those steps. If it is already running, you can assume that all the previous steps have been completed, so there is no need to rerun them. Instead, you can just have your script continue. Figure 10.5 shows the logic.

10.6.1 *Determining code logic and functions*

Chapter 2 mentioned a few basic rules to follow when creating functions. These include the following:

- A function can perform multiple related tasks but should be able to be restarted if an error occurs at any point.
- Do not include control logic inside of your functions. If you need your script to take specific actions based on certain results, it is best to define that in the script.

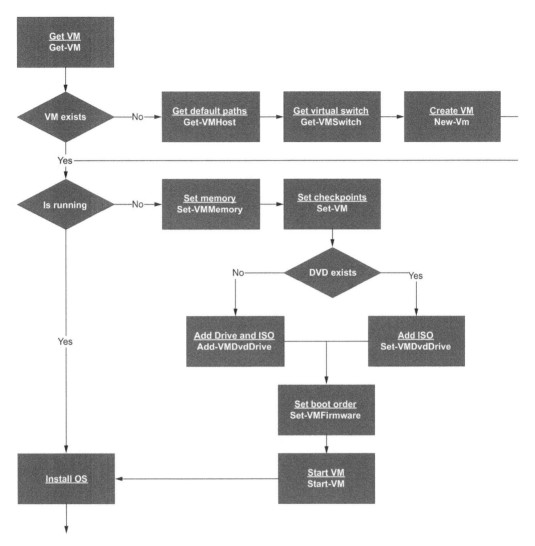

Figure 10.5   If the virtual machine does not exist, create it. If the virtual machine is not running, configure the settings (memory, drives, etc.) and then start it. Once it is created and running, move on to the operating system install.

Considering these, you can determine the best way to structure your script.

The first thing you need to do for the virtual machine provisioning is check whether the virtual machine exists and, if it does not, create it. Since this is control logic, you will want it in your main script. However, when it comes to creating the virtual machine, you can create a single function that will get the disk path and the virtual switch and create the virtual machine.

Then, you need to check whether the machine is running. If it is not, then update the settings and start it. Again, this is control logic, so it goes in the main script. But updating the settings can be done in a single function because that section of code can be rerun from the beginning. Then, you can call the command to start the virtual machine. The steps are shown in figure 10.6.

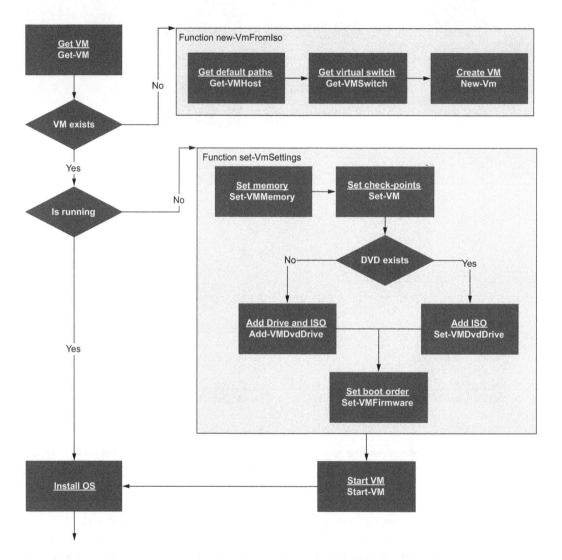

Figure 10.6 Virtual machine creation organized with functions and checks. The first check that confirms whether the virtual machine exists is performed in the script. If it doesn't exist, a function is called to perform the creation process. Once it is confirmed that it exists or has been created, a running check will tell you whether you can set the configuration or not. Finally, if the configuration is performed, you know it is not running, so turn it on—but outside the function, in case you need to perform additional configuration later.

You may notice that there is a check in the update settings to see whether a DVD drive has already been added. While this may seem like control logic, it does not directly impact the execution of the script. So, it is acceptable to include conditions inside your functions, just not something that would change the execution of the script.

Another way to look at it is through the function calls themselves. Having nested functions, or functions calling functions, can make for maintenance and trouble-shooting nightmares. For example, if you put the virtual machine running check inside the `Set-VmSettings` function in figure 10.6, your script will always execute it. This can cause errors because the `Start-VM` cmdlet will always run and return an error if the virtual machine is already running. So, you can put the logic inside the function to only turn it on if it is not running to avoid that. Now, say that 6 months from now, you want to add a new function to perform some additional configurations. Of course, it cannot perform them if the virtual machine is running, but if the virtual machine is started by the `Set-VmSettings` function, you will need to make some significant changes to get this new functionality implemented.

As you can see, this can get complex quickly, and unfortunately, there is no golden rule for it. But by being aware of these challenges during the initial build process, you can save yourself lots of work in the long run.

10.7   Waiting for automations

Once the virtual machine starts, you will need to wait for the operating system to finish installing before you can do anything else. You have two options here. You can just have the script stop and then go back and start it again once the installation is complete, but that requires manual intervention. So instead, you can have your script wait and monitor for completion using a `while` loop.

Whenever you build a `while` loop, you need to be 100% certain that it will end. In this instance, you need to find a way to tell your script that the operating system installation has been completed. Since the host machine cannot tell that, you can use the `Invoke-Command` cmdlet to execute a remote command inside the virtual machine. Once that command completes successfully, you know the operating system is installed. However, if the operating system installation fails, your script could theoretically run forever. So, to prevent that from happening, you need to build a fail-safe into your loop.

There are two ways to build a fail-safe. One is to check for a `failed` condition as well as a `success` condition. For example, if you are monitoring data transferring from one place to another, you know that transfer will either succeed or fail. So, all you need do is monitor for the transfer to end and then get the results. Unfortunately, with the operating system installation, you only know when it is successful. There is no way for PowerShell to know whether the operating system installation failed or is just still running.

If you cannot monitor all possible conditions, you should include a time limit on your while loop. You can do that using the .NET Stopwatch class you first learned about in chapter 3. The Stopwatch class will create a timer that will continue to run as long as your script is executing. So, you can use it to check the elapsed time and take appropriate actions if the time is exceeded. In chapter 3, you used it to ensure that job executions would not overlap and that you could control when a script terminates. In this automation, it will be used as a fail-safe for when other conditions cannot be checked.

For the operating system installation loop, you can set the time limit to 30 minutes. If, after 30 minutes, your installation has not been completed, then throw a terminating error. This will alert you to the problem so you can resolve it manually.

This technique can be used in any situation where PowerShell is not able to tell the condition of the object it is waiting on. The best part is that since you made this script resumable, after you fix the operating system installation, all you have to do is restart the script, and it will pick up where it left off.

Listing 10.10   Waiting for the operating system install to finish

```
$OsInstallTimeLimit = 30
$Command = @{                      ◁──  Command to return the VM
    VMId        = $VM.Id                 guest hostname. It will be used
    ScriptBlock = { $env:COMPUTERNAME }  to determine that the OS install
    Credential  = $Credential            has been completed.
    ErrorAction = 'Stop'
}

$timer = [system.diagnostics.stopwatch]::StartNew()   ◁──  Include a timer or
                                                            counter to ensure that
                                                            your script doesn't end
                                                            after so many minutes.

$Results = $null                                         ◁──  Set the variable before the while loop
while ([string]::IsNullOrEmpty($Results)) {                   to $null to ensure that past variables
    try {                                                     are not causing false positives.
        $Results = Invoke-Command @Command   ◁──  Run the command to
    }                                             get the hostname.
    catch {
        if ($timer.Elapsed.TotalMinutes -gt    ◁──
            $OsInstallTimeLimit) {
            throw "Failed to provision virtual machine after 10 minutes."
        }                                      If the timer exceeds the
    }                                          number of minutes, throw
}                                              a terminating error.
```

Once the operating system installation is finished, there is only one step left: attaching a second VHD.

10.8   *Think of the next person*

In this last step, you will create a new VHD and attach it to the virtual machine. Then, you will execute a remote command on the virtual machine to initialize, partition, and format the new disk. This sounds like many steps that can get complicated quickly when you start thinking about making the script resumable. There is no problem with making complicated logic when needed, but you need to think about the next person who might use this script or even yourself six months down the line. Are they going to be able to follow it? To make things easier on them and yourself, you can follow these best practices.

10.8.1   *Do not overcomplicate it*

Keeping in mind that you will want to resume the script from any point, you will need to build some checks into it to ensure that you don't just add new hard disks every time you restart it. But, at the same time, you do not want to go overboard by creating a whole bunch of different nested if statements that make it nearly impossible for someone else to understand.

To add a second drive to your virtual machine, you need to perform the following steps:

1   Determine the path and name of the VHD.
2   Create the VHD.
3   Attach the VHD to the virtual machine.
4   Add the disk inside the guest operating system.

Figure 10.7 shows the process. Now think about restarting the automation after each step. For instance, step 1 of getting the path and name must run every time the script runs, so no additional logic is needed. However, step 2, create the VHD, will fail if the disk exists. Therefore, you need to check if the disk exists before creating it. So, you can use the Test-Path cmdlet and an if statement to determine whether the disk needs to be created.

Now, on step 3, if the disk exists, it does not mean it was attached to the virtual machine. But, if it is already attached, trying to attach it again will cause an error. So, before attaching the VHD, you can check the virtual machine object and see whether the VHD is already attached.

Finally, once the VHD is attached, you need to initialize, partition, and format the new disk in the guest operating system. The difficult part here is determining whether this has already been done. This is because the guest operating system has no idea what VHD is attached to it. It just knows that it has this disk. Trying to solve situations like this can cause others to make things overly complicated. They will try to do things like writing a file to the new disk in the guest operating system as a mark of it being added. The problem here is that there is no way to know if someone removed that file, if the disk was added but failed to write the file, how you

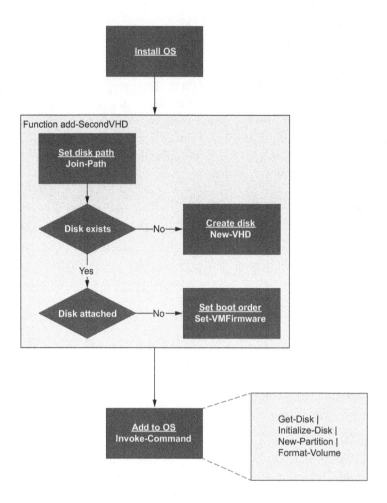

Figure 10.7   Process to add a second VHD to a virtual machine and configure the disk in the guest operating system

would handle adding a third disk, etc. In reality, all you need to do is check the guest operating system for any raw disks.

The existence of a raw disk lets you know that a disk has not been added to the operating system. So, using the Get-Disk cmdlet, you can check for any disk with the partition style of raw. Then, using pipelines, you can pass that disk to the Initialize-Disk cmdlet, then to the New-Partition cmdlet, and finally to the Format-Volume cmdlet. You can run this command as many times as you like because it only returns raw disks. Therefore, you do not need to build any fancy logic or checks into the script in the next listing. The simple Where-Object filter after the Get-Disk cmdlet is all you need.

Listing 10.11   Adding a second VHD

```
Function Add-SecondVHD{
    param(
        $VM
    )
    $Path = @{                          ◁──── Set the path for the
        Path      = $VM.Path                  second hard drive.
        ChildPath = "$($VM.Name)-Data.vhdx"
    }
    $DataDisk = Join-Path @Path                     If the VHD does not
                                                    exist, create it.
    if (-not(Test-Path $DataDisk)) {    ◁────
        New-VHD -Path $DataDisk -SizeBytes 10GB | Out-Null
    }
                                                    If the VHD is not
    $Vhd = $VM.HardDrives |             ◁──── attached to the
        Where-Object { $_.Path -eq $DataDisk }      VM, attach it.
    if (-not $Vhd) {
        $VM | Get-VMScsiController -ControllerNumber 0 |
            Add-VMHardDiskDrive -Path $DataDisk
    }
}

Add-SecondVHD -VM $VM        Script block to initialize,
                            partition, and format the
$ScriptBlock = {            ◁──── new drive inside the guest OS
    $Volume = @{
        FileSystem        = 'NTFS'
        NewFileSystemLabel = "Data"
        Confirm           = $false
    }
    Get-Disk | Where-Object { $_.PartitionStyle -eq 'raw' } |
    Initialize-Disk -PartitionStyle MBR -PassThru |
    New-Partition -AssignDriveLetter -UseMaximumSize |
    Format-Volume @Volume
}                           Run the command on
                            the guest OS to set up
$Command = @{               ◁──── the new drive.
    VMId         = $VM.Id
    ScriptBlock = $ScriptBlock
    Credential  = $Credential
    ErrorAction = 'Stop'
}
$Results = Invoke-Command @Command
$Results
```

10.8.2   Comment, comment, comment

Sometimes making complex logic in your automation is unavoidable. In these cases, you will want to ensure that you leave proper comments in your script following a few best practices.

DO NOT STATE THE OBVIOUS

Do not comment on anything that someone familiar with PowerShell will already know. For example, above the New-VHD cmdlet, you do not need to put the comment "Create a new VHD." However, if you nest the New-VHD cmdlet inside of an if statement that checks whether the disk already exists, it might warrant a brief command such as "If the VHD does not exist, create it."

Also, if you create such a mess of nested if/else and foreach statements that you feel the need to add a comment to the end of each block, you may want to consider rethinking the logic or building some functions to handle it.

USE REGIONS TO SEPARATE CODE LOGICALLY

PowerShell lets you create regions that allow you to create a grouping of lines. To create a new region, all you have to do is enter #region at the start of a line and then, to end it, create another line with #endregion. Most editors, including VS Code and ISE, will allow you to collapse the entire code section between these two lines. You can also include a title next to the region declarations to identify the section quickly.

You can see an example in the screenshot in figure 10.8, where I put the commands to create the virtual machine into a region. Then, in the second screenshot, in figure 10.9, I collapsed it.

```
340    #region Create VM
341    # Attempt to see if the virtual machine already exists
342    try {
343        $VM = Get-VM -Name $VMName -ErrorAction Stop
344    }
345  > catch { ...
354    }
355
356    # If the VM is not found then create it
357  > if ($null -eq $VM) { ...
365    }
366
367    # Check if the VM is running
368  > if ($VM.State -ne 'Running') { ...
377    }
378    #endregion Create VM
```

Figure 10.8   PowerShell code to create a virtual machine added to a region

```
339
340  > #region Create VM...
378    #endregion Create VM
379
380  > #region Wait for OS install...
413    #endregion Wait for OS install
414
```

Figure 10.9   The same code as figure 10.8, but collapsed

Also, if you find your script becoming so long that you need to create multiple regions, it might be a good sign that you need to break them up into separate files and create a custom module instead of a single script.

AVOID MULTIPLE-LINE COMMENTS

There should never be more comments than code. Try to keep your comments short and to the point. If you need to explain a section in depth, I recommend creating a region and placing the multiple-line comment at the beginning of the region.

Also, place your multiple-line comments between a less-than hash (<#) and greater-than hash (#>) instead of putting a hash at the start of every line. This way, you can collapse the entire comment block when working on the script:

```
#region Section the requires explaining
<#
This is where I would put a multiple-line
comment. It is also best to use the less than hash
and hash greater than when creating multiple-line
comments, as it allows you to collapse the entire
comment section.
#>

... your code

#endregion
```

10.8.3 Include help and examples on all scripts and functions

Nothing can be more frustrating than coming across a script or function that does not contain the help section at the beginning. You may think the name and parameters are obvious, but remember, you are the one writing it. You need to think about the next person who will use it.

You can generate the help section template using VS Code by entering ## at the top of a script or inside a function. It will even include a line for each parameter. For example, the following snippet shows what VS Code was generated when I entered ## on the first line of this function:

```
Function New-VmFromIso {
    <#
    .SYNOPSIS
    Short description

    .DESCRIPTION
    Long description

    .PARAMETER VMName
    Parameter description

    .PARAMETER VMHostName
    Parameter description
```

```
.EXAMPLE
An example

.NOTES
General notes
#>
[CmdletBinding()]
param(
    [Parameter(Mandatory = $true)]
    [string]$VMName,
    [Parameter(Mandatory = $true)]
    [string]$VMHostName
)


}
```

Unlike the comments in your code, you want to be as verbose as possible in the help section. You want to ensure that everyone knows exactly what this script or function does and how to use it. If you have optional parameters, explain when they are required and include examples of them being used.

On top of showing how to use the parameters, also show examples of the parameter values. The only thing more frustrating than no help is help that does not explain what it is doing. For example, instead of making an example like `Set-VmSettings -VM $VM -ISO $ISO`, show what those values are. It is useless unless the person knows what the `$VM` and `$ISO` values are. Instead, make your examples like the following snippet:

```
.EXAMPLE
$ISO = 'D:\ISO\Windows11.iso'
$VM = Get-VM -Name 'Vm01'
Set-VmSettings -VM $VM -ISO $ISO
```

10.8.4 *Have a backup plan*

Throughout this chapter and this book, I have talked multiple times about keeping things as simple as possible. However, that does not mean you can't get fancy. But if you do, have a backup plan.

To show what I mean by this, we can get fancy about obtaining the login credentials for the new virtual machine. Since you saw how to set and encode the default password in the first automation, you can also decode it. To do that, you can create a function that will mount the ISO, find the autounattend.xml file, and import it to PowerShell. Then retrieve the password value, decode it, and build a credential object.

Shown in listing 10.12 is a pretty slick bit of code that is more of a nicety to have than a required step in the automation process. Of course, you could just simply prompt the person running the script to enter the username and password, but where is the fun in that? So, you can go ahead and include the fancy function to extract the password, but include a fail-safe in it.

If the function cannot find the password in the ISO file, then have it prompt the user to enter the username and password using the Get-Credential cmdlet. This way, if something goes wrong, your automation can continue to work.

Listing 10.12 Get-IsoCredentials

```
Function Get-IsoCredentials {
    param($ISO)

    $DiskImage = @{              ◄──┤ Mount the
        ImagePath = $ISO             ISO image.
        PassThru  = $true
    }
    $image = Mount-DiskImage @DiskImage

    $drive = $image |           ◄────┤ Get the new
        Get-Volume |                   drive letter.
        Select-Object -ExpandProperty DriveLetter

    $ChildItem = @{             ◄────┐ Attempt to find the
        Path   = "$($drive):"          autounattend.xml in
        Filter = "autounattend.xml"    the ISO image.
    }
    $AutounattendXml = Get-ChildItem @ChildItem
                                              ┌ If the autounattend.xml is found,
    if ($AutounattendXml) {     ◄─────────────┤ attempt to extract the password.
        [xml]$Autounattend = Get-Content $AutounattendXML.FullName
        $object = $Autounattend.unattend.settings |
            Where-Object { $_.pass -eq "oobeSystem" }
        $AdminPass = $object.component.UserAccounts.AdministratorPassword
        if ($AdminPass.PlainText -eq $false) {
            $encodedpassword = $AdminPass.Value
            $base64 = [system.convert]::Frombase64string($encodedpassword)
            $decoded = [system.text.encoding]::Unicode.GetString($base64)
            $AutoPass = ($decoded -replace ('AdministratorPassword$', ''))
        }
        else {
            $AutoPass = $AdminPass.Value
        }
    }
                                       ┌ Dismount
                                         the ISO.
    $image | Dismount-DiskImage | Out-Null   ◄─┘

    $user = "administrator"     ◄──────────┐ If the password is returned,
    if ([string]::IsNullOrEmpty($AutoPass)) {  create a credential object;
        $parameterHash = @{                     otherwise, prompt the user
            UserName = $user                    for the credentials.
            Message  = 'Enter administrator password'
        }
        $credential = Get-Credential @parameterHash
    }
    else {
        $pass = ConvertTo-SecureString $AutoPass -AsPlainText -Force
        $Object = @{
```

```
        TypeName    = 'System.Management.Automation.PSCredential'
        ArgumentList = ( $user , $pass )
    }
    $credential = New-Object @Object
}

$credential
}
```

10.9 *Do not forget about the presentation*

I'm sure most of you have, at some point, watched a cooking show and seen the judges critique a contestant about their presentation. The food may have tasted wonderful, but they still lost because it was ugly. The same can be said for your code. If your script is a jumbled mess of 300-character-long single-line commands, nobody will want to touch it.

Please don't fall into the trap of trying to make your script three lines shorter because of the misconception that the shorter the script, the better it is. Sure, it is fun to see how efficient you can make your code, but the number of lines does not directly correlate with efficiency. Break up those one-liners. And, if you want to keep all the pipes, remember PowerShell allows line breaks after pipes. For example, PowerShell treats both of the following commands in the exact same way:

```
Get-Service -Name Spooler | Stop-Service

Get-Service -Name Spooler |
    Stop-Service
```

Use splatting to handle cmdlets with a bunch of parameters. My typical rule of thumb is to use splatting if my parameters make my script scroll horizontally. On a typical widescreen monitor, that's around 150–180 characters. Manning, the publishers of this book, limits a code line to 76 characters, which is why you see so much splatting in this book.

Finally, group your code logically. For example, don't mix functions and script code together. Your script should be the help section, parameters, functions, and then the code. Also, if you have a lot of functions, consider grouping them into regions.

So, taking everything we have covered in this chapter, you can put together the final script, which leads to my last tip. Once you have your completed script, open it in VS Code, right-click, and select Format Document. This will ensure that all your commands have the proper spacing and indentations.

Since the final code of this chapter is quite long, I have decided to leave it out of the text in the book. Instead, you can find the completed script in the source code provided with this book or in the GitHub repository (https://mng.bz/m2W0). The logic is illustrated in figure 10.10.

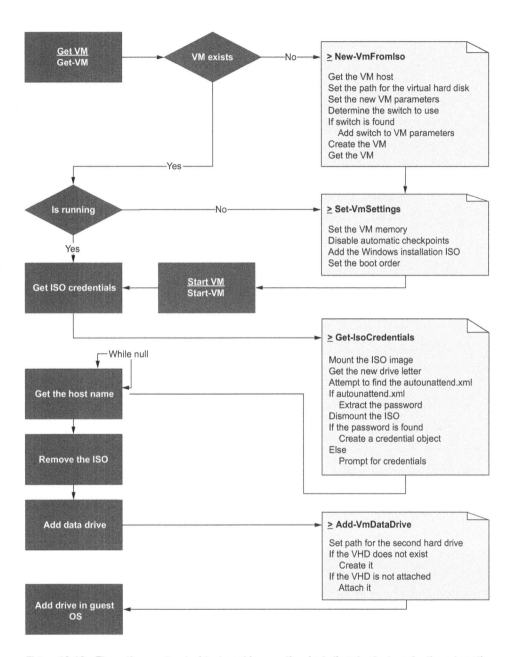

Figure 10.10 The entire zero-touch virtual machine creation, including checks to make the automation restartable by seeing whether the virtual machine exists before attempting to create it, and checking if it is running before configuring the settings. It includes a loop to monitor the operating system installation and adds the second drive to both the virtual machine and the guest operating system after the installation.

Summary

- Converting tasks from manual to automations is not always a one-to-one conversion. There may be things you do not even realize you are doing. Therefore, it is always a good idea to walk through it step by step.
- When updating structured data, import it to PowerShell instead of trying to manipulate a text file.
- Functions should not contain logic that would change the execution of the overall script. Instead, that logic should be done in the main script body.
- Not all applications and operating systems behave the same way. As a result, you may need to use additional logic when interfacing with external tools.
- You should always try to make multistep automations restartable if there is a failure at any one part.
- Think about the next person to use the script and comment and document it appropriately.

Part 3

Creating an automation for yourself is all well and good, but to see the true potential that automation has to offer, you need to be able to share it. In this section, you will learn how to easily share scripts with your colleagues. You will also see how you can create a frontend to implement an automated process that anyone can use. And, finally, you will learn how you can maintain your automations through the use of source control and unit testing.

11

End-user scripts and forms

This chapter covers

- Creating a web frontend for a PowerShell automation
- Processing automation requests
- Writing PowerShell to execute on client machines

So far, most scripts in this book are *backend scripts* (e.g., ones you would run locally, on a dedicated machine, or shared with others familiar with PowerShell). However, this is not always the case. PowerShell can assist others in your organization who may not even know what PowerShell is. In this chapter, you will see how you can build and design PowerShell automations to help not just yourself but the entire organization.

In this chapter, we will cover two main scenarios related to end-user scripts. The first is providing an automation mechanism to the business. A very common example of this is user account provisioning and deprovisioning. There is a wealth of resources out there on creating users in Active Directory, Exchange, Office 365, and other environments. But you cannot just provide HR a copy of a PowerShell script and expect them to know how to execute it. Instead, you will want to give them a frontend interface to submit requests for automations.

The second scenario is using PowerShell to manage end-user devices. Anyone who has worked in IT long enough knows that there are some things that just cannot be handled by application installers, group policy, mobile device management, or whatever configuration management system you might be using. And, in most cases, you will need to execute the script across hundreds or thousands of machines. To help you when these situations arise, you will learn how to mimic and test the execution of scripts so you will be able to design a working script for these tasks.

11.1 Script frontends

When designing scripts that require user input, you have two choices. First, you can package the automation as a script or module and provide a copy to the person. Or you can create a frontend.

Providing someone with a script assumes that the person is familiar with PowerShell, knows how to provide parameters, and has the correct modules and versions installed. It might be safe to assume that members of your team can handle this. But what about nontechnical people? For them, the better choice is to provide a frontend.

As you know, PowerShell itself does not have a frontend. Instead, it is entirely command-line driven. If you search around the web, you will find plenty of resources around creating custom forms using PowerShell and .NET. However, these still require that the person has the correct version of PowerShell installed, along with any required modules and, even more important, the correct permissions.

On top of that, designing a form can be a long and arduous task. Having to account for things like different screen resolutions, not to mention different platforms, can turn a simple task into a major project. To prevent this from happening to you, you can leverage existing platforms to create web-based forms and then have PowerShell pick up the data submitted by the form and perform the appropriate actions. Most IT service management platforms have a web portal that you can leverage, or, as you will see in this case, you can do something as simple as a SharePoint form that takes less than 10 minutes to create.

By using a platform like SharePoint, you can bring its capabilities to your automations. For instance, when you create a list in SharePoint, it automatically includes a form to add and edit items. Also, since it is a web platform, someone could submit a request from their mobile phone or any other device with a browser. And, if that is not enough to convince you, SharePoint (and other similar platforms) also provide built-in security.

11.1.1 SharePoint trial tenant

The following two sections in this chapter will require a SharePoint Online tenant. If you do not have an existing SharePoint tenant or would prefer to do your testing outside your company's environment, you can sign up for the Microsoft 365 Developer Program. Doing this will give you a free sandbox tenant prepopulated with 25 users.

To set up your demo tenant, go to the Microsoft 365 Developer Program (http://mng.bz/QnpG), click the Join Now button, and log in using any Microsoft personal account (hotmail.com, live.com, outlook.com, msn.com, etc.). Then, follow the prompts to enter your region and contact information. When you reach the page to set up your Microsoft 365 E5 sandbox, select Instant Sandbox.

Next, you will need to provide an admin user name and password. Keep these somewhere handy, as you will need them throughout the following two sections.

Once you complete the setup wizard, your sandbox environment will start provisioning, and you can continue to the next section, where you will create a custom SharePoint form.

11.2 Creating a request form

Anyone who has ever maintained a SharePoint, Teams, or Groups environment knows that site sprawl can be a huge problem. You can choose to give individuals throughout the company access to create sites, but you will lose control of the settings and maintenance of these sites. The other option is to restrict anyone from creating sites, which shifts a burden onto the people who can create them. So, to provide a happy middle ground, you can create a form for people to request sites and then have an automation perform the actual creation.

By having people submit a form, you can track the owners, know the state of the sites, and if you choose, you can even use the built-in approval processes in SharePoint. Another added benefit is that you can control exactly how each site is created.

Throughout this section, we will be using the PnP PowerShell module. This module is a cross-platform solution with over 600 cmdlets to manage Microsoft 365 environments, including SharePoint Online. The PnP PowerShell module is a successor to the SharePoint PnP modules that have been around for over 10 years. While it came from the SharePoint Pnp module, it has grown to include commands for managing Microsoft Teams, Project, Security & Compliance, and Azure Active Directory.

Before getting started, you need to ensure that you have the PnP PowerShell installed and imported:

```
Install-Module PnP.Powershell
Import-Module PnP.Powershell
```

Then you need to connect to your SharePoint Online site. If you signed up for a development environment, your tenant's name will be a random alphanumeric subdomain on the onmicrosoft.com domain. This will make your SharePoint URL the subdomain .SharePoint.com. For example, 57pzfq.onmicrosoft.com would be 57pzfq.SharePoint .com. For now, you can use the interactive login to access with an administrator account:

```
Connect-PnPOnline -Url "https://<subdomain>.SharePoint.com" -UseWebLogin
```

Finally, before we get started, go ahead and create a new site specifically for this exercise so you can keep everything self-contained in case you want to remove it later:

```
$PnPSite = @{
    Type        = 'CommunicationSite'
    Title       = 'Site Management'
    Url         = "https://<subdomain>.sharepoint.com/sites/SiteManagement"
    Owner       = "<your-username>@<subdomain>.onmicrosoft.com"
    SiteDesign  = 'Blank'
}
New-PnPSite @PnPSite
```

If you navigate to the URL of the site, you should see a new blank SharePoint site, shown in figure 11.1.

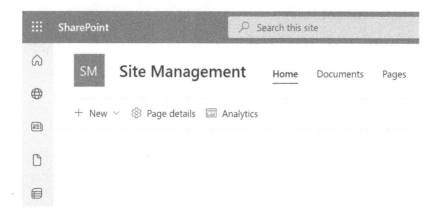

Figure 11.1   A blank SharePoint site created to host the form for submitting new site requests

Next, you need to switch your PowerShell session to this new site, so everything you do is on it and not on your main SharePoint page:

```
Connect-PnPOnline -Url "https://<subdomain>.SharePoint.com/sites
➡ /SiteManagement" -UseWebLogin
```

You are now ready to create the list to gather the request information.

11.2.1 *Gathering data*

Ensuring that you get the correct data for your automation is the most critical step in the process. The best way to determine the data you need is to look at the cmdlets to create the site. In this case, you will use the `New-PnPTenantSite` cmdlet to create the sites.

Using the following snippet, you can list the parameters for the `New-PnPTenantSite` cmdlet:

```
$commandData = Get-Command 'New-PnPTenantSite'
$commandData.ParameterSets |
```

```
Select-Object -Property @{l='ParameterSet';
    e={$_.Name}} -ExpandProperty Parameters |
    Where-Object{ $_.Name -notin
        [System.Management.Automation.Cmdlet]::CommonParameters } |
Format-Table ParameterSet, Name, ParameterType, IsMandatory
```

You should see 4 required parameters and 10 optional parameters. Just because something is a parameter or even a required parameter does not mean it needs to be a field in the form for the user to fill in. You may be able to perform lookups or calculations or set default values for some parameters. Using table 11.1, you can determine which parameters you want to include and where you will get that data.

Table 11.1 The parameters for the New-PnPTenantSite that will be used to help determine the fields you need in your form

Parameter	Data type	Required
Title	string	TRUE
Url	string	TRUE
Owner	string	TRUE
Lcid	uint	FALSE
Template	string	FALSE
TimeZone	int	TRUE
ResourceQuota	double	FALSE
ResourceQuotaWarningLevel	double	FALSE
StorageQuota	long	FALSE
StorageQuotaWarningLevel	long	FALSE
RemoveDeletedSite	switch	FALSE
Wait	switch	FALSE
Force	switch	FALSE
Connection	PnPConnection	FALSE

Starting with the required parameters, the most obvious one we will need is the Title. This can be a simple text field for the user to fill out. Next is the Url. Per SharePoint requirements, a site's URL can't contain symbols other than an underscore, dash, single quotes, and period (_, -, ', and ., respectively). Also, you will most likely want the URL to reflect the site's name. For this reason, you can use the Title to determine the Url and remove any illegal characters in your PowerShell. This way, you do not have to rely on the user to know these limitations.

For Owner, you have a couple of options. You can have the user select the owner or have the owner automatically set to the person who created the request—or even a combination of both. We will keep it simple and just get the person who created the request.

The final required parameter, TimeZone, has multiple ways to address it. If you are a small company with offices in a single time zone, you can just set a default value. However, a lot of companies have offices in multiple time zones. Therefore, you can create a drop-down list of different time zones for users to choose from. The nice thing about this is that you can customize it to your company. So, you don't need to list all 93 different time zones in the drop-down—just the ones you know you need. You can also make this optional and set a default value when not selected. To keep things short and simple here, we will just have the automation use the same time zone as the main SharePoint site.

For the optional parameters, you know you will want the users to choose a template, so we will include the Template parameter. These will need to be a prepopulated list of options. If you run the Get-PnPWebTemplates cmdlet, you will see all the available templates:

```
Get-PnPWebTemplates | Select-Object Name, Title, DisplayCategory
Name                     Title                                 DisplayCategory
----                     -----                                 ---------------
STS#3                    Team site (no Microsoft 365 group)    Collaboration
STS#0                    Team site (classic experience)        Collaboration
BDR#0                    Document Center                       Enterprise
DEV#0                    Developer Site                        Collaboration
OFFILE#1                 Records Center                        Enterprise
EHS#1                    Team Site - SharePoint Online         Enterprise
BICenterSite#0           Business Intelligence Center          Enterprise
SRCHCEN#0                Enterprise Search Center              Enterprise
ENTERWIKI#0              Enterprise Wiki                       Publishing
PROJECTSITE#0            Project Site                          Collaboration
PRODUCTCATALOG#0         Product Catalog                       Publishing
COMMUNITY#0              Community Site                        Collaboration
COMMUNITYPORTAL#0        Community Portal                      Enterprise
SITEPAGEPUBLISHING#0     Communication site                   Publishing
SRCHCENTERLITE#0         Basic Search Center                  Enterprise
visprus#0                Visio Process Repository             Enterprise
```

The tricky part here is that the name values that you need for the New-PnPTenantSite cmdlet are not easy to figure out independently. So, you will want to make your drop-down show the title instead of the name. However, the title of a template is not immutable, meaning it can change. Therefore, you will not want to create a drop-down of just the titles. Instead, you can create a second list to hold the title and the name properties. Then, use that list as a lookup. This will allow you to display the clean title value for the people submitting the form and refer back to the internal name inside your automation.

For the other parameters, you can just let SharePoint use the default values. So, our final parameters are shown in table 11.2.

Table 11.2 Final parameters for what will need to be gathered for creating a new SharePoint site

Parameter	Value
Title	A text box on the form
Url	Derived from the title in the script
Owner	Created by user from the SharePoint entry
Template	Look up from another list
TimeZone	Use the same as the main SharePoint site

REPORTING STATUS

Before you create the list in SharePoint, you need to consider how you will let the user know about the status of the automation. If they just submit a form and it takes them to a blank page or shows them the SharePoint list, there is no way for them to know what is happening. Therefore, at a minimum, you will want to include a status field in your list, as in figure 11.2. Then, as your automation runs, you can update it so they know what is happening.

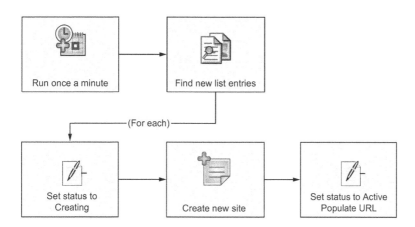

Figure 11.2 New SharePoint site creation workflow with status updates so the submitter knows the status of their request

Also, since you are generating the site URL in the automation, you will need to let the user know what it is. So, you will want to add another field for the URL.

11.2.2 Creating a SharePoint form

Creating a form in SharePoint can be as simple as creating a list and using the default SharePoint forms, or you can use custom JSON or Power App to really customize them. For our purposes, the automatically generated form will work.

To create a SharePoint list, you can use the `New-PnPList` cmdlet. Then, you can customize it by using the `Set-PnPList` cmdlet and adding additional fields using the `Add-PnPField` cmdlet.

Starting with the list to hold the template selections, you can create the list and then add a text column for the Name property. There is no need to create a column for the title because a Title field is included by default when you create a list:

```
$templateList = New-PnPList -Title 'Site Templates' -Template GenericList
Add-PnPField -List $templateList -DisplayName "Name" -InternalName "Name" -Ty
➥pe Text -AddToDefaultView
```

Since this is going to be a prepopulated list, you can get the list of templates again using the `Get-PnPWebTemplates` cmdlet. Then, you can loop through each one and add it to the list using the `Add-PnpListItem` cmdlet:

```
$WebTemplates = Get-PnPWebTemplates
foreach($t in $WebTemplates){
    $values = @{
        Title = $t.Title
        Name = $t.Name
    }
    Add-PnpListItem -List $templateList -Values $values
}
```

If you navigate to the site and click Site Contents, you should now see a list named Site Templates, shown in figure 11.3. Inside it, you will see the list of templates you just imported.

Site Templates ☆	
Title ⌄	Name ⌄
Team site (no Microsoft 365 group)	STS#3
Team site (classic experience)	STS#0
Document Center	BDR#0

Figure 11.3   Site Templates list in SharePoint that will be used as a drop-down for the new site creation form

Now you can repeat the process to create the new site request list. However, there are a few additional things that are necessary for creating this list.

First, when creating the list, this time, you will want to include the `OnQuickLaunch` switch so the list is added to the navigation pane on the site. Also, by default, SharePoint

enables attachments on a list. Since there is no need for attachments, you can use the
`Set-PnPList` cmdlet to disable them:

```
$list = New-PnPList -Title 'Site Requests' -Template GenericList -OnQuickLaun
ch
Set-PnPList -Identity $list -EnableAttachments $false
```

Like with the previous list, the Title field is created by default. But this time, let's use
the `Set-PnPField` cmdlet to change the field's display name to Site Name. This way,
it will be more obvious to the person submitting the form what they need to put in
the field:

```
Set-PnPField -List $list -Identity "Title" -Values @{Title="Site name"}
```

Next, you can add the new fields you will need to the site, starting with the Site URL
and Status fields. The Site URL field will be set to the type of URL, so SharePoint will
make it a link, and Status will be a choice because you should have your statuses predefined. When you create a choice list, you can include the fields for the drop-down
in a string array.

   Now, there are two more things to consider with these fields. First, since any field
added to a list in SharePoint is automatically added to the submission form, it gives
users the ability to change it. To prevent that, you can create a custom form or simply
set the columns to Hidden. This way, they will not show on the form. However, since
the user will need to see them, you can include the `-AddToDefaultView` switch when
creating them. This way, even though they will not be on the form, they will show
when the user looks at the list. And, finally, on the Status field, you will want to include
a default value:

```
Add-PnPField -List $list -DisplayName "Site URL" -InternalName "SiteURL" -Typ
e URL -AddToDefaultView
Set-PnPField -List $list -Identity "SiteURL" -Values @{Hidden=$True}

Add-PnPField -List $list -DisplayName "Status" -InternalName "Status" -Type C
hoice -AddToDefaultView -Choices "Submitted","Creating","Active","Retired",'P
roblem'
Set-PnPField -List $list -Identity "Status" -Values @{DefaultValue="Submitted
"; Hidden=$True}
```

The last field to add is the Lookup field. Lookup fields are a little more complicated
to make with PowerShell. They require that you create the XML required to perform
the lookup. Since this chapter is more about the automation than the creation of
SharePoint lists, I'll spare you the details of each value in the XML. All you need to
know is the List field is the GUID of the lookup list—in this case, the Site Templates
list. The SourceId is the GUID of the list to add the field to, and the ID just needs to
be any random GUID. If you followed all the previous code examples, you can run the
following snippet without making any changes:

```
$xml = @"
<Field
    Type="Lookup"
    DisplayName="Template"
    Required="TRUE"
    EnforceUniqueValues="FALSE"
    List="{$($templateList.Id)}"
    ShowField="Title"
    UnlimitedLengthInDocumentLibrary="FALSE"
    RelationshipDeleteBehavior="None"
    ID="{$(New-Guid)}"
    SourceID="{$($list.Id)}"
    StaticName="Template"
    Name="Template"
    ColName="int1"
    RowOrdinal="0"
/>
"@
Add-PnPFieldFromXml -List $list -FieldXml $xml
```

After creating everything, go back to the site and navigate to the Site Requests list. If you click the New button, you should see the form shown in figure 11.4 with the site name and template drop-down.

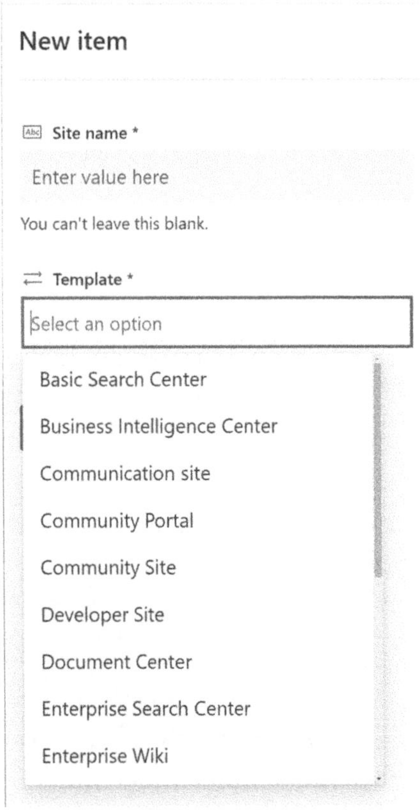

Figure 11.4   The New item form that is created automatically by SharePoint, based on the list you created

Go ahead and submit a new entry so you have something to test with in the next section.

11.3   Processing requests

Now that you have your nice form, you need to trigger your automations. There are several ways to do this. You can use something as simple as Task Scheduler or Cron to run the script every 5–10 minutes to check for new entries. Some cloud platforms like Power Apps and Logic Apps have integrations for SharePoint that can use webhooks and Azure Automation or Azure Functions to trigger a PowerShell script, but those include additional costs for either consumption, licensing, or both. No matter which you choose, the script behind it will remain the same, so for now, we will just concentrate on the script to perform the automation.

11.3.1   Permissions

Like you have had to do many times throughout this book, we once again need to figure out a way to securely provide the script access to the resources it needs. Luckily, the PnP PowerShell module can help with this too. The cmdlet `Register-PnPAzureADApp` can create a service principal (Azure AD App) with all the permissions required to manage SharePoint sites. It also can generate the certificate for authentication and save it to the user or machine stores.

To create the Azure AD App with the default permissions, you can run the following snippet. The default permissions include everything you need to perform the steps of this automation. You will be prompted to log in. Then, it will pause for 60 seconds before asking you to approve the permissions:

```
Register-PnPAzureADApp -ApplicationName 'PnP-SiteRequests' -Tenant
➥ '<subdomain>.onmicrosoft.com' -Store CurrentUser -Interactive
WARNING: No permissions specified, using default permissions
Certificate added to store
Checking if application 'PnP-SiteRequests' does not exist yet...Success.
    Application 'PnP-SiteRequests' can be registered.
App PnP-SiteRequests with id 581af0eb-0d07-4744-a6f7-29ef06a7ea9f created.
Starting consent flow.

Pfx file               : C:\PnP\PnP-SiteRequests.pfx
Cer file               : C:\PnP\PnP-SiteRequests.cer
AzureAppId/ClientId    : 34873c07-f9aa-460d-b17b-ac02c8e8e77f
Certificate Thumbprint : FBE0D17755F6321E07EFDBFD6A046E4975C0277C
Base64Encoded          : MIIKRQIBAzCCCgEGCSqGSIb3DQEHAaCCCfIEggnu…
```

Now, to authenticate with SharePoint, you will need the `AzureAppId/ClientId` and `Certificate Thumbprint` and the certificate installed locally on the machine:

```
$ClientId = '<Your Client GUID>'
$Thumbprint = '<Your Certificate Thumbprint>'
$RequestSite = "https://<subdomain>.sharepoint.com/sites/SiteManagement"
$Tenant = '<subdomain>.onmicrosoft.com'
Connect-PnPOnline -ClientId $ClientId -Url $RequestSite -Tenant $Tenant
➥ -Thumbprint $Thumbprint
```

Make sure to store the certificate files in a secure location. I would also recommend storing the client ID and thumbprint in the Secret Store. For more information on this, you can refer to chapter 4 for best practices around handling sensitive information in scripts, but it is not necessary at this step in the process.

11.3.2 Monitoring for new requests

To make this a truly hands-free automation, you need to be able to monitor the Share-Point list for new entries. However, since you do not want the site creation process interfering with the monitor, you can use the watcher and action script concept we covered in-depth in chapter 3. This is the concept where you will have one script that monitors for new entries and initiates a second script to create the site.

In this situation, the watcher script will check the SharePoint list for entries with a status of Submitted. For each one found, it will set the status to Creating and then initiate an action script to perform the creation process, as shown in figure 11.5. By updating the status in the watcher script, you are preventing it from potentially submitting the same request twice.

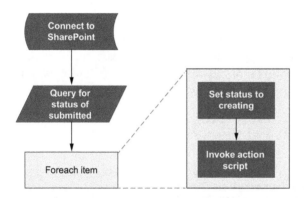

Figure 11.5 SharePoint list watcher script to check for new entries, then submit an action script to perform the automation on new entries

Another benefit to using a tool like SharePoint is that you do not have to worry about passing all the values between the watcher and action scripts. Instead, you can pass the ID of the list item and have the action script look up all the data it needs.

This also helps when making changes to the script. For example, say you want to add a drop-down for the time zone. By just having the action script pass the ID, you only need to change the watcher script. Therefore, the watcher script in the next listing connects to SharePoint, queries the list for new entries, updates the status, and initializes the action script.

Listing 11.1 Monitoring for new site requests

```
$ClientId = '<Your Client GUID>'                          Your connection
$Thumbprint = '<Your Certificate Thumbprint>'             information
```

```
$RequestSite = "https://<subdomain>.sharepoint.com/sites/SiteManagement"
$Tenant = '<subdomain>.onmicrosoft.com'

$ActionScript = ".\Listing 2.ps1"          ◄──┐  The action script
                                               │  that will perform
                                               │  the site creation
$RequestList = 'Site Requests'          ◄──────┘

$PnPOnline = @{                  ◄──┐  The name of
    ClientId   = $ClientId          │  the list
    Url        = $RequestSite
    Tenant     = $Tenant         Connect to the Site
    Thumbprint = $Thumbprint     Management site.
}
Conneact-PnPOnline @PnPOnline

$Query = @'        ◄──┐  Query to get all entries on
<View>                │  the Site Request list with
  <Query>             │  the status of Submitted.
    <Where>
      <Eq>
        <FieldRef Name='Status'/>
        <Value Type='Text'>Submitted</Value>
      </Eq>
    </Where>
  </Query>
</View>
'@
$submittedSites = Get-PnPListItem -List $RequestList -Query $Query

foreach ($newSite in $submittedSites) {
    $Arguments = "-file ""$ActionScript""",     ◄──┐  Set the arguments
    "-ListItemId ""$($newSite.Id)"""               │  from the action
                                                    │  script.
    $jobParams = @{
        FilePath      = 'pwsh'
        ArgumentList  = $Arguments
        NoNewWindow   = $true
        ErrorAction   = 'Stop'
    }
                                 │  Set the status
    $PnPListItem = @{       ◄─────┘  to Creating.
        List     = $RequestList
        Identity = $newSite
        Values   = @{ Status = 'Creating' }
    }
    Set-PnPListItem @PnPListItem
                                                        Confirm that the
                                                        action script can
    try {                                               be found.
        if (-not (Test-Path -Path $ActionScript)) {  ◄──┘
            throw ("The file '$($ActionScript)' is not recognized as " +
                "the name of a script file. Check the spelling of the " +
                "name, or if a path was included, verify that the path " +
                "is correct and try again.")
        }
```

```
        Start-Process @jobParams -PassThru          Invoke the
    }                                                action script.
    catch {
        $PnPListItem['Values'] =                     If it errors trying to
        @{ Status = 'Problem' }                      execute the action script,
        Set-PnPListItem @PnPListItem                 then report a problem.

        Write-Error $_
    }
}
```

11.3.3 *Processing the request*

The next step is to create the script to perform the actual site creation. To do this, you will need to gather the information from the SharePoint list, define the lookup values, and, finally, write the completed data back to the original request.

Since this script will be running in a different context from the watcher script, it will need to authenticate again and look up the entry. However, you don't need to do any XML queries this time because you are expecting the item ID from the watcher script, which you can pass to the Get-PnpListItem cmdlet.

When using the Get-PnpListItem cmdlet, it does not create properties for the different fields. Instead, all the fields and their values are added to a hashtable. So, you reference them using square brackets with a string set to the field's internal name. For example, to get the title for the list item with the ID of 1, it would look like the following snippet:

```
$item = Get-PnpListItem -List 'Site Requests' -Id 1
$item['Title']
$item['Author']
$item['Template']
Posh Tester

Email                          LookupId   LookupValue
-----                          --------   -----------
user@<sub>.onmicrosoft.com     6          Matthew Dowst

LookupId LookupValue           TypeId
-------- -----------           ------
      15 Communication site    {f1d34cc0-9b50-4a78-be78-d5facfcccfb7}
```

As you can see, the title is a simple string you can work with, but the template and author are lookup values. To set the owner, you only need the email address, so you can just use the Email property. But for the template, you need to look up the internal name you wrote to the Site Templates list. Therefore, you need to use the Get-PnpListItem cmdlet again, this time to get the value for the template name:

```
$templateItem = Get-PnpListItem -List 'Site Templates' -Id $item['Template'].
➥LookupId
$templateItem['Name']
SITEPAGEPUBLISHING#0
```

Next, you set the URL based on the title. Keeping in mind that you can only have letters, numbers, underscores, dashes, single quotes, and periods, you will need to sanitize the string. The best way to do this is by using regular expressions (regex).

Now, I know the word *regex* can be a dirty word to some people, and there are varying reasons for this. The syntax of it can be difficult to grasp and, if not done right, can lead to problems in your code like returning the wrong information or dropping information it should have. There are others who say the overreliance on regex is bad coding practice and should only be used when there is no other option. But like most things in life, a little regex in moderation is not bad and can save you a lot of time and hassle.

In a case like this, where you need to remove illegal characters from the URL, it is really the best way to handle it. Since there is no way that you can list all illegal characters, you can use the regex replace method with a NOT clause to list the characters you will allow. This will replace any that do not match with nothing. So, for example, `my-page (name)` would become `my-pagename`. The following snippet shows the command and regex we will use:

```
[regex]::Replace($string, "[^0-9a-zA-Z_\-'\.]", "")
```

The `$string` variable is the original string you want to clean up, followed by the regex to find the characters that need to replaced. The final value is the value to replace them with, which in this case is nothing.

The regex itself looks like gibberish to those not familiar with regular expressions but is quite straightforward when you break it down. The square brackets [] create a matching list. This tells regex to match against any character inside the brackets. Then, by adding the caret ^, you turn it into a NOT match. By using that along with a `Replace`, you are telling it to replace any characters that don't match the criteria. Then, the rest is the values you want to allow:

- `[`   Starts matching list.
- `^`   Does not match.
- `0-9`   Any digit between 0 and 9.
- `a-z`   Any lowercase letter between A and Z.
- `A-Z`   Any uppercase letter between A and Z.
- `_`   Any underscore.
- `\-`   Any dash. Since dashes can mean something else in regex, the slash is an escape character telling it to view the dash as a literal dash.
- `'`   Any single quote.
- `\.`   Any period (full-stop) escaped, so it is viewed as literal, like the dash.
- `]`   Ends the matching list.

Once you have the URL, you will check that no other sites are already using it. And, if there are, you will add a `while` loop to add a number to the end until a unique URL is found. Also, keep in mind that this is an automation, so you should also include a fail-safe in the `while` loop. For instance, if the count reaches 100, there might be something else going on, so this should be investigated. Therefore, if the loop reaches 100 iterations, it should throw a terminating error. Then, you can get the time zone from the parent site and finally create the new site.

Once the site is created, you can add additional commands to perform customizations specific to your needs. Then, update the original request in the SharePoint list with the status of Active and the URL, as in figure 11.6. This way, the person submitting the request knows their site is ready and how to get to it. You can see the script in listing 11.2.

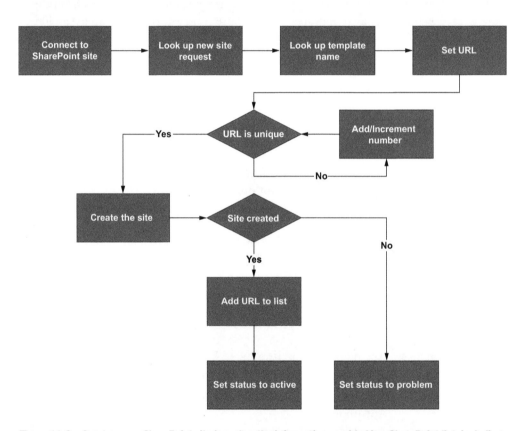

Figure 11.6   Create a new SharePoint site based on the information provided in a SharePoint list, including the automatic creation of a unique URL and recording the URL and status back to the original request.

Listing 11.2   Creating a new SharePoint site

```
param(
    [Parameter(Mandatory = $false)]
    [int]$ListItemId = 1
)
```

```
$ClientId = '<Your Client GUID>'
$Thumbprint = '<Your Certificate Thumbprint>'
$RequestSite = "https://<subdomain>.sharepoint.com/sites/SiteManagement"
$Tenant = '<subdomain>.onmicrosoft.com'
```

Your connection information

```
$RequestList = 'Site Requests'
$TemplateList = 'Site Templates'
```

The name of the list

```
$SiteProblem = @{
    List     = $RequestList
    Identity = $ListItemId
    Values   = @{ Status = 'Problem' }
}
```

Set the parameters to set the status to Problem if anything goes wrong during the script execution.

```
$PnPOnline = @{
    ClientId   = $ClientId
    Url        = $RequestSite
    Tenant     = $Tenant
    Thumbprint = $Thumbprint
}
Connect-PnPOnline @PnPOnline
```

Connect to the Site Management site.

```
$PnPListItem = @{
    List = $RequestList
    Id   = $ListItemId
}
$siteRequest = Get-PnPListItem @PnPListItem
```

Get the site request details from SharePoint.

```
$PnpListItem = @{
    List = $TemplateList
    Id   = $siteRequest['Template'].LookupId
}
$templateItem = Get-PnpListItem @PnpListItem
```

Look up the name of the template from the Site Templates list.

```
$web = Get-PnPWeb -Includes 'RegionalSettings.TimeZone'
```

Get the current web object. It will be used to determine URL and time zone ID.

```
$URI = [URI]::New($web.Url)
$ParentURL = $URI.GetLeftPart([System.UriPartial]::Authority)
$BaseURL = $ParentURL + '/sites/'
```

Get the top-level SharePoint URL from the current website URL.

Get the site URL path from the title.

```
$regex = "[^0-9a-zA-Z_\-'\.]"
$Path = [regex]::Replace($siteRequest['Title'], $regex, "")
$URL = $BaseURL + $Path
```

```
$iteration = 1
do {
    try {
        $PnPTenantSite = @{
            Identity    = $URL
            ErrorAction = 'Stop'
        }
        Get-PnPTenantSite @PnPTenantSite
        $URL = $BaseURL + $Path +
            $iteration.ToString('00')
        $iteration++
    }
```

If the site is not found, then trigger the catch.

If it is found, then add a number to the end and check again.

```
    catch {
        if ($_.FullyQualifiedErrorId -ne
            'EXCEPTION,PnP.PowerShell.Commands.GetTenantSite') {
            Set-PnPListItem @SiteProblem
            throw $_
        }
        else {
            $siteCheck = $null
        }
    }
    if ($iteration -gt 99) {
        Set-PnPListItem @SiteProblem
        throw "Unable to find unique website name for '$($URL)'"
    }
} while ( $siteCheck )

$PnPTenantSite = @{
    Title    = $siteRequest['Title']
    Url      = $URL
    Owner    = $siteRequest['Author'].Email
    Template = $templateItem['Name']
    TimeZone = $web.RegionalSettings.TimeZone.Id
}
try {
    New-PnPTenantSite @PnPTenantSite -ErrorAction Stop

    $values = @{
        Status  = 'Active'
        SiteURL = $URL
    }
    $PnPListItem = @{
        List     = $RequestList
        Identity = $ListItemId
        Values   = $values
    }
    Set-PnPListItem @PnPListItem
}
catch {
    Set-PnPListItem @SiteProblem
}
```

If error ID does not match the expected value for the site not being there, set the Status to Problem and throw a terminating error.

Final fail-safe: If the iterations get too high, something went wrong, so set the Status to Problem and terminate the script.

Set all the parameter values.

Create the new site.

Update the original request with the URL and set the status to Active.

If something goes wrong in the site-creation process, set the status to Problem.

After running the script with your test entry, you should see the URL and Status updated in the original list, as in figure 11.7.

Figure 11.7   Test site request list submission after the automation ran and updated the URL and status of the request

You can now schedule the watch script to run every few minutes to check the list for new entries, and your automation will be fully functional. Next, we will look at a situation in which you need a script to execute on the user's local machine.

11.4 Running PowerShell script on end-user devices

While it is best to offload the processing of scripts to backend systems, there are times when you will need to run a PowerShell script on a local client device. There are several reasons you may need to do this. For example, there are still third-party software vendors who create horrible installers that cannot run without some extra finagling. Even Microsoft themselves is guilty of this. Only a few years ago, they provided a PowerShell script to enroll devices in Update Compliance before they had the settings in Group Policy or Intune. So, in this section, I will show you some tips and tricks on writing and testing PowerShell scripts for execution on client devices.

The first thing to consider with executing scripts on client devices is what mechanism to use. PowerShell remoting is disabled by default in Windows 10/11. And, for security reasons, it is never a good idea to enable remote PowerShell execution on client devices. It is a different story for servers because you have greater control over them. But client devices can be in and out of all sorts of places that you have no control over. Also, with the ever-increasing prevalence of remote working, there is no way to guarantee you can connect to every machine like you used to do over a WAN. For this reason, I strongly recommend investing in a systems management solution. There are several options out there, just to list a few:

- System Center Configuration Manager
- Microsoft Intune
- Ivanti UEM
- ManageEngine Desktop Central
- Jamf Pro
- Quest KACE
- Symantec Client Management Suite

Regardless of which solution you choose, you need to write and test your PowerShell scripts to run through them. If you have ever tried debugging a script through one of these solutions, you know what a pain it can be.

For example, to test a PowerShell script through Intune, you must upload it to Intune and deploy it to a test machine. It sounds simple, but then you realize that the test machine must be enrolled in Intune. So, now you need to join it to your Azure AD domain. Then, to deploy it, the machine has to be a member of an Azure AD group. So, you have to create a one-off group with just this machine in there to test. Once you have all that done, you can force a sync on the test machine by digging down through five or six layers of settings. Then, all you can do is wait and hope that the machine updates its policies, finds the script, executes it, and reports straight back to Intune. And, to be fair to Intune, every platform has its quirks and enrollment requirements.

But the point is that testing through these solutions can be a huge time suck. Luckily, there are ways to replicate how they execute scripts, allowing you to test and make adjustments in seconds. Of course, once you finish your local testing, you will still need to do a final test through the platform, but if you did all your debugging locally first, it should go much smoother. So, let's take a look at some ways to do that.

11.4.1 *Custom Git Install*

To demonstrate how you can build and test the scripts to execution under different contexts, you will create a script to install and configure Git. In this script, you will perform the following tasks:

1. Install Git.
2. Enable auto CRLF to prevent line-ending issues between Windows and other operating systems.
3. Set the default branch to use the name main in the user's configuration.

Since Winget does not support system-based installation, this script will use Chocolatey to perform the installation. If you are not familiar with Chocolatey, it is a package manager similar to Winget, apt, or Homebrew. You can refer to their documentation (docs.chocolatey.org) for the latest installation instructions.

Also, this section will focus on Windows due to the nature of how different operating systems handle user- and system-based execution. But keep in mind that while the commands might be different on Linux or macOS, the general process behind this section will remain the same.

Installing Git with Chocolatey can be as simple as entering the command choco install git.install -y. But there are additional parameters you can supply to customize the installation. One parameter that you should consider is NoAutoCrlf.

When you use a Windows computer and add a new line to a file by pressing the Enter key, two hidden characters are added to the file. These are the carriage return (CR) and line feed (LF), hence CRLF. However, only a line feed is added on Unix-based systems like Linux and macOS. This can cause issues when you share files with people using different operating systems. To prevent this, you can have Git automatically convert CRLF line endings to LF.

However, if you read the documentation for the NoAutoCrlf parameter, it will only apply to new installs. Since you are using Chocolatey, it can detect if existing versions of Git are installed and either upgrade them or skip the install. In these cases, the NoAutoCrlf parameter will be ignored. So, instead of building a bunch of logic into your script to detect existing versions, you can just run the following command to enable the CRLF to LF conversion automatically after the installation:

```
git config --system core.autocrlf true
```

Using the --system parameter tells Git to use this setting for all users on the computer and all repositories. But let's say you want to create a setting at the user level. In that case, you would use the `--global` parameter. This will apply the settings specific to all repositories for the user who ran the command. Since you may need to change the default branch name for different users, you will want to set that value at the user level and not the system level. This can be done with the following command, with `<name>` being a placeholder for the default name:

```
git config --global init.defaultBranch <name>
```

You can put these commands together into a single script to test this installation. However, keep in mind that you just installed Git, so the Git executable will most likely not be in the path environment variable. Therefore, you will need to supply the full path to the executable. Fortunately, PowerShell allows you to create aliases, so you can use the `git` command just as you would if it had been previously installed. You can do this by setting an alias of `git` to the full path of the git.exe.

Create a script named git-install.ps1 based on the following listing and save it to a test machine.

> **Listing 11.3   git-install.ps1**

```
param(
    $branch
)
choco install git.install -y          ←⎯ Install Git.

$alias = @{            ←⎯  Set an alias to the
    Name = 'git'            full path of git.exe.
    Value = (Join-Path $Env:ProgramFiles 'Git\bin\git.exe')
}
New-Alias @alias -force                         Enable Auto
                                                CRLF to LF
git config --system core.autocrlf true    ←⎯   conversion.

git config --global init.defaultBranch $branch   ←⎯  Set the default branch
                                                     at the user level.
```

Typically, the best way to test is to use a virtual machine that you can take snapshots of and revert between tests. However, since I know that may not be possible for everyone, I've included the uninstall and clean-up commands in the following snippet. You can use these to remove Git and clear out the customizations between installs:

```
choco uninstall git.install -y
Remove-Item "$($env:USERPROFILE)\.gitconfig" -force
Remove-Item "$($env:ProgramFiles)\Git" -Recurse -force
```

11.4.2   *Running as system versus the user*

Most systems management solutions can run scripts as the logged-on user or as the system account. Both ways have their advantages and disadvantages. For instance, some actions require elevated permissions that might not be available when running as the local user. However, it can be difficult to set user-specific settings when running as the system. Therefore, you will need to test the different methods to see how your script will behave.

An excellent way to approach testing is by first testing the installation method as an administrator. Get it all working, so you know your commands are good and produce the desired outcome. Then, once you know your script is working, move to testing it as a standard user and under the system context. You may find that your script doesn't work entirely in either. But that's okay; since you know your commands are good, there are ways you can mix the two types of executions. Start by opening an elevated PowerShell window and executing the git-install.ps1:

```
.\git-install.ps1 -branch 'main'
Chocolatey v0.12.1
Installing the following packages:
git.install
By installing, you accept licenses for the packages.
Progress: Downloading git.install 2.35.1.2... 100%

chocolatey-core.extension v1.3.5.1 [Approved]
chocolatey-core.extension package files install completed. Performing ot...
 Installed/updated chocolatey-core extensions.
 The install of chocolatey-core.extension was successful.
  Software installed to 'C:\ProgramData\chocolatey\extensions\chocola...

git.install v2.35.1.2 [Approved]
git.install package files install completed. Performing other installa...
Using Git LFS
Installing 64-bit git.install...
git.install has been installed.
Environment Vars (like PATH) have changed. Close/reopen your shell to
 see the changes (or in powershell/cmd.exe just type `refreshenv`).
 The install of git.install was successful.
  Software installed to 'C:\Program Files\Git\'

Chocolatey installed 2/2 packages.
 See the log for details (C:\ProgramData\chocolatey\logs\chocolatey.log).
```

What you are checking for here is that the software installs without any interactions required and that the expected configurations are set. To check the configuration, open a second PowerShell window and enter the following command. Then, check the output to ensure that your settings match the expected outcomes. The ones you set are bolded in the output:

```
git config --list --show-scope
diff.astextplain.textconv=astextplain
system   filter.lfs.clean=git-lfs clean -- %f
system   filter.lfs.smudge=git-lfs smudge -- %f
system   filter.lfs.process=git-lfs filter-process
system   filter.lfs.required=true
```

```
system  http.sslbackend=openssl
system  http.sslcainfo=C:/Program Files/Git/mingw64/ssl/certs/ca-bundle.crt
system  core.autocrlf=true
system  core.fscache=true
system  core.symlinks=false
system  pull.rebase=false
system  credential.helper=manager-core
system  credential.https://dev.azure.com.usehttppath=true
system  init.defaultbranch=master
global  init.defaultbranch=main
```

You should see that the autocrlf is set to true at the system level, and the default branch is main at the global level. If you see that, you know your commands are good, and it is time to move on to testing under the user and system contexts. Go ahead and run the uninstall commands or restore a snapshot to ensure that Git is not installed and the settings have been cleared.

Testing as a user is usually pretty straightforward. Log on to the test machine with an account with standard user permissions, run your script, and see what happens. Of course, in this case, I'm sure most of you will already know that you will be met with User Access Control (UAC) prompts and errors trying to write the system-level configuration. So, to save you some time, I'll just tell you that it won't work.

If the script was just running the last command to set the branch, it would, but the installation and setting of the system configuration require administrator permissions. Table 11.3 details the context in which a script can be executed and the resources it will have access to.

Table 11.3   The different contexts a script can run under and the resources it will be able to access

	Standard user	Administrator	System
User Profile	Read/Write	Read/Write	N/A
User Registry (HKCU)	Read/Write	Read/Write	N/A
Program Files	Read	Read/Write	Read/Write
Program Data	Read	Read/Write	Read/Write
Machine Registry (HKLM)	Read	Read/Write	Read/Write

As you can see, the only context that has the permissions to write to both the system and user areas is an administrator. Since you should never give your users local administrator rights, this is not really a viable option. So, it is best to avoid user-based scripts that perform installations. They work great for setting user-based settings, but not system-wide settings. Therefore, in our case, we can skip right to testing as the system.

Running a script under the system context is not the same as running from an elevated prompt. The script considers the system to be the user when running under the system. Therefore, it will not have access to the user's profile or registry hive. It is also not something that you can do by right-clicking the PowerShell icon. There are two easy ways to test a script as a system in PowerShell. The first is to use the Sysinternals Tool PSExec to open PowerShell as system using the /s switch. The other option is to use the Invoke-CommandAs module created by Marc R. Kellerman.

The downside to the Invoke-CommandAs module is that it is designed for Windows PowerShell 5.1. However, since we are building this script specific to Windows, we can use Windows PowerShell 5.1.

To test under the system context, open an elevated Windows PowerShell 5.1 prompt, install the Invoke-CommandAs module, and then import it. Then, you can use the Invoke-CommandAs cmdlet with the -AsSystem switch and the -ScriptBlock parameter pointed to the git-install.ps1:

```
Install-Module -Name Invoke-CommandAs
Import-Module -Name Invoke-CommandAs
Invoke-CommandAs -ScriptBlock { . C:\git-install.ps1 } -AsSystem
Progress: Downloading git.install 2.35.1.2... 100%


git.install v2.35.1.2 [Approved]
git.install package files install completed. Performing ot...
Using Git LFS
Installing 64-bit git.install...
git.install has been installed.
WARNING: Can't find git.install install location
  git.install can be automatically uninstalled.
Environment Vars (like PATH) have changed. Close/reopen your shell to
 see the changes (or in powershell/cmd.exe just type `refreshenv`).
 The install of git.install was successful.
  Software installed to 'C:\Program Files\Git\'


Chocolatey installed 1/1 packages.
 See the log for details (C:\ProgramData\chocolatey\logs\chocolatey.log).
```

Now, just like last time, open a new PowerShell prompt and check the configuration:

```
git config --list --show-scope
system  diff.astextplain.textconv=astextplain
system  filter.lfs.clean=git-lfs clean -- %f
system  filter.lfs.smudge=git-lfs smudge -- %f
system  filter.lfs.process=git-lfs filter-process
system  filter.lfs.required=true
system  http.sslbackend=openssl
system  http.sslcainfo=C:/Program Files/Git/mingw64/ssl/certs/ca-bundle.crt
system  core.autocrlf=true
system  core.fscache=true
system  core.symlinks=false
system  pull.rebase=false
system  credential.helper=manager-core
system  credential.https://dev.azure.com.usehttppath=true
system  init.defaultbranch=master
```

If you receive an error message that `git` cannot be found, this can be because installing under the system did not cause your environment variables to update. You can force them to update using the following command or reboot:

```
$env:Path = [System.Environment]::GetEnvironmentVariable("Path","Machine") +
";" + [System.Environment]::GetEnvironmentVariable("Path","User")
```

Either way, when you run the configuration check, you'll notice that the user's default branch is not set. This is because it technically ran as the system user. So, to handle installers that need to run under both the system and the user, you can use a technique known as Active Setup.

11.4.3   Using Active Setup with PowerShell

Active Setup is a method to execute commands once per user during the login process. It is similar to the RunOnce mechanism, but Active Setup runs before the desktop loads and at a higher privilege level. This allows you to perform tasks that might otherwise require administrator privileges.

You use Active Setup by creating a registry key under the path `HKEY_LOCAL_MACHINE` `\SOFTWARE\Microsoft\Active Setup\Installed Components`. Since this is the local machine hive, you can write to it while running as the system. The key you create will have two values under it: one with the version number and one with the command to execute.

The command writes a copy of the version value under the same path in the current user hive. Then, every time you log into Windows, it compares the user values version to the machine values and runs any new commands or ones with updated version numbers.

While Active Setup itself is a function of Windows and not PowerShell, we can use PowerShell to overcome some of its limitations. The most significant limitation is that since Active Setup runs before the desktop is loaded, there is no way to see error messages. The only way to confirm it ran is by checking the registry key in the current user hive, and that only tells you that it ran, not whether it ran successfully. Also, if it executes a script file, there is no record of that script other than its name. If the script is removed or changed, it can be difficult or impossible to tell what was done.

To avoid the issue of not knowing if the command was executed successfully, we will use a wrapper script to record a log of the commands executed. This can be done natively in PowerShell using the `Start-Transcript` cmdlet.

To keep consistent records of all scripts and versions, you can create a folder under the Program Data directory to store each one along with the name of the Active Setup registry key and version number. Then, have the log file for each user written to a folder in their local application data folder with the same name. This way, you will have a one-for-one mapping between the registry keys, scripts, and log files.

We will put all this together in a reusable function you can use any time you need to use Active Setup. Then, all you need to do is supply a name, a version number, and the commands you want to execute, and the function will take care of the rest.

Starting with the wrapper script, you will use the `Start-Transcript` cmdlet to record the outputs from the script execution. You can include the timestamp of when it ran using the `-IncludeInvocationHeader` switch and record multiple runs to the same log file by including the `-Append` and `-Force` switches.

Also, to ensure that you capture any error messages, you will wrap the entire script in a `try/catch/finally` block. The code you want to execute will go inside the `try` block. If there is a terminating error in your code, the `catch` block will be triggered instead of just stopping. Inside the `catch` block, you will output the error message to record it in the transcript log. Then, whether there was an error or not, the `finally` block will execute, and it will have the `Stop-Transcript` cmdlet to cleanly close the transcript log, marking the end of the execution process.

To create this script, you will need to combine two different script strings, the wrapper code and the code you need to execute. There are several ways to create and combine strings in PowerShell, but when converting code to a string, you need to account for certain things, like line breaks, special characters, and keywords.

When dealing with line breaks in a string, the best option is to use a here-string. Here-strings allow you to include line breaks in your string without PowerShell thinking they are new lines of code. Like regular strings, PowerShell will treat here-strings with single quotes as a literal, while double quotes will evaluate any variables. So, if you use double quotes, you will need to escape any characters that would be evaluated when the script executes. A single-quote here-string is a good option for your wrapper script because it is relatively static but can be a hassle with the code you are adding to the wrapper. Luckily, there is a third option, which is to use a script block.

PowerShell allows you to declare script blocks inside a script and save them to a variable by adding curly brackets at the beginning and end of the code. These script blocks are just saved and not executed. Plus, they can be converted to strings by using the `ToString()` method. The advantage you get with script blocks over here-strings is that the code you enter will still take advantage of syntax highlighting, IntelliSense, and code analysis to help identify errors.

Once you have the string with the script code in it, you need to write it to the local machine. This function will create the folder ActiveSetup in the Program Data directory and save the script inside of it. The script name will be based on the name and version of the application. So, for the script in listing 11.4, the path will be `C:\ProgramData\ActiveSetup\Git_v1.0.ps1`.

To create the Active Setup registry values, you first need to make the key, `HKLM:\Software\Microsoft\Active Setup\Installed Components\Git`. Then, populate `Version` with the version number and `StubPath` with the command to execute.

When populating `StubPath`, you cannot just enter the command as you would to run it from the command prompt. Since it runs before the user profile is fully loaded, it does not contain all the environment variables you would see in a standard session. So, you will need your script to write the literal path to the script file. Also, when providing a path, you must escape the slashes by doubling them (`\\`).

In addition, when calling a PowerShell script, you will want to bypass the system execution policy to prevent it from blocking your script. Luckily, since Active Setup runs at a higher privilege, you can bypass the execution policy just for this command by including the argument -ExecutionPolicy bypass.

Listing 11.4 `New-ActiveSetup`

```
Function New-ActiveSetup {
    param(
        [string]$Name,
        [System.Management.Automation.ScriptBlock]$ScriptBlock,
        [version]$Version = '1.0.0.0'
    )

    $ActiveSetupReg =
    'HKLM:\Software\Microsoft\Active Setup\Installed Components'

    $Item = @{
        Path  = $ActiveSetupReg
        Name  = $Name
        Force = $true
    }
    $ActiveSetup = New-Item @Item | Select-Object -ExpandProperty PSPath

    $DefaultPath = 'ActiveSetup\{0}_v{1}.ps1'
    $ChildPath = $DefaultPath -f $Name, $Version
    $ScriptPath = Join-Path -Path $env:ProgramData -ChildPath $ChildPath
    $ScriptFolder = Split-Path -Path $ScriptPath

    if (-not(Test-Path -Path $ScriptFolder)) {
        New-Item -type Directory -Path $ScriptFolder | Out-Null
    }

    $WrapperScript = {
        param($Name,$Version)
        $Path = "ActiveSetup\$($Name)_$($Version).log"
        $log = Join-Path $env:APPDATA $Path
        $Transcript = @{ Path = $log; Append = $true;
        IncludeInvocationHeader = $true; Force = $true}
        Start-Transcript @Transcript
        try{
            {0}
        }
        catch{ Write-Host $_ }
        finally{ Stop-Transcript }
    }

    $WrapperString = $WrapperScript.ToString()
    $WrapperString = $WrapperString.Replace('{','{{')
    $WrapperString = $WrapperString.Replace('}','}}')
    $WrapperString = $WrapperString.Replace('{{0}}','{0}')
```

The path to the Active Setup registry keys

Create the Active Setup registry key.

Set the path for the script.

Create the ActiveSetup folder if it does not exist.

Declare the Wrapper script code.

Convert wrapper code to string and fix curly brackets to all for string formatting.

```
$WrapperString -f $ScriptBlock.ToString() |         ◁──┐  Add the script block
    Out-File -FilePath $ScriptPath -Encoding utf8        │  to the wrapper code
                                                         │  and export it to the
$args = @{                      ◁──┐  Set the registry      script file.
    Path  = $ActiveSetup           │  values for the
    Force = $true                  │  Active Setup.
}
$ActiveSetupValue = 'powershell.exe -ExecutionPolicy bypass ' +
"-File ""$($ScriptPath.Replace('\', '\\'))""" +
" -Name ""$($Name)"" -Version ""$($Version)"""
Set-ItemProperty @args -Name '(Default)' -Value $Name
Set-ItemProperty @args -Name 'Version' -Value $Version
Set-ItemProperty @args -Name 'StubPath' -Value $ActiveSetupValue
}
```

You can now include the code in the next listing in the original script from listing 11.3 to the call default branch setting command with Active Setup.

Listing 11.5   Git install with Active Setup

```
Function New-ActiveSetup {
    <#
    Code from listing 4
    #>
}

choco install git.install -y       ◁──┤  Install Git.

$alias = @{               ◁──┤  Set an alias to the
    Name = 'git'                 │  full path of git.exe.
    Value = (Join-Path $Env:ProgramFiles 'Git\bin\git.exe')
}
New-Alias @alias -force                    ┌  Enable Auto
                                           │  CRLF to LF
git config --system core.autocrlf true  ◁─┘  conversion.

$ScriptBlock = {                        ◁──┐  Set the default branch
    git config --global init.defaultBranch main  │  at the user level using
    git config --global --list               │  Active Setup.
}

New-ActiveSetup -Name 'Git' -ScriptBlock $ScriptBlock -Version '1.0'
```

Once you have it all put together, remove Git again and run the install as system:

```
choco uninstall git.install -y
Remove-Item "$($env:USERPROFILE)\.gitconfig" -force
Remove-Item "$($env:ProgramFiles)\Git" -Recurse -force
Invoke-CommandAs -ScriptBlock { . C:\git-install.ps1 } -AsSystem
```

When the install completes, open a second PowerShell prompt and check the Git config. Like the previous time, the global setting for default should be missing:

```
$env:Path = [System.Environment]::GetEnvironmentVariable("Path","Machine") +
➥ ";" + [System.Environment]::GetEnvironmentVariable("Path","User")
git config --list --show-scope
system   diff.astextplain.textconv=astextplain
system   filter.lfs.clean=git-lfs clean -- %f
system   filter.lfs.smudge=git-lfs smudge -- %f
system   filter.lfs.process=git-lfs filter-process
system   filter.lfs.required=true
system   http.sslbackend=openssl
system   http.sslcainfo=C:/Program Files/Git/mingw64/ssl/certs/ca-bundle.crt
system   core.autocrlf=true
system   core.fscache=true
system   core.symlinks=false
system   pull.rebase=false
system   credential.helper=manager-core
system   credential.https://dev.azure.com.usehttppath=true
system   init.defaultbranch=master
```

Now log off and back on, and then check the config once more. This time, you should see that the global setting for the default branch is set to main:

```
git config --list --show-scope
system   diff.astextplain.textconv=astextplain
system   filter.lfs.clean=git-lfs clean -- %f
system   filter.lfs.smudge=git-lfs smudge -- %f
system   filter.lfs.process=git-lfs filter-process
system   filter.lfs.required=true
system   http.sslbackend=openssl
system   http.sslcainfo=C:/Program Files/Git/mingw64/ssl/certs/ca-bundle.crt
system   core.autocrlf=true
system   core.fscache=true
system   core.symlinks=false
system   pull.rebase=false
system   credential.helper=manager-core
system   credential.https://dev.azure.com.usehttppath=true
system   init.defaultbranch=master
global   init.defaultbranch=main
```

Now that you know your script can run under the system context and still make user-level changes, you are ready to test through your system management platform.

Summary

- Instead of designing a custom frontend, you can utilize existing platforms and integrate your PowerShell automations with them. These can include platforms like SharePoint, CRM, an ITSM catalog, and others.
- If an automation does not need to run on a user's local machine, you should set up a backend system to execute it. This will help to ensure that you have the correct modules and allow you better control over permissions.
- When running a script on a local machine, it can execute as the logged-on user or as system. Depending on what the script is doing, it may require executing under the user context or the system context.

- Scripts running under the system context will not have access to the user-based folders and registry hives. However, script running as the user will not be able to access system folders and registry hives.
- If a script needs to make changes to both system and user resources, you can use Active Setup to execute the part of the scripts for the user-based resources.
- There is no way to interact with scripts that run through Active Setup, so properly log their execution to make troubleshooting easier.

Sharing scripts
among a team

12

This chapter covers

- Using GitHub Gist to share scripts
- Creating a module to share with a team
- Using a GitHub repository to store and manage
  a module

How often have you spent time writing a script to perform a task, only to find out someone else on your team had already done something similar? If you are like me, the answer is more times than you can count. And this problem only continues to grow as things like working from home and bringing your own device become more prevalent. So, in this chapter, we will explore some ways that you can share scripts as a team.

Depending on which source you look at, you will see reports that 20–50% of service desk calls are for repetitive issues. These can be things like password resets, fixing permissions, freeing up disk space, troubleshooting connection issues, or any other number of issues. So, it would only make sense for you to arm your team with tools to resolve these problems quickly, and one of the best ways to do this is by creating a PowerShell module that they can use. In this chapter, you will learn how to use GitHub to share individual scripts and an entire module.

To get started, you will need a GitHub account. A free account will do. You will also need to install the Git command-line tools and the GitHub CLI. You can download and install Git from git-scm.com/downloads, and GitHub CLI can be downloaded and installed from cli.github.com. Or, if you prefer, you can run the GitSetup.ps1 included in the Helper Scripts for this chapter to have them installed for you.

Once the installations are complete, you will need to close and reopen your PowerShell window to ensure that the environment is updated. Then, you can configure your computer to use your GitHub account. The first two commands in the following snippet will set your email and name. The name is what you want GitHub to display. It does not have to be your username. The last command will open your default browser to have you log into your account and confirm you want to connect it to your computer:

```
git config --global user.email "you@example.com"
git config --global user.name "Your Name"
gh auth login --web
```

WARNING You must complete these steps before continuing with this chapter.

Also, if you prefer, you can switch the default editor for Git from vim to VS Code using the following command:

```
gh config set editor "code -w"
```

12.1 *Sharing a script*

When it comes to sharing an individual script, you have many options. You can upload it to a network share or a collaboration platform like SharePoint or Teams or even email it to someone. However, each of these methods has its drawbacks. Network shares require LAN or VPN access. Platforms like SharePoint and Teams will often block scripts from being uploaded. Most email clients also block scripts, plus once you email it, you no longer have any way to update the script or ensure the people you shared it with are using the most current version. The best option, and the one we will cover in this section, is using a dedicated code platform. There are multiple different options out there like Azure DevOps, Bitbucket, and the one we will be using, GitHub.

I chose GitHub for a few reasons. First and foremost, the free tier contains all the functionality you will need in this chapter. The paid tiers offer additional functionality like more storage space, single sign-on, and better collaboration tools, none of which you will need here. Second, it is based on Git, the most widely used version control system out there. Since Git is open source, many platforms utilize it. GitHub is just a place for storing Git repositories. Therefore, many of the lessons in this chapter can be applied to the other platforms like Azure DevOps and Bit-Bucket, which can also use Git.

If you are not familiar with GitHub or any code repository platforms, they can seem intimidating with all the different options. Or you may think, I just need a single script; why would I create an entire code repository? And the answer to that is you don't. GitHub, along with being a place for code repositories, complete with branching, continuous testing, and pull requests, has a service named Gist.

A gist is a single code snippet that you can create and share in a few seconds. And the best part is that it has built-in version control. This way, you can track your changes over time. On top of that, a gist can be public or private, have syntax highlighting in the browser, and allows others to add comments, and you can run a gist script locally with a one-liner in PowerShell.

12.1.1 Creating a gist

You can create a gist in the browser at gist.github.com or use the GitHub CLI to upload an existing script. To demonstrate this, you can use a command from back in chapter 9 to return information about a local PC. Save the code in the following listing to your local machine as Get-SystemInfo.ps1.

Listing 12.1 Get-SystemInfo.ps1

```
Get-CimInstance -Class Win32_OperatingSystem |
    Select-Object Caption, InstallDate, ServicePackMajorVersion,
    OSArchitecture, BootDevice, BuildNumber, CSName,
    @{l='Total_Memory';e={[math]::Round($_.TotalVisibleMemorySize/1MB)}}
```

After saving the script, open a command-prompt window and navigate to the folder with the Get-SystemInfo.ps1 script. Then, enter the following command to upload the file to a GitHub Gist. Including the --web switch will tell it to open the newly created gist in your web browser after creation, as shown in figure 12.1:

```
gh gist create Get-SystemInfo.ps1 --web
- Creating gist Get-SystemInfo.ps1
√ Created gist Get-SystemInfo.ps1
Opening gist.github.com/2d0f590c7dde480fba8ac0201ce6fe0f in your browser.
```

And that is it! You have just created your first gist.

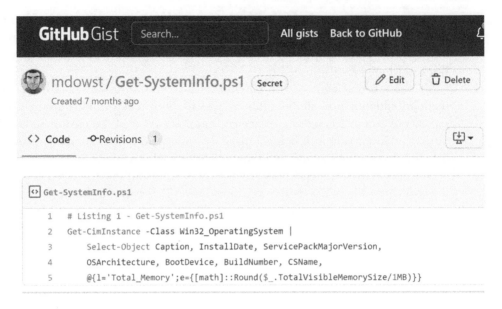

Figure 12.1 Creating a gist using the GitHub CLI and viewing it in the browser

12.1.2 Editing a gist

Just like when creating gists, you can edit them via the command line or directly in the web browser. When using the command line, you will need to know the ID of the gist you want to edit. You can quickly find that using the View option with the GitHub CLI:

```
gh gist list
0d0188e13b8c1be453cf1   Autounattend.xml        1 file   secret   about 25 days ago
116626205476f1df63fe3   AzureVM-Log4j.ps1       1 file   public   about 7 days ago
a1a9a69c0790d06eb8a53   Get-SystemInfo.ps1      1 file   secret   about 1 month ago
e0a176f34e2384212a3c1   PoshAutomator.ps1       1 file   secret   about 1 month ago
a7e6af4038444ff7db54d   Get-OSData.ps1          1 file   secret   about 1 month ago
ffc62944a5a429375460a   NewDevServer            1 file   secret   about 4 months ago
3aafcd16557f952e58c6f   Out-GridViewCode        1 file   public   about 3 months ago
```

Then, copy the ID of the gist you want to update, and add it to the end of the edit command:

```
gh gist edit <Your ID>
```

This will open the gist in the default editor you set in the configuration. You can make all your edits and run tests in the editor. Once you save and close the file, it will upload the changes to GitHub and automatically create a new version of the gist.

12.1.3 Sharing a gist

The gist you just created is private. This means that if someone looks at your GitHub profile, they will not see a listing for this gist. However, you can still share it using the direct URL. You can also choose to make a gist public by using the `--public` switch at the time of creation. And you can switch between public and private after creation through the web interface:

```
gh gist create --public Get-SystemInfo.ps1
```

One downside to Gist is that while it does allow for collaboration, there is no way to approve changes. Therefore, I recommend using full repositories when you have a script that multiple people will work on (more on that later). However, you can allow comments to be made on a gist, so you can at least receive feedback on it.

12.1.4 Executing a gist

As I mentioned earlier, one of the great benefits of gists is the ability to execute them directly from a URL without needing to download the file. The way to do this is to combine the `Invoke-Expression` and `Invoke-RestMethod` cmdlets. This is also another reason why you do not want to allow others to be able to edit your gists.

To see this in action, open the gist you just created in your web browser. In the top right corner of the gist, you will see the Raw button. Click on the Raw button, and it will open your gist as a plain text file. If you pass this URL to the `Invoke-RestMethod` cmdlet, it will display your script as a string:

```
Invoke-RestMethod -Uri 'The Gist Raw URL'
# Listing 1 - Get-SystemInfo.ps1
Get-CimInstance -Class Win32_OperatingSystem |
    Select-Object Caption, InstallDate, ServicePackMajorVersion,
    OSArchitecture, BootDevice, BuildNumber, CSName,
    @{l='Total_Memory';e={[math]::Round($_.TotalVisibleMemorySize/1MB)}}
```

Since the output of the `Invoke-RestMethod` is a string, you can pass it to the `Invoke-Expression` cmdlet, and it will convert the string to PowerShell and execute it:

```
Invoke-Expression (Invoke-RestMethod -Uri 'The Gist Raw URL')
Caption                 : Microsoft Windows 11 Enterprise
InstallDate             : 10/21/2021 5:09:00 PM
ServicePackMajorVersion : 0
OSArchitecture          : 64-bit
BootDevice              : \Device\HarddiskVolume1
BuildNumber             : 22000
CSName                  : DESKTOP-6VBP512
Total_Memory            : 32
```

This method works great when you need to share a one-off or a specialized script with someone. But, as you can imagine, remembering that URL could, in some cases, be even more difficult than remembering the command. I also advise against using a URL shortener, because the Raw URL will change with each version. So, a shortened URL may point to an old version. That is not to say it doesn't have its benefits. For example, there are often times when a client or colleague needs help with a specific issue I have scripted a resolution for in the past. I can keep these as gists and just send them the link when needed. However, if there are commands that you run often, a better solution is to create a shared module.

12.2 *Creating a shared module*

When it comes to creating a module to share with your team, the creation process is the same as it is with any other module you create. However, what is different is how you share it. Suppose your module contains functions specific to your company. You would not want to upload it to some place like the PowerShell Gallery, where anyone can find and download it. You could create a private repository using a network share, but this can cause issues for remote employees. Or you could set up a NuGet server to use as a private repository, but this involves additional overhead and can still be an issue for remote employees unless you host it somewhere externally or allow access through your firewall. Also, while a NuGet server does have some version control, it does not have all the capabilities that a code repository does.

In this section, you will create a GitHub repository for a shared PowerShell module. We will then add some custom code to replicate the installation functionality you get with a repository. And, finally, we will make it so the module can update itself.

To get started, create the module code just like we have done many times throughout this book. However, you will not include a version folder this time, as you can see in the next listing, because we will use GitHub for version control. Also, since we have covered it many times before, I have included the code to import the functions in the psm1.

Listing 12.2   Create a PoshAutomator module

```
Function New-ModuleTemplate {
    [CmdletBinding()]
    [OutputType()]
    param(
        [Parameter(Mandatory = $true)]
        [string]$ModuleName,
        [Parameter(Mandatory = $true)]
        [string]$ModuleVersion,
        [Parameter(Mandatory = $true)]
        [string]$Author,
        [Parameter(Mandatory = $true)]
        [string]$PSVersion,
        [Parameter(Mandatory = $false)]
        [string[]]$Functions                      ⟵┐ Do not include the version
    )                                                │ path since GitHub will take
    $ModulePath = Join-Path .\ "$($ModuleName)"   ⟵┘ care of the version controls.
    New-Item -Path $ModulePath -ItemType Directory
    Set-Location $ModulePath
    New-Item -Path .\Public -ItemType Directory
```

```
    $ManifestParameters = @{
        ModuleVersion     = $ModuleVersion
        Author            = $Author
        Path              = ".\$($ModuleName).psd1"
        RootModule        = ".\$($ModuleName).psm1"
        PowerShellVersion = $PSVersion
    }
    New-ModuleManifest @ManifestParameters

    $File = @{
        Path     = ".\$($ModuleName).psm1"
        Encoding = 'utf8'
    }
    @'
$Path = Join-Path $PSScriptRoot 'Public'
$Functions = Get-ChildItem -Path $Path -Filter '*.ps1'

Foreach ($import in $Functions) {
    Try {
        Write-Verbose "dot-sourcing file '$($import.fullname)'"
        . $import.fullname
    }
    Catch {
        Write-Error -Message "Failed to import function $($import.name)"
    }
}
'@ | Out-File @File
    $Functions | ForEach-Object {
        Out-File -Path ".\Public\$($_).ps1" -Encoding utf8
    }
}

$module = @{
    ModuleName    = 'PoshAutomator'
    ModuleVersion = "1.0.0.0"
    Author        = "YourNameHere"
    PSVersion     = '5.1'
    Functions     = 'Get-SystemInfo'
}
New-ModuleTemplate @module
```

Go ahead and autopopulate the functionality to import the function scripts.

Get all the ps1 files in the Public folder.

Loop through each ps1 file.

Execute each ps1 file to load the function into memory.

Set the parameters to pass to the function.

The name of your module

The version of your module

Your name

The minimum PowerShell version this module supports

The functions to create blank files for in the Public folder

Execute the function to create the new module.

Once you create the module, go ahead and populate the Get-SystemInfo function script in the following listing.

Listing 12.3 Get-SystemInfo

```
Function Get-SystemInfo{
    Get-CimInstance -Class Win32_OperatingSystem |
        Select-Object Caption, InstallDate, ServicePackMajorVersion,
        OSArchitecture, BootDevice, BuildNumber, CSName,
        @{l='Total_Memory';e={[math]::Round($_.TotalVisibleMemorySize/1MB)}}
}
```

You should now be able to test the module and ensure the Get-SystemInfo function works:

```
Import-Module .\PoshAutomator.psd1
Get-SystemInfo
Caption                 : Microsoft Windows 11 Enterprise
InstallDate             : 10/21/2021 5:09:00 PM
ServicePackMajorVersion : 0
OSArchitecture          : 64-bit
BootDevice              : \Device\HarddiskVolume1
BuildNumber             : 22000
CSName                  : DESKTOP-6VBP512
Total_Memory            : 32
```

12.2.1 *Uploading the module to a GitHub repository*

Now that you have your module's initial files and structure, let's create a GitHub repository to store it. Like with Gist, this can all be done via the command line. You also have the ability to make a GitHub repository private or public. If you make it private, you can invite other users to a repository and allow them to contribute to the code base.

Open a command prompt and navigate to the folder with the module files to get started. Then, start by initializing the repository using the following commands. This will create a folder named .git in the directory with all the configuration files for the repository:

```
git init
Initialized empty Git repository in C:/PoshAutomatorB/.git/
```

These commands create a local repository in the current folder, add all of the files to the repository, commit the changes, and apply the changes to the main branch.

Next, you can add all the files in the directory to the repository. Just because a file is placed in the folder, it does not mean that it is in the Git repository. You have to tell Git to add the file or files. By using a period at the end of the add, you are telling Git to add all files and folders in the current directory:

```
git add .
```

Then, it is time to save the changes to the repository by committing them. Commits provide you with a current snapshot of all the files. They also allow you to see the changes over time:

```
git commit -m "first commit"
[master (root-commit) cf2a211] first commit
 4 files changed, 261 insertions(+)
 create mode 100644 Install-PoshAutomator.ps1
 create mode 100644 PoshAutomator.psd1
 create mode 100644 PoshAutomator.psm1
 create mode 100644 Public/Get-SystemInfo.ps1
```

Then, finally, you will want to ensure that your local branch is named *main* and all changes have been saved. You do not have to name your branch *main*, but it is pretty much an unwritten rule that the default branch is named *main*:

```
git branch -M main
```

Next, you will create the remote repository in GitHub using the following command. Note the URL of the command's output. In the next step, you will need it to connect the local repository to the remote repository:

```
gh repo create PoshAutomator --private --source=. --remote=upstream
✓ Created repository mdowst/PoshAutomator on GitHub
✓ Added remote https://github.com/mdowst/PoshAutomator.git
```

Once the remote repository is created, you need to add it to your local repository using the URL from the `create` command:

```
git remote add origin https://github.com/<yourProfile>/PoshAutomator.git
```

Finally, you will sync your local files to the remote repository using the push command:

```
git push -u origin main
Enumerating objects: 7, done.
Counting objects: 100% (7/7), done.
Compressing objects: 100% (6/6), done.
Writing objects: 100% (7/7), 3.56 KiB | 3.56 MiB/s, done.
Total 7 (delta 0), reused 0 (delta 0), pack-reused 0
To https://github.com/mdowst/PoshAutomator.git
 * [new branch]      main -> main
Branch 'main' set up to track remote branch 'main' from 'origin'.
```

You can verify everything synced correctly by navigating to the repository in your web browser. Figure 12.2 shows an example.

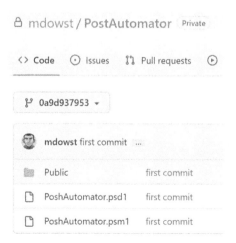

Figure 12.2 Initial commit and sync with the remote repository on GitHub

12.2.2   *Giving access to the shared module*

If you created the repository as public, then there is nothing else that needs to be done. However, if the repository is private, you will need to give your team members access to it before they can download or contribute to the module.

You can share a GitHub repository by opening it in your web browser and going to Settings > Collaborators > Manage Access. You can then share the project with your team by adding their GitHub accounts as collaborators.

12.2.3   *Installing the shared module*

Since you are using GitHub instead of the PowerShell repository, you will need to create a way for your team to easily install this module. You can do that by creating an installation script that will sync the module files to their local machine and link the files to their default PowerShell module path.

To make things as simple as possible for your team, the installation script will need to check if the Git executable is installed and, if not, install it. Since different operating systems have different ways of installing applications, I recommend using a package manager, one that you know your team will have installed. In this example, we will assume winget for Windows, Homebrew for macOS, and APT for Linux. Therefore, the installation script will need to perform the following steps:

1 Check if Git is installed.
2 Install Git if it is not found, based on the operating system.
3 Clone the remote repository to the local machine.
4 Create a symbolic link between the repository folder and the PowerShell module path.

> **NOTE** The choice of package manager is completely up to you. Just make sure that is it something that is supported in your environment.

The way that PowerShell works is that any module found in the PSModulePath is automatically recognized by PowerShell and can be imported just by using the name. To have the repository module recognized in this manner, it must be inside one of the folders listed in the PSModulePath environment variable. The tricky part is that this path is different for different operating systems. This means you can run into all sorts of issues trying to get the repository to clone to one of the folders under it. For example, you can update the environment variable on Windows machines but not Linux. Likewise, you can have the PowerShell profile add it, but each version of PowerShell and each console have their own profiles. Therefore, the best way is to create a symbolic link under one of the folders in the PSModulePath environment variable. This way, the repository can be located anywhere on the machine but still automatically loaded into any PowerShell session.

The first thing you need to do is determine how to test whether Git is installed. Luckily, Git has a switch to return the installed version. Therefore, you can test the installation by creating a function that will run to check the Git version and confirm it returns data. You can do this by simply passing the command to the `Invoke-Expression` cmdlet and using a `try`/`catch` to determine whether the executable exists.

Since you will technically be running an executable and not a PowerShell expression, there is no way to tell the command to stop on an error. Therefore, you can't force the `catch` to run if the executable is not found. To work around this, you can overwrite the global error action preference to stop execution on any errors. But when you do this, be sure to set it back to the way it was before, as in the next listing, or you may cause issues with other commands expecting the default error action.

Listing 12.4 `Test-CmdInstall`

```
Function Test-CmdInstall {
    param(
        $TestCommand
    )
    try {
        $Before = $ErrorActionPreference          ← Capture the current
        $ErrorActionPreference = 'Stop'           ← ErrorActionPreference.
        $Command = @{                                Set ErrorActionPreference
            Command = $TestCommand                   to stop on all errors, even
        }                                            nonterminating ones.
        $testResult = Invoke-Expression @Command
    }
    catch {
        $testResult = $null      ← If an error is returned,
    }                              set results to null.
    finally {
        $ErrorActionPreference = $Before   ← Reset the
    }                                        ErrorActionPreference
    $testResult                             to the original value.
}
```

Attempt to run the command.

Once you have your function, you can build the command to perform the installs if required based on the operating system. One thing you will want to ensure is that you reload the `Path` environmental variable if you perform the Git installation. This way, the commands after it know how to find them since the `Path` is only updated when you load your session:

```
$env:Path = [System.Environment]::GetEnvironmentVariable("Path","Machine") +
    ";" + [System.Environment]::GetEnvironmentVariable("Path","User")
```

The remainder of the script will be the functionality to download the files and create the symbolic link. The `Git clone` command will copy the files from GitHub to the local computer, and the `New-Item` cmdlet will create the symbolic link. Figure 12.3 illustrates the process.

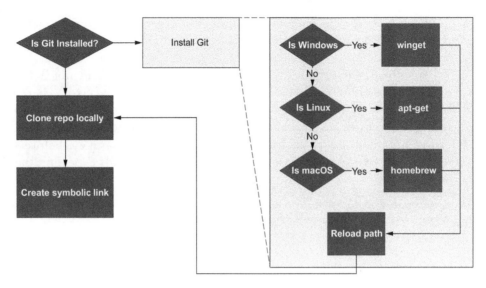

Figure 12.3 `Install-PoshAutomator` **flow including the ability to automatically install Git**

Create a new file named Install-PoshAutomator.ps1 and enter the code in the next listing. Be sure to update the $RepoUrl variable with the URL for your repository.

Listing 12.5 `Install-PoshAutomator.ps1`

```
$RepoUrl =                                                    ◄──────    The URL to
    'https://github.com/<yourprofile>/PoshAutomator.git'                 your GitHub
Function Test-CmdInstall {                                               repository
    param(
        $TestCommand
    )
    try {
        $Before = $ErrorActionPreference
        $ErrorActionPreference = 'Stop'
        $testResult = Invoke-Expression -Command $TestCommand
    }
    catch {
        $testResult = $null
    }
    finally {
        $ErrorActionPreference = $Before
    }
    $testResult
}
                                         Reload the Path
                                         environment
Function Set-EnvPath{                    variables.
    $env:Path =                 ◄────────
        [System.Environment]::GetEnvironmentVariable("Path", "Machine") +
        ";" +
        [System.Environment]::GetEnvironmentVariable("Path", "User")
}
```

```
$GitVersion = Test-CmdInstall 'git --version'        ◄── Check for Git.exe
if (-not ($GitVersion)) {                                and install if not
    if($IsWindows){                                      found.
        Write-Host "Installing Git for Windows..."
        $wingetParams = 'winget install --id Git.Git' +
            ' -e --source winget --accept-package-agreements' +
            ' --accept-source-agreements'
        Invoke-Expression  $wingetParams
    }
    elseif ($IsLinux) {
        Write-Host "Installing Git for Linux..."
        apt-get install git -y
    }
    elseif ($IsMacOS) {
        Write-Host "Installing Git for macOS..."           Reload environment
        brew install git -y                                variables to ensure
    }                                                      Git is available.
    Set-EnvPath                               ◄────────
    $GitVersion = Test-CmdInstall 'git --version'
    if (-not ($GitVersion)) {
        throw "Unable to locate Git.exe install.
            Please install manually and rerun this script."
    }
    else{
        Write-Host "Git Version $($GitVersion) has been installed"
    }
}
else {
    Write-Host "Git Version $($GitVersion) is already installed"
}


if($IsWindows){                          ◄──────   Set the location
    Set-Location $env:USERPROFILE                  to the user's
}                                                  profile.
else {
    Set-Location $env:HOME
}
                                                        Clone the
                                                        repository locally.
Invoke-Expression -Command "git clone $RepoUrl"    ◄──

                                                   Get the first folder listed
$ModuleFolder = Get-Item './PoshAutomator'         in the PSModulePath.
$UserPowerShellModules =                       ◄──
    [Environment]::GetEnvironmentVariable("PSModulePath").Split(';')[0]
$SimLinkProperties = @{
    ItemType = 'SymbolicLink'
    Path     = (Join-Path $UserPowerShellModules $ModuleFolder.BaseName)
    Target   = $ModuleFolder.FullName
    Force    = $true
}
New-Item @SimLinkProperties
```

Create the
symbolic link.

Once you have this put together, you can upload it to a gist:

```
gh gist create Install-PoshAutomator.ps1 --web
```

Then, you can use the Raw link to create a one-line installation command you can share with your team. But we will come back to that in a little bit.

12.3   *Updating a shared module*

The best part of using a code repository to store your module files is that they provide branching, code reviews, automated testing, and version control. We will cover creating automated tests and code reviews in later chapters. For now, we will just look at how to create a separate branch for developing your changes and then how to create a pull request to update the main branch.

Creating separate branches allows you to create copies of the repository to make code changes and test with, without having to make changes to code that is currently in use. Then, once you have finished and tested all of your changes, you can merge them into the main branch so that two people or teams can be working on different parts at the same time without interfering with each other. You can see an example of this in figure 12.4.

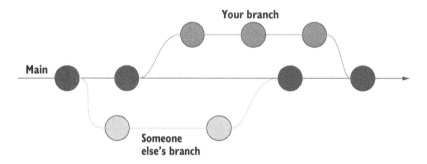

Figure 12.4   Simple branch model with a single main branch

Once again, open a command prompt and navigate to the folder with the repository files. Use the following snippets to create a new branch and pull down the main repository from GitHub. This ensures that your local branch has the most recent version of all the files and you are not working from an older codebase:

```
git checkout -b develop
Switched to a new branch 'develop'
git pull origin main
From https://github.com/mdowst/PoshAutomatorB
 * branch            main        -> FETCH_HEAD
Already up to date.
```

Now you can make any changes you want to the existing files or add new files. To see how this works, go ahead and open PoshAutomator.psd1. Then, change the version number to 1.0.0.1 and save the file. Next, using Git, you will commit the changes:

```
git add .
git commit -m "versioned PoshAutomator.psd1"
[develop 6d3fb8e] versioned PoshAutomator.psd1
 1 file changed, 1 insertion(+), 1 deletion(-)
```

Then, push the change to GitHub:

```
git push origin develop
Enumerating objects: 5, done.
Counting objects: 100% (5/5), done.
Compressing objects: 100% (3/3), done.
Writing objects: 100% (3/3), 322 bytes | 322.00 KiB/s, done.
Total 3 (delta 2), reused 0 (delta 0), pack-reused 0
remote: Resolving deltas: 100% (2/2), completed with 2 local objects.
remote:
remote: Create a pull request for 'develop' on GitHub by visiting:
remote:        https://github.com/mdowst/PoshAutomator/pull/new/develop
remote:
To https://github.com/mdowst/PoshAutomator.git
 * [new branch]      develop -> develop
```

Since there is no branch named *develop* in the GitHub repository, it will be automatically created for you. Then, if you make more changes and push again, it will update the branch. So now, if you navigate to the repository in GitHub and click on branches, you should see the main and develop branches.

When you have finished all your updates, you will merge the develop branch into the main branch using a pull request. The pull request allows you to review all differences between the branches side by side so you can see exactly what will change before committing anything to the main codebase. But before we do that, let's look at how you can ensure that your team members are always using the most recent version of the module.

12.3.1 *Make the module self-update*

Since this is a shared module, you will want to ensure that everyone using it has the most recent version installed. The fact that the module is stored in GitHub gives you the capability to have the module check for and automatically sync changes. Once again, this can be done using the Git executables.

To make the module self-update, you will add the code in listing 12.6 to the Posh-Automator.psm1 file. As you know, the psm1 file is executed when the module is imported to PowerShell. So, we will add some commands to it to check that the code on the local machine matches the latest version on GitHub. This time, you will use the `Start-Process` cmdlet to execute the Git commands. This cmdlet will allow you to ensure that the Git executable is running in the correct directory and capture the output so it can check if an update is required. The code will perform the following functionality:

1 Get the current local branch to ensure the local repository is set to main:

```
git branch --show-current
```

2 If it is not on main, switch to main:

```
git checkout main
```

3 Update the metadata for the main branch on GitHub:

```
git fetch
```

4 Compare the local version of main against the remote version:

```
git diff main origin/main --compact-summary
```

5 If the output from the `diff` command shows differences, then sync to ensure that the local files match the remote ones:

```
git reset origin/main
```

Since you are using the `Start-Process` cmdlet to execute the command, you will need a local file to capture the output. You can use the `New-TemporaryFile` cmdlet to create one for you and then have your code delete it after the checks are complete.

One last thing you will want to do is provide the user a message letting them know the module was updated and recommending that they restart PowerShell. This is because any changes to the psm1 and psd1 files will not be picked up until the next time the module is loaded, and a module cannot reload itself.

Listing 12.6 PoshAutomator.psm1

```
$gitResults = New-TemporaryFile               ◁          Create a temporary file to
$Process = @{                                  ◁          capture command outputs.
    FilePath                = 'git.exe'
    WorkingDirectory        = $PSScriptRoot               Set the default parameters
    RedirectStandardOutput  = $gitResults                 to use when executing the
    Wait                    = $true                       Git command.
    NoNewWindow             = $true
}
$Argument = 'branch --show-current'           ◁          Get the current
Start-Process @Process -ArgumentList $Argument           branch.
$content = Get-Content -LiteralPath $gitResults -Raw
                                                         Check if the current
                                                         branch is main.
if($content.Trim() -ne 'main'){               ◁
    $Argument = 'checkout main'                ◁          Set the branch
    Start-Process @Process -ArgumentList $Argument        to main.
}
$Argument = 'fetch'                           ◁          Update the metadata
Start-Process @Process -ArgumentList $Argument           for the main branch
$Argument = 'diff main origin/main --compact-summary'    on GitHub.
Start-Process @Process -ArgumentList $Argument
$content = Get-Content -LiteralPath $gitResults -Raw
```

**Compare the local version of
main against the remote version.**

If a difference is detected, force the module to download the newest version.

```
if($content){
    Write-Host "A module update was detected. Downloading new code base..."
    $Argument = 'reset origin/main'
    Start-Process @Process -ArgumentList $Argument
    $content = Get-Content -LiteralPath $gitResults
    Write-Host $content
    Write-Host "It is recommended that you reload your PowerShell window."
}

if(Test-Path $gitResults){                    ⟵——  Delete the
    Remove-Item -Path $gitResults -Force            temporary file.
}

$Path = Join-Path $PSScriptRoot 'Public'       Get all the ps1 files
$Functions = Get-ChildItem -Path $Path -Filter '*.ps1'   in the Public folder.

Foreach ($import in $Functions) {      ⟵——  Loop through each ps1 file.
    Try {
        Write-Verbose "dot-sourcing file '$($import.fullname)'"
        . $import.fullname                 ⟵   Execute each ps1 file to load
    }                                           the function into memory.
    Catch {
        Write-Error -Message "Failed to import function $($import.name)"
    }
}
```

Go ahead and save your changes to the psm1 file and run the following commands to sync the changes with GitHub. Then, you will be able to make a pull request to move your changes to the main branch:

```
git checkout develop
git add .
git commit -m "added self-updating to PoshAutomator.psm1"
git push origin develop
```

12.3.2 Creating a pull request

Once you have completed and tested all of your changes to a development branch, you can update the main branch via a pull request. You can create a pull request using the GitHub CLI, but you should use the browser to approve and complete a pull request. Then, you can quickly review all adds, deletes, and updates to the code with the browser. But first, start by creating the pull request:

```
gh pr create --title "Develop to Main" --body "This is my first pull request"
? Where should we push the develop' branch? mdowst/PoshAutomator

Creating pull request for develop into main in mdowst/PoshAutomator

Branch 'develop' set up to track remote branch 'develop' from 'upstream'.
Everything up-to-date
https://github.com/mdowst/PoshAutomator/pull/1
```

This command will create a pull request for the branch you are on to the main branch. It will also output the URL for the pull request. Go ahead and copy that URL and open it in GitHub.

The pull request is designed to show you the history of commits made to the branch and the file differences between the two branches. When a pull request is completed, the changes are merged into the destination branch.

The pull request will also show you if there are any merge conflicts. These can arise when a file has been updated in both branches. To prevent accidentally overwriting someone else's work, you will need to manually review the conflicting files and determine which one to keep. You can review the difference between the files on branch under the Files Changed tab, shown in figure 12.5.

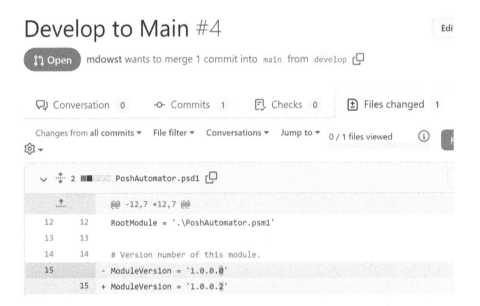

Figure 12.5   The Files Changed tab of the pull request shows the difference between the two branches. The new lines start with a plus sign (+) and are highlighted in green, and removed/ updated lines start with a minus sign (•) and are highlighted in red.

If all the changes look good, click the Merge Pull Request button back on the Conversation tab. When the merge completes, you will be given the option to delete the develop branch. It is usually a good idea to do so to prevent having a bunch of old branches sitting around. Plus, all of your commits have been merged with the main branch, so you don't have to worry about losing data.

We have just scratched the surface of what is possible with pull requests. You can do many different things with them, like have reviewers approve changes, create continuous integration tests, and create custom code checks. Some of this will be covered in later chapters.

12.3.3 *Testing the self-update*

Now that you have everything put together, the only thing left is to test the self-updating functionality. To do this, you will install the module using the installation script from section 11.2.2. Then, make a change to the main branch and reload the module. This should trigger the module to update itself.

Start by opening the gist for the Install-PoshAutomator.ps1 script, then click the Raw button. Next, copy the raw URL and execute it using the `Invoke-Expression`/`Invoke-RestMethod` cmdlets. Then, test importing and using the module:

```
Invoke-Expression (Invoke-RestMethod -Uri 'Your Gist Raw URL')
Import-Module PoshAutomator
Get-SystemInfo
```

Open the repository in your browser and confirm you are on the main branch. Next, click the PoshAutomator.psd1 file. Click the pencil icon to edit the file and change the version to 1.0.0.2. Scroll to the bottom of the page and click Commit Changes.

Normally you would not want to update the main repository in this manner. In fact, with the paid versions of GitHub, you can lock down the main branch to prevent someone from accidentally committing to it. However, for testing and learning purposes, it is much quicker than creating a new branch and merging a pull request.

Once you save the changes, go back to your command prompt and import the PoshAutomator module with the `-Force` switch to ensure it reloads:

```
Import-Module PoshAutomator -Force
```

Then, if you run it once more, it should load without downloading anything.

From here, the possibilities are endless. You and your team can continue to add new functionality to the module, and the changes will automatically sync for everyone.

Summary

- You can use a GitHub Gist to share individual scripts or code snippets quickly and easily.
- You can execute a gist directly from the URL using the `Invoke-Express` and `Invoke-RestMethod` expressions.
- A GitHub repository can be used to store a PowerShell module that can be shared among the members of your team.
- Using the Git and GitHub CLI executables, you can automate much of your codebase's development and updating processes.

Testing your scripts

This chapter covers

- Writing unit tests using Pester
- Creating mocks to ensure consistency in testing
- Writing integration tests with Pester

If you asked me what one key takeaway I would like people to get from this book, it would be to plan for the future. Throughout this book, we have discussed things like creating functions and modules with your reusable code. By making things modular and extensible, you are giving yourself a great foundation. However, there will come a time when you may need to make changes to these foundational parts. If you have a function or module used across multiple automations, you need to ensure that your changes do not break existing functionality. The best way to do that is by creating unit and integration tests, and there is no better way to do that in PowerShell than by using Pester.

Pester is the predominant test and mock framework for PowerShell. It is one of PowerShell's most prominent community-owned extensions, with over 130 contributors and an Open Collective group. It has been such the gold standard for PowerShell testing that Microsoft includes it in the default PowerShell installation. Like many things in PowerShell, it is simple to get started but is also very powerful once you start diving deep into it.

In this chapter, we will work through a scenario I'm sure many of you have faced: reconciling a vulnerability report against the actual state of a machine. Anyone who has dealt with vulnerability scanners knows there can be many false positives. One of the most common false positives is caused by security patches being superseded.

For example, say you missed the February patch but installed the March one. Since they are cumulative, your machine is up to date. However, some vulnerability scanners will still consider the February patch missing.

To help save you time and frustration when this happens, you will create a script that can search the Microsoft Update Catalog for a particular patch and return the supersedence information. You can then check the computer to see whether any of the patches that superseded the original patches are installed.

As you build this functionality, you will use Pester to create different tests, allowing you to confirm each piece of your script along the way. But before we dive right in, let's have a brief overview of Pester.

13.1 Introduction to Pester

Pester provides a framework to create repeatable tests in PowerShell. This provides you with assurance that your code will still work after making changes. It will also allow you to mock the behavior of any PowerShell command, which, as you will see, can come in very handy.

Before getting started, you want to ensure that you have at least Pester version 5.3.1 installed. By default, PowerShell includes Pester version 3.4.0. So, you will need to include the `-SkipPublisherCheck` switch to allow it to upgrade:

```
Install-Module Pester -Scope AllUsers -Force -SkipPublisherCheck
```

Unlike the rest of PowerShell, Pester does not use cmdlets. It uses keywords. The keywords are used to organize, execute, and confirm the unit tests. At the top level is the `Describe` keyword. `Describe` is used to group your tests into logical categories. Below `Describe` is `Context`. The `Context` allows you to group similar tests inside of a `Describe` section. You are not required to include Context in your script, but it can be helpful to keep things organized. Each `Describe` and `Context` block can be given a label that will be included in the test results.

Also, Pester commands cannot be run interactively. They must be saved to a ps1 file and run all at once:

```
Describe "Test 1" {
    Context "Sub Test A" {
        # Test code
    }

    Context "Sub Test B" {
        # Test code
    }
}
```

Inside of the `Describe` and `Context` blocks are `It` blocks that contain the actual test commands. Then, the `Should` command is used to confirm the results:

```
Describe "Boolean Test" {
    Context "True Tests" {
        It '$true is true' {
            $true | Should -Be $true
            $true | Should -Not -Be $false
            $true | Should -BeTrue
            $true | Should -BeOfType [System.Boolean]
        }
    }

    Context "False Tests" {
        It '$false is false' {
            $false | Should -Be $false
            $false | Should -Not -Be $true
            $false | Should -BeFalse
            $false | Should -BeOfType [System.Boolean]
        }
    }
}
```

The important thing to know is that the commands written inside an `It` block are entirely self-contained. This means that you cannot share variables or commands between `It` blocks like you would in a standard PowerShell script. To share code between tests, you must use the `BeforeAll` or `BeforeEach` commands.

The `BeforeAll` or `BeforeEach` commands can be declared at the top of the script or nested inside of `Describe` and `Context` blocks. Like their names state, the `Before-All` runs once before running all tests, and the `BeforeEach` reruns the commands before each test:

```
Describe "Boolean Test" {
    Context "True Tests" {
        BeforeAll{
            $var = $true
        }

        It '$true is true' {
            $var | Should -BeTrue
        }

        It '$true is still true' {
            $var | Should -BeTrue
        }
    }
}
```

The `BeforeAll` or `BeforeEach` commands are also where you will include your `Mock` commands.

13.2 Unit testing

For those unfamiliar with software testing terminology, a *unit test* is designed to test the logic in your code. In PowerShell terms, a unit test would be a test for a single function. Since you are testing the logic in your code, you should use mocks to ensure consistent data is sent to your functions.

A mock is a way to "fake" a call to something outside of your function. For example, in our scenario of checking for vulnerabilities, we will need to get the results from the Get-HotFix cmdlet, as shown in figure 13.1. Your unit test aims to test that your function handles the response from this cmdlet in the way you designed. To ensure this, you will mock the call to the Get-HotFix cmdlet in your test to return the values you want to test against.

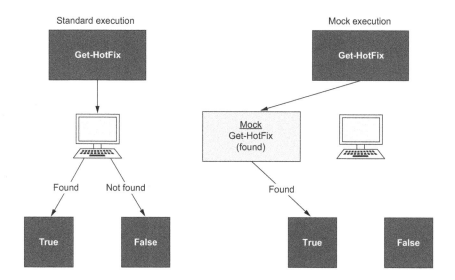

Figure 13.1 Standard execution will call the actual cmdlet, making your unit test dependent on the local machine being appropriately configured. Instead, you can mock the cmdlet to return exactly what you are expecting in any scenario.

Before you create your first test, you need code to test. So, let's create a function to test whether a computer has a particular patch installed. The Get-HotFix cmdlet returns the Microsoft patches installed on a Windows computer. To test for a specific patch, you use the -Id parameter with the patch's knowledge base (KB) number. You can also check remote machines using the -ComputerName parameter. However, if you use the -Id parameter and the patch is not installed on the computer, the Get-HotFix cmdlet will return an error. So, to prevent your script from returning a bunch of errors when searching for patches, you can wrap the Get-HotFix cmdlet in a try/catch block.

If an error triggers the catch block from the Get-HotFix cmdlet, you can confirm whether the error was from the patch not being found or something else. If it is something else, throw an error; otherwise, just return `false`. If the patch is found, the `catch` block will not be triggered, and the return value will be set to `true`. Go ahead and create the function to test using the following listing.

Listing 13.1 `Get-HotFixStatus`

```
Function Get-HotFixStatus{
    param(
        $Id,
        $Computer                      Set the initial
    )                                  value to false.

    $Found = $false                    Attempt to return the
    try{                               patch and stop execution
        $HotFix = @{                   on any error.
            Id            = $Id
            ComputerName  = $Computer
            ErrorAction   = 'Stop'          If the previous
        }                                   command did not        If the catch block is
        Get-HotFix @HotFix | Out-Null       error, then it is safe to   triggered, check to
        $Found = $true                      assume it was found.   see if the error was
    }                                                              because the patch
    catch{                                                         was not found.
        $NotFound = 'GetHotFixNoEntriesFound,' +
            'Microsoft.PowerShell.Commands.GetHotFixCommand'
        if($_.FullyQualifiedErrorId -ne $NotFound){
            throw $_
        }                              Termination execution
    }                                  on any error other
    $Found                             than the patch not
}                                      found
```

You can test this out with a couple of patches you have installed on your computer, and then with a couple that you know are not installed. Save this function to your local computer in a file named Get-HotFixStatus.ps1. Then, create a new file in the same folder named Get-HotFixStatus.Unit.Tests.ps1. This is the file that will contain the code for performing the Pester tests.

13.2.1 BeforeAll

The first thing you will need to do in your Pester test is to set any global variables and commands. Since `Get-HotFixStatus` is a custom function, PowerShell and, by extension, Pester will not know about it unless you import it to the current session. So, to ensure that all tests are aware of the function, you will put a `BeforeAll` block at the very top of the script, outside of any `Describe` or `Context` blocks. This `BeforeAll` will call the Get-HotFixStatus.ps1 file to import the function into the current session:

```
BeforeAll {
    Set-Location -Path $PSScriptRoot
    . .\Get-HotFixStatus.ps1
}
```

Remember that the `BeforeAll` block will be inherited by all `Describe` or `Context` blocks below. This way, all tests will have the `Get-HotFixStatus` function.

13.2.2 Creating tests

Now it is time to create your tests. First, we will create a simple test to ensure the function behaves as expected when a patch is installed.

We will get to mocks shortly, but for now, you can run the command `Get-HotFix` without any parameters and choose a KB number to test with.

Below the `BeforeAll` in the Pester script, create a Describe block with the label `Get-HotFixStatus`. Then, inside of that, you can create an It block with the `Get-HotFixStatus` command set to a KB number you know is installed. Then, confirm it returns `true` by using a `Should` assertion:

```
Describe 'Get-HotFixStatus' {
    It "Hotfix is found on the computer" {
        $KBFound = Get-HotFixStatus -Id 'KB5011493' -Computer 'localhost'
        $KBFound | Should -Be $true
    }
}
```

Save the Get-HotFixStatus.Unit.Tests.ps1 file and execute it. You should see an output similar to the following snippet if everything worked:

```
Starting discovery in 1 files.
Discovery found 1 tests in 5ms.
Running tests.
[+] D:\Chapter13\Pester\Get-HotFixStatus.Unit.Tests.ps1 185ms (158ms|22ms)
Tests completed in 189ms
Tests Passed: 1, Failed: 0, Skipped: 0 NotRun: 0
```

You can also add a test for a patch you know is not installed, this time using a KB number you know is not installed and checking that the result is `false`:

```
It "Hotfix is not found on the computer" {
    $KBFound = Get-HotFixStatus -Id 'KB1234567' -Computer 'localhost'
    $KBFound | Should -Be $false
}
```

Then, you can add one final test that will throw a terminating error. Since the function is designed to terminate on any error other than the patch not being found, you can pass it a machine name that does not exist and then confirm that it throws an error:

```
It "Hotfix is found on the computer" {
    { Get-HotFixStatus -Id 'KB5011493' -Computer 'Srv123' } | Should -Throw
}
```

Now your Get-HotFixStatus.Unit.Tests.ps1 should look like the next listing. Go ahead and save it, and run it once more to confirm that all tests pass as expected.

Listing 13.2   Get-HotFixStatus.Unit.Tests.ps1 local check

```
BeforeAll {
    Set-Location -Path $PSScriptRoot          ◁──┤ Import your
    . .\Get-HotFixStatus.ps1                       function.
}

Describe 'Get-HotFixStatus' {              ◁──┘ Pester tests
    It "Hotfix is found on the computer" {
        $KBFound = Get-HotFixStatus -Id 'KB5011493' -Computer 'localhost'
        $KBFound | Should -Be $true
    }

    It "Hotfix is not found on the computer" {
        $KBFound = Get-HotFixStatus -Id 'KB1234567' -Computer 'localhost'
        $KBFound | Should -Be $false
    }

    It "Unable to connect" {
        { Get-HotFixStatus -Id 'KB5011493' -Computer 'Bad' } | Should -Throw
    }
}
```

These tests will run and pass on your local computer where you verified the KB numbers. However, the test will fail if you run it on a computer without the first patch installed—and this failure would be a false positive because the function did what it was supposed to. So, let's look at how you can prevent that by using mocks.

13.2.3 Mocks

Mocks can be a very powerful tool when it comes to unit testing. They allow you to intercept the call to any PowerShell command and return predetermined results. This allows you to control the exact data that your tests will receive. Remember, your unit test is not testing the commands that it calls but rather the behavior that you designed the function to take based on the results of those commands.

For example, say you want to check Active Directory users for passwords about to expire. If a password is within a week of expiring, you want to send the user an email. If it is within three days of expiring, you want to send them and their manager an email. To test this function, you need to have user accounts that meet those exact specifications. So, instead of manually manipulating user accounts to meet each scenario, you can mock the call to the Get-AdUser cmdlet. Inside of that mock, you can create PowerShell objects that match the expected return of the cmdlet.

In our scenario, you will want to mock the Get-HotFix cmdlet that is executed inside the Get-HotFixStatus function. By doing this, you can ensure that your tests will behave as expected regardless of where they are run.

To create a mock, you need to declare it using the Mock command, followed by the command you want to mock and a script block of what you want to return. Typically, you will declare a mock inside a BeforeAll or BeforeEach command, as you can see in figure 13.2.

You also need to take into consideration the level of the mock. For instance, if you added a mock to the BeforeAll at the top of the script or inside the Describe block, it would apply to both the found and not found It blocks. Therefore, you will want to use a Context block inside the Describe block to ensure the Mock only applies to the correct tests.

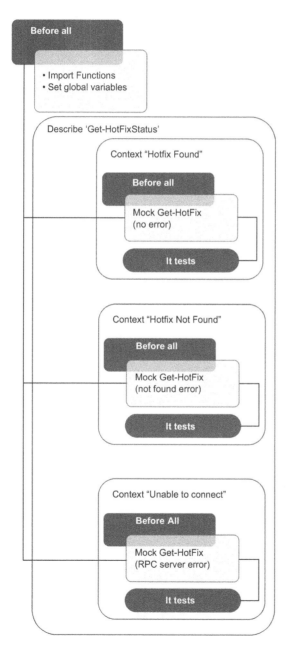

Figure 13.2   Pester mocking example showing that BeforeAll blocks are inherited down but not between different Context or Describe blocks

The way the `Get-HotFixStatus` function is written, as long as the `Get-HotFix` cmdlet does not return an error, it considers the patch found. So, in this case, you can create a `Mock` that returns nothing:

```
Mock Get-HotFix {}
```

For the next test, we need to simulate a patch not being found. In this case, the `Get-HotFixStatus` function expects a specific error message, which you can easily reproduce using a `throw` command:

```
Mock Get-HotFix {
    throw 'GetHotFixNoEntriesFound,Microsoft.PowerShell.Commands.GetHotFixCommand'
}
```

And, finally, you can test an error where the `Get-HotFix` cmdlet cannot connect to the remote machine:

```
Mock Get-HotFix {
    throw 'System.Runtime.InteropServices.COMException,Microsoft.PowerShell
     .Commands.GetHotFixCommand'
}
```

Your script will look like the next listing when you put this all together. Save this and run it again. You should see all tests pass.

Listing 13.3   Get-HotFixStatus.Unit.Tests.ps1 with mocking

```
BeforeAll {
    Set-Location -Path $PSScriptRoot          ←─┤ Import your
    . .\Get-HotFixStatus.ps1                     │ function.

    $Id = 'KB1234567'          ←─┤ Set a default
}                                 │ value for the ID.

Describe 'Get-HotFixStatus' {          ←── Pester tests
    Context "Hotfix Found" {
        BeforeAll {
            Mock Get-HotFix {}
        }
        It "Hotfix is found on the computer" {
            $KBFound = Get-HotFixStatus -Id $Id -Computer 'localhost'
            $KBFound | Should -Be $true
        }
    }

    Context "Hotfix Not Found" {
        BeforeAll {
            Mock Get-HotFix {
                throw ('GetHotFixNoEntriesFound,' +
                    'Microsoft.PowerShell.Commands.GetHotFixCommand')
            }
        }
```

```
        It "Hotfix is not found on the computer" {
            $KBFound = Get-HotFixStatus -Id $Id -Computer 'localhost'
            $KBFound | Should -Be $false
        }
    }

    Context "Not able to connect to the remote machine" {
        BeforeAll {
            Mock Get-HotFix {
                throw ('System.Runtime.InteropServices.COMException,' +
                    'Microsoft.PowerShell.Commands.GetHotFixCommand' )
            }
        }

        It "Unable to connect" {
            { Get-HotFixStatus -Id $Id -Computer 'Bad' } | Should -Throw
        }
    }
}
```

As you can see, mocks can be very useful in unit testing. But, as you will learn in the next section, you need to be careful not to rely on them too much.

13.3 Advanced unit testing

So far, you have written a function that can check a computer for an installed patch, but this does not account for superseded patches. Say your vulnerability report shows that a computer is missing the March 2022 patch. When you check the computer, it has the April 2022 patch installed. Since this patch is cumulative and supersedes the March patch, you know it is a false positive on the vulnerability report. However, when you have hundreds or thousands of computers to do this on, checking each one could be a full-time job. So, let's look at how we can include some superseded checks and integrate those checks into your Pester tests.

Unfortunately, Microsoft does not have a searchable API for all patches. You can install Windows Server Update Services (WSUS) and sync the entire patch catalog locally to search, but this is a massive amount of overhead. In addition, there are hundreds of applications in WSUS, and it constantly needs to be updated to include new ones. So, unless you have some really beefy hardware, you would be better off finding another way to search for patch information.

The Microsoft Update Catalog website (https://www.catalog.update.microsoft.com/) allows you to search for every patch released by Microsoft. The downside to this website is that there is no publicly available backend for you to search. However, all is not lost. You can still get the information you need from this site by using some web scraping. And to help with this, you will want to install the PowerHTML module from the PowerShell Gallery.

The PowerHTML module includes the `ConvertFrom-Html` cmdlet. This cmdlet can take an HTML input and convert it to an object you can navigate using XPath queries. And don't worry if you have no idea how to write XPath queries or even what one is. We will let your browser do most of the work for you:

```
Install-Module PowerHTML
```

13.3.1 Web scraping

The trick to web scraping is to use the developer tools available in most modern web browsers. This section was written using Edge, but the process is the same for Chrome and Firefox. To get started, open the Microsoft Update Catalog website in your browser (https://www.catalog.update.microsoft.com/). Then, search for a patch that you know has been superseded. If you do not know one off the top of your head, you can use KB4521858, as in the example in figure 13.3.

When you search for KB4521858 on the site, you will see in the address bar that the URL for the search results is https://www.catalog.update.microsoft.com/Search.aspx?q =KB4521858. You will also see that there are three results because this patch applies to Windows Server 2016 and Windows 10, both x64 and x86. So, you know you will need to account for multiple results.

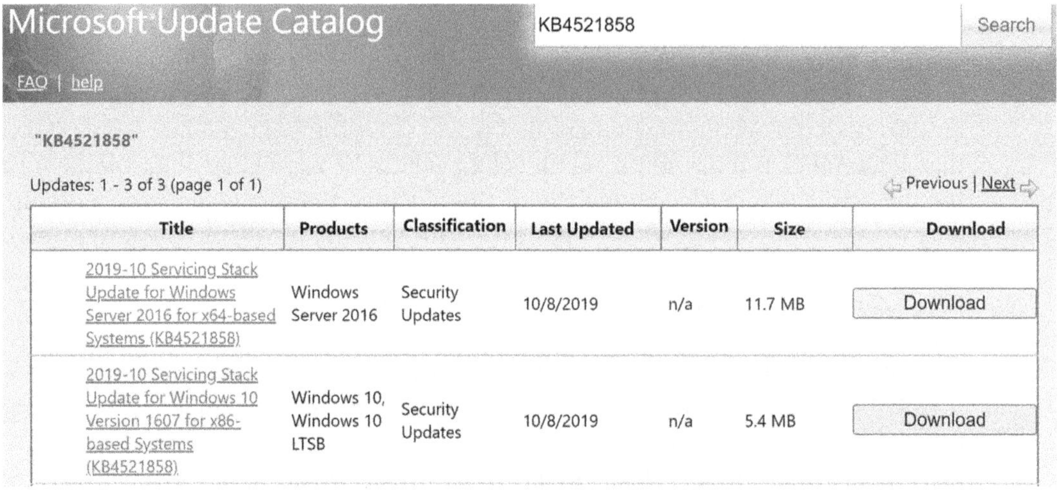

Microsoft Update Catalog   KB4521858   Search

FAQ | help

"KB4521858"

Updates: 1 - 3 of 3 (page 1 of 1)   Previous | Next

Title	Products	Classification	Last Updated	Version	Size	Download
2019-10 Servicing Stack Update for Windows Server 2016 for x64-based Systems (KB4521858)	Windows Server 2016	Security Updates	10/8/2019	n/a	11.7 MB	Download
2019-10 Servicing Stack Update for Windows 10 Version 1607 for x86-based Systems (KB4521858)	Windows 10, Windows 10 LTSB	Security Updates	10/8/2019	n/a	5.4 MB	Download

Figure 13.3   Search results for the patch KB4521858 in the Microsoft Catalog showing that there can be multiple results for one KB number

Each of the links shown in figure 13.3 will open a new window with that patch's details, including the superseded information. If you click on one of them, it opens a new window with the patch's details, shown in figure 13.4, including the superseded information.

So, the first thing you need to do is extract the links from the search results. Then, extract the data from the page that each one of those links opens. This is where PowerShell and the `ConvertFrom-Html` cmdlet will come in handy.

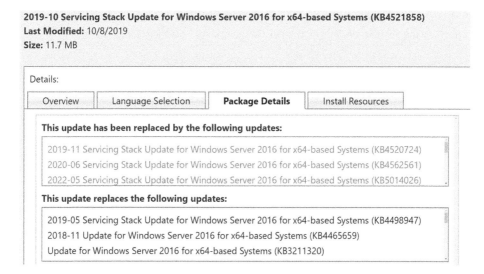

Figure 13.4 Clicking on the search results opens a new window that contains the information you need to collect.

We will start by creating a command that will let you build the search results URL and pass that URL to the ConvertFrom-Html cmdlet:

```
$KbArticle = 'KB4521858'
$UriHost = 'https://www.catalog.update.microsoft.com/'
$SearchUri = $UriHost + 'Search.aspx?q=' + $KbArticle
$Search = ConvertFrom-Html -URI $SearchUri
```

If you look at the output for the $Search variable, it will just show you the top node of the page, which in this case is document:

```
NodeType Name      AttributeCount ChildNodeCount ContentLength InnerText
-------- ----      -------------- -------------- ------------- ---------
Document #document 0              5              51551         ...
```

Here is where XPath queries will help you find what you need. In the web browser, right-click on the first link and select Inspect. This will open the developer console and navigate right to the section with the code for this link. If you then right-click on the code, you will be presented with several copy options, one of which is Copy XPath.

If you copy the XPath and paste it to Notepad or VS Code, you will see something like the following snippet:

```
//*[@id="83d7bc64-ff39-4073-9d77-02102226aff6_link"]
```

You may have noticed that the ID here is the same one in the URL when clicking on the link. However, if you look at the other links, you will see different IDs. This shows that you cannot just search for the ID because you have no idea what it will be. So right-click on the code again, and this time, select Copy Element:

```
<a id="83d7bc64-ff39-4073-9d77-02102226aff6_link"
   href="javascript:void(0);"
   onclick="goToDetails(&quot;83d7bc64-ff39-4073-9d77-02102226aff6&quot;);"
   class="contentTextItemSpacerNoBreakLink">
2019-10 Servicing Stack Update for Windows Server 2016 for x64-based Systems
   (KB4521858)
</a>
```

Here you get the entire section of the web page that contains the link information. You can create an XPath query on any and all values inside the element. If you copy the element from the other two links, you will see that the class and href have the same values in each one. Therefore, you can build any XPath query to search for elements containing both values. You can then pass the XPath query to the `SelectNodes` method on the `$Search` variable, and you should see the three elements that correspond with the three links:

```
$xPath = '//*[' +
    '@class="contentTextItemSpacerNoBreakLink" ' +
    'and @href="javascript:void(0);"]'
$Search.SelectNodes($xPath) | Format-Table NodeType, Name, Id, InnerText
NodeType Name AttributeCount ChildNodeCount ContentLength InnerText
-------- ---- -------------- -------------- ------------- ---------
Element  a    4              1              144           …
Element  a    4              1              148           …
Element  a    4              1              148           …
```

You can then take this further by extracting the ID from each element:

```
$Search.SelectNodes($xPath) | ForEach-Object {
    $_.Id
}
83d7bc64-ff39-4073-9d77-02102226aff6_link
3767d7ce-29db-4d75-93b7-34922d49c9e3_link
250bfd45-b92c-49af-b604-dbdfd15061e6_link
```

Back in the web browser, if you click on the first link, you will see that the URL is https://www.catalog.update.microsoft.com/ScopedViewInline.aspx?updateid=83d7bc64 -ff39-4073-9d77-02102226aff6, which nearly matches the ID from the first element. It is not perfect because the ID contains _link at the end, but that can easily be resolved using a `Replace` method. You can now build the URL for each link using the extracted ID and then pass that to the `ConvertFrom-Html` cmdlet:

```
$Search.SelectNodes($xPath) | ForEach-Object {
    $Id = $_.Id.Replace('_link', '')
    $DetailsUri = $UriHost +
        "ScopedViewInline.aspx?updateid=$($Id)"
```

```
    $Details = ConvertFrom-Html -Uri $DetailsUri
    $DetailsUri
}
https://www.catalog.update.microsoft.com/ScopedViewInline.aspx?updateid=
    83d7bc64-ff39-4073-9d77-02102226aff6
https://www.catalog.update.microsoft.com/ScopedViewInline.aspx?updateid=
    3767d7ce-29db-4d75-93b7-34922d49c9e3
https://www.catalog.update.microsoft.com/ScopedViewInline.aspx?updateid=
    250bfd45-b92c-49af-b604-dbdfd15061e6
```

Now that you have the URL for each update, it is time to extract the data you need from that web page. Unfortunately, during my testing, I discovered that the results for this particular URL did not work with the ConvertFrom-Html cmdlet. This was because this web page requires a header setting the return language. You can use the Invoke-WebRequest and pass the results to the ConvertFrom-Html cmdlet to get around that:

```
$Headers = @{"accept-language"="en-US,en;q=0.9"}
$Request = Invoke-WebRequest -Uri $DetailsUri -Headers $Headers
$Details = ConvertFrom-Html -Content $Request
```

Getting header values

The header values I provided in the Invoke-WebRequest snippet are for US English results. To find what the language values should be for your language, open your web browser and press F12 to open the Developer Tool. Then, click the Network tab in the Developer tools and confirm they are recording. Next, navigate to one of the links for a KB article. You should see an entry for ScopedViewInline.aspx in the console. Click it and then the Headers tab. There, you will see the value sent for the Accept Language entry. You can copy that value and update your script with your preferred language.

Now, open one of the links in your browser. On the Overview tab, there are values for the architecture and the supported products. Starting with the architecture value, right-click it and select Inspect. You will see the value is inside a div with the ID of archDiv. You can right-click the div and Copy XPath.

   Next, paste that XPath into your script and return the InnerText property. Then, you can use a Replace to remove the "Architecture:" part at the front and remove any white space with the Trim method:

```
$xPath = '//*[@id="archDiv"]'
$Architecture = $Details.SelectSingleNode($xPath).InnerText
$Architecture.Replace('Architecture:', '').Trim()
AMD64
```

You can then do the same thing for supported products, but if you are using a link that has more than one product, you may see some results like the following:

```
$xPath = '//*[@id="productsDiv"]'
$Products = $Details.SelectSingleNode($xPath).InnerText
$Products = $Products.Replace('Supported products:', '')
$Products
```

Windows 10

'

Windows 10 LTSB

As you can see, there is a lot of white space between the two products. Since a `Trim` only removes from the beginning and the end, it will not remove the space and line breaks between the two products. Luckily, you can rectify this by splitting the values into an array and then trimming the individual values. Also, this makes your data cleaner and easier to parse later on because, with an array, you can use `-contains` and `-in` operators. In contrast, a string with multiple values would require you to use `-like` or `-match` operators, which are not as accurate:

```
$xPath = '//*[@id="productsDiv"]'
$Products = $Details.SelectSingleNode($xPath).InnerText
$Products = $Products.Replace('Supported products:', '')
$Products = $Products.Split(',').Trim()
$Products
Windows 10
Windows 10 LTSB
```

Back in the web browser, go to the Package Details tab. Then, right-click in the box for This Update Has Been Replaced by the Following Updates and choose Inspect.

You will see an ID named `supersededbyInfo`. This is a good indication that this box has a nice ID label you can use. You can also see that each link underneath is inside of an a element that is inside a `div`. So, you will use the `Elements` method after the XPath to parse through each level. Right-click on the `supersededbyInfo` ID and Copy XPath and add the path to your script:

```
$xPath = '//*[@id="supersededbyInfo"]'
$DivElements = $Details.SelectSingleNode($xPath).Elements("div")
$SupersededBy = $DivElements.Elements("a")
$SupersededBy | Format-Table NodeType, Name, InnerText
NodeType Name InnerText
-------- ---- ---------
  Element a    2019-11 Servicing Stack Update for Windows Server...(KB4520724)
  Element a    2020-03 Servicing Stack Update for Windows Server...(KB4540723)
  Element a    2020-04 Servicing Stack Update for Windows Server...(KB4550994)
  Element a    2020-06 Servicing Stack Update for Windows Server...(KB4562561)
  Element a    2020-07 Servicing Stack Update for Windows Server...(KB4565912)
  Element a    2021-02 Servicing Stack Update for Windows Server...(KB5001078)
  Element a    2021-04 Servicing Stack Update for Windows Server...(KB5001402)
  Element a    2021-09 Servicing Stack Update for Windows Server...(KB5005698)
  Element a    2022-03 Servicing Stack Update for Windows Server...(KB5011570)
```

Let's take it one step further and get the GUIDs and KB article numbers from the results. If you look at the URL of the a elements, you will see the path is the same as the ones you just built with the GUID from the search results. So, all you need to do is get the value after the equals sign.

Next, you can extract the KB number from the InnerText using a regular expression. Since all KB numbers start with the letters KB followed by a seven-digit number, your regular expression will be KB[0-9]{7}. And, finally, you can build this all into a PowerShell object and save it to a variable:

```
$xPath = '//*[@id="supersededbyInfo"]'
$DivElements = $Details.SelectSingleNode($xPath).Elements("div")
$SupersededBy = $DivElements.Elements("a") | Foreach-Object {
    $KB = [regex]::Match($_.InnerText.Trim(), 'KB[0-9]{7}')
    [pscustomobject]@{
        KbArticle = $KB.Value
        Title     = $_.InnerText.Trim()
        ID        = $_.Attributes.Value.Split('=')[-1]
    }
}
$SupersededBy

KbArticle Title                                                      ID
--------- -----                                                      --
KB4520724 2019-11 Servicing Stack Update for Window...(KB4520724)    447b628f...
KB4540723 2020-03 Servicing Stack Update for Window...(KB4540723)    3974a7ca...
KB4550994 2020-04 Servicing Stack Update for Window...(KB4550994)    f72420c7...
KB4562561 2020-06 Servicing Stack Update for Window...(KB4562561)    3a5f48ad...
KB4565912 2020-07 Servicing Stack Update for Window...(KB4565912)    6c6eeeea...
KB5001078 2021-02 Servicing Stack Update for Window...(KB5001078)    ef131c9c...
KB5001402 2021-04 Servicing Stack Update for Window...(KB5001402)    6ab99962...
KB5005698 2021-09 Servicing Stack Update for Window...(KB5005698)    c0399f37...
KB5011570 2022-03 Servicing Stack Update for Window...(KB5011570)    c8388301...
```

Now that you have all the elements you need, you can build this into the function in the following listing, which returns a custom PowerShell object for each search result.

Listing 13.4 Find-KbSupersedence.ps1

```
Function Find-KbSupersedence {
    param(
        $KbArticle
    )

    $UriHost = 'https://www.catalog.update.microsoft.com/'
    $SearchUri = $UriHost + 'Search.aspx?q=' +
        $KbArticle
    $Search = ConvertFrom-Html -URI $SearchUri          ◁─┐ XPath query for the
                                                           │ KB articles returned
    $xPath = '//*[' +                                   ◁─┘ from the search
    '@class="contentTextItemSpacerNoBreakLink" ' +
    'and @href="javascript:void(0);"]'
```

```
            ┌──▷  $Search.SelectNodes($xPath) | ForEach-Object {          ┐ Get the title and GUID
      Parse  │        $Title = $_.InnerText.Trim()                 ◁──┤ of the KB article.
      through│        $Id = $_.Id.Replace('_link', '')
      each search
      result.│        $DetailsUri = $UriHost +                          ◁──┤ Get the details page
             │           "ScopedViewInline.aspx?updateid=$($Id)"          ┘ from the Catalog.
             │        $Headers = @{"accept-language"="en-US,en;q=0.9"}
             │        $Request = Invoke-WebRequest -Uri $DetailsUri -Headers $Headers
             │        $Details = ConvertFrom-Html -Content $Request

      Get the  ┌──▷  $xPath = '//*[@id="archDiv"]'
   Architecture.│      $Architecture = $Details.SelectSingleNode($xPath).InnerText
              │        $Architecture = $Architecture.Replace('Architecture:', '').Trim()

      Get the  ┌──▷  $xPath = '//*[@id="productsDiv"]'
     Products. │        $Products = $Details.SelectSingleNode($xPath).InnerText
              │        $Products = $Products.Replace('Supported products:', '')
              │        $Products = $Products.Split(',').Trim()

      Get the  ┌──▷  $xPath = '//*[@id="supersededbyInfo"]'
    Superseded │        $DivElements = $Details.SelectSingleNode($xPath).Elements("div")
    By Updates.│        if ($DivElements.HasChildNodes) {
              │            $SupersededBy = $DivElements.Elements("a") | Foreach-Object {
              │                $KB = [regex]::Match($_.InnerText.Trim(), 'KB[0-9]{7}')
              │                [pscustomobject]@{
              │                    KbArticle = $KB.Value
              │                    Title     = $_.InnerText.Trim()
              │                    ID        = [guid]$_.Attributes.Value.Split('=')[-1]
              │                }
              │            }
              │        }
                                                          ┐ Create a PowerShell
                   [pscustomobject]@{                  ◁──┤ object with search
                       KbArticle    = $KbArticle          ┘ results.
                       Title        = $Title
                       Id           = $Id
                       Architecture = $Architecture
                       Products     = $Products
                       SupersededBy = $SupersededBy
                   }
               }
           }
```

Now that you have your function, test it with a couple of KB numbers to check the results. Then we can build some Pester tests for it.

13.3.2 *Testing your results*

To get started, you can build a simple test like in the next listing to confirm the function works and returns the data you are expecting. You can start with a test to search for KB4521858 and ensure it does not return null and that three results are returned.

Listing 13.5   Find-KbSupersedence.Unit.Test.ps1 initial

```
BeforeAll {
    Set-Location -Path $PSScriptRoot
    . ".\Listing 04 - Find-KbSupersedence.ps1"
}

Describe 'Find-KbSupersedence' {
    It "KB Article is found" {
        $KBSearch = Find-KbSupersedence -KbArticle 'KB4521858'
        $KBSearch | Should -Not -Be $null
        $KBSearch | Should -HaveCount 3
    }
}
```

Now, this test will work as long as the information for the KB article remains the same and your machine running the test has internet access. But for it to be a proper unit test, you will want to mock the results from the Microsoft Catalog.

13.3.3 Mocking with parameters

In the previous section, you built a mock for the Get-HotFix cmdlet to ensure that you receive consistent test results. In this case, you will want to mock the Convert-From-Html cmdlet. However, this mock will not be as simple as the previous one.

For instance, in the previous test, you knew that the Get-HotFix either returns the patch or throws an error. This makes the mocking super simple. On the other hand, to mock the results of the ConvertFrom-Html cmdlet, you would need to build an object with HtmlAgilityPack.HtmlNode classes, which is not something most people would know how to do. But there are other ways you can create mock data.

You can use cmdlets like ConvertFrom-Json or Import-CliXml to easily create PowerShell objects from a file or string. But in this case, the object returned from the ConvertFrom-Html cmdlet is too complex for these. We will come back to them in chapter 14.

Fortunately, the ConvertFrom-Html cmdlet can import data from a URI, a string, or a file. This means that you can export the results of the command, save them, and import them back in when needed. Taking some snippets from the Find-KbSupersedence function, as in the following listing, you can create an HTML file for each search result.

Listing 13.6   Export HTML to file

```
$KbArticle = 'KB5008295'                          Build the search URL.

$UriHost = 'https://www.catalog.update.microsoft.com/'
$SearchUri = $UriHost + 'Search.aspx?q=' + $KbArticle

$Search = ConvertFrom-Html -URI $SearchUri
```

Get the
search
results.

```
$Search.OuterHtml | Out-File ".\$($KbArticle).html"
```

← **Output the HTML of the page to a file named after the KB.**

```
$xPath = '//*[' +
'@class="contentTextItemSpacerNoBreakLink" ' +
'and @href="javascript:void(0);"]'
```

← **XPath query for the KB articles returned from the search**

Parse through each search result. →

```
$Search.SelectNodes($xPath) | ForEach-Object {
    $Id = $_.Id.Replace('_link', '')
    $DetailsUri = $UriHost +
        "ScopedViewInline.aspx?updateid=$($Id)"
    $Header = @{"accept-language"="en-US,en;q=0.9"}
    $Details = Invoke-WebRequest -Uri $DetailsUri -Headers $Header |
        ConvertFrom-Html

    $Details.OuterHtml | Out-File ".\$($Id).html"
}
```

← **Get the ID and use it to get the details page from the Catalog.**

← **Output the HTML of the page to a file named after the ID.**

Another way to do this is to open each page in your web browser, right-click, and choose View Page Source. From there, you can copy and paste the contents into a file on your local machine. To save you some time, no matter which way you choose, I've included the search results for KB4521858 in the Helper Scripts folder for this chapter.

Now you can build the mock similar to the ones from before, but this time you will need to use a parameter filter. The parameter filter on the mock can be used to determine where in the script to call the mock. You can see the logic in figure 13.5.

There are currently two places in the script that call the ConvertFrom-Html cmdlet. The first one is to get the search results, and the second is to get the KB article details. The first time it is called to get the search results, it uses the URI parameter. However, the second call is piped from the Invoke-WebRequest cmdlet, which maps to the Content parameter. Therefore, in the second instance, you will want to mock the Invoke-WebRequest cmdlet because it is the one that is making the call to the external source.

So, we will tell it to only call the mock when the ConvertFrom-Html cmdlet uses the URI parameter. Then, mock the Invoke-WebRequest cmdlet for the second call. This way, when you use the Content parameter for the second call, Pester will ignore it.

Also, when you call a mock, the values passed to the parameters are available inside it. So, for our specific case, I named the files the same as the last part of the URI after the equals sign. This allows the mock to choose the correct file dynamically, based on the URI.

The ConvertFrom-Html mock can import the file directly using the Path parameter. However, the Invoke-WebRequest cmdlet returns a PowerShell object that the actual ConvertFrom-Html will use to convert the content to a HtmlAgilityPack .HtmlNode class. In this case, the ConvertFrom-Html cmdlet only needs the Content

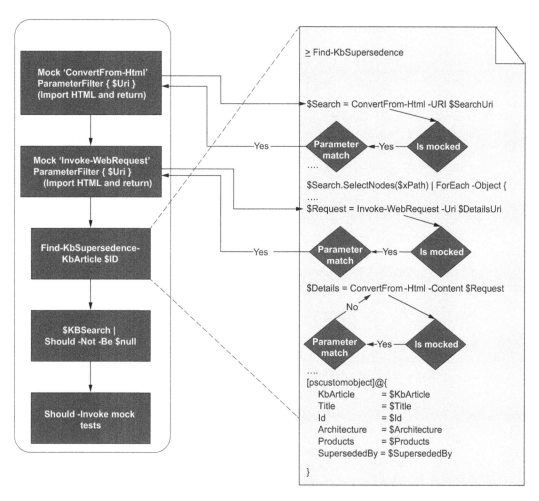

Figure 13.5 Creating a mock with a parameter filter can help ensure a command used multiple times is only mocked when needed.

property, so you can build a custom object to pass the results back in the way the script needs:

```
Mock ConvertFrom-Html -ParameterFilter{ $URI } -MockWith {
    $Path = Join-Path $PSScriptRoot "$($URI.AbsoluteUri.Split('=')[-1]).html"
    ConvertFrom-Html -Path $Path
}

Mock Invoke-WebRequest -MockWith {
    $Path = Join-Path $PSScriptRoot "$($URI.AbsoluteUri.Split('=')[-1]).html"
    $Content = Get-Content -Path $Path -Raw
    [pscustomobject]@{
```

```
        Content = $Content
    }
}
```

Finally, you will want to ensure that the Mock is actually being called. Previously, with the mock of the Get-HotFix, it would have been pretty easy to tell if it was not being used, but with the ConvertFrom-Html, it will be more difficult. So, you can use the Should -Invoke test to count the number of times a mock is invoked instead of the actual command.

By including the Should -Invoke test, you can ensure that your parameter filters are working as expected and that the mock is not being triggered when it should not. The ConvertFrom-Html cmdlet mock should have been called one time for this test (once for the search), and the Invoke-WebRequest mock should have been called three times (once for each search result). If it gets called more times, you know your parameter filter is too broad, and if it gets called fewer times, your filter is too restrictive.

Update the Find-KbSupersedence.Unit.Tests.ps1 script with the code in the following listing, and ensure the test HTML files are in the same folder as the script.

Listing 13.7   Find-KbSupersedence.Unit.Tests.ps1 with mock test files

```
BeforeAll {
    Set-Location -Path $PSScriptRoot
    . ".\Find-KbSupersedence.ps1"
}

Describe 'Find-KbSupersedence' {
    BeforeAll {
        Mock ConvertFrom-Html -ParameterFilter{       ◁──┐  Build the mock for
            $URI } -MockWith {                              ConvertFrom-Html.
            $File = "$($URI.AbsoluteUri.Split('=')[-1]).html"
            $Path = Join-Path $PSScriptRoot $File
            ConvertFrom-Html -Path $Path
        }

        Mock Invoke-WebRequest -MockWith {            ◁──┐  Build the mock for
            $File = "$($URI.AbsoluteUri.Split('=')[-1]).html"  Invoke-WebRequest.
            $Path = Join-Path $PSScriptRoot $File
            $Content = Get-Content -Path $Path -Raw
            [pscustomobject]@{            ◁───┐  Build a custom PowerShell
                Content = $Content              object to mock what the
            }                                   cmdlet would return.
        }
    }

    It "KB Article is found" {        ◁──┐  Find-KbSupersedence
        $KBSearch = Find-KbSupersedence -KbArticle 'KB4521858'   should use the mock.
        $KBSearch | Should -Not -Be $null
        $KBSearch | Should -HaveCount 3      ◁──┐  Confirm the mocks were
                                                   called the expected
        $cmd = 'ConvertFrom-Html'            ◁──┘  number of times.
        Should -Invoke -CommandName $cmd -Times 1
```

```
        $cmd = 'Invoke-WebRequest'
        Should -Invoke -CommandName $cmd -Times 3
    }
}
```

Now, you need to be careful what you mock in your tests. There are some situations you may not be able to account for with mocks—for instance, if Microsoft changes the backend of the Catalog website and the data cannot be found using the correct paths. Your tests would continue to pass, but in the real world, the code would fail. This is where integration testing comes in, which we will cover in the next section.

13.3.4 *Unit vs. integration tests*

In cases like this, where your function has some complex logic and multiple places where something can go wrong, you need to determine what is a unit test versus an integration test. Remember that a unit test should be self-contained and not dependent on external systems. To illustrate this, let's stick with the KB article KB4521858.

We have already tested that the function will return data, but let's take a closer look at the data returned. Since this function does things like web scraping and string manipulation, you will want to ensure that the properties are populated with the expected results.

For instance, you can check that the results contain a particular GUID or that there are two Windows 10 as the products and two AMD64 as the architecture. You can even check individual results like whether a particular GUID should be a specific product or that it is superseded the expected number of times. These tests will help you test changes that might affect the parsing of the data:

```
$KBSearch = Find-KbSupersedence -KbArticle 'KB4521858'
$KBSearch.Id | Should -Contain '250bfd45-b92c-49af-b604-dbdfd15061e6'
$KBSearch | Where-Object{ $_.Products -contains 'Windows 10' } | Should -HaveCount 2
$KBSearch | Where-Object{ $_.Architecture -eq 'AMD64' } | Should -HaveCount 2
$KB = $KBSearch | Where-Object{ $_.Id -eq '83d7bc64-ff39-4073-9d77-02102226aff6' }
$KB.Products | Should -Be 'Windows Server 2016'
```

Since this particular patch is over two years old, there is a pretty good chance that it will not change, but it is not guaranteed. Therefore, building a test with this level of detail should be done as a unit test with mocks. Remember, the unit test is just testing your logic.

Then, when you get to the integration tests, you can make broader tests. For example, you can check that any GUID was returned instead of checking for a specific GUID. Or, instead of checking for AMD64 only, you can check that the architecture is AMD64, x86, or ARM. By making the integration tests broader, your tests would not be at the mercy of a third party changing something like a GUID value. However, it still would catch situations in which the external source changed, and the GUID was no longer in the same place.

So, for your unit tests, you've tested that the function returns data and that the data is what is expected. The only remaining thing to do is test what happens when a patch is not superseded. To help with this, I've included the mock files for the patch KB5008295 in the helper scripts, which, at the time I captured them, was not superseded by any other patches.

In this test, you want to ensure that the superseded results are `null` for both patches with this KB number. Go ahead and update the Find-KbSupersedence.Unit.Tests.ps1 script with the code in the following listing containing these final tests, and confirm everything passes.

Listing 13.8   Find-KbSupersedence.Unit.Tests.ps1 in-depth with mocks

```
BeforeAll {
    Set-Location -Path $PSScriptRoot
    . ".\Find-KbSupersedence.ps1"
}

Describe 'Find-KbSupersedence' {
    BeforeAll {                                      Build the mock for
        Mock ConvertFrom-Html -ParameterFilter{      ConvertFrom-Html.
            $URI } -MockWith {
            $File = "$($URI.AbsoluteUri.Split('=')[-1]).html"
            $Path = Join-Path $PSScriptRoot $File
            ConvertFrom-Html -Path $Path
        }

        Mock Invoke-WebRequest -MockWith {
            $File = "$($URI.AbsoluteUri.Split('=')[-1]).html"
            $Path = Join-Path $PSScriptRoot $File
            $Content = Get-Content -Path $Path -Raw
            [pscustomobject]@{
                Content = $Content
            }
        }
    }
                                                Find-KbSupersedence
    It "KB Article is found" {                   should use the mock.
        $KBSearch = Find-KbSupersedence -KbArticle 'KB4521858'
        $KBSearch | Should -Not -Be $null
        $KBSearch | Should -HaveCount 3

        $cmd = 'ConvertFrom-Html'                       Confirm the mocks were
        Should -Invoke -CommandName $cmd -Times 1       called the expected
        $cmd = 'Invoke-WebRequest'                      number of times.
        Should -Invoke -CommandName $cmd -Times 3
    }

    It "In Depth Search results" {
        $KBSearch = Find-KbSupersedence -KbArticle 'KB4521858'
        $KBSearch.Id |
            Should -Contain '250bfd45-b92c-49af-b604-dbdfd15061e6'
        $KBSearch |
            Where-Object{ $_.Products -contains 'Windows 10' } |
            Should -HaveCount 2
```

```
        $KBSearch |
            Where-Object{ $_.Architecture -eq 'AMD64' }  |
            Should -HaveCount 2
        $KB = $KBSearch |
            Where-Object{ $_.Id -eq '83d7bc64-ff39-4073-9d77-02102226aff6' }
        $KB.Products  | Should -Be 'Windows Server 2016'
        ($KB.SupersededBy | Measure-Object).Count | Should -Be 9
    }

    It "SupersededBy results" {
        $KBMock = Find-KbSupersedence -KbArticle 'KB5008295'

        $KBMock.SupersededBy |
            Should -Be @($null, $null)

        $cmd = 'ConvertFrom-Html'
        Should -Invoke -CommandName $cmd -Times 1
        $cmd = 'Invoke-WebRequest'
        Should -Invoke -CommandName $cmd -Times 2
    }
}
```

Run the Find-KbSupersedence for the not superseded update.

Confirm there are no superseding updates for both updates returned.

Confirm the mocks were called the expected number of times.

These tests will all pass for any update that has superseded patches, but what about ones that do not?

13.4 Integration testing

So far, in this chapter, all the tests you have built are unit tests. This means that they test individual parts of your code (e.g., functions). The next step is to build *integration tests* that test how everything works together. To accomplish this, we'll go ahead and create one more function. This function will check a computer for a particular patch, and if not found, it will check each superseded update until it finds one installed.

Go ahead and save the next listing as the file Get-VulnerabilityStatus.ps1 in the same folder as the other functions. Then, you will be ready to start building some integration tests.

Listing 13.9 Get-VulnerabilityStatus.ps1

```
Function Get-VulnerabilityStatus{
    param(
        [string]$Id,
        [string]$Product,
        [string]$Computer
    )
    $HotFixStatus = @{
        Id       = $Id
        Computer = $Computer
    }
    $Status = Get-HotFixStatus @HotFixStatus

    if($Status -eq $false){
        $Supersedence = Find-KbSupersedence -KbArticle $Id
```

First check is the patch is installed.

If it is not installed, check for any patches that supersede it.

```
          $KBs = $Supersedence |
              Where-Object{ $_.Products -contains $Product }
          foreach($item in $KBs.SupersededBy){
              $Test = Get-HotFixStatus -Id $item.KbArticle -Computer $Computer
              if($Test -eq $true){
                  $item.KbArticle
                  break
              }
          }
      }
      else{
          $Id
      }
  }
```

Check each superseded patch to see if any are installed. *(annotation pointing to the `foreach` line)*

If a superseded patch is found, there is no need to check for additional ones, so go ahead and break the foreach loop. *(annotation pointing to the `break` line)*

When building integration tests, your goal is to ensure that all the code works together as expected. To ensure this, you should not mock any of your custom code. In this case, that refers to the functions Get-HotFixStatus, Find-KbSupersedence, and Get-VulnerabilityStatus. However, you can still mock items outside of these functions. For example, to ensure the Get-VulnerabilityStatus function works when a patch is installed, you do not want to mock the function Get-HotFixStatus. Instead, you will want to mock the Get-HotFix cmdlet. This way, the Get-HotFixStatus function will be called, and you can ensure that it returns the expected results to the other function. You will also want to build a test to check for the condition where a patch is not installed but is still required because a patch that supersedes it is also not installed.

The final test you will build will test for the condition where a patch is not installed. However, a patch that supersedes it is installed. So, while it is not installed, it is also no longer needed. Let's start by finding a patch that has superseded updates. For that, you can use KB4521858 again:

```
$KB = Find-KbSupersedence -KbArticle 'KB4521858' |
    Where-Object{ $_.Products -contains 'Windows Server 2016' }
$KB.SupersededBy
KbArticle Title                                                      ID
--------- -----                                                      --
KB4520724 2019-11 Servicing Stack Update for Windows...(KB4520724)  6d4809e8-
KB4540723 2020-03 Servicing Stack Update for Windows...(KB4540723)  14075cbe-
KB4550994 2020-04 Servicing Stack Update for Windows...(KB4550994)  d43e862f-
KB4562561 2020-06 Servicing Stack Update for Windows...(KB4562561)  2ce894bd-
KB4565912 2020-07 Servicing Stack Update for Windows...(KB4565912)  0804dba3-
KB5001078 2021-02 Servicing Stack Update for Windows...(KB5001078)  99e788ad-
KB5001402 2021-04 Servicing Stack Update for Windows...(KB5001402)  95335a9a-
KB5005698 2021-09 Servicing Stack Update for Windows...(KB5005698)  73f45b23-
KB5011570 2022-03 Servicing Stack Update for Windows...(KB5011570)  3fbca6b8-
```

Let's select the fifth KB article from the list, KB4565912, to test with. To make this work, you will create two Mock blocks for the Get-HotFix cmdlet. The first mock will return the Hotfix Not Found error for any ID other than KB4565912. Then, the second will mock a good return if the ID is KB4565912. This time, you want to test that when you pass the ID of KB4521858 to `Get-VulnerabilityStatus`, it will return KB4565912. You will also want to include the mock of the `ConvertFrom-Html` in the test so you can control the results from the Microsoft Catalog.

Also, since KB4565912 is the fifth KB in the list, you can confirm that the `break` in `Get-VulnerabilityStatus` works and that it did not continue checking for other patches after finding the installed one. You can do this once again using the `Should -Invoke`. This time, you will check that the first mock ran four times and the second one ran once. You can see the script in the next listing.

Listing 13.10   Get-VulnerabilityStatus.Integration.Test.ps1

```
BeforeAll {
    Set-Location -Path $PSScriptRoot          ◁──┐ Import all your
    . ".\Get-HotFixStatus.ps1"                     │ functions.
    . ".\Find-KbSupersedence.ps1"
    . ".\Get-VulnerabilityStatus.ps1"
}

Describe 'Find-KbSupersedence not superseded' {
    BeforeAll {
        $Id = 'KB4521858'
        $Vulnerability = @{
            Id = $Id
            Product = 'Windows Server 2016'
            Computer = 'localhost'
        }                                              ┐ Build the mock for
        Mock ConvertFrom-Html -ParameterFilter{   ◁──┘ ConvertFrom-Html.
            $URI } -MockWith {
            $File = "$($URI.AbsoluteUri.Split('=')[-1]).html"
            $Path = Join-Path $PSScriptRoot $File
            ConvertFrom-Html -Path $Path
        }
    }
    Context "Patch Found" {                     Mock Get-HotFix so the
        BeforeAll {                    ◁──┐     integration test thinks
            Mock Get-HotFix {}                  the patch is installed.
        }

        It "Patch is found on the computer" {
            $KBFound = Get-VulnerabilityStatus @Vulnerability
            $KBFound | Should -Be $Id
        }
    }
                                        ┐ Mock Get-HotFix so the integration test
                                        │ thinks the patch is not installed, and
    Context "Patch Not Found" {         │ neither is one that supersedes it.
        BeforeAll {                ◁──┘
            Mock Get-HotFix {
                throw ('GetHotFixNoEntriesFound,' +
                    'Microsoft.PowerShell.Commands.GetHotFixCommand')
            }
        }
        It "Patch is not found on the computer" {
            $KBFound = Get-VulnerabilityStatus @Vulnerability
```

```
                    $KBFound | Should -BeNullOrEmpty
                }
            }

            Context "Superseding Patch Found" {
                BeforeAll {
                    Mock Get-HotFix {
                        throw ('GetHotFixNoEntriesFound,' +
                            'Microsoft.PowerShell.Commands.GetHotFixCommand')
                    } -ParameterFilter { $Id -ne 'KB4565912' }

                    Mock Get-HotFix { } -ParameterFilter {
                        $Id -eq 'KB4565912' }
                }
                It "Superseding Patch is found on the computer" {
                    $KBFound = Get-VulnerabilityStatus @Vulnerability
                    $KBFound | Should -Be 'KB4565912'

                    $cmd = 'Get-HotFix'
                    Should -Invoke -CommandName $cmd -ParameterFilter {
                        $Id -ne 'KB4565912' } -Times 4
                    Should -Invoke -CommandName $cmd -ParameterFilter {
                        $Id -eq 'KB4565912' } -Times 1
                }
            }
        }
    }
```

Annotations:

Mock Get-HotFix so that not installed is returned for any patch other than KB4565912. →

Mock Get-HotFix so that installed is returned only for KB4565912. →

Add the same ParameterFilters to the Should -Invoke to confirm they execute the expected number of times. →

13.4.1 Integration testing with external data

In the last integration test, you were still mocking the results from the Microsoft Catalog because you were testing that your full automation worked the way you designed it. However, when working with external data sources, you should also build tests to ensure that the data is what is expected. For instance, if Microsoft changes the format on its website, it could break your web scraping in the Find-KbSupersedence function.

When building unit tests for external data, you can build them slightly more generically. For example, in listing 13.7, you tested that the KB search results returned a specific GUID. However, you could just test that the result is a GUID, not a specific GUID. You can also check that the product field is populated:

```
$KBSearch.Id |
    Should -Match ("(\{){0,1}[0-9a-fA-F]{8}\-[0-9a-fA-F]{4}\-[0-9a-fA-F]" +
    "{4}\-[0-9a-fA-F]{4}\-[0-9a-fA-F]{12}(\}){0,1}")
$KBSearch.Products | Should -Not -Be $null
```

Some other tests can get a little more specific to ensure that you receive the expected data. Like with the architecture, you know the return data will be x86, AMD64, or ARM. So for this, you can use a Where-Object filter to exclude any results that do not match one of those three. Then, test that the number of results matches the number of search results. If there are fewer than expected, you know that one of the fields was populated with something different.

You can also test that something meets the minimum or maximum value by using BeGreaterOrEqual or BeLessThan in your assertions. For example, since we know that KB4521858 has been superseded nine times, you can assert that it should be equal to or greater than nine. Therefore, if another patch is released to supersede it, your test will continue to pass, but if it fails to return the superseded patches, then it will fail. You can save the code in the next listing in the Tests folder and confirm that your function is still working when talking to the Microsoft Catalog.

Listing 13.11   Find-KbSupersedence.Integration.Tests.ps1 integration tests

```
BeforeAll {
    Set-Location -Path $PSScriptRoot
    . ".\Find-KbSupersedence.ps1"
}

Describe 'Find-KbSupersedence' {
    It "KB Article is found" {                          ◁── Find-KbSupersedence
        $KBSearch =                                          without a mock.
            Find-KbSupersedence -KbArticle 'KB4521858'
        $KBSearch | Should -Not -Be $null
        $KBSearch | Should -HaveCount 3
        $GuidRegEx = '(\{){0,1}[0-9a-fA-F]{8}\-' +      ◁── Confirm the
            '[0-9a-fA-F]{4}\-[0-9a-fA-F]{4}\-[0-9a-fA-F]{4}\' +   ID is a GUID.
            '-[0-9a-fA-F]{12}(\}){0,1}'
        $KBSearch.Id | Should -Match $GuidRegEx
        $KBSearch.Products | Should -Not -Be $null     ◁── Confirm products
        $KBSearch |                                         are populating.
            Where-Object{ $_.Architecture -in 'x86','AMD64','ARM' } |
            Should -HaveCount $KBSearch.Count
        $KB = $KBSearch | Select-Object -First 1       ◁──┐ Confirm there are at
        ($KB.SupersededBy | Measure-Object).Count |          least nine SupersededBy
            Should -BeGreaterOrEqual 9                       KB articles.
    }
}
```

Confirm the number of results that have the expected architecture matches the number of results.

13.5   *Invoking Pester tests*

Another fantastic feature of Pester is the ability to run multiple tests at once. The command Invoke-Pester will invoke every file in the current folder that ends in .Tests.ps1.

If you followed along with all the listings in this chapter, you should have a folder with the following files:

- 6fcd8832-c48d-46bc-9dac-ee1ec2cdfdeb.html
- 9bd3bbf6-0002-4c0b-ae52-fc21ba9d7166.html
- Find-KbSupersedence.ps1
- Find-KbSupersedence.Unit.Tests.ps1
- Find-KbSupersedence.Integration.Tests.ps1
- Get-HotFixStatus.ps1
- Get-HotFixStatus.Unit.Tests.ps1

- Get-VulnerabilityStatus.ps1
- Get-VulnerabilityStatus.Integration.Tests.ps1

If you open a new PowerShell window and navigate to that folder, you can run `Invoke-Pester`, and it will run all the test files in the folder:

```
Invoke-Pester
Starting discovery in 4 files.
Discovery found 10 tests in 25ms.
Running tests.
[+] D:\Ch13\Find-KbSupersedence.Integration.Tests.ps1 10.81s (10.78s|28ms)
[+] D:\Ch13\Find-KbSupersedence.Unit.Tests.ps1 84ms (54ms|25ms)
[+] D:\Ch13\Get-HotFixStatus.Unit.Tests.ps1 48ms (15ms|25ms)
[+] D:\Ch13\Get-VulnerabilityStatus.Integration.Tests.ps1 17.05s
      (17.02s|23ms)
Tests completed in 28.01s
Tests Passed: 10, Failed: 0, Skipped: 0 NotRun: 0
```

One other excellent function of the `Invoke-Pester` cmdlet is that you can customize how the tests run, display, and even write the results to a test results file. This is done by creating a Pester configuration using the `New-PesterConfiguration` cmdlet and then customizing the settings to meet your needs.

For example, the following snippet will write the details of each test run and write the test results to a file named testResults.xml. The test results file contains the details of the test results in an NUnit schema. NUnit is an industry-standard unit-testing framework. As you will see in the next chapter, these test files can be used to report on automated tests:

```
$config = New-PesterConfiguration
$config.TestResult.Enabled = $true
$config.Output.Verbosity = 'Detailed'
Invoke-Pester -Configuration $config
Pester v5.3.1

Starting discovery in 4 files.
Discovery found 10 tests in 63ms.
Running tests.

Running tests from 'D:\Ch13\Find-KbSupersedence.Integration.Tests.ps1'
Describing Find-KbSupersedence
  [+] KB Article is found 3.73s (3.73s|1ms)

Running tests from 'D:\Ch13\Find-KbSupersedence.Unit.Tests.ps1'
Describing Find-KbSupersedence
    [+] KB Article is found 139ms (137ms|2ms)
    [+] In Depth Search results 21ms (20ms|0ms)
    [+] SupersededBy results 103ms (103ms|0ms)

Running tests from 'D:\Ch13\Get-HotFixStatus.Unit.Tests.ps1'
Describing Get-HotFixStatus
 Context Hotfix Found
    [+] Hotfix is found on the computer 8ms (4ms|4ms)
```

```
Context Hotfix Not Found
  [+] Hotfix is not found on the computer 5ms (4ms|1ms)
Context Not able to connect to the remote machine
  [+] Unable to connect 10ms (10ms|1ms)

Running tests from 'D:\Ch13\Get-VulnerabilityStatus.Integration.Tests.ps1'
Describing Find-KbSupersedence not superseded
 Context Patch Found
  [+] Patch is found on the computer 9ms (7ms|3ms)
 Context Patch Not Found
  [+] Patch is not found on the computer 10.46s (10.46s|1ms)
 Context Superseding Patch Found
  [+] Superseding Patch is found on the computer 4.27s (4.27s|1ms)
Tests completed in 18.99s
Tests Passed: 10, Failed: 0, Skipped: 0 NotRun: 0
```

The goal of this chapter was to give you a good general overview of how to get started with Pester. I encourage you to continue using Pester for any custom functionality you write. The following links are to some additional resources you can use to explore Pester further:

- https://pester.dev/docs/quick-start
- https://github.com/pester/pester

Summary

- Pester is the ubiquitous test and mock framework for PowerShell.
- You can create mocks to ensure consistency when testing.
- Mocks work great for unit testing because you are only testing the logic inside of your function.
- You can use mocks with integration tests, but be sure not to mock any of your custom code, as you want to ensure that everything functions together as expected.
- Pester tests can be saved to files for reporting and recording historical results.

Maintaining your code

Throughout this book, I have stressed the importance of building code that you can easily maintain and share. You have seen how to accomplish this through the use of functions and modules. Then, in chapter 12, you saw how to use GitHub to store your code and control the changes to it through pull requests. And, in chapter 13, you saw how to build unit and integration tests to ensure that your code functions as expected. Now, in this chapter, you will see how to bring this all together.

In chapter 11, you created the module PoshAutomator and stored it in GitHub. This module contains the function `Get-SystemInfo`, which returns information about the local computer. However, the focus of the chapter was more on GitHub and source control than the code itself. Therefore `Get-SystemInfo` is a fairly basic function. It uses the `Get-CimInstance` cmdlet to gather data, which only works on

Windows machines. So, in this chapter, we are going to expand it to include the same information for Linux-based machines.

Now, don't worry, you will not have to create a bunch of different virtual machines to test against all the different Linux distributions. Instead, we will use Pester to simulate the return values from a few different distros. And, luckily for you, I created a bunch of virtual machines with different Linux distros and captured that data for you. Then we will take it all one step further and create a GitHub workflow to automatically run your Pester tests any time there is a code change.

It is okay if you haven't read chapters 11 and 13. If you are already familiar with using Git and Pester, it should not be a problem if you skip them. However, if you have not read chapter 11, you will not have the code and GitHub repository to update. So, I have provided some scripts in the Helper Scripts folder for this chapter that you can use to create these quickly. Refer to the GitHub-Setup.md file for instructions on setting up git and GitHub.

Assuming you either completed the exercises from chapter 11 or ran the script, you will want to open the PoshAutomator folder in VS Code and create a new branch named add_linux. Then you will be ready to perform all the exercises in this chapter:

```
git checkout -b add_linux
```

14.1 Revisiting old code

One of my favorite things to do is to go back and look at the scripts I wrote two or more years ago. Without fail, every time I do this, I will find one bit of code that makes me say, "What was I thinking?" But aside from cringing at my code, I can also see how my skills and knowledge have grown. Even after 15 years of writing PowerShell, I am still finding new and better ways to accomplish things. Of course, this makes it very tempting to go back and "fix" all this past code, but you need to be careful that you do not break something that might still be relying on that code.

The function `Get-SystemInfo` from chapter 11 can return information about the local Windows operating system. Now, we want to expand that to include information about Linux-based operating systems. You can see the code and the output from this function in the following snippet:

```
Function Get-SystemInfo{
    Get-CimInstance -Class Win32_OperatingSystem |
        Select-Object Caption, InstallDate, ServicePackMajorVersion,
        OSArchitecture, BootDevice, BuildNumber, CSName,
        @{l='Total_Memory';e={[math]::Round($_.TotalVisibleMemorySize/1MB)}}
}
Get-SystemInfo
Caption                  : Microsoft Windows 11 Enterprise
InstallDate              : 10/21/2021 5:09:00 PM
ServicePackMajorVersion  : 0
OSArchitecture           : 64-bit
BootDevice               : \Device\HarddiskVolume3
```

```
BuildNumber             : 22000
CSName                  : MyPC
Total_Memory            : 32
```

Before you just dive right in and start changing code, you need to ensure that updating this function will not break anything else that may rely on it. The best way to do this is to create a Pester test for the function as it is right now. Then, make your changes and finish by creating new tests for any new functionality.

14.1.1 Test before changing

To ensure that your code changes do not affect anything else that may be using this code, you should always start by making a few Pester tests of the function. Since this function is part of a module, I suggest that you create a new folder inside the module folder named Test. Then, you can store all test scripts and files there.

To start, create a test that executes the `Get-SystemInfo` function where data is returned for each property. You can do this with a simple `Should -Not -BeNullOrEmpty` after each property to check. As long as the data is returned, the test will pass. It doesn't matter if it was run on Windows 10, 11, or even XP. However, if you run it on a Linux machine, it would fail because no information would be returned, which is the expected result at this time.

Then, you can create one more test to check the actual return values, as shown in figure 14.1. To do this, you can mock the data returned from the `Get-CimInstance` cmdlet, and once again, PowerShell has a couple of nifty cmdlets to help you do that.

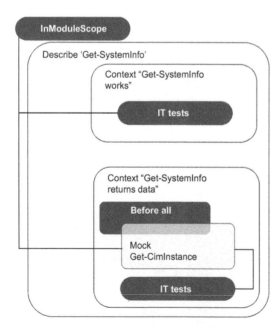

Figure 14.1 `Get-SystemInfo` **unit test that checks to see if the function returns data and then mocks the return data to ensure the expected values are returned**

The cmdlets `Export-Clixml` and `Import-Clixml` can be used, respectively, to export and import a PowerShell object. The best thing about these cmdlets is that they store information about the object types. Therefore, when you import them back in, it is nearly identical to the original object. This is opposed to something like JSON, where PowerShell just makes its best guess as to what the object type should be.

So, to create the mock, all you need to do is pipe the results from `Get-CimInstance` into `Export-Clixml` and save it as an XML in the Test folder. Then, when you create your mock, you will call the `Import-Clixml` cmdlet and import the file:

```
Get-CimInstance -Class Win32_OperatingSystem | Export-Clixml -Path
    .\Test\Get-CimInstance.Windows.xml
```

You can even help make your assertions by running the `Get-SystemInfo` function and looping through the properties to populate the names and values in a string. Then, you can copy and paste the output into your `It` block:

```
$Info = Get-SystemInfo
$Info.psobject.Properties | ForEach-Object{
    "`$Info.$($_.Name) | Should -Be '$($_.Value)'"
}
```

This trick will work for any PowerShell object, but you will want to go back and fix any values that have a specific data type. For instance, remove the quotes around any numbers and use the `Get-Date` cmdlet to convert strings to `DateTimes` where applicable.

There is one more thing you will need to add to your mocks. Since you are testing a cmdlet inside a module, you need to tell Pester that the mocks will be inside the module. You can do this by wrapping your entire test in an `InModuleScope` block. The `InModuleScope` block tells Pester to assume that all mocks are in the context of the module. This is the preferred method when you are testing your module code.

You can also use the `-ModuleName` argument directly on your mock commands, but this should be reserved for tests outside the current module. By wrapping the entire test in the `InModuleScope` block, you ensure that your module functions are being tested.

Go ahead and create a file named Get-SystemInfo.Unit.Tests.ps1 in the Test folder based on the next listing. Be sure to update the values in the `Get-SystemInfo` Windows `11` block with the data from your local machine.

> **Listing 14.1** `Get-SystemInfo` **test before updating**

```
$ModulePath = Split-Path $PSScriptRoot
Import-Module (Join-Path $ModulePath 'PoshAutomator.psd1') -Force

InModuleScope -ModuleName PoshAutomator {          Set the module scope to the
  Describe 'Get-SystemInfo' {                       module you are testing.
    Context "Get-SystemInfo works" {
      It "Get-SystemInfo returns data" {            Test Get-SystemInfo
        $Info = Get-SystemInfo                       generic results to ensure
        $Info.Caption | Should -Not -BeNullOrEmpty   data is returned.
```

Import the module.

```
      $Info.InstallDate | Should -Not -BeNullOrEmpty
      $Info.ServicePackMajorVersion | Should -Not -BeNullOrEmpty
      $Info.OSArchitecture | Should -Not -BeNullOrEmpty
      $Info.BootDevice | Should -Not -BeNullOrEmpty
      $Info.BuildNumber | Should -Not -BeNullOrEmpty
      $Info.CSName | Should -Not -BeNullOrEmpty
      $Info.Total_Memory | Should -Not -BeNullOrEmpty
    }
  }

  Context "Get-SystemInfo returns data" {        ⟵   Test Get-SystemInfo results
    BeforeAll {                                        with mocking to ensure data
      Mock Get-CimInstance {                           that is returned matches the
        Import-Clixml -Path ".\Get-CimInstance.Windows.xml"   expected values.
      }
    }
    It "Get-SystemInfo Windows 11" {
      $Info = Get-SystemInfo
      $Info.Caption | Should -Be 'Microsoft Windows 11 Enterprise'
      $Date = Get-Date '10/21/2021 5:09:00 PM'
      $Info.InstallDate | Should -Be $Date
      $Info.ServicePackMajorVersion | Should -Be 0
      $Info.OSArchitecture | Should -Be '64-bit'
      $Info.BootDevice | Should -Be '\Device\HarddiskVolume3'
      $Info.BuildNumber | Should -Be 22000
      $Info.CSName | Should -Be 'MyPC'
      $Info.Total_Memory | Should -Be 32
    }
  }
  }
}
```

Once you've created this, ensure the Get-CimInstance.Windows.xml is in the Test folder, and run the test. It should return two tests passed:

```
.\Get-SystemInfo.Unit.Tests.ps1
Starting discovery in 1 files.
Discovery found 2 tests in 19ms.
Running tests.
[+] D:\PoshAutomator\Test\Get-SystemInfo.Unit.Tests.ps1 178ms (140ms|22ms)
Tests completed in 181ms
Tests Passed: 2, Failed: 0, Skipped: 0 NotRun: 0
```

14.1.2 *Updating the function*

To add the Linux functionality, the first thing you need to do is determine whether a machine is Windows or Linux. This can be done with the $IsWindows and $IsLinux variables. These variables were introduced in PowerShell 6 to return a Boolean value based on the operating system. There is also an $IsMacOS for macOS devices. Before you go off and just make some if/else logic, you need to take into consideration PowerShell versions.

Since these variables do not exist in Windows PowerShell 5.1, you will break backward compatibility if you make your function completely dependent on them. However, since versions before PowerShell 6 only run in Windows, you can have your script check if it is Linux because it will return `false` if the variable does not exist. If it is, run the Linux commands; else, run the Windows commands. You could even put an `if/else` between them to display that you do not support macOS yet (sorry, I don't own a Mac to test with).

However, there is one more thing to consider, and that is creating mocks. The `IsLinux`, `IsMacOS`, and `IsWindows` are read-only variables. This means you cannot override them for your testing. You also can only create mocks for the PowerShell commands and not variables. So, to allow you to mock different operating systems, you can use the `Get-Variable` cmdlet to return the value of each variable. It will have the same behavior as just putting the variable there, but it has the added benefit of using a mock:

```
If(Get-Variable -Name IsLinux -ValueOnly){
    <# Linux commands #>
}
ElseIf(Get-Variable -Name IsMacOS -ValueOnly){
    Write-Warning 'Support for macOS has not been added yet.'
}
Else{
    <# Windows commands #>
}
```

Now comes the fun part of getting the data for the Linux operating systems. Since there is no single command to get this information in Linux, you will need to build the return data by combining the output of several commands. To save you the time researching this, I have listed the different properties in table 14.1 along with the command or file that the information can be returned from in most major Linux distros.

Table 14.1 Linux properties

Property	Command/file
Caption	/etc/os-release (PRETTY_NAME)
InstallDate	stat /
ServicePackMajorVersion	/etc/os-release (VERSION)
OSArchitecture	uname -m
BootDevice	df /boot
BuildNumber	/etc/os-release (VERSION_ID)
CSName	uname -n
Total_Memory	/proc/meminfo (MemTotal)

Starting with the two files (/etc/os-release and /proc/meminfo), you have a couple of different ways to get the data. You can use the `Get-Content` cmdlet to return all the data in the file, or you can use the Select-String cmdlet to return the line that matches a specific pattern. In this case, we will use both.

The file /etc/os-release is formatted using a pattern of key equals sign value, which also happens to be the same format that the ConvertFrom-StringData cmdlet uses. This cmdlet works much like the ConvertFrom-Json, where it will take a formatted string and turn it into a hashtable. The following snippet shows an example of the contents from an Ubuntu server:

```
Get-Content -Path /etc/os-release
NAME="Ubuntu"
VERSION="20.04.4 LTS (Focal Fossa)"
ID=ubuntu
ID_LIKE=debian
PRETTY_NAME="Ubuntu 20.04.4 LTS"
VERSION_ID="20.04"
HOME_URL="https://www.ubuntu.com/"
SUPPORT_URL="https://help.ubuntu.com/"
BUG_REPORT_URL="https://bugs.launchpad.net/ubuntu/"
VERSION_CODENAME=focal
UBUNTU_CODENAME=focal
```

You can pipeline the output to the ConvertFrom-StringData cmdlet and save it to a variable. Then, you can access the properties directly. You may need to do some cleanup of the quotes using a replace, but other than that, you have a good chunk of the information you need:

```
$OS = Get-Content -Path /etc/os-release | ConvertFrom-StringData
$OS.PRETTY_NAME
$OS.PRETTY_NAME.Replace('"','')
"Ubuntu 20.04.4 LTS"
Ubuntu 20.04.4 LTS
```

The next file you need to get data from is /proc/meminfo. This file is not formatted in a way that PowerShell recognizes, so you will need to do some more data manipulation to get the value you need. We know the line with the number you want starts with MemTotal. So, we can use the Select-String cmdlet to only return the line that starts with that:

```
Select-String -Path /proc/meminfo -Pattern 'MemTotal'
/proc/meminfo:1:MemTotal:        4019920 kB
```

Then you can use a regular expression to extract the number from the line:

```
Select-String -Path /proc/meminfo -Pattern 'MemTotal' |
    ForEach-Object{ [regex]::Match($_.line, "(\d+)").value}
4019920
```

Next, you will need to use some commands to return information about the operating system. We had previously discussed that you can run external commands directly in PowerShell, which you could do here. But you would run into the problem that you will not be able to mock them. So, to ensure that you can adequately mock the results for your testing, you can use the `Invoke-Expression` cmdlet to run these external commands. Then, you can mock the `Invoke-Expression` cmdlet in your Pester tests.

Like when you extracted the data from the files, you will need to do some data manipulation to get the results from the command output. Once again, you can use the `Select-String` to help get what you need. For example, you can run the command `stat /` to get the installation date. However, this command returns multiple lines with different data. So, as with the memory total, we'll narrow it down to the line we want and then extract the value we want:

```
$stat = Invoke-Expression -Command 'stat /'
$stat | Select-String -Pattern 'Birth:' | ForEach-Object{
    Get-Date $_.Line.Replace('Birth:','').Trim()
}
Wednesday, 26 January 2022 15:47:51
```

You can do something similar for the boot device by returning the first value of the last line from the command `df /boot`. You can do this by splitting on the line breaks `` `n ``, then getting the last one by using the number `[-1]`, then splitting on the spaces and getting the first value:

```
$boot = Invoke-Expression -Command 'df /boot'
$boot.Split("`n")[-1].Split()[0]
/dev/sda1
```

Fortunately, the last two commands to get the architecture and name can be retrieved using a command that only outputs the value you need, so there is no need to manipulate the output. Go ahead and update the Get-SystemInfo.ps1 with the updated function in the following listing.

Listing 14.2   Get-SystemInfo.ps1

```
Function Get-SystemInfo{
    [CmdletBinding()]                              Check if the machine
    param()                                        is running a Linux-
    if(Get-Variable -Name IsLinux -ValueOnly){  ◄  based OS.
        $OS = Get-Content -Path /etc/os-release |  ◄── Get the data from
            ConvertFrom-StringData                       the os-release file,
                                                         and convert it to a
        $search = @{                                     PowerShell object.
   ┌──►      Path    = '/proc/meminfo'
   │
   Search the meminfo file for the MemTotal
   line and extract the number.
```

Run the stat command, parse the output for the Birth line, then extract the date.

Build the results into a PowerShell object that matches the same properties as the existing Windows output.

```
                    Pattern = 'MemTotal'
                }
            $Mem = Select-String @search |
                ForEach-Object{ [regex]::Match($_.line, "(\d+)").value}

            $stat = Invoke-Expression -Command 'stat /'
            $InstallDate = $stat | Select-String -Pattern 'Birth:' |
                ForEach-Object{
                    Get-Date $_.Line.Replace('Birth:','').Trim()
                }

            $boot = Invoke-Expression -Command 'df /boot'
            $OSArchitecture = Invoke-Expression -Command 'uname -m'
            $CSName = Invoke-Expression -Command 'uname -n'

            [pscustomobject]@{
                Caption                 = $OS.PRETTY_NAME.Replace('"',"")
                InstallDate             = $InstallDate
                ServicePackMajorVersion = $OS.VERSION.Replace('"',"")
                OSArchitecture          = $OSArchitecture
                BootDevice              = $boot.Split("`n")[-1].Split()[0]
                BuildNumber             = $OS.VERSION_ID.Replace('"',"")
                CSName                  = $CSName
                Total_Memory            = [math]::Round($Mem/1MB)
            }
        }
        else{
            Get-CimInstance -Class Win32_OperatingSystem |
                Select-Object Caption, InstallDate, ServicePackMajorVersion,
                OSArchitecture, BootDevice, BuildNumber, CSName,
                @{l='Total_Memory';
                    e={[math]::Round($_.TotalVisibleMemorySize/1MB)}}
        }
    }
```

Run the df and uname commands, and save the output as is.

Original Windows system information commands

14.1.3 Post update test

After making the updates, you will first want to run the original test script to ensure that you did not break anything. If all the tests pass, you can start building your new ones.

To test the Linux output, you will need to create several mocks. You will need to mock the data returned from the /etc/os-release and /proc/meminfo files and the results from the df, stat, and uname commands. With the exception of the /etc/os-release file, the output for all the other commands remains the same between different Linux distros. Therefore, if you place all the tests inside the same context, you only need to mock these once. Then, inside each It test block, you can mock the results for the individual /etc/os-release file.

I have included several text files that start with the name test in the Helper Scripts for this chapter to save you a lot of time and hassle. These files contain output examples for the different distros and commands. You can import the data from these files inside the mock statements to replicate the results from running these commands on a Linux server.

If you are interested in creating additional test files, all you need to do is run the command in Linux and then pipe it to the `Out-File` cmdlet to save the output in a text file:

```
stat / | Out-File .\test.stat.txt
```

To ensure that you are calling the correct mock for each command, you must use parameter filters. For example, to mock the `df /boot` command, you will mock `Invoke-Expression` with the parameter filter of the command equal to the `df` command. Then, you can mock the individual `os-release` files inside of the `It` blocks:

```
Mock Invoke-Expression -ParameterFilter { $Command -eq 'df /boot' } -MockWith {
    Get-Content -Path (Join-Path $PSScriptRoot 'test.df.txt')
}
```

You will also want to test the invoke assertions to ensure that your mocks are being properly called. For example, to ensure that the `df` mock was called, you would add the following assertion:

```
Should -Invoke -CommandName 'Invoke-Expression' -ParameterFilter {
    $Command -eq 'df /boot' } -Times 1
```

Since you have seven mocks, you will also want to include seven invoke assertions. When testing against three different distros, that is 21 tests, just to confirm the tests are running. Then, counting the other tests, each `It` block will be around 22 lines long. Now imagine that in a few months you decide to add a new property to the function. You will need to update every single `It` block with this new test. Digging through hundreds of lines of code to ensure that you updated everything would be a huge pain. So, instead of creating separate `It` blocks for each distro, you can use a `foreach` loop to pass the expected values for each distro, as shown in figure 14.2.

All you need to do is create a hashtable for each distro and populate it with the data expected. Pester will then loop through each test case, allowing you to perform multiple tests with one `It` block. Update Get-SystemInfo.Unit.Tests.ps1 with the additional tests in listing 14.3, and ensure everything passes.

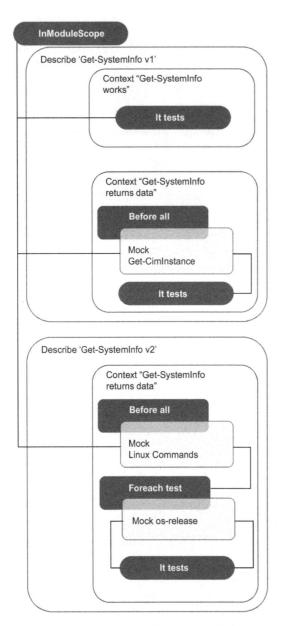

Figure 14.2 `Get-SystemInfo` unit tests after updating the function to include Linux. Include `foreach` to check multiple different Linux distros with a single `It` block.

Listing 14.3 `Get-SystemInfo` test after the updates

```
$ModulePath = Split-Path $PSScriptRoot
Import-Module (Join-Path $ModulePath 'PoshAutomator.psd1') -Force

InModuleScope -ModuleName PoshAutomator {
    Describe 'Get-SystemInfo v1' {
```

Set the module scope to the module you are testing.

The tests from before you made any changes

Import the module.

```
        <#
          Copy Tests from Listing 1 here to ensure they all still pass
        #>
    }
```

Mock the Get-Variable command to return true if IsLinux variable.

New tests for the Linux distros

```
    Describe 'Get-SystemInfo v2' {
        Context "Get-SystemInfo for Linux" {
            BeforeAll {
                Mock Get-Variable -MockWith { $true }        ←──
```

Mock each on the Linux system commands to control the data that is returned.

```
                Mock Select-String -ParameterFilter {        ←──
                    $Path -eq '/proc/meminfo' } -MockWith {
                    [pscustomobject]@{line = 'MemTotal:        8140600 kB' }
                }
                Mock Invoke-Expression -ParameterFilter {
                    $Command -eq 'df /boot' } -MockWith {
                    Get-Content -Path (Join-Path $PSScriptRoot 'test.df.txt')
                }
                Mock Invoke-Expression -ParameterFilter {
                    $Command -eq 'stat /' } -MockWith {
                    Get-Content -Path (Join-Path $PSScriptRoot 'test.stat.txt')
                }
                Mock Invoke-Expression -ParameterFilter {
                    $Command -eq 'uname -m' } -MockWith {
                    'x86_64'
                }
                Mock Invoke-Expression -ParameterFilter {
                    $Command -eq 'uname -n' } -MockWith {
                    'localhost.localdomain'
                }
            }
```

Test the different Linux distros using a foreach so you do not need to recreate the It block for each distro.

```
            It "Get-SystemInfo Linux (<Caption>)" -ForEach @(     ←──
```

Build hashtables with the values needed to test each distro.

```
                @{ File = 'test.rhel.txt';
                   Caption = "Red Hat Enterprise Linux 8.2 (Ootpa)";
                   ServicePackMajorVersion = '8.2 (Ootpa)';
                   BuildNumber = '8.2'
                }
                @{ File = 'test.Ubuntu.txt';
                   Caption = "Ubuntu 20.04.4 LTS";
                   ServicePackMajorVersion = '20.04.4 LTS (Focal Fossa)';
                   BuildNumber = '20.04'
                }
                @{ File = 'test.SUSE.txt';
                   Caption = "SUSE Linux Enterprise Server 15 SP3";
                   ServicePackMajorVersion = '15-SP3';
                   BuildNumber = '15.3'
                }
            ) {
                Mock Get-Content -ParameterFilter {
                    $Path -eq '/etc/os-release' } -MockWith {
                    Get-Content -Path (Join-Path $PSScriptRoot $File)
                }
```

Run the Get-SystemInfo while mocking the Linux results.

```
                $Info = Get-SystemInfo
```

<table>
<tr><td>

Confirm the expected mocks are being called.
</td><td>

```
$cmd = 'Get-Content'
Should -Invoke -CommandName $cmd -ParameterFilter {
    $Path -eq '/etc/os-release' } -Times 1
Should -Invoke -CommandName 'Get-Variable' -ParameterFilter {
    $Name -eq 'IsLinux' -and $ValueOnly } -Times 1
Should -Invoke -CommandName 'Select-String' -ParameterFilter {
    $Path -eq '/proc/meminfo' } -Times 1
Should -Invoke -CommandName 'Invoke-Expression' -ParameterFilter {
    $Command -eq 'df /boot' } -Times 1
Should -Invoke -CommandName 'Invoke-Expression' -ParameterFilter {
    $Command -eq 'stat /' } -Times 1
Should -Invoke -CommandName 'Invoke-Expression' -ParameterFilter {
    $Command -eq 'uname -m' } -Times 1
Should -Invoke -CommandName 'Invoke-Expression' -ParameterFilter {
    $Command -eq 'uname -n' } -Times 1
```
</td></tr>
<tr><td>

Confirm the results match the expected values.
</td><td>

```
$Info.Caption | Should -Be $Caption
$Date = Get-Date '2021-10-01 13:57:20.213260279 -0500'
$Info.InstallDate | Should -Be $Date
$Info.ServicePackMajorVersion | Should -Be $ServicePackMajorVersion
$Info.OSArchitecture | Should -Be 'x86_64'
$Info.BootDevice | Should -Be '/dev/sda2'
$Info.BuildNumber | Should -Be $BuildNumber
$Info.CSName | Should -Be 'localhost.localdomain'
$Info.Total_Memory | Should -Be 8
        }
    }

    }
}
```
</td></tr>
</table>

This time you should have five tests that pass.

14.2 Automating your testing

Now that you have your changes made to the module, you are almost ready to sync them with the remote GitHub repository and create a pull request to move them into production. However, before you do that, let's create a GitHub workflow to run these Pester tests for you automatically.

GitHub workflows are a continuous integration and continuous delivery (CI/CD) platform that allows you to automate your build, test, and deploy your code. You can create workflows that run your Pester tests automatically every time a pull request is submitted. This will help you to ensure that everything still works as expected. Workflows can also be used to deploy code automatically. For example, you can upload modules directly to the PowerShell Gallery or to a private repository.

GitHub workflows are written in YAML, yet another data-serialization language, like JSON and XML. YAML is used by many CI/CD platforms, including GitHub workflows and Azure DevOps Pipelines. If you have never even heard of YAML before, don't worry; the syntax is very straightforward. The biggest challenge for someone who uses languages like PowerShell is that YAML uses indentions to signify nesting, similar to Python.

14.2.1 Creating a GitHub workflow

A GitHub workflow is not designed specifically with Pester testing in mind. However, what it does have is the ability to run shell commands. These shell commands support PowerShell and have the Pester modules installed. This allows you to call your Pester tests from within the workflow, and the results will be reported back to you.

To create a GitHub workflow, you need to create the YAML and place it in the folder .github/workflows/ in your repository (and yes, that is a period in front of GitHub). Create the folder structure in your local repository and create a new file named Get-SystemInfo.yaml.

The first thing you need to do in the YAML is name the workflow and define the triggers. The triggers are defined using the key on and tell GitHub when to run a workflow automatically. In this case, you want the workflow to run when a pull request is opened or reopened. So, the start of your file will look like the following snippet:

```
name: PoshAutomator Pester Tests
on:
  pull_request:
    types: [opened, reopened]
```

Next, you need to define your jobs. Jobs are used to define the environment you want to run the test in. A workflow can be made up of several jobs that can run concurrently or sequentially. We only need a single job to execute the tests in our case.

You need to define the operating system you want it to run on when you define a job. There are several options, including Windows Server, Ubuntu, and macOS, and they all have PowerShell and Pester installed. In most cases, you will want to use the Windows image.

If you need to test against Windows PowerShell 5.1, it is only available in Windows. Even if you are using PowerShell 6 or 7, some cmdlets are only available on Windows. For instance, the Get-CimInstance cmdlet does not exist on Linux operating systems. Even though you are mocking the results of it, it can cause issues if the host machine does not think the cmdlet exists. So, to make things easier, you can run it on a Windows image.

Under the job, you will define the steps for the workflow to take. To run the Pester test, you only need two steps, as you can see in the next listing—one to check out the repository code, making it available to the job, and a second one to run the Pester script.

Listing 14.4 Get-SystemInfo.yaml

```
name: PoshAutomator Pester Tests
on:
  pull_request:                        ◁─┐  Set to run when
    types: [opened, reopened]           │  a pull request is
                                        │  opened or reopened
jobs:                                   │  automatically
  pester-test:
    name: Pester test
```

Run on
Windows.

```
runs-on: windows-latest
  steps:
    - name: Check out repository code      ⟵   Check out the code for
      uses: actions/checkout@v3                the workflow to access.
    - name: Run the Get-SystemInfo.Unit.Test.ps1 Test File
      shell: pwsh
      run: |
        Invoke-Pester .\Test\Get-SystemInfo.Test.ps1 -Passthru
```

Invoke
the Pester
scripts.

Once the Get-SystemInfo.yaml file is updated, commit and sync your changes to GitHub:

```
git add .
git commit -m "added Linux support and Pester workflow"
git push origin add_linux
```

Then, create a new pull request between the add_linux branch and main:

```
gh pr create --title "Add Linux Support" --body "Updated Get-SystemInfo
➥function to work on major Linux distros. Add workflows for testing"
```

If you open the pull request in your web browser, as shown in figure 14.3, you should see that the workflow has triggered and is running.

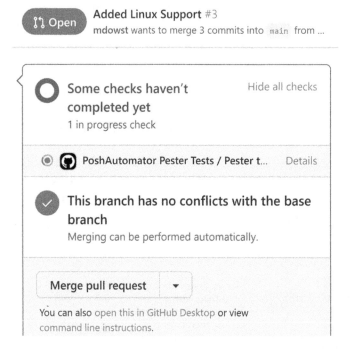

Figure 14.3   GitHub pull request showing that there are workflow checks that are running

If you click on the details, you can watch the execution and see the detailed outcome of the tests. After it finishes, you will be able to view the results from right within the pull request, as in figure 14.4.

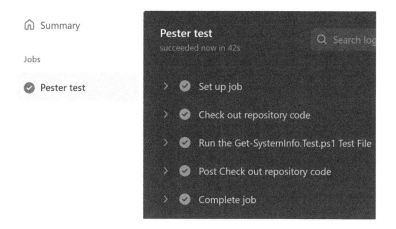

Figure 14.4   The results of the Pester tests running through the GitHub workflow

Once you approve and merge this pull request with the main branch, these Pester tests will be run any time someone makes a change.

Along with testing against changes to your code, these types of tests can be used to ensure that platform-level changes don't affect your code. With new versions of Power-Shell being released every few months, you will want make sure that the updates do not introduce any breaking changes to your code to ensure your continued success on your automation journey.

14.3   *Avoiding breaking changes*

The example in the last section was very specific to that particular function. Unfortunately, there is no one way for me to say how you should update your code in other situations. It all depends on what the code is and what you need it to do. But there is one thing you need to be aware of no matter what, and that is creating a breaking change.

A number of factors can cause a breaking change, but two of the most common I see are the renaming of properties and parameters. For example, when I look back at the code in the function, it bothers me that I left the computer's name as `CSName`. I really should have made it `HostName`. However, if I just decide to change it because

I don't like it, I could potentially break someone else's automation that was expecting the CSName property.

That is not to say that you cannot introduce breaking changes. It's just that they should have a more valid reason than that I don't like the name of that property. And if you do introduce a breaking change, you had better be sure that everyone is aware and has time to prepare.

14.3.1 *Parameter changes*

There are several types of parameter changes that can affect existing automations. These include adding and removing parameters, renaming, and changing the type. Fortunately, there are multiple ways you can ensure that your parameter changes will have as little impact as possible on existing automations.

Removing a parameter is usually the best way to break existing automations. PowerShell will throw an error whenever you pass a parameter that does not exist. So, it is best to avoid removing parameters whenever possible.

An excellent example of this can be seen in the Invoke-WebRequest cmdlet. In Windows PowerShell 5.1 and older, this cmdlet used the user's Internet Explorer profile when connecting to a remote endpoint. To overwrite this and connect using just the basic connection, you could include the switch UseBasicParsing. With the move to cross-platform, this cmdlet was uncoupled from Internet Explorer, making the Use-BasicParsing switch obsolete. However, to support backward capability, the parameter remains in PowerShell 6 and 7. As long as it is not hurting anything, you can leave obsolete parameters in your functions.

On the other end, adding parameters may seem innocuous, but it will break all existing automations if it is set to required. Therefore, when adding a parameter, it is best to make it optional, at least at first. I will also recommend the same approach with renaming parameters. If you need to add a required parameter or rename a parameter, it should be done slowly.

An excellent example of this can be seen in the Azure PowerShell modules. The cmdlet Get-AzManagementGroup originally had a parameter named GroupName. However, if you look at a management group in the Azure portal, there is no management group name field. Instead, there is an ID field and a display name field. The value the GroupName parameter expected was the ID. So, people were obviously confused. Before Microsoft completely removed the GroupName parameter, they released an update that would display a warning anytime it was used to let you know the parameter was changing. They also included an alias so both would work for a period of time. This gave people plenty of time to update their scripts before this parameter was removed entirely.

You can do this yourself by adding an alias declaration to the parameter and making the alias the original value. You can then use the ValidateScript attribute to display a warning any time the parameter is used. This will give people a heads-up to change the parameter and time to do it before it is permanently removed. For example, say you want to change the parameter in the following snippet from Name to HostName:

```
param(
    [string]$Name
)
```

When making the change, the parameter's name should always be the new name, and the old name should become the alias. Then, you will need to update all references to the old name in the function's code. This way, when it comes time to remove the old parameter name, you can just remove the alias, and you are done:

```
param(
    [Alias('Name')]
    [string]$HostName
)
```

You can also use the ValidateScript attribute to display a warning when the parameter is used. Since the ValidateScript only runs when a parameter is used, it will only display when used. So all you have to do is include a Write-Warning cmdlet followed by $true. The $true is because the ValidateScript is technically designed to test the value of a parameter, so if you use it, it must return $true for your function to execute:

```
param(
    [Alias('Name')]
    [ValidateScript({
        Write-Warning "The parameter Name is being replaced with HostName. Be
    sure to update any scripts using Name";
        $true}
    )]
    [string]$HostName
)
```

14.3.2 Output changes

Changing the output of a function can be a lot trickier than changing the parameters because there is no good equivalent of the alias. The data you return is the data that is sent back to the invoking command. Things like adding a property usually do not harm things, but removing and renaming properties can have massive impacts.

If you need to change the output from a command, the best course of action is to create an entirely new function. Then, you can put a warning on the old one stating that it is being replaced. Once you've given people enough time to make the changes, you can remove the old function. You can also add an alias for the old function name to the new function in a module's psm1 file. Then, if something is still using the old name, it will be automatically mapped to the new function. When doing this in a module, you need to include the `Export-ModuleMember` command so the alias is available to the user and not just inside the module:

```
New-Alias -Name Old-Function -Value New-Function
Export-ModuleMember -Alias * -Function *
```

As I mentioned at the beginning of this section, I really wish I had made the computer's name `HostName` and not `CSName`. But as long it is not causing confusion, I cannot justify changing it because I'm not too fond of it. However, if it were causing issues, my suggestion would be to include both properties for some time. Then, like with the others, provide a warning that the property will eventually be changing.

Summary

- Be sure not to introduce breaking changes without proper notice and an investigation of the impact.
- Before updating old code, you should create unit tests for it to ensure that you do not break any existing functionality.
- You can include unit and integration tests in your GitHub repository to automatically test your code any time a pull request is submitted.

appendix
Development
environment set up

One of the biggest challenges I faced when writing this book was how to make example automations that could appeal to large audiences. Therefore, for the most part, I tried to stick with base operating systems tasks or with software that almost everyone already has, like Office. Otherwise, the tools used in this book are either free or open source. The only exception is the cloud-based items, but they all offer free trials that you can use.

The majority of the examples in this book can be done using a single machine. However, to get the benefits and to be able to create every automation in this book, you will need three machines. These can all be any combination of physical or virtual machines. The three machines you will need are

1. *Development machine (required)*—Windows 10, Windows Server 2016, or newer
2. *Automation server (optional)*—Windows Server 2016 or newer
3. *Linux machine (optional)*—Ubuntu 20.04 or newer

I have provided you with three options for setting up your environment. You can download and install the applications manually. You can use Chocolatey to perform most installs or use the Lab Setup kits provided in the GitHub repository to automate the setup.

A.1   Development machine

The majority of the script development and testing can be done on a single Windows 10/11 or Windows Server 2016/2019/2022 or newer machine. You can install and configure the entire machine using the DevelopmentMachine.ps1 script in the GitHub repository Practical-Automation-with-PowerShell:

```
Set-ExecutionPolicy Bypass -Scope Process -Force;
Invoke-Expression (Invoke-RestMethod 'https://raw.githubusercontent.com/
➥mdowst/Practical-Automation-with-PowerShell/main/LabSetup/DevelopmentMac
➥hineSetup.ps1'))
```

Everything you need is provided in the following list if you prefer to install and configure the applications manually:

- PowerShell 7
  - Direct install: http://mng.bz/690o
- Chocolatey
  - Direct install: https://chocolatey.org/install
- Git
  - Direct install: https://git-scm.com/download/win
  - Choco install: https://community.chocolatey.org/packages/git
- Visual Studio Code
  - Direct install: https://code.visualstudio.com/
  - Choco install: https://community.chocolatey.org/packages/vscode
- Visual Studio Code extensions
  - PowerShell
  - Direct install: http://mng.bz/o5nd
- GitHub Pull Requests and Issues
  - Direct install: http://mng.bz/neoa

A.1.1   *Clone the book repository*

A GitHub repository for this book contains all of the code examples and snippets from the book. It also includes a preconfigured workspace, so you do not have to manually configure the Visual Studio Code extensions. These steps are not necessary if you ran the automated installation script:

1 In Visual Studio Code, click the Source Control extension button on the far left.
2 Click the Clone Repository button.
3 In the message box, enter the URL https://github.com/mdowst/Practical-Automation-with-PowerShell.git.
4 Click Clone from URL.
5 Select where to save the repository, and click OK.
6 Wait for the clone to finish.
7 Once finished, go to File > Open Workspace.
8 Navigate to the repository, and select the PoSHAutomate.code-workspace file.

A.2   Automation Server

The automation server will host the different applications and platforms that your automation will interact with. This machine should be Windows Server 2016 or newer. You can download a 180-day trial of Windows Server from Microsoft.

You can install and configure most of the requirements using the Automation-Machine.ps1 script in the GitHub repository Practical-Automation-with-PowerShell. However, there will be additional setups that you must perform to configure Jenkins:

```
Set-ExecutionPolicy Bypass -Scope Process -Force;
Invoke-Expression (Invoke-RestMethod 'https://raw.githubusercontent.com/
➥mdowst/Practical-Automation-with-PowerShell/main/LabSetup/Automation
➥Server.ps1'))
```

Everything you need is listed next if you prefer to install and configure the applications manually:

- PowerShell 7
  - Direct install: http://mng.bz/49Gw
- Chocolatey (not required unless you want to use Choco installs)
  - Direct install: https://chocolatey.org/install
- Jenkins CI 2.222.4 or newer
  - Direct install: https://www.jenkins.io/download/
  - Choco install: https://community.chocolatey.org/packages/jenkins

A.2.1   Set up Jenkins

Jenkins is used in several examples throughout the book, but no automations are dependent on it. So, it is up to you if you want to install it and go through those examples:

1. Open a web browser on the server, and navigate to http://localhost:8080.
2. Select Install Suggested Plugins.
3. Create the first user.
4. Click Manage Jenkins.
5. Under the System Configuration section, click Manage Plug-Ins.
6. Select the Available tab.
7. Search for and select PowerShell.
8. Click Install Without Restart.

A.3   Linux environment

A few examples in this book are designed specifically for Linux. All examples in this book were tested using Ubuntu 20.04:

- Direct install: http://mng.bz/5m2q
- Snap install: `snap install powershell –classic`

- Visual Studio Code
  - Direct install: https://code.visualstudio.com/docs/setup/linux
  - Snap install: `snap install code --classic`
- Git
  - Direct install: https://git-scm.com/book/en/v2/Getting-Started-Installing-Git
  - Snap install: `snap install git-ubuntu --classic`

index

RELATED MANNING TITLES